City of Capital

City of Capital

POLITICS AND MARKETS
IN THE
ENGLISH FINANCIAL REVOLUTION

Bruce G. Carruthers

PRINCETON UNIVERSITY PRESS

PRINCETON, NEW JERSEY

Library of Congress Cataloging-in-Publication Data

Carruthers, Bruce G.
City of capital : politics and markets in the
English financial revolution / Bruce G. Carruthers
p. cm.
Includes bibliographical references and index.
ISBN 0-691-04455-4 (cl : alk. paper)
1. Capital market—History—17th century.
2. Capital market—History—18th century.
3. Great Britain—Politics and government—1689–1702.
4. Great Britain—Politics and government—18th century.
5. Bank of England—History—18th century.
6. East India Company—History—18th century.
7. South Sea Company—History—18th century.   I. Title.
HG5432.C37   1996
332'.0414—dc20   95-53190   CIP

For my parents, Janet Wilson Greenhow and
Bruce Magoffin Carruthers; to my wife,
Wendy Nelson Espeland; and to my children,
Esther Jane Carruthers Espeland and
Samuel Nelson Espeland Carruthers.

Life goes on.

CONTENTS

FIGURES

TABLES

ACKNOWLEDGMENTS

SOCIOLOGICAL RESEARCH is a collective enterprise for which an individual author gets the credit or blame. Acknowledgments are an opportunity to spread that credit and blame around to those who truly deserve it. As this research moved forward, people too numerous to thank individually have examined and criticized various parts. Those who read a whole version may have already suffered enough, but nevertheless I must implicate Sarah Babb, Wendy Espeland, Carol Heimer, Christopher Jencks, Richard Lachmann, Karl Monsma, Charles Ragin, Peter Siegelman, Arthur Stinchcombe, and Richard Swedberg for their careful readings and constructive comments. As members of my dissertation committee, John Padgett, Theda Skocpol, and the late James Coleman helped to launch this project. John and Theda have continued to provide valuable advice and support, and I remain inspired by the high standard of scholarly rigor set by their own work. In timely conversations, Mark Granovetter and Michael Burawoy helped me to clarify various of my arguments, but in time-honored fashion I must fall on my sword and accept responsibility for all remaining errors.

The past and present members and staff of the Northwestern University Sociology Department have provided a truly supportive and friendly environment in which to undertake scholarship and have a family. Managing both has been much easier thanks to my colleagues but also, and especially, because of Heather Jones and Carmen Cranston. Thanks are due to two classical scholars, Jonathan Swift and Polly Hoover, for introducing me to Eumenes. Thanks also to Adam Gebler and Kate Wilson for their research assistance and to Ken Dauber for his graphic prowess. Working with Peter Dougherty and Bill Laznovsky at Princeton University Press has been a pleasure I recommend to all. For financial support, I am grateful to the American Bar Foundation (then directed by William L. F. Felstiner) and the Northwestern University Research Grants Committee.

During my time in England, I received ample assistance from the staffs of the Bodleian Library, Bank of England Archives, British Library, Centre for Socio-Legal Studies, Corporation of London Record Office, Guildhall Library, India Office Library, Public Record Office, and the Royal Bank of Scotland Archives. P.G.M. Dickson, Evelyn Cruikshanks, and Henry Roseveare provided helpful advice, although I'm sure I didn't follow enough of it.

In addition to many other fine qualities, my friends have helped me remain sane and enjoy life, two necessary conditions for getting research done. Thanks to Peter and Sean, Edwin, Lis, Alfred, Durkin, Ingrid and Bob,

Kathy and Nick, Sunita, Tom and Polly, Blair, Terry and Holly, Art and Carol, Mark, Maureen, Dennis and Susan, Bob and Lisa, Tessie, and Charles and Mary. For similar reasons, I thank my family, including Elspeth and Andrew, Mary and Erika, Anne and John, Scotty, Wendy, Mandy, Mark and Annie, Amos, Esther (I), and Obert. I am also deeply indebted to Samuel and Esther (II) for helping me to keep my work in proper perspective. Finally, I owe more than I can ever say to Wendy Espeland, for many, many reasons.

Throughout this book, I have used the masculine "he" as a generic pronoun because the overwhelming majority of persons I am referring to were male. Early modern England was a patriarchal society, so an analysis of political and economic elites necessarily deals mostly with men. Parts of chapter 7 are reprinted from Bruce G. Carruthers, "Homo Economicus and Homo Politicus: Non-Economic Rationality in the Early 18th Century London Stock Market," *Acta Sociologica* (1994), vol. 37, pp. 165–94, by permission of Scandinavian University Press, Oslo, Norway.

City of Capital

_____

Chapter One

INTRODUCTION

> Eumenes, however, perceiving that, while they despised
> one another, they feared him and were on the watch for an
> opportunity to kill him, pretended to be in need of money,
> and got together many talents by borrowing from those
> who hated him most, in order that they might put confi-
> dence in him and refrain from killing him out of regard
> for the money they had lent him. The consequence
> was that the wealth of others was his body-guard, and
> that, whereas men generally preserve their lives by
> giving, he alone won safety by receiving.
> —Plutarch

> It [the Bank of England] acts, not only as an ordinary bank,
> but as a great engine of state.
> —Adam Smith

EUMENES OF CARDIA was principal secretary to Alexander the Great and a member of his army. As a Greek general in a Macedonian force, Eumenes was regarded with suspicion and contempt. Those who served under him had to respect his martial abilities but this made the Macedonians fear and hate him even more. With the death of Alexander, Eumenes lost his sponsor and his situation suddenly became rather precarious. As Plutarch explained, Eumenes' response consisted of an unusual hostage strategy. He borrowed as much money as he could, especially from his bitterest rivals. As creditors, Eumenes' enemies acquired a financial interest in his ability to repay them, something which he could not do if he were dead. As a debtor, Eumenes made reluctant allies out of his creditors. He had, in effect, taken their money hostage.

The story of Eumenes points out an important fact about debtor-creditor relations. Debtors may depend on creditors for money but after the loan is made, creditors are in a sense beholden to their debtors. Their interests become aligned with the debtor because the creditor now has a stake in the ability of the debtor to repay. Since at least the fourth century B.C., debt has been one way to win friends and influence people.

Without knowing it, many have followed the same strategy. In this book, I am going to concentrate on how one group of debtors has exploited Eumenes' idea to create a financial constituency with an interest in their political survival. These are the sovereign debtors—the kings, rulers, states, and governments which have over the centuries obtained large sums of money from their creditors. It is natural to suppose that the point of borrowing money is to be able to fund activities that one cannot otherwise afford. But debt is not just about raising money, it is also about creating allies, and particularly when the debtor is sovereign, lending money takes on an inevitably political complexion. Sovereign creditors have a financial interest in the ability of sovereigns to repay their debts, and therefore they acquire a political interest in the survival of the sovereign regime. They become its allies.

Now imagine that Eumenes was a financial sophisticate who used negotiable promissory notes to borrow from his creditor-enemies. They would be able to sell the notes on the market and so could have alienated their financial claims, or accumulated more if they wished. In the market, Eumenes' notes might have been viewed as a financial commodity like other negotiable securities but it is certainly possible that the larger meaning of debtor-creditor relationships would affect trade in his notes. Some people might invest in his notes as a way to signal their support for Eumenes, while others might sell out as a sign of antipathy. In fact, Eumenes' debts were not alienable commodities but sovereign obligations frequently are. The political character of sovereign debtor-creditor relationships can shift to another level when the sovereign's debts become commodities that traders buy and sell. Political support and opposition can structure ownership and trading in sovereign debt and thereby politics enters into the marketplace.

If politics is concerned with power, markets are concerned with profit. One imagines that market traders who deal in sovereign debt are mostly apolitical profit-maximizers. Indeed, much of classical economic and sociological theory recommends this simple assumption, and no matter what their other disagreements, Adam Smith and Karl Marx both concurred that profit-seeking was the prime mover in market society. Following this line of argument, one might conclude that traders were unwilling to let politics interfere with business, and that the political significance of sovereign debt simply evaporated in the market. Certainly, the exclusion of politics from the market was recognized as an important feature. Adam Smith's self-interested man, the "prudent man": ". . . is averse to enter into any party disputes [and] hates faction" (Smith 1976 [1790]: 353).[1] The inherently apolitical nature of the market is still celebrated by Smith's disciples: "No one who buys bread knows whether the wheat from which it is made was grown by a Communist or a Republican, by a constitutionalist or a Fascist, or, for that matter, by a negro or a white. This illustrates how an impersonal market separates economic activities from political views. . . ." (Friedman 1962: 21).[2] Furthermore, the development of economic markets is understood as a process in which they become increasingly differentiated from noneconomic relationships and institutions. Extending Milton Friedman's argument, we would conclude that developed markets are less likely to be political than undeveloped ones, and that being apolitical signaled a market's "maturity."

In early modern Britain, sovereign debtor-creditor relations displayed both the real and imaginary aspects of Eumenes' situation. The national debt grew by leaps and bounds at the end of the seventeenth century and the number of sovereign creditors rose enormously. The post-Glorious Revolution regime acquired many allies by borrowing so heavily. At the same time, government debt became a highly liquid financial commodity, easily traded on an active London stock market. Unlike Eumenes' creditors, Crown creditors could buy and sell their government's debts by trading in joint-stock company shares.

The stock ledgers of the East India Company record a profusion of trading activity in company shares for the year 1712, chronicling the famous propensity of merchants to truck, barter, and exchange. The well-known merchant John Hopkins, nicknamed "Vulture" Hopkins for his mercantile temperament, traded twenty-one times for a total of £13,300 worth. Even busier was the London goldsmith Thomas Martin, who in one hundred and twenty-eight trades transacted stock worth over £100,000. The market where they bought and sold was located in Exchange Alley, near Lombard Street in central London. Information about shares was easy to obtain because daily prices were published in a number of newspapers, and standardized contracts to execute share transfers were common. Transactions were so commonplace that to trade in shares was very much "business as usual." The value of the shares these men traded was substantial, making it unlikely that their decisions were rash or ill-considered. Buying and selling was serious business, even for the sober-minded. Yet to conclude that the stock market was just a market, pure and simple, would be premature, for beneath the commercial hustle and bustle flowed strong political currents.

Like most of their colleagues, these two individuals had partisan loyalties, and many of their trades had a political angle. Thomas Martin showed strong Whig support by voting for the straight Whig ticket in both the 1710 and 1713 London parliamentary elections. Sixty-seven of his trades were with persons whose politics are unknown but of the remaining sixty-one trades, fifteen were with Tories and forty-six were with Whigs. Since this proportion roughly mirrors the proportion of Tory-to-Whig shareholders, Martin seemed not to care much about the politics of his trading partners. "Vulture" Hopkins was a Whig member of parliament. Only one of his trades was with a Tory, seven were with Whigs, and the remaining thirteen were with people whose political allegiances cannot be determined. His reputation for commercial acumen notwithstanding, Hopkins seemed to favor fellow party supporters when trading.

Like Eumenes' rivals, Hopkins and Martin were (indirectly) sovereign creditors. The East India Company traded with the far east but it also loaned large sums of money to the British government. As shareowners, Hopkins and Martin had in effect lent their money to a sovereign debtor but it is hard to know why they traded the way they did. Perhaps they were acting on their personal political preferences; or perhaps situational factors encouraged them to trade more with the supporters of one party than the other. Or it could be that the partisanship of trading partners was an irrelevant aspect of trading activity that all simply ignored. At the same time, Joseph Addison remarked on the ability of the Royal Exchange to erase social and national differences, and to draw together a highly diverse group of people who would otherwise never congregate.[3] This suggests that partisanship didn't matter in the market.

One naturally assumes that people trading shares were trying to turn a profit and that their chief goal was an economic one. But can this make sense of the apparent partisanship of John Hopkins, or the relative indifference of Thomas Martin? More generally, can the assumption of economic rationality account for such behavior in the early modern London stock market? My intention here is to set aside such assumptions and reconsider the relationship between polity and market. Are there circumstances where political goals can be pursued in the marketplace? Does evidence of political action mean that the market is inefficient, irrational, or undeveloped? Friedman's argument suggests that it would be unwise even to try to achieve political aims through economic action, for a competitive market would automatically punish such an attempt. The eighteenth-century journalist and commentator Richard Steele suggested that traders knew better than to be diverted by such concerns, for: ". . . as Gain is the chief End of such a People, they never pursue any other" (Ross 1982: 447).[4] How could a market be a suitable location for the pursuit of political goals?

This book is about how politics and political conflict influence economic institutions. For modern capitalist societies, it is common to follow Friedman's reasoning and suppose that markets and polities are distinct and that each sphere has behavior that is uniquely appropriate to it: people lobby and vote in politics but they buy and sell in the marketplace; they exercise their voice in the polity and use the exit option in the market.[5] Furthermore, the separation of the two social spheres is compelling for mixed modes are intellectually and even morally troublesome. To buy and sell political influence is a form of corruption, and to let politics interfere with the market is considered inefficient if not irrational.[6] It is easy to envision a substantial compartmentalization of the two spheres. Persons may devotedly vote for the same political party, year after year, while in business paying no attention to political allegiances, buying and selling to all. Their lives would comprise distinct political and economic roles, and they would switch between them depending on the situation.

The current theoretical interchange between economics and sociology is relevant for understanding this issue. In recent years, there has been a growing interest within sociology in the rational choice perspective that is at the heart of neoclassical economics.[7] As well, economists have increasingly taken on questions and topics that formerly were considered within the realm of sociology (e.g., marriage, crime, and discrimination) and have provided rational choice explanations of social institutions.[8] Gary Becker's simple claim that the economic approach applies: ". . . to all human behavior" (Becker 1976: 8) exemplifies the trend. All of this creates the impression that economics has something to say to sociology but not the other way around, and is reinforced by the widespread belief that the modern market is an autonomous system with its own internal economic logic.[9] Along with Granovetter (1985, 1992, 1993), Zelizer (1989, 1994), Smelser and Swedberg (1994), Stinchcombe (1983), and others, however, I believe that sociologists can offer important insights into economic phenomena.

To argue this point I focus upon that most economic of institutions, the stock market, and show how its growth and dynamics were influenced by political relationships. To understand what happened in this market, we must look outside to its partisan context. The London stock market is well suited as a case with which to assess economic and sociological perspectives.[10] As a capital market in a capitalist economy, it forms the empirical core for economic theorizing. If the economic approach works anywhere, it is in capital markets.

Most people studying the relationship between politics and economics in capitalist democracies suppose that political action is used to serve an economic interest, or that the economy is the "base" and politics the "superstructure." For example, people "vote their pocketbooks" and support the political candidate or party they believe will best raise their incomes or lower their taxes. Or they pressure the government to pass legislation favorable to their economic interests, as when an industry pushes for high tariffs to protect it from foreign competition. They let their economic interests dictate their politics. Similarly, one can interpret the political tensions of class struggle as rooted in the contradictory economic interests of workers and capitalists.

The relationship between politics and economics is not, however, a unilateral one. To be sure, economic interests shape political action but that is only half the story. When people pursue their political goals in the marketplace, political interests influence economic action.[11] People can let political considerations influence their decisions to buy and sell. What makes this logical possibility seem empirically improbable, however, is the fact that economic competition compels market participants to keep their eyes on the bottom line. In the heat of economic battle, dabbling in politics is a luxury most cannot afford, for someone who plays political favorites can be underpriced by those who don't.[12] To indulge in political distractions is the kind of inefficiency that competitive markets are supposed to punish. In this book I consider a situation where politics did influence economics, despite the competitiveness of the market. By understanding how and why political conflict conditioned economic behavior, I consider how effectively market forces like competition can keep politics out.[13]

The connection between politics and economics rests on more than just idiosyncratic preferences. I will not argue that the English had a peculiar taste for politics which was expressed, however inappropriately, in the stock market. There were strong institutional linkages joining the stock market to the English state and the two political parties who were competing for control. So basic were these connections that development of the state went hand in hand with development of the market. In 1672, there was no stock market in London, and England was a weak nation-state and second-rate military power. In 1712, only forty years later, the shares of many joint-stock companies were traded on an active and highly organized capital market that had emerged in London. Furthermore, Great Britain had become one of the major military powers in Europe and had successfully checked French expansion in the War of the Spanish Succession. These two dramatic changes, one economic and the other political-military, were intimately related and it is their connection which made it possible for the Bank of England to act as a "great engine of state."

The sheer intensity of partisan conflict also helped to forge a connection between politics and economics. This period of English history was striking for the hostility between Whigs and Tories, and their intense rivalry was an undeniable feature of political life. Of course, the mere fact of political competition doesn't necessarily mean it had any influence on market behavior. Indeed, quite the opposite was claimed at the time, for one of the arguments made in support of capitalism was that cool-headed economic self-interest would help to subdue a whole variety of passions, political and otherwise.[14] Commerce would affect politics rather than vice versa. By contrast, I will show that Whig-Tory conflict contingently and subtly shaped the London stock market. In explaining why and how it did, I will highlight the nexus of institutional links that joined the state, public debt, the major joint-stock companies, and which then extended to control over joint-stock companies and finally to trading on the stock market. It will become clear how these links managed to "transmit" political conflicts into a rational marketplace.

This book is also about state formation in the early modern era, and how social elites became attached to the state. Financial capacity was a central part of the story.[15] The power of the state grew as its ability to mobilize economic resources expanded. Taxing and borrowing were two ways in which states extracted the money they needed to fight wars and secure control over their own territories: taxes and loans paid for a bureaucratic and military apparatus. Yet the role of public financial machinery was not simply an extractive one, for it was also political. Schumpeter pointed out that "the spirit of a people, its cultural level, its social structure, the deeds its policy may prepare—all this and more is written in its fiscal history" (Schumpeter 1991: 101). In early modern England, spirit and culture mattered less than social structure and policy.

Most historical sociologists and historians suppose that early modern state-builders constructed alliances with elites by using "political" institutions. For example, in the British case landed elites co-governed through the instruments of Parliament and local government. In other countries, elites were granted state offices, assimilated into clientage networks, or participated in government through estates, councils, or other representational institutions. These were all ways in which early modern elites were incorporated and co-opted by an expanding state.[16] Here, I propose that elites also became attached to states and regimes through the less-obviously "political" means of debtor-creditor relationships. Under certain circumstances (particularly war), states and regimes had to borrow money, and those from whom states borrowed entered into a financial relationship with them. Creditors acquired a vested financial interest in the continuation of the state, government, or regime to whom they loaned money, and public debtor-creditor relations concerned what Robert Brenner (1993) has aptly called "politically constituted property rights."

Debtor-creditor relationships are "contractual" in that two parties voluntarily participate in a transaction where the creditor loans a sum to the debtor, in exchange for a stream of repayments extending into the future. It is not a simultaneous exchange (or "spot transaction") in which each party comes away from the transaction with what the other gave them. The debtor gets his money right away but the creditor isn't repaid until later. This presents two problems for the creditor. First, he wants the debtor's commitment to repay the debt to be a credible one, which is why creditors prefer legally enforceable debt contracts. But the creditor also gains an interest in the ability of the debtor to repay, and in the very existence of the debtor. He doesn't want the debtor to, for example, drop dead before the money gets repaid, and so the creditor acquires an interest in the health, financial and otherwise, of his debtor. The same obligation that binds the debtor to the creditor also, in a curious way, binds the creditor to the debtor. This creates the potential for a complex balance of power between debtors and creditors, and modifies the usual picture of a debtor beholden to his or her creditors.

Now consider the situation when the debtor also happens to be a sovereign ruler or government. As before, the ruler receives a lump sum from the creditor, and promises in return to make a series of payments to the creditor over a period of time. But the credibility of the ruler's promise was often doubtful because the laws that could bind a debtor usually did not apply to sovereigns.[17] Furthermore, creditors of the sovereign acquired an interest in the political health of the regime to whom they had loaned money, for they were among the biggest losers if the regime "died." It is rare, for example, that post-revolutionary regimes live up to the financial obligations of the regime they have overthrown.[18] In a sense, creditors became *politically* obliged to the debtor-regime just as the regime was *financially* obliged to them.

Creditors must necessarily be drawn from those who have money to lend. Domestic sovereign creditors came from the economic elite of British society but British elites were neither united nor monolithic. In the early eighteenth century they consisted (roughly) of a traditional landed elite and a new and growing monied elite. Divisions within the elite were reflected in political conflict between Whig and Tory parties. In general, the landed gentry sided with the Tories while the commercial and mercantile classes supported the Whigs. Competition between Whigs and Tories mirrored the conflict between landed and mercantile elites, and party strife was sufficiently fierce to raise fears of a return to civil war. It was this political conflict which penetrated into the stock market.

As the vehicle through which a government borrowed, the national debt was an economic means to establish a political relationship between elites and the state. In Britain, it was used to bring into the fold an elite which was otherwise largely excluded. Parliament was, and continued to be for many centuries, dominated by traditional landed elites (gentry and aristocracy).[19] Traders and mercantile capitalists represented a new form of wealth, a new propertied class, but one which had little voice in parliament. Through the national debt, their financial interests were joined to that of the post-1688 regime.[20] And so, as the public debt grew from £6.1 million in 1694 to £78 million in 1750, as the total number of public creditors grew from about five thousand in 1694 to approximately sixty thousand by the middle of the eighteenth century, more and more of the political nation became financially bound to the government.[21] By creating and expanding this financial constituency, the ruling regime was better able to face the serious threats posed to its sovereignty by Louis XIV's France and his sponsorship of Jacobite Pretenders to the British throne.[22]

WHY THIS CASE?

To understand how politics can influence economics requires a careful examination of the institutional linkages between these two spheres, and a close inspection of individual economic behavior. The trade-off between historical detail and sample size is a familiar one but selection of an appropriate case can remedy many of the problems that face a study with a sample of one.

Most discussions of the emergence of market society are set in terms of the transition from feudalism to capitalism.[23] While it remains an open question whether market forces eroded feudal social structures, or if feudal class structures engendered markets, it is obvious that the spread of markets was a central part of this change. Rather than reconsider the "which came first" questions that have traditionally been at the center of this debate, I focus instead upon the process of market formation. Where do markets come from? How are they organized?

To answer these questions I will look at late seventeenth- and early eighteenth-century England, where an organized and centralized market emerged rapidly. I have selected 1672 and 1712 as two dates to highlight so as to examine the case before and after the rise of the market (and the emergence of political parties), and better understand the formative process. In 1672, a major default by Charles II, namely, the Stop of the Exchequer, exemplified one of the major problems with sovereign borrowing, but also left behind many useful records related to public finance. After the stock market developed, 1712 was a year when the market was perhaps least influenced by national elections, financial crises, or major changes in joint-stock companies. Internal dynamics rather than external shocks determined how the market operated, and what happened cannot be dismissed as atypical or aberrant. The years 1672 and 1712 are comparable to one another in the sense that England faced similar kinds of fiscal problems and political controversies at both points, although with one crucial difference—there were two political parties in 1712 but none in 1672.

The choice of a capital market is especially appropriate for several reasons. Capital markets possess more than just etymological significance in capitalist economies, and to study their emergence can provide additional insight into the larger historical process of the emergence of capitalism. The credit institutions that developed in the seventeenth and eighteenth centuries made an important contribution to Britain's Industrial Revolution,[24] although the "transition" literature has focused mostly upon agriculture and agrarian class relations or upon trade. Additionally, the relevance of a sociological approach to economic phenomena will be clearer if it can be demonstrated for something as central to economic theorizing as capital markets, the *sanctus sanctorum* of economic rationality and efficiency.

Modern capital markets have enjoyed pride of place in economic theory. Compared to other markets, they have many informed buyers and sellers trading in homogeneous commodities with low transaction costs, and so come close to satisfying the conditions of perfect competition.[25] Capital markets were used to develop rational expectations theory and the enormously influential efficient markets hypothesis.[26] The people who participate in stock and bond markets have a richly deserved reputation for being concerned to make money. If *homo economicus* has a home, it is surely the capital market.

The recent "institutional turn" in economics and the "law and economics" school of jurisprudence reflect a greater awareness of the importance of the

institutional framework for markets.[27] Markets are no longer thought to be
self-sustaining but rather are understood to depend on legal and political
institutions which, for example, maintain property rights and enforce contracts. The recent experience of trying to help Eastern European nations
build a market economy has given economists renewed appreciation for the
importance of institutions. Many of the legal, political, and economic institutions now common to capitalist democracies appeared first in England, and
help explain the rise of the London stock market. Early modern England
was a country with vigorous markets. It was the first country to make the
transition from feudalism to capitalism; it was a leader in the development
of capitalist agriculture, and later was the first country to industrialize.[28] By
virtue of England's role in worldwide economic development, the process of
market formation in England possesses historic importance.

The seventeenth century also witnessed the birth of political economy. As
both Appleby (1978) and Agnew (1986) have argued, English social commentators were struck by the distinctive character of the market. They understood it as an autonomous sphere, differentiated from the rest of society
and possessing its own comprehensible order. The market was a separate
entity with an internal logic, and the goal of political economy, and later
economics, was to discern that logic. Unlike the Church or State, the market
had no hierarchical organization or centralized governance: it was a diffuse
and decentralized institution animated by the pursuit of individual self-
interest. In sharp contrast to gift exchange, which in virtually all societies
is used to establish social relations and maintain status differences, market exchange appeared to be asocial and largely unencumbered by such
considerations.[29]

William Reddy observed that in the seventeenth century:

> The idea that monetary exchange was a politically free form of relationship was
> found to dovetail nicely with the idea that gain was the operative motive in all
> exchanges. In both notions one particular kind of exchange came to serve as an
> implicit paradigm. In this exchange, money and tangible commodity are virtu-
> ally the only things that pass between the two parties, who are indifferent to
> each other in every other respect and perfectly free of other entanglements
> with each other. (Reddy 1987: 74)

In this period there was a heightened consciousness of the significance of
market society, precisely because of the market's novelty, dynamism, and
distinction. The market was disrespectful of traditional social statuses and
obligations, for it valued economic efficiency above all else.[30] The social
meaning of the market inevitably influenced the political response to those
"monied men" who helped create London's stock market. At the same time
that the market challenged the old social order, monied men were considered a threat to traditional ruling elites.

The evidence for the rise of the London stock market is impressive. According to one measure, the number of trades in East India Company stock rose from an average of 44 per annum in the early 1660s to over 650 in the late 1680s.[31] After borrowing the techniques of the Dutch, who were then the world's foremost capitalists, the London market quickly acquired many of the features of a modern stock market. It was highly centralized (located in Exchange Alley in central London) and became organized around a group of financial specialists and brokers. A financial press developed that disseminated inexpensive and accurate information on share prices, exchange rates, interest rates, and so on. Standardized financial contracts were used to execute trades, including options and futures contracts. The overall size of the market grew very rapidly, both in the number of different securities traded and the numbers of trades and traders. Econometric research suggests that it was an efficient capital market, as well.[32]

THE STATE AND THE MARKET

How can one account for the sudden emergence of a market that even today plays an important role in international finance? Economic explanations frequently stress the role of property rights and there is an extensive literature on how this occurs. It points to changes in property rights as a key element in the rise of markets.[33] Commodities are defined as "bundles of rights" over things, not the things themselves, and so without well-established property rights there is nothing to exchange. And without exchange, of course, there is no market. Government typically plays a central role in the articulation and protection of property rights, and so processes of state-formation become intertwined with processes of market formation.

In the British legal tradition, property rights structure the relations between individuals and the objects they possess. Owners have a bundle of specific rights and powers over the objects they own, and according to Sir William Blackstone's classic formulation, property is: ". . . that sole and despotic dominion which one man claims and exercises over the external things of the world" (Blackstone 1765: 2). However, because they structure social relations, property rights are also about associations among people. The connection between property ownership and social stratification (or class, in the Marxist sense) is an obvious illustration of this fact. Relations between different social classes are based on systematic differences in the property rights held by groups of people, with the primary distinction being between those who do and those who do not own the means of production. Here, I examine the financial property rights that gave legal shape to the relations between debtors and creditors. The property rights of sovereign creditors were especially troublesome because they were so hard to enforce. A monarch who defaulted on a loan could seldom be sued in the royal courts of law.

The significance of formal property rights cannot be ignored but I will argue that partisan politics also affected how the stock market grew. Whig-Tory rivalry helped to propel the market forward by injecting into it a set of political incentives, and partisanship influenced how formal property rights were used in practice.[34] At its heart, the reason for this was simple: the joint-stock companies whose shares were traded on the stock market were heavily involved in public debt. The three biggest companies (the Bank of England, the South Sea Company, and the East India Company) made large loans to the government. Since there were no general laws of incorporation, each company received at its founding a special royal or parliamentary charter. In exchange for the exclusive privileges granted in such a charter, companies loaned large sums of money to the government. Funding public expenditures through loans embroiled the joint-stock companies in politics and in the struggle between Whig and Tory parties.

If, as North (1981) would have it, property rights are the key to economic growth, and if the state is the foundation for property rights, then to understand markets one must consider the state.[35] Early modern England possessed a distinctively "weak" state along with its "strong" markets.[36] A state's strength may be gauged by its ability to intervene in the social, economic, and political activities of civil society.[37] A strong state can more easily extract domestic resources and build up its military strength. By this measure, post-feudal English monarchs were weak because they had to share power with the gentry.[38] Decentralized and unbureaucratic, heavily reliant upon the participation of local elites, the English state would appear to have been at a disadvantage when it came to war-making. War is expensive, and but for the English Channel it is easy to believe that England might have become a French province.

The connection between states and wars and between state-building and war-making is fundamental. As Weber underscored in his famous definition, a state monopolizes the means of coercion (Weber 1946: 78).[39] Such coercive powers were applied both internally and externally. External wars required the extraction of resources needed to maintain armies and navies, but these coercive forces could in turn be used internally on domestic populations to extract more resources, a fact that made the English wary of "standing armies."[40] Building up a military apparatus was a key part in building a state apparatus. Being able to fight a war and possessing a strong state, were virtually two sides of the same coin.

Many others have commented on the connection between states and capitalism in the early modern era and why military power played such an important role. Charles Tilly (1990), Michael Mann (1986), and Otto Hintze (1975) have outlined the important reciprocal relationship between war-making and state-building.[41] Wars necessitated the mobilization of resources to pay for the army and navy, which required the buildup of a substantial fiscal apparatus whose exactions were partly enforced through domestic application of the very military force they helped to fund. A more commercialized economy generally made resource extraction easier, and so economic development was also implicated in the process. The state's coercive powers also gave it a special role in the protection of property rights, as North (1981) has argued.

Discussions of state strength often focus upon how much political power is centralized or dispersed. By this standard, the difference between seventeenth-century England and France was substantial. The English monarch shared power with the Common Law Courts, Parliament, and local government.[42] Judicial, legislative, and executive powers were separate, and executive power was itself fragmented between central and local government. In absolutist France, by contrast, Louis XIV concentrated in his royal personage legislative, judicial, and executive powers. Sovereignty belonged exclusively to the King, who was also the supreme judge and above the law.[43] Louis headed a French state organization with a far greater ability to intervene in the lives of his subjects than Charles II of England. For example, the total number of royal officials in all the counties of England was much less than the number in a single French province.[44]

The attempts by Charles II and James II to imitate Louis XIV's absolutist monarchy reflected the discrepancy between England and France.[45] Charles, for example, modeled his standing army directly after the French army and through the secret Treaty of Dover (1670) received a French subsidy to help reduce his financial dependence upon Parliament.[46] The same strategy was behind the Third Dutch War (1672–74), which Charles launched with the intention of boosting royal revenues by extracting a substantial war indemnity as well as commercial concessions. In the same vein, he issued the Declaration of Indulgence (1672) to make dissenting Protestants directly dependent on the king. Again, the intention was to reduce Charles's dependency on Parliament and make him more like Louis XIV.[47] Both Charles II and James II were envious of Louis's power and autonomy, but their admiration was not reciprocated. To Louis, England seemed a weak vacillating country plagued by a troubled political past, and the situation of English monarchs was not one he wished to emulate.[48]

Less than a decade after the start of James II's reign, England and its allies were caught in a great military struggle with France. For all of the apparent weakness of its state, England under William III and later Queen Anne sustained an unprecedented military effort on land and at sea. England supported armies totaling 170,000 troops in 1710–11, while France, a nation with almost four times the population, managed to amass an army of about 250,000 troops. At the same time, the English navy outgunned and outmanned the French navy.[49] In a short time, England went from second-rate status to being one of the Great Powers,[50] and this rapid growth in strength was crucial for Britain's later defeat of France in the struggle for world hegemony.[51] The emergence of the British "fiscal-military state" is well worth examining for it underscores the importance of economic markets for state strength.

Douglass North (1981) and Margaret Levi (1988) propose that the primary goal of early modern rulers was to maximize revenue, and that the main instrument for this was the system of property rights. Property rights set the rules for the production, use, and exchange of valuable resources, and give to some persons (owners) the right to exclude others from use of their property. Property rights must ultimately be maintained through coercive power, and so the organization controlling coercion in a given society, the state, played a central role. Rulers sought to increase their revenues but they understood that outright confiscation of a nation's wealth would not work in the long run, even when it was possible.[52] Rulers used their control over property rights to facilitate market activity, encourage economic growth, and ultimately give themselves a larger tax base. But if forced to choose between revenues and economic growth, they took the former.

Jack Goldstone and Brian Downing both consider the political consequences of warfare and its effect on public finance. For Goldstone (1991, 1986), strained state finances are a major contributor to political revolution. In combination with other factors, fiscal distress makes a state vulnerable to political challenge.[53] According to Downing (1992), warfare required the buildup of a state apparatus to extract resources, and the more intensive and expensive the warfare, the harder the state had to squeeze. In its political consequences, exploitation of a domestic economy was antidemocratic. The representative institutions and political machinery inherited from medieval times could not easily survive in a harsh environment of ruthless war-making and fiscal exaction. Thus, countries in competitive geopolitical circumstances, such as Prussia, became un- and even antidemocratic; whereas democracy in some form survived in countries like England, protected from Continental predators by the English Channel. By Goldstone's and Downing's arguments, the financial developments that helped England to pay for its wars also fostered its democratic institutions and enhanced its political stability.

All of these arguments are concerned with the causes or consequences of the state's ability to mobilize resources within the territories it governs. In the early modern period, warfare was the main activity to which economic resources were devoted, and taxation was the most obvious way in which states secured resources. Taxes can be obtained with or without the consent of the taxed, although agreement made the process easier. Such consent was obtained through representative institutions like parliaments, parlements, or estates. When taxes were actively opposed by the taxed population, or were assessed without consent, collection became much harder. Part of the growing strength of the English state came from the increased participation of Parliament in fiscal policy, a political change whose importance many others have noted.[54] It was harder to resist taxes which Parliament had authorized.

No matter how effective an early modern tax system might be, however, it could never adequately deal with the onslaught of spending associated with war. This became particularly true after the Military Revolution of the early seventeenth century, when the size of armies and the scale of combat grew much larger.[55] At least in the short run, expenditures exceeded tax revenues, and borrowing was necessary to fill the breach. This points to yet another important part of the increased strength of Britain's fiscal-military state: its ability to borrow on an unprecedented scale. When it couldn't tax enough, or soon enough, to cover military spending, Britain was able to induce those with capital to invest in the national debt. Taxing is easier with consent, but borrowing *requires* the consent of lenders.[56] Lenders voluntarily provide money to a debtor in exchange for a future stream of repayments. The financial machinery necessary to borrow on a large scale was erected in this period and once created, it could be used for other purposes.

In subsequent chapters, I show how the processes of market formation and state development were linked together. The London capital market was central to the improvements in public finance that gave strength to this weak state. But the market did not only help fund the military adventures of British monarchs, nor provide a home for *homo economicus*. Because of the connections between political parties and public finance, the market was also used to pursue other kinds of interests. It wasn't simply that English rulers encouraged the market because it enlarged the tax base, as North's argument would have it, but also that the English ruling elite, divided along party lines, turned the market into a political battlefield.

The two dates I have selected, 1672 and 1712, span England's rise to international prominence, and also some important domestic political changes. The two most noteworthy were the shift in power from monarch to Parliament that occurred during the Glorious Revolution of 1689, and the formation of two political parties (Whig and Tory) starting at the end of the 1670s. The shift in power gave greater political importance to the House of Commons, while the rise of parties organized Parliament's power. Party conflict became the chief organizing principle of English politics in the late seventeenth and early eighteenth century. Conflict was intense and party cleavages penetrated into the Church and into municipal and local government, in addition to the House of Commons and House of Lords.

Joint-Stock Companies in Political Context

The connections among politics, public finance, and the stock market can be traced on two levels. At the institutional level, political parties were centrally involved in the establishment of the three major joint-stock companies (the Bank of England, the New East India Company, and the South Sea Company), and the attempted (but unsuccessful) founding of the Land Bank. The shares of these companies constituted the majority of all shares traded, and so they dominated the London stock market. The same companies also extended large long-term loans to the government and thereby played an important role in public finance. They embodied, in effect, the connection between the private capital market and public finance.

Contemporaries generally regarded debtor-creditor relationships as one-sided, with creditors enjoying the balance of power. Many believed that as a crucial source of much-needed money, joint-stock companies had leverage over the government. By the end of the War of the Spanish Succession in 1713, the government had borrowed in excess of £16 million from these three companies, more than from any other source. It also borrowed substantial sums from individual investors in the form of annuities and lottery loans, but that money came from a large number of dispersed creditors who could not act in a politically organized fashion, even if they wanted to. If Parliament's control over public purse strings gave it a voice in government policy, then the companies' control over loans also granted them some influence, or so many thought. For political parties whose goal it was to determine policy, this created a powerful incentive to try to seize the joint-stock companies and exploit the political leverage they possessed. In addition, such control brought financial rewards. With government spending at wartime levels, public finance provided many profitable opportunities for those with the right connections. Investment in government debt was an attractive alternative to overseas trade, which even in peacetime was a risky investment, and to landed property, which at the end of the seventeenth century was burdened by a heavy land tax and high interest rates.[57] Control over joint-stock companies conferred both political and economic advantages to the party that could seize it.

Political Trading

Individual market behavior also reflected the influence of politics. Participation in a stock market involves buying and selling a financial commodity. Ordinarily, we suppose that the point of the buying and selling is to make money or assemble an optimal investment portfolio. Those who become distracted by other goals are eventually bankrupted by those who keep their eyes on the bottom line. Using data on stock transfers, derived from the stock ledgers of the Bank and East India Company, I study patterns of share ownership and share trading for the East India Company and Bank of England in 1712.[58]

How would one know that a particular trade in a market was politically, as opposed to economically, motivated? Can we tell if a trader was more concerned about partisanship than about pounds, shillings, and pence? There are several things to consider before answering in the affirmative. First, it must be clear that there *could be* some kind of political goal that a trader might have pursued through the market. If there was no plausible political end to be served this way, then one can hardly suppose that people in the market were intentionally behaving "politically." Second, one must have a clear idea of what it meant to be apolitical in the market. That is, one must understand what pattern of behavior would arise if people were uninterested in politics or did not let it influence their trading decisions.

Control over joint-stock companies brought with it the opportunity to influence government policy and provide financial rewards to the party faithful. Political ends could be served in the stock market because decisions about share trading ultimately influenced who controlled the company. Voting and economic rights were both in the bundle of property rights that constituted a company share. A shareholder had claims on profits (in the form of dividends) but he or she also had a right to vote for company directors, and thus could help choose company management. If Whig and Tory parties were struggling for control over the joint-stock companies, then their best strategy was to buy blocks of shares (and avoid selling them to the other party) and use their voting rights to elect Whig or Tory company directors. Thus, political goals could be pursued through the buying and selling of shares.

Apolitical traders will focus upon their economic goals and ignore extraneous concerns and distractions. Traders such as these behave rationally in an economically self-interested way and are the familiar inhabitants of economics textbooks. In competitive markets with secure property rights and homogeneous goods, economically rational traders behave in accordance with the Law of Indifference, enunciated by W. Stanley Jevons (1931). Markets populated by rational traders are anonymous and impersonal. Traders focus on the price and quantity of goods but are indifferent to the social characteristics of the people they deal with. So long as the other person's "money is green," a rational trader will trade with anyone. Early eighteenth-century London had the kind of capital market to which this law applies. Indeed, historians have noted a number of "marriages of convenience" between kings and their financiers which strongly suggest that political differences could be set aside in the pursuit of mutual economic interests.[59]

The Law of Indifference predicts patterns of trading in which social boundaries are regularly transgressed. Indifferent traders ignore differences

in status, gender, class, nationality, race, religion, ethnicity, political allegiances, or whatever other social characteristic one can think of. The pursuit
of self-interest compels them to trade across all these lines, and the market
such traders create does not respect traditional social distinctions. Under
certain circumstances, however, it may be economically rational to pay attention to the social identity of a trading partner. But with secure property
rights and homogeneous goods in a competitive market, these circumstances
do not apply.

To discriminate is, in economic terms, not to be indifferent.[60] It means
treating different categories of people differently. Discriminatory economic
behavior occurs, for example, when a buyer or seller responds to some economically irrelevant social characteristic of a potential supplier, client, trading partner, or customer. Gender and race are two common bases for economic discrimination. Refusing to sell goods to someone from another racial
group, or refusing to hire a woman (even though she is as qualified for the
job as a man) are instances of discrimination. Together, discriminating buyers and sellers reproduce social boundaries in the market.

Although it may seem irrational to discriminate, some explanations have
been offered to show how and when discrimination can be economically
rational. If social features can be used to indicate other hard-to-measure
characteristics, then it may be sensible to discriminate. This is what economists call "statistical discrimination." If gender, for example, could be used
to estimate job commitment, then employers might rationally discriminate
against women on the grounds that they tended to be less committed to
their work than men.[61] Or it may be that because of a faulty legal system, it
is important that trading partners be trustworthy. If people cannot trust
contract law to enforce their agreements, it would be rational to look for
other means of enforcement. People will prefer to trade with others they
find trustworthy, and this often means trading with people who are members of the same social group. Common group membership provides the
basis for informal sanctions that compensate for the absence of formal legal
sanctions.[62]

Such explanations suggest that discrimination in a market (trading that
reproduces group boundaries) could be economically rational. In the case of
the London stock market, if the Law of Indifference is violated because of
political discrimination, it is necessary to be sure that such discrimination
was not just solving an economic problem (minimizing transaction costs,
providing informal sanctions to compensate for faulty contract law, etc.) before concluding that traders were trying to achieve political goals. But after
considering this alternative explanation, I will show how domestic political
allegiances and international political commitments influenced patterns of
share trading.

My general point is that more than just economic behavior takes place in a market. Although it is considered the primary locus for the single-minded pursuit of profits, a market can be a setting in which to pursue other kinds of ends and enact other kinds of social relationships. People bring to markets a rich set of economic and noneconomic motivations. Markets are not populated solely by *homines economici,* and so to understand the structure and dynamics of the market one must look outside to the social context.

In taking up this line of reasoning, I am extending arguments made by Mark Granovetter (1985, 1992, 1993) and others. Granovetter points out that economic relationships are *embedded* in social relationships, and that one cannot understand economic behavior outside of its social context. His programmatic declaration (1985) left unresolved *how* and *why* economic behavior was embedded in social relations, or in *which* social relations it was embedded. But by tracing out the connections that joined partisan conflict over public policy, the use of the national debt to fund the war, company loans to the government, control over joint-stock companies, votes in directors' elections, and trading in company stock, I will answer these how, why, and which questions for the case of the London stock market.

OUTLINE OF THE ARGUMENT

To understand how politics influenced economic institutions, it is first necessary to understand politics. Chapter 2 surveys English politics between 1672 and 1712 and discusses political institutions and how they changed. This was an eventful period that witnessed the growth of Parliamentary power and the formation within Parliament of two political parties, Whigs and Tories. In 1672, there were no political parties in England and Charles II clearly had the upper hand over an occasionally unruly Parliament. In contrast, by 1712 there were two parties and Parliament and Crown were much closer to equal partners. Britain was governed by the King-in-Parliament rather than the King alone. Perhaps the best indicator of the change was Parliament's increased role in public finance. After the Glorious Revolution of 1688, Parliament controlled the public purse strings. Before then, monarchs like Charles II and James II enjoyed more financial independence from Parliament, although not as much as they wanted. When William and Mary took the throne, William immediately brought England into the war with France, for reasons that will become obvious. English foreign policy kept it involved in warfare for most of the next twenty-five years. This militaristic stance forced the Crown to turn to Parliament for more money, and motivated many of the changes in public finance.

The Whig party was born in the Exclusion Crisis of the late 1670s, with the Tories forming in reaction. Religion was at the heart of the Exclusion Crisis, for what united the new Whig party was the conviction that James Duke of York, Charles II's younger brother, was a Catholic and as such should not inherit the throne. The Whigs received strong support from voters in the three general elections of the crisis period but failed to convince Charles that he should alter the line of succession. They survived their failure to exclude James, and the conflict between Whig and Tory parties continued into the eighteenth century. Religion remained an important point of contention but other key issues included foreign policy, public finances, and immigration.

The formation of the two parties altered English politics by changing how politics was organized. Their conflict also served as a reminder of the deep divisions among English political elites, which against the backdrop of the Civil War explains why institutionalized political conflict was never fully legitimate.[63] How elites became allied with the state mirrored their political divisions. The landed interest, which predominantly was a Tory constituency and the traditional ruling elite, joined the state through parliament. The monied interest, Whig constituents and a rising threat to the traditional ruling class, joined the state through financial ties.

In chapter 3, I examine the fiscal and political buildup of the British state from 1672 to 1712, tracing in detail what Tilly (1990) calls the "capitalized coercion" path of state formation. Britain became a great power without a large state apparatus. How did it do this? I discuss the war-driven changes in public revenues and public borrowing. Public revenues improved as the state relied less on tax farming and shifted to direct collection.[64] Public borrowing altered with the differentiation of short-term from long-term debt and the tremendous growth of the latter during the wars with France. The ability to borrow allowed Britain to finance its expenses. Through the development of its financial machinery, the British state greatly expanded its capacity to mobilize domestic resources. But through the growth of the national debt, the state also managed to create alliances with Britain's mercantile and commercial classes. Those who invested in the national debt acquired a financial stake in the political viability of the regime.

The point of comparison for 1712 will be 1672, when Charles II defaulted on his loans in the "Stop of the Exchequer." A detailed analysis of the Stop shows how it was that in subsequent years the government avoided similar defaults, even though it was borrowing much more than Charles II ever did. As well, the Stop allows us to investigate the structure of public debt and the social composition of public creditors.

Chapter 4 puts Britain's experience in a comparative context and surveys the public financial systems of four other European countries: France, the Dutch Republic, Spain, and Sweden. The comparisons will help determine which were the crucial ingredients for successful state-building, and also outline different variants of the "Eumenes effect." The primary contrasts will be between Britain, on the one hand, and France and the Dutch Republic, on the other. These two were Britain's main political and commercial rivals. Spain and Sweden are also included because they were both military powers in decline, and allow for a consideration of countries whose fiscal systems were unable to match Britain's success.

The Dutch Republic is a natural comparison for several reasons. First, the English learned most of their financial techniques from the Dutch. The London stock market was modeled after the Amsterdam Bourse, and long-term funded public debt first developed in Holland and was later emulated in Britain. Furthermore, as in Britain, the financial interests of wealthy elites were allied to the state through public debt. Second, the Dutch were paragons of indifference and notoriously reluctant to let politics interfere with trade. Not only would the Dutch happily loan money to governments at war with each other, thus making money on both sides of a conflict, but, even more impressive, the Dutch were willing to trade with their own enemies, even as war raged.[65] Commentators trying to explain the success of the Dutch often touched on the connection between commerce and toleration: those who would traffic without prejudice were bound to be more successful.[66] Dutch trading, in other words, appeared to conform to the Law of Indifference.

The Dutch followed an extreme path of state formation, what Tilly (1990) calls "capital intensive." With a small population and few natural resources, the Dutch erected a remarkable state apparatus whose fiscal power was only partly offset by the radically decentralized nature of Dutch national government. By following the Dutch example and learning to exploit capital markets, the British state was able to join the ranks of the great powers.[67]

France is the other major point of comparison. France was Britain's greatest enemy, and it was Britain's ability to check French power that signaled its entry into the circle of great powers. Absolutist France was the quintessential "strong state," complete with massive national bureaucracy and without divided political powers, checks, or balances. A King ruled France, not a King-in-Parlement. Not surprisingly, French public finances were constructed along very different lines from Britain and the Dutch Republic. There was no developed capital market upon which the state could market its debt. Rather, France raised money through a complex and cumbersome system of tax farms, private bankers, and venal offices. France provides a sharp contrast for how public financial machinery can lead to "state strength," and also for the way that this machinery could be used to build political alliances with domestic elites. Chapter 4 concludes by underscoring the importance of developed markets for state-building.

Chapter 5 considers why markets developed so quickly in Britain. Property rights are a key factor in many explanations of economic change and so I address English public and private financial property rights, and how these might account for the changes described in chapter 3. I begin with a discussion of the most compelling property rights analysis of this period, offered by

North and Weingast (1989). In their argument, North and Weingast pay more attention to constitutional politics than to law, an imbalance I propose to redress. There were two relevant legal developments, one having to do with public finance and the other with private finance. The first concerned a lawsuit filed by a group of public creditors in the wake of the 1672 Stop of the Exchequer, which amounted to a unilateral suspension of debt repayments by Charles II. At issue in this case, known as the "Bankers' Case," were the property rights of public creditors. The second development had to do with the law of financial instruments. A mature capital market includes many kinds of financial instruments: promissory notes, company shares, bills of exchange, and so on, and their use is influenced by how enforceable they are in a court of law. They were traditionally employed only by merchants, who utilized a special kind of law, the *lex mercatoria* or law merchant. Common-law courts did not ordinarily recognize the validity of these contracts. This changed, however, when in the latter part of the seventeenth century the law merchant was "absorbed" into the common law, and financial contracts became enforceable in the ordinary courts.

Joint-stock companies like the Bank of England, East India Company, and South Sea Company played an important role in Britain's "Financial Revolution" (Dickson 1967). Chapter 6 discusses the changes in private finance which allowed each company to make long-term loans to the government. This period was marked by the emergence of an organized, centralized, and active capital market in London, and the liquidity of the market made company shares an especially attractive investment. Merchants and financiers from the London area were particularly active in the stock market. The political reaction to this new market was colored by the fact that financial wealth represented a new basis for power, rivaling traditional landed wealth, and involved many people from marginal social groups (Huguenots, Jews, foreigners, nonconforming Protestants, etc.). For a variety of reasons, the new "monied interest" allied itself with the Whig party and was attacked most strongly by the Tories.

Chapter 6 also considers the partisan context in which joint-stock companies were established and operated. The incorporation of the Bank of England in 1694, the New East India Company in 1698, the South Sea Company in 1711, and the attempted formation of a Land Bank in 1696, were all deeply political events. Contemporary political pamphlets remarked on the strong connections between the Bank, New East India Company, and the Whig party, and between the Old East India Company, Land Bank, South Sea Company, and the Tories. The rivalry between the New and Old East India Companies was not merely a commercial one, it was also a political one. For example, the Tory Old East India Company organized a politically inspired run on the Whiggish Bank of England. The minutes of the company director's meetings show how carefully each of these companies managed its

relations with Parliament through a continual stream of petitions and dele-
gations sent to influence Parliamentary policy, buttressed by the fact that
company men were also MPs. The overall effect was that the joint-stock
companies were almost as much political organizations as they were economic ones.[68]

Chapter 7 considers the pattern of market behavior at the individual level,
analyzing data from 1712. Having argued in chapter 6 that joint-stock companies were embroiled in politics at the organizational level, I now consider
how politics influenced the behavior of individuals trading company
shares.[69] The thread of political influence ran through company directors
and the votes needed to elect them in the annual directors' elections. Such
votes were attached to company shares.

Chapter 7 analyzes individual shareholding and trading in Bank of England and East India Company shares (the relevant records for the South
Sea Company have not survived). I assess the social characteristics of investors, including their political affiliations. Linking individual financial records
and voting records, I have constructed a unique political-economic data set
that shows for a sizable proportion of all shareholders whether they were
Whig or Tory supporters.[70] I analyze trading in Bank and East India Company stock and find that there was a significant pattern of "endogamous"
political trading in East India Company stock but not in Bank stock. Overall,
traders in East India stock discriminated politically and so favored trading
with members of the same party. Traders in Bank stock were, on the other
hand, indifferent about the politics of their trading partners.

I conduct additional analyses of active and inactive traders, and large and
small shareholders, to interpret political trading and be sure that it wasn't
just a reflection of some other kind of endogamy. I also analyze trading by
ethnic-religious group and by guild, to see if there was an economic ratio-
nale behind political discrimination. I conclude that the pattern of trading in
East India Company stock was genuinely political, and not motivated by
concern for transaction costs, unreliable contracts, or faulty property rights.
Such trading was induced by the voting rights attached to company shares,
and the way these could be used to choose directors and secure partisan
control over a company. The reason for the contrast between the East India
Company and the Bank was that the Bank was solidly in the hands of the
Whigs, whereas the East India Company was split between Whigs and Tories. Unless a huge block of Bank shares changed hands, there was virtually
no way for the Bank to fall under Tory control. However, there were both
Whig and Tory directors in the East India Company, and so even marginal
shifts in shareownership could be politically consequential because of their
effect on the balance of power within the company.[71]

One goal of this book is to show how political forces shaped a competitive,
efficient capital market at both the institutional and individual levels. There

was no hard and fast line separating the political from the economic: there was simply a *political economy* as economic relationships were connected to political relationships. Economic explanations of this type of correspondence attempt to show how external social organizations are appropriated within a market to serve some kind of economic end.[72] I argue just the opposite, namely, that the correspondence resulted from the fact that people were using the market to pursue noneconomic political ends. It may be true that *de gustibus non est disputandum*,[73] but people can have a "taste" for politics as well as profits. Furthermore, this "taste" was not some kind of primordial impulse but arose out of the articulation of political and economic institutions.

Although my results derive from a single historical case, they suggest more generally how politics can penetrate into a market and shape economic behavior. We already know that trading in contemporary capital markets has a network structure, and this raises the possibility that market structures are embedded in noneconomic social structures.[74] I do not claim that all markets are politically embedded but rather wish to determine how and under what circumstances such political "embedding" occurs. Organized boycotts offer a contemporary example of politics influencing economic behavior. A person who decides not to purchase a commodity because she disagrees with the labor, racial, or environmental policies of the company that manufactures it is making a politically informed decision. "Buy Black" campaigns in the African-American community, and "Buy American" campaigns are both economic ways to pursue political goals of racial solidarity and nationalism. Such political currents in the stream of commerce are easy to overlook because they are often only temporary measures whose symbolic effect is greater than their economic impact. To show how politics influenced longer-lasting economic institutions, such as a stock market, makes a more convincing demonstration of political embedding.

My other general aim is to reconsider state development and its connection to market development. The case of England underscores the strength of weak states, and of the need to reconceptualize state strength so as to downplay bureaucratic capacities. Rapid growth in British state strength rested on a modest development of specific bureaucratic capacities but more particularly on a massive development in market capacities. The capital market made a fundamental contribution to the financial power of the English state. It did more than expand extractive capacity, however, for the national debt also bound a significant number of the political nation to the post-1688 regime and it did so as a type of "politically constituted property right." State-building meant cultivating domestic elites as well as enlarging extractive capacity.

Chapter Two

BRITISH POLITICS FROM 1672 TO 1712

THIS CHAPTER explains the changing political context for public and private financial developments. To construct an embeddedness explanation for economic behavior, it is necessary to understand social context. Of course, much of the social environment of an economy may be irrelevant, and depending on how embeddedness works, it could be the kinship system, popular or elite culture, religion, ethnicity, politics, or any number of other factors, which matter most. What made politics so relevant in this case was a set of institutional connections joining the polity to the stock market. This and the next chapter describe the structure of those connections.

The seventeenth-century English polity was partly autonomous in the sense that politics cannot be fully reduced to religion, economics, ethnicity, family, or other relationships.[1] It was, for example, more than just conflict among aristocratic families for power, or a function of religious differences between dissenting and conforming Protestants, or between Protestants and Catholics. Much of politics was sui generis. Political dynamics were shaped by political institutions and organizations that did not derive from other social forces.[2] The late seventeenth century was marked by the emergence of political parties as the major form of political organization,[3] and by power shifts within the polity, from the Crown to Parliament.

English politics changed dramatically between 1672 and 1712, with important consequences for public finance. Organized political competition shaped financial evolution by reinforcing commercial rivalries with political ones. Political affiliation was such an important component of an individual's self-identity that it affected how people behaved, even in ostensibly "apolitical" social settings.[4] Political developments embroiled England in two expensive wars with France, with a resulting increase in public spending, taxing, and borrowing. Furthermore, at a general level, the foundation for the market was a political one.[5] Political authorities supply many of the prerequisites for a market: money, property rights, contract law, standardized weights and measures, and so on. In so doing, they also constructed a line of influence running between polity and economy.

By "political party" I mean an organized group of people who want to pursue a set of policies and so try to gain control over the government through electoral means.[6] Given the dependence of political parties on elections, management of elections and mobilization of the electorate are two of the main activities they undertake.[7] Parties seek the support of the electorate in a variety of ways. One is to promise legislation or policy that the electorate wants, but parties can also offer less universalistic benefits such as patronage: specific rewards given in exchange for a voter's support (e.g., money, a job, food and drink). English parties from this period provided a mixture of policy and patronage, with the emphasis changing over time. Since it was easier to use patronage to influence a small number of voters, the growth in the size of the electorate affected the balance between patronage and policy. Internally, early British parties were not bureaucratic organizations but cohered through the selective use of kinship relations, patron-client ties, political clubs, and informal caucuses and party whips.

Political parties competed for control over government. In seventeenth-century England, the Crown was at the center of national government. Besides the Crown, other important political institutions included the House of Lords, the House of Commons, the Privy Council, and various Offices of State (e.g., Lord Chancellor, Lord Treasurer, and Lord Admiral). Possession of the Crown was determined by primogenitural rules of succession, although these were modified in extraordinary circumstances.[8] Persons gained membership in the House of Lords either by inheritance (as the eldest son of a peer) or appointment (through nomination by the Crown to a bishopric, or through the creation of a new peerage).[9] Privy Councilors and State Officials were appointed by the reigning monarch and served at his or her pleasure. The House of Commons was the only institution for which electoral success was the criterion for membership. Consequently, the growth of political parties was closely connected to the rising importance of the Commons as a political institution.

Several types of evidence indicate the presence of political parties. Since parties try to win elections, if there are too few or no elections, it is unlikely that political parties exist. Furthermore, political parties organize the voting behavior of members of a legislative body, and so stable patterns along specific cleavage lines can indicate the presence of parties. When members of the legislature vote only as individuals, forming temporary coalitions with other members, parties are likely to be absent. Without continuous organization, such coalitions break down and are redrawn along different lines when another issue arises, and the overall pattern is unstable. There is no "party line" to organize voting patterns.[10]

The voting behavior of the electorate also reflects the presence or absence of parties. Through general and specific blandishments, parties try to influence how the electorate votes. Poll books from the seventeenth and eighteenth centuries provide evidence on how the English electorate voted, but it is important to understand the meaning of a vote. As Mark Kishlansky (1986) has shown, the process of parliamentary selection changed during the seventeenth century. To read an early poll book as a simple listing of which voters supported which candidates is to apply an anachronistic standard.[11]

In addition to voting behavior, one can also examine political commentary as evidence for parties. In an arena as self-conscious as politics, participants and commentators are aware of how things are organized. Discussions of political conflict commonly mention party positions and party strategies. One can understand politics by understanding how contemporaries perceived and discussed politics, for politics is in part political debate.

EARLY SEVENTEENTH-CENTURY POLITICS

In Conrad Russell's wonderful phrase, early Stuart parliaments were not so much ongoing institutions as they were irregular events.[12] The House of Lords and the House of Commons were discontinuous legislative bodies. The Crown called parliaments and could terminate them at any point by dissolving them (which meant a general election) or proroguing them (which ended the current session and lapsed any unpassed bills). The ability to convene, adjourn, prorogue, or dissolve parliament gave the Crown no small measure of political leverage.

Parliaments were called to do the Crown's business, which meant to pass laws, grant extraordinary taxes, and give counsel.[13] As an institution, parliament possessed the ability to consent to decisions that would bind those whom parliament represented.[14] A parliament was part of the process through which the Crown consulted with the political nation, and it was one of several channels (which also included the Privy Council and the Court) through which the state of the nation was communicated to the Crown. Members were free to give unsolicited advice on local matters, and when their counsel was solicited by the Crown, they could advise on matters of more general import.[15] Overall, however, government was the Crown's business, not Parliament's.

At the beginning of the century, a seat in the Commons was not a high political office. The politically ambitious sought connections at Court among the aristocracy, or tried to obtain local offices, for parliament in the early seventeenth century was not yet important enough to be worth their while. Selection to parliament was more a social than a political process, being one of several ways for English elites to achieve social distinction. The infrequency of contested elections, in which there was more than one candidate, provides a key to understanding this difference.

At the time, a contested election was a rare event.[16] In the 1604 elections, for example, there were only thirteen contests.[17] Was this because parliamentary seats were so politically unimportant as not to be worth the expense of an electoral struggle? In fact, a special premium was placed on uncontested elections and typically a substantial effort was expended on preventing a contest. A seat in the Commons was no great political vehicle, but it was a high social honor, particularly when it was uncontested.[18] Parliamen-

tary seats were granted in a way that both reinforced the social hierarchy of
the constituency and reflected on the status and other personal qualities of
the candidates. Gaining an uncontested seat garnered as much social honor
as losing an electoral contest brought dishonor. Furthermore, an uncontested election was good for the constituency as it documented the unity of
the community. Contests, in contrast, brought out the divisions within the
community and were therefore to be avoided. Prior consultations among
county and borough elites usually ensured that only one candidate would
come forward for an election.[19] Electoral contests were a sign that the normal political process had failed and resulted most often from misunderstand-
ings or mistakes. They did not necessarily indicate an ideological cleavage
dividing elites.

   Modern experience is misleading over the question of who could vote and
how. In the early part of the seventeenth century, voting procedures were
not at all systematic, partly because electoral contests were so rare. When a
parliamentary election went to a contest, there were three ways to determine who had the most support: "the shout,"[20] "the view,"[21] and the poll.
The poll was most like a modern vote. One by one, members of the electorate would state which candidate they supported, the votes were counted,
and a winner declared. Who was eligible to vote varied from constituency to
constituency, and in practice depended on which of the three methods of
voting was used. It was difficult to assess the eligibility of persons standing
in a crowd and shouting out names but it was much easier if they came forth
one by one. In county elections, the official criteria had been in effect since
the fifteenth century: freeholders of land worth at least forty shillings per
annum were eligible to vote.[22] When first established this was a fairly selective test of property ownership, but after the inflation of the sixteenth century even quite modest property owners could vote.[23] The county electorates were the largest and could number several thousand.

   Borough franchises were much more varied. There were eight major
types: burgage, corporation, freeholder, freeman, freeman and other, house-
holder, inhabitant, and scot and lot.[24] In burgage boroughs, for example, the
right to vote was attached to specific pieces of property. Sometimes it was
the owners who could vote, sometimes it was the tenants. In corporation
boroughs, voting rights were vested in the corporation (which typically
meant that the mayor, aldermen, and common councilmen voted). A freeman franchise meant that those who were free of the corporation voted. For
the Oxford and Cambridge parliamentary elections, only those holding an
MA degree from the university could vote. Borough electorates were as varied in number as they were in franchises. Some numbered fewer than
twenty, others were in the hundreds.[25]

   With so much uncertainty about electoral procedure and with the personal stakes of victory so high, it was not uncommon for an election result to

be disputed (by the loser, of course). Parliament had the right to adjudicate disputed elections and decide which of the candidates would sit in Parliament.[26] Since the involvement of ineligible voters was one of the commonest grounds to contest an election, this meant that Parliament itself ultimately decided who the eligible voters were.

The size of an electorate determined how easily elections could be controlled by political elites. Aristocratic patrons generally played a greater role in the boroughs, with their smaller electorates, than in the counties, although nowhere were they without influence.[27] Over the course of the seventeenth century, electorates grew in size.[28] Smaller electorates could more easily be controlled through patronage, bribery, or some other direct means, but as they grew, appeals had to be made on different grounds.

The period of the English Revolution resulted in some important political changes. Formerly just an occasional "event," parliament became by the 1640s a significant political institution that resisted the domineering tendencies of James I and Charles I, and electoral contests were more common. By the 1650s, parliament itself was the sovereign power in England. The restoration of Charles II in 1660 did not entirely reduce parliament to its former status, and so the political role of parliament was permanently enlarged. Nationally ambitious members of the elite no longer looked solely to the Court for opportunity for they could now find it in the House of Commons.

Over the century, the process of parliamentary selection changed as the frequency of electoral contests rose. This meant that electoral contests were more familiar, and no longer bore such negative connotations. When they happened, the poll replaced the older "shout" and "view." Selection became a more political and less social process as the personal qualities of the candidate (how honorable, prestigious, or pious he was) mattered less, and the ideological or political position he represented mattered more.[29]

ENGLISH POLITICS CIRCA 1672

Despite a vigorous polity, in the early 1670s political conflicts and issues were not organized by political parties. At the restoration of Charles II to the throne in 1660 many people imagined, or hoped, that things would return to "normal," and most of the old structures of national governance were restored.[30] In the early 1660s, Charles II's chief minister was Edward Hyde, the Earl of Clarendon, whose job it was to see that Parliament did the King's bidding. As an older politician, Clarendon did not fully appreciate the enhanced position of Parliament and simply assumed that Parliament would retake its former role.[31] His anachronistic reading of Parliament made him an ineffectual leader and he was forced to resign in 1667.[32] By the time of his fall, Clarendon had become a convenient scapegoat for Charles II's difficulties with the Commons, and was actively undermined by many rivals. A number of these headed opposition factions but their goal in opposing Clarendon's ministry was to supplant Clarendon, not to pursue different policies.[33]

Three political issues shifted the House of Commons from its royalist stance at the Restoration to a much more confrontational posture at the end of the 1660s: religion, foreign policy, and finance. Most of the Commons were opposed to any policy granting toleration to Catholics or dissenters (non–Church of England Protestants). At different times and for various reasons, Charles II tried to institute a measure of toleration but this caused him particular difficulty because his own supporters in the Commons were most strongly opposed to toleration.[34] In foreign affairs, Holland and France were considered enemies, although for different reasons. Holland was England's main commercial rival, while Catholic France was feared as a military (and religious) threat. Charles became embroiled in a number of expensive wars with Holland and formed a secret alliance with France. After an upsurge of patriotism at the start of a new war, the political enthusiasm of the Commons would usually flag, especially during expensive or losing efforts. The failure and cost of the Second Dutch War (1665–67) worsened Charles's relations with Parliament. Finance was another frequent battleground. At the outset of his reign, Parliament had voted a generous annual sum to Charles (£1.2 million) but had not provided adequate means to raise that amount. Even without war-related expenses, Charles would have had to summon Parliament for more money.

Until the late 1670s there were no political groups in Parliament that could be called parties. Furthermore, no general election took place between 1661 and 1679, and although there were by-elections as members of Parliament died or resigned, there was no general electoral effort upon which political parties typically thrive. Instead, there were a small number of members organized into several factions, and a large number of independent and relatively inactive members who were not organized at all. Factions were usually headed by a peer. The core of Clarendon's faction in the Commons, for example, was composed of his three sons and a cousin.[35] Another of the factions included the servants and employees of the Crown (who, naturally, were expected to support government legislation).

After the fall of Clarendon, from 1667 to 1673, an uneasy coalition of factions dominated politics. The five chief ministers in this period were called the Cabal.[36] The divisions within the ministry were cultivated deliberately as Charles did not appoint a single person as a leading minister. He preferred to have a set of rivals who could be played off against one another.[37] It was in this period that Charles tried to strengthen his position in relation to parliament by pursuing a policy with both foreign and domestic sides. In foreign policy, a secret agreement was signed with Louis XIV of France (the 1670 Treaty of Dover). Its terms promised English support for a French attack on Holland in exchange for military and financial assistance.[38] This represented a reversal from the Second Dutch War in which England battled Holland and its then-ally France, and repudiated the Triple Alliance of 1668 (a treaty joining England, Holland, and Sweden). The Third Dutch War began in March 1672 with England and France allied against Holland. The domestic side of the policy consisted of two prerogative measures, the Stop of the Exchequer and the Declaration of Indulgence, undertaken when Parliament was prorogued in 1672. The Stop involved a unilateral suspension of payments on the public debt, and the Declaration involved the suspension of penal laws against nonconformists and recusants.

The Parliamentary session of 1670 showed that Parliament would vote large sums of money for government if Charles followed the appropriate religious and foreign policies.[39] This meant adhering to a strongly anglican policy (no toleration for Catholics and nonconforming Protestants), and supporting the Triple Alliance. But Charles was eager to reduce his financial dependency on Parliament and to pursue a more tolerant religious policy. He addressed both of these goals at the same time.

The Treaty of Dover brought direct financial benefits in the form of a French subsidy. The government also hoped that the Third Dutch War would be like the first. Successfully prosecuted, a war with England's greatest commercial rival could result in the payment of a cash indemnity to the winner, and in long-term benefits like increased trade and higher customs revenues. A successful war could, in other words, more than pay for itself, and anything improving Charles's financial position would reduce his reliance on Parliament. The Stop of the Exchequer freed up revenues which had been earmarked for repayment of loans, and gave Charles cash to pay for the war. By pursuing toleration through the exercise of his prerogative powers rather than through parliamentary legislation, the Declaration of Indulgence ensured that dissenters were dependent on Charles alone for their benefits.[40] Both measures were enacted when Parliament was not in session, so there was no opportunity for it to respond. The hope was to present Parliament with a fait accompli: a successfully concluded war and a financially independent Crown.[41]

The Third Dutch War was both more expensive and less successful than Charles hoped. By the end of 1672 it was apparent that Charles would have to call Parliament and ask for more money. When he did in February 1673, it also became obvious that the war and the Declaration of Indulgence were both extremely unpopular in the House of Commons. The Declaration was interpreted as a sign of the growing influence of Catholicism in the Court, a perception strengthened by the alliance with Louis XIV. Thus, the issue of Catholicism came to the fore.[42]

Parliament's first concern was the Declaration of Indulgence. Although Charles referred explicitly in his Parliamentary address to the plight of the goldsmith-bankers whose repayments were halted, there was little interest in the Stop of the Exchequer. The Commons went to work on a bill against Catholics and made it clear that there would be no more money until the religious issue had been settled.[43] Charles was publicly committed to his Declaration but the strength of the opposition forced him to cancel it. Only then did the Commons consider funds for the war. Additionally, Charles consented to the Test Act of 1673, which was intended to force Catholic officeholders to resign or give up their religion.[44] It resulted in the resignations from office of both James Duke of York (Charles's younger brother and heir to the throne) and Sir Thomas Clifford. Sir Thomas Osborne was appointed to replace Clifford as the Lord Treasurer.[45]

The failure of its policies brought about the disintegration of the Cabal. Clifford was forced to resign by the Test Act while Arlington, Lauderdale, and Buckingham were attacked in the House of Commons. Ashley, now Earl of Shaftesbury, resigned from his post as Lord Chancellor and moved to join the political opposition.[46] Sir Thomas Osborne, soon elevated to the peerage as Danby, became the dominant politician after the Cabal period and before the Exclusion Crisis at the end of the 1670s.

Growing fears of Catholicism and recurrent financial struggles between Crown and Commons dominated the early 1670s. The parliamentary opposition did not consist of an organized political party for it came together as a largely spontaneous expression of backbench sentiment.[47] Charles's supporters consisted of an amalgam of factions, disorganized (in no small measure because of internal rivalries that Charles cultivated) and unable to steer legislation through the Commons.

THE EMERGENCE OF POLITICAL PARTIES

Danby drew some important lessons from the failures of Clarendon and the Cabal. To ensure the cooperation of the Commons, the King's ministers had to provide policy that was not too objectionable but more importantly the Commons had to be actively and aggressively managed.[48] Through the extensive and systematic use of patronage and family connections, Danby built up a Court group in the Commons.[49] His attempt to establish such direct control prompted a backlash as many began to worry about the independence of Parliament. The opposition to Danby was led by the Earl of Shaftesbury, the first to head a political party. Two political goals motivated Shaftesbury: in the short run, he sought the dissolution of Parliament and a general election; in the long run, he wanted to exclude James Duke of York from the line of succession to the throne.[50] The issue of Catholicism was closely tied up with the second goal.

By 1675, the Cavalier Parliament had been in existence for fourteen years and the House of Commons was increasingly unrepresentative of the country. From by-election results it was clear that the next general election would produce a large turnover of MPs. Danby had invested heavily in the construction of a Court group and so was opposed to a general election that would undoubtedly sweep it away.[51] Shaftesbury sought a general election for this very reason.

Several events raised the issue of Catholicism. James's resignation after the passage of the Test Act of 1673 confirmed suspicions of his Catholic sympathies. His marriage to Mary of Modena, a Catholic, raised the prospect of a Catholic dynasty on the English throne, for Charles had no legitimate heirs and James was next in line to the throne. Were James to have a male child by his new wife, a Catholic King would eventually inherit the throne, for James's new son would supersede his protestant daughters by his first marriage, Mary and Anne, in the line of succession. In a country where Catholicism and Absolutism were considered equivalent (as the example of Louis XIV of France suggested), this possibility was deeply troubling.[52] The Popish Plot of 1678 convinced many that there was a widespread Catholic plot to overthrow the government, and further inflamed anti-Catholic sentiment.[53] Shaftesbury organized the political opposition around the single long-term goal of excluding James Duke of York from the line of succession.

When the Commons learned at the end of 1678 of Danby's involvement in secret negotiations with Louis XIV, he fell from power and was impeached. The now unmanageable Cavalier Parliament was finally dissolved and the first general election in eighteen years occurred in March 1679. There were more contests in this election than in any other in the 1660–90 period. Danby's Court group was swept away and the majority of new members were actual or potential supporters of Shaftesbury.[54] Shaftesbury began to construct an opposition party among the MPs using Exclusion as his main issue.

The new Commons began its proceedings with an investigation of the Popish Plot. The first Exclusion bill was introduced in May 1679 and soon passed its second reading. Charles prorogued Parliament to slow down the passage of the bill, and then dissolved it, calling for elections in August and September 1679. In these, Shaftesbury organized an effective and systematic opposition effort. The number of contested elections was again high, although not as high as in March.[55] National political issues, specifically Exclusion, played a major role, and to a far greater extent than ever before, parliamentary selection was determined by political and ideological criteria rather than by social criteria. A sizable majority of Shaftesbury supporters were returned and Shaftesbury himself was the undisputed leader of the newly formed Whig party. The new parliament met in October, and was immediately prorogued by Charles. He moved against the opposition by purging Whigs from local political offices such as the commissions of the peace, militia, and lieutenancies.[56] Even though Parliament was not in session, Shaftesbury maintained the coherence and energy of the Whigs, so when Parliament finally convened in late 1680, the Commons immediately went to work on a second, harsher, Exclusion bill. This passed the Commons in November, but died in the Lords because of Charles's opposition.[57] The Whigs in the Commons refused to vote any money for Charles until the Exclusion bill passed, but Charles refused to let it pass, resulting in a political standoff. In early 1681 he again dissolved Parliament.

The issue of exclusion polarized the nation. A political group opposed to the Whigs was organized and became known as the Tory party.[58] The Tory party was independent of Charles, having among its core supporters the provincial gentry and anglican clergy, but it received the benefit of his favor.[59] Tories were supportive of monarchy and the Church of England, and became concerned that the Whigs were too extreme in their opposition to James (whose right to the Crown was, in the Tory view, incontestable given the rules of succession). The Whig coalition contained too many anti-monarchists and dissenters, and Tories feared that Whig intransigence could eventually lead to civil war.[60] The election of 1681 was more divisive than any other as the political nation split between Whigs and Tories. Whig electoral machinery was by now quite developed and made effective use of petitions, the press, political clubs, and voting lists.[61] Again, a majority of Whigs were returned to Parliament, and again Shaftesbury pressed for Exclusion. For the first time, however, the Tories tried to emulate Whig electoral technique, albeit without much success.[62]

Charles called Parliament to Oxford in order to remove it from the influence of London, where popular sentiments ran strongly in favor of the Whigs. Oxford was a royalist town, and Charles's choice signaled his displeasure with the Whigs. By quickly passing yet another Exclusion bill, the Whigs demonstrated their unwillingness to compromise with Charles, who proposed measures short of exclusion that would secure protestantism on the throne. In the eyes of many voters, the Whigs had gone too far, and Charles's strong reaction seemed justified. Parliament was dissolved at the end of March 1681 and Charles did not call another for the rest of his reign.

Without elections or a parliament, the Whigs lacked a political stage. Charles continued to purge them from local offices and initiated a judicial campaign. Shaftesbury was sent to the Tower of London on charges of treason and the Whigs were effectively suppressed. By revoking London's city charter, Charles attacked the Whigs in their greatest stronghold. He denied them a parliament in which to press for exclusion, removed them from local offices, and attacked the charters of the boroughs they controlled. Charles also moved to dismantle the Tory party because of his opposition to *all* independent political organizations.[63] Charles's financial position was strong enough for him to govern without a parliament because active overseas trade in the early 1680s meant high customs revenues.

Although they failed to exclude James from the succession, the Whigs constituted the first political party in England. Sitting in both the House of Commons and House of Lords, the Whigs were a group organized to seize political power through electoral means, in order to enact the policy of exclusion. Three general elections in two years afforded plenty of practice, and so they quickly became quite sophisticated in their electoral methods. Inadvertently, however, the Whigs created an opposing party in their own image. The very effectiveness of Whig political technique forced their Tory opponents to imitate it. Although they were not as good at electioneering as the Whigs, the Tories also learned a great deal.

The controversy around which the Whig party grew was fundamentally a religious one, but, once established, the party accumulated other interests, including economic ones. Religion, foreign and military policy, the independence of parliament, and public finance eventually formed an interwoven nexus of issues. Still, Charles's ability to rule without parliament demonstrated the limited power of a political party, even one as popular and well organized as the Whigs. For parties to matter more, Parliament had to matter more, and it was not until after the Glorious Revolution that Parliament really became a full partner in governance.

THE GLORIOUS REVOLUTION

The backlash against the Whigs was strong enough to overcome whatever fears James II's Catholicism had formerly raised, so when Charles died in 1685, James inherited the throne and a great deal of political support. This situation did not last long, however, for James quickly alienated his own allies. The Tory constituency provided the bulk of James's support, and was both pro-monarchy and pro-anglican. The direction of James's policies forced his supporters to choose between these two goals, and most Tories found that they could not endure such pro-Catholic religious policies. It was not so much Whig opposition that caused James's downfall as it was the loss of Tory support.

The reign began auspiciously enough, with James publicly promising to abide by the laws of the country. Privately, however, he intended to establish dominance over Parliament,[64] and was soon lifting the restrictions placed on English Catholics by the Test Acts of 1673 and 1678. For example, he enlarged the standing army and posted many Catholic officers into it.[65] This was an ominous move in the minds of the English public, for standing armies and Catholicism were the hallmarks of absolutist rule. James also tried to put Catholics into the local offices from which they had previously been excluded by law.[66] His freedom to pursue these unpopular measures depended largely on the buoyant state of the economy. Like Charles II, James was voted permanent revenues at the outset of his reign, and high levels of economic activity meant high customs revenues. A rosy financial situation gave James the political rope he used eventually to hang himself.[67]

The first parliament in James's reign was very supportive but this support soon dwindled in the face of his pro-Catholic maneuvering. The Tory-dominated Commons refused to repeal the Test Acts, and so James prorogued parliament and then dissolved it in 1687. Impatient with his own Tory supporters, James turned to dissenters and Whigs in the hope that they would be more sympathetic toward Catholics.[68] James surveyed his justices of the peace to determine who would support a repeal of the Test Acts, and purged Tories from local offices, replacing them with Whigs and dissenters.[69] The displacement of so many of the local gentry from their traditional offices greatly increased dissatisfaction with James. Another strategy he used to gain a cooperative Commons was to reorganize the boroughs. By revoking borough charters, he was able to put borough seats into cooperative hands.[70] This kind of explicit "gerrymandering" raised fears that James intended to eliminate all parliamentary independence. James also pressured the judiciary to obtain favorable legal rulings.

James's actions were especially problematic because they were aimed at bringing Catholicism back to England. Little that stood in his way seemed safe: neither property, political rights, nor the Anglican Church.[71] Catholicism was the issue that turned his supporters against him. It was unlikely that he could ever make allies out of the Whigs who had opposed his right to the throne, and so his overtures to them were ineffectual and only further angered the Tories. Nevertheless, the prospect of a Protestant successor to James encouraged Tories to tolerate his behavior, for they felt that things would return to normal when the throne passed to his daughter, Princess Mary.

By 1687 William of Orange, who was both James's nephew and the husband of the heir to the throne, was plotting to invade England and overthrow James. He received many encouraging signs of support from a variety of English politicians and his English followers carried out an extensive propaganda campaign criticizing James.[72] The pregnancy of James's Catholic wife became public knowledge by late 1687, and she gave birth to a son in June 1688. This meant that under the normal rules of succession James would be followed by a Catholic son, not a Protestant daughter. Three weeks later, seven leading Whig and Tory politicians invited William to invade. In November 1688, William successfully landed an army at Torbay, on the south coast of England. James's army disintegrated, his political support crumbled, and he fled the country to France, where he was granted safe haven by Louis XIV. James later led French troops to join Catholic rebels in Ireland, but this military venture was eventually quashed. What followed his departure from the throne was a protracted political debate in England on how to shift the throne to William and Mary, and on what terms.

Although members from both parties had invited William to England, Whig and Tory differences were never completely resolved. Elections took place in January 1689 for the Convention,[73] and there was a big swing back to the Whigs. Whigs gained a majority in the Commons, while the House of Lords remained more evenly split between the parties. After the Convention assembled, some important party differences emerged. The Commons resolved that James had abdicated the throne and so the central political question concerned who should have title to the now vacated throne. The Tories were opposed to any arrangement in which William would be the sole monarch, and some pushed for Mary alone as sovereign. They were also hesitant to acknowledge that Parliament could alter the line of succession.[74] Nottingham, a Tory peer, argued for an arrangement in which James would retain the title to the throne while being divested of all executive powers. The Whigs were opposed to the return of James under any circumstances, and were eager for a speedy resolution of the situation.[75] The parties split over how to deal with those who had collaborated with James's regime and how to compensate those who suffered under it, but both Houses came together for a resolution to disinherit Catholic kings.

The Convention decided to bestow the Crown on William and Mary together, with William having executive power. The Convention also presented to William and Mary a Declaration of Rights: a formal statement of many of the legal rights of royal subjects which James had violated. Three things in particular were mentioned: the legislative supremacy of Parliament, the necessity of parliamentary consent for a standing army in peacetime, and a list of grievances against James's rule. When William and Mary accepted the Crown, they promised to uphold these rights. The Crown had been placed within the framework of law, and was no longer "above the law."

THE REIGN OF WILLIAM AND MARY

Vested with full regal powers, William converted the Convention into a Parliament. One of the first issues it faced was the religious one: would there be toleration for dissenting Protestants? Radical Whigs wanted to put dissenters on an equal footing with the Anglican Church, while the Tories did not want toleration in any form. The Tory Nottingham introduced two bills: a comprehension bill paired with a toleration bill. The first specified conditions under which Dissenters might rejoin the Church of England, the second granted limited toleration for those dissenters who did not rejoin. For various reasons, only the toleration bill passed.[76] The Toleration Act of 1689 allowed Dissenters freedom of worship (so long as they took oaths of supremacy and allegiance, and declared against transubstantiation). It did not give them equal access to public office but nevertheless represented a major change, and the number of dissenting places of worship grew quickly during the 1690s.[77]

William predictably declared war on France in May 1689. As the Dutch leader, he had been fighting France for twenty years and the English throne gave him new military assets to exploit. William hoped that the revenues granted to James would simply continue but Parliament opposed this idea and the financial settlement became one of the major developments of the Glorious Revolution.[78] William's wish was to be granted revenues for life, like Charles and James had at the start of their reigns. The Commons, however, was in no mood to rush a financial settlement, and so as a sign of good faith (and to expedite matters) William voluntarily gave up the unpopular hearth tax.[79] Nevertheless, his gesture failed to speed up the Commons' deliberations, for Parliament was mindful of the lessons of James's reign: a financially independent monarch could be very dangerous. Eventually they voted the excise revenues for life, but the customs revenues for a period of only three years. They also voted some extraordinary supplies for the war effort. William needed more revenue than this, and realized that he would not get it from Parliament. In early 1690 he dissolved parliament, and indicated that he favored moderate Tories in the forthcoming elections.[80]

The election of 1690 was highly contested and national issues again played a major role. The Tories gained the upper hand and so the new parliament was less Whiggish than before. In his opening speech William stressed the need for a quick financial settlement. This time, Parliament turned first to public finances but only reaffirmed its earlier decision to grant the excise revenues for life and the customs revenues for a limited period (although they extended it from three to four years). The Commons also voted the hereditary revenues for life and authorized loans using them as security.

The revenues provided to William in 1690 were insufficient to cover even the normal expenses of government.[81] A major portion of the revenues (the customs) expired after a short period and would have to be voted on again. And a portion of these revenues were saddled with new debts to fund the war.[82] The inadequacy of these measures was no accident, for the purpose was to make the Crown fiscally dependent on Parliament. Never again would a monarch be financially autonomous. The Crown would have to seek additional funds from Parliament, which ensured that Parliament would have to be called frequently, and that it could use control of the purse strings to influence policy. The Declaration of Rights stated the independence of parliament but it was public finance that really increased Parliament's power over the Crown.

Political lines were confused between 1689 and 1702. Whig and Tory parties realigned as part of the old Whig coalition joined the Tory party.[83]

Cross-cutting the Whig-Tory cleavage was another division between Court and Country.[84] Court influence was built up using the methods perfected by Danby in the 1670s: securing cooperation by granting offices, pensions, and other forms of patronage to MPs. In the 1680s, Whigs had formed the Country opposition and the Tories the Court party. In the 1690s, William drew his ministers from both political parties, which meant that the Court group was composed of both Whigs and Tories, as was the Country opposition.[85] William's strategy did not always work, and he often had to put his government into the hands of a single party, usually the Whigs.[86] Later, under Anne, the Whigs were more firmly in place as the Court party, and the Tories as the Country party. Over time, the Whigs moved from their initial position as Country opposition over to the Court, and the Tories shifted in the other direction.[87] Thus, the Court and Country difference eventually came into alignment with party distinctions.

There were a number of other important political developments in William's reign. One was the passage of the Triennial Act of 1694 (6 & 7 William & Mary, c.2), which ensured that parliamentary elections would be held at least once every three years. Like the financial settlement, the purpose of this measure was to secure frequent parliaments that would remain independent of Crown control. The durability of the Cavalier Parliament allowed Danby to cultivate a constituency beholden to the Crown, but frequent elections would undercut such strategies. As a consequence, the period until 1715 had more general elections than any other in the eighteenth century and party competition rose to new heights.[88]

The second major political development resulted from the war with France. William's primary purpose in invading England in 1688 was not to restore the liberties of Englishmen. He intended to assert his and his wife's claims to the throne but mainly England was a resource in William's lifelong battle with Louis XIV. English money, armies, and the navy could now be thrown into the fray, and so one of William's first acts as king was to declare war on France. The Nine Years' War, lasting from 1689 to 1697, forced William to recall Parliament frequently to ask for more money. In so doing, the war reinforced the new dependency of Crown upon Parliament institutionalized by the financial settlement. It also required the Commons to gain some measure of expertise in the area of government finance.[89]

Throughout William's reign, the Whig party was much more supportive of the war effort than were the Tories. Traditional Tory xenophobia and isolationism combined with the Jacobite element within the Tory party and the Dissenter element within the Whig party to pull the two parties in sharply different directions. Jacobites were hesitant to support a war against Louis XIV, James's host.[90] If there was to be a war, the Tories preferred that it be fought at sea and they were happier funding the navy than the army.

Louis XIV's Revocation of the Edict of Nantes in 1685 had started an exodus of Huguenots out of France, with many settling in England. Foreign-born dissenters, especially Huguenots, were virulently anti-French, and their support for the Whig party colored Whig support for the war.

THE REIGN OF ANNE

During Queen Anne's reign (1702–14), party competition intensified as the Court-Country distinction became clearer. The Whigs were firmly entrenched at the Court end and the Tories at the Country end.[91] At the outset, Anne's reign raised Tory hopes, for she was a lifelong Anglican and a legitimate heir of James II. With her as monarch, Tories could embrace wholeheartedly their ideals of passive obedience and nonresistance. Yet Anne did not give herself over completely to the Tories. She selected as her premier ministers moderate politicians such as Godolphin and Oxford (as Lord Treasurers), and the Duke of Marlborough (as Captain-General). Godolphin and Marlborough started out as moderate Tories but became allied to the Whigs during their 1702–10 ministry. Oxford (the former Robert Harley), whose ministry lasted from 1710 to 1714, had been a Country Whig in the early 1690s, but migrated with other Country Whigs over to the Tory party. All three men were averse to the idea of party government and tried to balance their ministries between the two parties.

As during William's reign, domestic politics were profoundly affected by involvement in a foreign war. In most respects, the War of the Spanish Succession (1702–13) was simply a continuation of the Nine Years' War, for France under Louis XIV was again the primary enemy. The English were allied with the Dutch and the Austrians, and Flanders was the primary military theater. The war started after the reigning monarch of Spain, Carlos II, died without an heir. Two of Europe's major ruling families had claims to the Spanish throne; Louis XIV's grandson the Duke of Anjou represented the interests of the Bourbons, and the archduke Charles of Austria, son of the Emperor Leopold I, had a claim on behalf of the Habsburgs. The Bourbon claim would unify the crowns of Spain and France and create an overwhelmingly powerful political entity within Europe, and so the Habsburgs opposed the Bourbons. For England as well, such an outcome would be extremely dangerous. Additionally, when James II died in 1701, Louis XIV recognized his son, James III, as the legitimate heir to the English throne. This challenged Anne's right to the throne and so shortly after gaining the throne she declared war on France.

The War of the Spanish Succession entailed unprecedented levels of expenditure. Britain maintained a "double forward commitment": armies in both Flanders and Spain, and a navy at sea.[92] So long as the war went well, the English public was more or less content to foot the bill, but as the war dragged on, and as the Spanish campaign suffered disastrous failures, public support waned.[93] Serious peace negotiations were initiated by the French, who at the end of 1708 were suffering badly, but these broke down in May 1709. The Whig ministry and allies tried to exact too high a price, and France rejected the proposed peace terms.[94] The battle of Malplaquet signaled French determination to continue the war, whatever the cost.[95] Meanwhile, popular support for the war continued to diminish in Britain. The war began to wind down in 1712 and peace negotiations resumed. A final treaty was signed between Britain and France in early 1713. Taken together, the Nine Years' War and the War of the Spanish Succession constituted two decades of full-scale military effort, and they marked Britain's emergence as a world power. War-driven expenses also forced the rapid development of Britain's system of public finance.

The war set the stage for politics under Anne but the succession issue again had important political ramifications. The problem was that Anne's only child, a son, died in 1700 when she was in her mid-thirties and unlikely to bear any more children. Except for the unrecognized descendants of James II, there were no more direct Stuart heirs after Anne. To remedy this situation, the Act of Settlement of 1701 placed the line of succession on the House of Hanover.[96] Tories once again faced a situation where Parliament settled the line of succession, a matter which according to Tory doctrine belonged to the realm of the divine right of kings. A second and related problem consisted in the fact that Scotland remained a separate country with a separate Parliament. Although Anne was Queen of both England and Scotland, Scotland did not pass an Act of Settlement and so it was likely that the thrones of the two countries would separate after the Hanoverian succession.[97] To defuse this dangerous possibility, England and Scotland merged to become Britain as the Treaty of Union was concluded in 1706, followed by the Act of Union in 1707. The Act was basically a Whig accomplishment, and political unification meant that Scottish MPs and Lords now sat in the House of Commons and House of Lords. This ensured that the Hanoverians would inherit the joint throne of a politically unified England and Scotland.[98]

ENGLISH POLITICS CIRCA 1712

In 1708, the Whigs won a great electoral victory on the strength of a failed French-Jacobite invasion of Scotland. The popular backlash against the Tories, who were forever being labeled Jacobites, gave the Whigs the electoral issue they needed to win.[99] The Whig ministry led by Godolphin and Marlborough lasted until 1710 when the next general election swept the Tories back into power. The Tory victory, which was even greater, resulted from general disillusionment with the war, the trial of Dr. Henry

Sacheverell, and Anne's decision to turn to the Tories for her government. Led by Robert Harley (who was granted a peerage as Earl of Oxford in 1711), the Tory ministry ruled from 1710 until shortly before Anne's death in 1714.

War-weariness was widespread by 1709. The fighting in Flanders had offered no recent victories, and progress was extremely slow.[100] Further-more, it seemed to many British subjects that the excessive demands of the Whigs had caused French peace initiatives to fail, and that the Whigs actually wanted to prolong the war. The Whig-sponsored parliamentary resolution that there be no peace without Spain, even though military pros-pects there were virtually nil, helped to confirm this suspicion.[101] Why would Whigs want to continue the fight? In Tory eyes the reason was obvious: the Whigs profited politically and financially from the war.[102] War-related expenses, the expansion of the state bureaucracy, and the army and navy, all provided vast opportunities for patronage, profiteering, and corruption.

The issue of religion also played into the hands of the Tories, although the Whigs raised it. In the wake of the Toleration Act of 1689, thousands of meeting places for dissenters had been licensed. Supporters of the Church of England were dismayed at the apparently rapid spread of dissent, and periodically the condition of the Anglican Church became a politi-cal issue. "The Church is in Danger" campaigns were usually unleashed when the Whigs were in power, or were about to gain it.[103] In 1709, the Tory Lord Mayor of London invited Dr. Henry Sacheverell to speak before the city fathers at a public service in St. Paul's cathedral. Sacheverell was a pro–Church of England minister, and completely opposed to toleration. Sacheverell used the public occasion to give a scorching critique of the Whig government and Whig policy.[104] Such a direct and public attack on the Whigs could not go unanswered and the Whigs in the House of Commons impeached Sacheverell for high crimes and misdemeanors.[105] What they had hoped would be a quick trial in the House of Lords turned into three and a half weeks of political theater. The impeachment of Sa-cheverell by the Whigs was soon perceived as a Whig attack on the Church, and "the Church is in Danger" became the theme of the Sacheverell trial and the subsequent general election.[106] Sacheverell was found guilty by the Lords but received a very light sentence, which was tantamount to acquittal.

The Anglican clergy and Tory party capitalized on the trial's outcome with an outpouring of anti-Whig propaganda. They convinced Anne that the Whigs no longer enjoyed popular support and that there should be an elec-tion immediately. Anne signalled her own preferences by replacing a num-ber of her Whig ministers with Tories. Whig prospects sank further when a delegation from the Bank of England met with Anne to suggest that public credit would suffer if there were any more changes in the ministry. This backfired, for not only did Anne proceed with the changes but the intervention created the distinct impression that the Whiggish Bank of England was telling the Queen how to govern.[107] Parliament was dissolved and in the elections of 1710 the Tories won a huge victory. Speck (1970) estimates that after 1708 the Commons contained 222 Tories and 291 Whigs. After the election of 1710, there were 332 Tories and 181 Whigs, and the House of Lords was the sole remaining Whig bastion.[108] The new Tory government was headed by Robert Harley, soon to be the Earl of Oxford.

The Tory victory was so complete that it presented something of a problem for Harley. Like Anne's previous parliamentary manager Godolphin, Harley was anxious not to be beholden to the extremists of either party. Harley opposed the idea of party government and envisioned a ministry composed of moderates from both sides, but leaning toward the Tories.[109] However, the Tory victory was so large that Harley had to rely on the Tories alone, and faced the difficult task of managing the hard-liners and Jacobites who formed the October Club.

The October Club was a peculiar feature of the 1710–13 Parliament. It was an organization of about 150 extremist backbench Tories and marked the first time that the largest bloc within the Tory party, the usually unorganizable country Tories, were organized. The club included most of the parliamentary Jacobites, and was independent of Harley.[110] Club members were intent on pursuing a radical Tory program. They soon became dissatisfied with Harley's attempts at moderation and began to exert themselves starting in early 1711. Their strategy was to show that October Club cooperation was necessary to the ministry, and they demonstrated this by obstructing business.[111]

Harley's response was to try to placate club members with various gestures: installing many of them on the commissions of the peace while simultaneously removing Whigs;[112] making secret overtures to the Pretender in order to ensure the cooperation of his parliamentary followers;[113] supporting a Qualifying of Members Bill (9 Anne, c.5);[114] supporting a repeal of the Naturalization Act;[115] appointing selected club members to various offices;[116] consenting to the attack on Robert Walpole, the former Whig Secretary at War;[117] and all the while deferring action on more radical October Club proposals until peace with France was negotiated.[118] Harley maintained a delicate political balance. In order to preserve government credit, he had to maintain reasonable terms with the largely Whiggish financiers of the Bank of England. At the same time, however, he had to keep the Tory backbenchers happy in order to protect his parliamentary position.

Oxford was equally subtle and duplicitous in the peace negotiations with France, for he simultaneously undertook several sets of secret negotiations. His goal was to bargain a secret bilateral peace with France, and then go through the official multilateral negotiations with the allies and France. During these some, but not all, of the details of the previous bilateral deal would be presented to the other allies, and unless they acquiesced, the allies would face the prospect of fighting France alone.[119] To keep the Jacobites at bay, Oxford simultaneously engaged in secret flirtations with the Pretender. The peace that was finally negotiated guaranteed British commercial access to the markets of the Spanish Empire, and granted a trade concession to the newly established South Sea Company. As part of the agreement, Louis XIV recognized Anne as the lawful sovereign of Britain. The Treaties of Peace and Commerce between Britain and France were signed in March 1713.

WHIGS AND TORIES

The Whig-Tory conflict organized politics during Anne's reign. From 1702 to 1714 there were five general elections and many contested constituencies.[120] The "view" and the "shout" were things of the past and contested elections went to the poll. The eligibility of each voter was ascertained,[121] and his vote recorded, so the voting process was more systematic and precise than ever before.[122] Both parties directed their strategies at the electorate. Poll books were used to determine supporters and opponents, and various means were developed to "get out the vote." The returning officer for an election was usually the sheriff, and so candidates tried to put into that office a fellow party member. They also tried to exploit their connections with local magnates and elites. Whenever possible, peers and lord lieutenants were brought in to rally support.

Both parties exploited the events of the day in their propaganda. The Whigs, for example, focused on the Jacobite invasion of Scotland in the 1708 election, while the Tories used Sacheverell's trial to great effect in 1710, and the peace treaty in 1713. Extensive efforts were made during and between elections to manage public opinion. In this regard, both parties were helped by the expiration of the Licensing Act in 1695, which effectively ended press censorship. What followed was an outpouring of newspapers, books, political tracts, and pamphlets directed at public opinion.[123] Some of the finest writers of the day were involved in the production of political pamphlets (e.g., Swift, Defoe, Addison, and Steele). Political poems, ballads, and prints were also common.[124] The Tories had the advantage of possessing an ally in the anglican clergy, for the pulpit was frequently used to give parishioners political as well as spiritual guidance.

The electorate was composed of hard-core Whig and Tory supporters, floating voters (who switched parties) and casual voters (who voted only occasionally). Analyses of poll books show that most of the electorate voted for the same party in successive elections, and there was little ticket-splitting.[125] Partisan electioneering tried to ensure that party supporters voted, that opponents did not, and that floating and casual voters shifted to the party side. Much of the propaganda was directed at the latter two groups. Parties believed that by stressing certain themes or discussing certain policies, they could swing over voters. Regular patronage was also used to encourage supporters and discourage opponents. In this, manipulation of local offices like the commissions of the peace could be very effective.[126] However, the growth in the electorate during the seventeenth century made it harder to rely on patronage alone.

Given its newly expanded role in government, control over the Commons became an important step toward control of the government. But there remained two other elements: the House of Lords, and the Crown. Whig-Tory party differences also divided the House of Lords. In fact, party leaders were usually aristocrats for they possessed the wealth and social status necessary for political leadership. If a party leader was not a peer, he could often expect to become one in the normal progression of his political career. A peerage was frequently granted in recognition for political service, as the example of Robert Harley attests.[127] Since only the Crown could create peerages and appoint bishops, the monarch had some control over the House of Lords.

The Crown was still free to appoint ministers, but given the practical necessity of obtaining financial supplies, Anne's ministers needed the cooperation of the Commons. A minister who did not enjoy its confidence could not be effective. But the Commons did not choose the government for that was still the prerogative of the Crown. Because Anne adhered to the ideal of nonparty government, she selected as her premier ministers moderate men like Godolphin and Oxford who tried to balance government between the two parties. Whenever possible, she avoided appointing to office Whig or Tory extremists.[128]

The majority of members of the House of Commons and the House of Lords belonged either to one party or the other. Since party membership was not formalized, parliamentary lists provide the best evidence. There were no official records kept of parliamentary votes, but parliamentary managers devised lists to classify MPs or Lords by party, or to predict how they would vote on a specific issue.[129] Other lists recorded the results of divisions (formal votes).[130] The very existence of these lists documents the importance of managing Parliament effectively, and also the level of public interest in parliamentary decisions. Some division lists were published and distributed for political purposes. "White" and "black" lists enumerated the supporters and foes of specific bills, and were distributed to the electorate so that they would vote for (or against) particular candidates.[131]

A large number of division lists have been collected and analyzed, and the evidence is overwhelming that voting occurred along party lines.[132] The majority of MPs and Lords voted consistently as Whigs or as Tories, with little cross-over voting (although the Whigs were generally more disciplined than the Tories). Even in the reign of William III, when the party lines were not so sharply drawn, most MPs voted consistently as either Whigs or Tories.[133] Major collapses of party discipline were usually the result of some careful strategy by the other party to split their opposition.[134]

Several features contributed to party coherence.[135] Unlike modern political parties, the Whigs and Tories did not have a single recognized leader, but consultations among party leaders, who were usually peers, helped to coordinate party strategy. Once the leadership had ironed out their differences, they had to get their party members in both Houses to cooperate and ensure that the members would actually attend Parliament.[136] Meetings between party leaders and party members at the outset of a new session were used to inform the membership of the current political strategy. Social clubs were also used as settings in which to coordinate party leaders and members.[137]

To ensure attendance and disciplined voting, the leaders of both parties exploited linkages between members of the House of Commons and peers in the House of Lords. Many of the peers had a personal "connection," a following in the Commons joined to them in a variety of ways. These included friendship, kinship and marriage, professional patronage, and electoral patronage.[138] The first two are self-evident: a peer could usually mobilize his personal friends and relatives in the House of Commons.[139] A peer could also mobilize members in the Commons who relied upon him for either professional or electoral patronage. Someone who controlled military offices, for example, had considerable leverage over MPs who were naval or army officers.[140] More important, a peer who controlled a parliamentary seat could manage the occupant of that seat. Such peer-commoner links would be used to ensure that votes followed party strategy. Independent members who did not owe their seat to a patron, were the most difficult to discipline.[141]

There were systematic differences between the two parties in their level of organization, policy goals, and supporters. Without a doubt, the Whigs were better organized. Led by a small group of peers (the Whig Junto),[142] the Whigs were better able to coordinate their personnel and other political assets and follow a coherent political strategy. The Whig leadership met much more frequently than the Tory leadership and worked hard to achieve a consensus among themselves. In contrast, Tory leaders were frequently divided. Even when the Tories won huge majorities in the Commons, the party was often rent by struggles among its leaders. For example, the battle between Oxford and Bolingbroke for Tory leadership set up the electoral disaster of 1715.[143] As a group, the Whig Junto were extremely ambitious and capable. The talent of their leadership aside, the Whigs had fewer independent country members than the Tories, and so discipline was easier to maintain. The Tory party included many men predisposed against organized voting.[144] Tory backbenchers were usually late to arrive for a parliamentary session and early to depart. Even the peer groups which could coordinate action between the Lords and Commons were both more numerous in the Tory party and less effective than those of the Junto.[145]

The Tories were also hard to organize because they were split over some basic political issues. The question of the succession divided the Tories into Jacobites (who supported the return of James the Pretender), and Hanoverians (who supported the Hanoverian succession), with many Tories somewhere in the middle. In addition, it was hard for a Tory government to conduct successful foreign and financial policy when so many of its supporters were opposed to the war and the taxes necessary to pay for it.

The Whig party was generally supported by dissenters, merchants, businessmen, and financiers (the so-called "monied interest"). The Tories were less sympathetic to commerce and so, for example, Carmarthen and Nottingham's Tory ministry got the blame for the disastrous loss of the Turkey merchant fleet in 1693. The Tory party counted as the core of its supporters the Anglican clergy and the landed gentry (the "landed interest").[146] The Whigs did better in the boroughs, and the Tories better in the counties. Both parties enjoyed support among the aristocracy, although the Whigs made more of that support than did the Tories. Numerically, the Tory party was preponderant. The Tories gained a majority in the Commons in four of the five general elections during Anne's reign. Yet, through superior organization the Whigs were frequently able to overcome this Tory advantage. And the Whigs were also able to use their strength in the House of Lords to compensate for their weakness in the Commons. Tory legislation would frequently pass the Commons and then die because of Whig opposition in the Lords.

Ideologically, the two parties took opposing views on many issues. Whigs supported the war and the military effort on the Continent. Tories were generally against the war, and preferred a naval war over a land war. Partly this was due to Tory isolationism, and partly because the land tax, one of the most obvious war-related burdens, fell heavily on the landed gentry. It was also because the Whigs were able to enjoy most of the patronage and profits the war generated. The Whigs were simply more effective at raising money to pay for the war, and so despite her sympathies to the contrary, Anne often had no choice but to work with a Whiggish ministry. Hence, Whigs often occupied the high public offices which in an early modern bureaucracy brought substantial rewards. To the Tories and their supporters, it seemed that they paid for a war that benefited their political enemies.

Whigs and Tories differed over religious questions. The Whigs supported some measure of toleration for dissenting Protestants while the Tories were staunchly pro–Church of England. They opposed toleration and sought additional measures to prevent dissenters (usually Whigs) from eluding the remaining religious restrictions. Both parties opposed toleration for Catholics, but because of the Jacobite contingent within the Tory party, the Whigs often accused the Tories of harboring papists. Strongly xenophobic, the Tories were deeply suspicious of Britain's military allies and of the foreign-born merchants who played such a prominent role in public finance and in the stock market.[147]

Electoral self-interest motivated the Whig preference for narrower franchises and the Tory preference for broader franchises. The Whigs did better in the smaller electorates that could be more easily managed by a patron while the Tories were popular among large county electorates. The Tories were also supportive of an independent Commons, one that could resist the influence wielded by Whig aristocrats and ministers. The Whigs were strongly supportive of the Hanoverian succession, whereas the Tories were fatally divided between Hanoverians and Jacobites. Neither party conceded much legitimacy to their opponent. It was hard for a true Tory to think that what he considered a godless, foreigner-loving, corrupt Whig could still be a good citizen. Likewise, Whigs thought little of the parochial, rebellion-minded Jacobites which they believed infested the Tory party.

CONCLUSION

The forty years between 1672 and 1712 witnessed a substantial change in how politics was organized. There was some continuity of political issues as religion, foreign policy, and public finance remained important throughout the period. Yet, the political organizations through which these issues were pursued and expressed, were transformed. Parliamentary politics, a factionalized and fluid undertaking in the early 1670s, was reorganized by the emergence of two competing political parties. After the Glorious Revolution, and in the context of two expensive wars, the Commons gained in importance as a political institution. Parliament went from being *a* political arena to being *the* political arena. Ambitious men learned that the high road to political power ran through the Commons.

Party divisions went deep into British society as virtually every sphere of life felt the effects of the Whig-Tory split. Not surprisingly, the Houses of Commons and Lords were divided, but so was the Church of England. The lower ranks of the Church were heavily populated by Tories, while Whigs dominated the upper positions.[148] Local government offices bore some of the

brunt as purges of the commissions of the peace and lord lieutenancies followed changes in party fortunes. Furthermore, social life was politicized as
Whigs and Tories began to move in different social circles. The publishing
boom in London increased the number of newspapers (many of which were
highly partisan) and helped fuel the political consciousness of the reading
public.[149] Even members of the lower class, who could not vote, were influenced by party conflict. For example, participants in the London riots that
broke out during the trial of Dr. Henry Sacheverell included many too poor
to vote.[150] During the Exclusion Crisis, Whig street crowds battled Tory
street crowds in London.[151] The poor were not immune from political sentiment, even if they were excluded from formal political participation. Partisanship was not confined to political elites.

Despite these political changes, it is important to recognize what stayed
the same. Party formation meant organized political conflict among English
elites. The English upper class was a divided elite but it nevertheless remained a ruling elite. It was not until much later that other social classes
made significant inroads into the major institutions of governance.[152] In particular, despite much anxiety about the rising "monied interest," merchants
and financiers never displaced landed gentlemen from control over the
Commons or the Lords.

Many social institutions served as the battleground for the competition
between Whig and Tory. The Church, local government, national government (including both the House of Commons and the House of Lords),
the armed forces, and the major joint-stock companies were all sites of
struggle. Elections, a main focus of party activity, were in abundance during
Anne's reign. And both parties became adept at wooing electorates through
whatever means possible. The growth in electorates meant that patronage
alone was no longer adequate, and wider appeals were necessary. Whigs
and Tories sought to gain power, not simply for power's sake, but to control
policy. When given the opportunity, that is exactly what they did.

Whig-Tory conflict emerged out of a number of related issues, including
religion, foreign policy, public finance, the succession, and the independence of Parliament. Not surprisingly, political conflict played itself out
in many different arenas. These included formal political institutions
like Parliament, local and municipal government, and others such as the
Church and the armed forces, and even such things as charitable institutions and parish poor relief.[153] It seems fairly obvious, for example, why
Tories who wanted to enact a particular religious policy would want to control the Church, or why Whigs who supported a foreign policy initiative
would want to control the army. So it is not surprising that the Church and
army became politicized. Where the connection between institution and
policy end was direct, party supporters would try to seize control of the
institution.

Sometimes there was no obvious connection. For example, elite social life was drawn along party lines, although it is not clear what could be gained by having this split.[154] At other times, the institution operated according to a logic that resisted politicization. A good example of this was the market, where efficiency criteria and considerations of profit shaped behavior. In the market, it would be harder to reconcile partisanship with profitability than to focus on the latter alone. Nevertheless, as we shall see, market behavior and economic institutions were pulled into the political storm.

Chapter Three

FINANCE AND STATE-FORMATION

... it [credit] is the principal mover in all business, and if
there should be a total stagnation in this nerval juice, a
dead palsy would forthwith seize the body-politic.
—Charles Davenant

WHIGS AND TORIES contended for control of many different institutions, but
chief among them was the apparatus of central government. The content
and stakes of their conflict changed as the size and financial power of the
British state grew, but this process occurred in a peculiar fashion. State
strength as measured by the ability to wage external wars increased many-
fold. England was rightly considered a marginal player in European politics
during Charles II's reign, but under Queen Anne, Britain achieved great
power status and was a force to be reckoned with. During the Financial
Revolution, Britain became a world power. At the same time, however, the
ability of the English state to regulate or control internal matters changed
very little, and, if anything, may even have diminished. The reaction to
James II's reign meant that British citizens enjoyed after 1689 even stronger
protections against arbitrary government than before. The spectacular increase in the external strength of the state was not matched by a similar rise
in its internal strength.[1] How could one occur without the other?

A state apparatus is fueled by money, and finance becomes particularly
important during war. Without cash, naval vessels aren't built or repaired,
and troops cannot be provisioned or paid for. The explanation for the curious
English combination of external strength and internal weakness lies in public finance. Thus, I examine here the major developments in public finance
occurring at the end of the seventeenth century and the beginning of the
eighteenth. I focus on how public monies were raised through taxes and
loans, as well as the organization of public financial institutions. These financial developments were connected to the political changes discussed earlier.
Partly, this was because public finance involves the deployment of economic
resources for political ends but in this case more was involved.[2] Three joint-
stock companies—the Bank of England, East India Company, and South
Sea Company—are worthy of particular attention for not only did they play
a central role in public finance, but they possessed a partisan character. As

Adam Smith noted about the Bank, they were all important as "engines of state," but they were also very political engines.

Spending figures give a rough measure of the growth of the English state. Shortly after the Restoration, in 1662, total public spending was about £1.6 million per annum. In 1672, the Third Dutch War pushed this figure up to £2.5 million, and simply overwhelmed the fiscal capacity of the state (about £1.2 million of the total was military-related spending). The result was the Stop of the Exchequer. By contrast, Britain spent in 1712 almost £7.9 million (with £4.8 million going to the military), but there was small chance of another Stop of the Exchequer.[3] Prices changed so little that adjusting for inflation accounts for very little of the difference between these sums.[4] The increase was real, not nominal.

A similar change occurred on the income side, although it was not as large. Net public income in 1662 was about £1.5 million, and increased up to £2.3 million in 1672. Public income in 1712 totaled £5.7 million, a considerable rise which nevertheless failed to keep pace with spending. Borrowing made up the difference, and it was the development of a national debt which really enlarged the fiscal capacity of the English state. Public financial machinery underwent a substantial improvement, and consequently Britain could fund and deploy more military resources. Despite the fact that France's population was four times greater, Britain was able to defeat it in the War of the Spanish Succession. Fiscal strength was demonstrably the basis for external strength.

For the first half of the seventeenth century, England's financial system remained undeveloped. England avoided most of the diplomatic entanglements of the Continent and so did not have to fund any major external military efforts.[5] As the Military Revolution unfolded and as the cost of war spiraled upward, England was less affected than most other European powers.[6] Without the financial pressures of warfare, England's fiscal system underwent no major overhaul and continued to stand on largely feudal foundations until the late seventeenth century.

Charles Tilly (1975, 1985, 1990) has argued convincingly that war was the major force shaping state finances, and John Brewer (1989, 1994) has elaborated this point in the case of England.[7] During the early modern era, the fiscal problem posed by warfare was simple. As expenses climbed, tax revenues had to be increased, and when they couldn't be expanded as quickly, which was most of the time, then it was necessary to borrow.[8] Warfare meant raising taxes and borrowing to cover the often considerable difference between revenues and expenditures. A ruler had to decide which taxes to increase and how, and also from whom to borrow and on what terms. As practical matters, these were seldom easy questions to answer. Which taxes to increase, for example, invariably became a political issue because it affected who was to bear the tax burden. It also affected borrowing since higher taxes made borrowing unnecessary.

In the feudal model of English government, the king was charged with the provision of justice and defense.[9] To fund these responsibilities, the Crown received ordinary revenues, ideally in the form of income from the Crown's own landed estates. It was understood, however, that a sustained military campaign in defense of the realm would require more than ordinary revenues could provide. Therefore, the king's subjects were obliged to supply additional financial aid so that the monarch could mount an adequate defense. National taxes were intermittent, appearing only to meet the occasional demands of war, and were supplied with the consent of Parliament.

Even with a cooperative Parliament, it was impossible to raise taxes fast enough to match wartime increases in spending. Inevitably there was a shortfall, if only a temporary one, that had to be bridged with a short-term loan. Such a loan would cover immediate expenses, and could be repaid as tax revenues flowed in. Thus, throughout most of the Middle Ages, English kings made fairly regular use of credit. Finding someone willing to loan money to the Crown was not easy, for sovereign debt presented an unusual problem. Lenders want their money back and ordinarily if a debtor defaults on a loan, they can initiate legal proceedings and take the debtor to court. Or lenders obtain security for a loan, and when the debtor defaults simply take possession of the collateral. Neither of these strategies worked well when the debtor was a sovereign ruler.[10] In general, the king could not be sued in his own courts of law and so lenders had no satisfactory legal redress. In addition, seizing collateral was difficult given the political and military position of a monarch. These problems made lending to sovereigns a risky undertaking, and to compensate, lenders often charged high rates of interest.[11] Hence, it was hard for sovereigns to borrow cheaply.

The traditional financial philosophy was reasserted for the last time in 1660 when Charles II was expected to "live of his own." Parliament recognized that Charles could not possibly fund ordinary expenses using the income of his own landed estates, and so it granted permanent revenues which it hoped would provide an annual income of £1.2 million.[12] Parliament's hopes proved to be overly optimistic, for over the course of his reign Charles's ordinary revenue generated on average only about £945,000 per year.[13] Not surprisingly, Charles was under constant financial pressure and frequently had to turn to Parliament for extraordinary funds (which made him politically dependent). In practical terms, the distinction between ordinary and extraordinary revenues was roughly equivalent to the difference between indirect and direct taxes.[14] Extraordinary revenues were usually granted as a direct tax.

ENGLISH PUBLIC FINANCE IN 1672

The Stop of the Exchequer is particularly helpful in marking the fiscal limits of the English state and highlighting the dangers of sovereign lending. In 1672, England could not manage both to pay for the new war with the United Provinces and meet its prior obligations to creditors. Charles was financially constrained by his debts, and so to free himself he defaulted. By unilaterally suspending Exchequer payments to Crown creditors in January 1672, Charles II made tax revenues available to cover his military spending. The bulk of the suspended debt, which totaled over £1.2 million, was owed to a small group of London goldsmith-bankers.[15] Most, but not all, crown debts were affected by this action.

The certainty of war precipitated the Stop, but the default demonstrated both the shaky condition of public finances and the weak position of public creditors. By the standards of later wars, the Third Dutch War was cheap, involving only about £5 million of military spending over three and a half years.[16] This compares with an expenditure of over £10 million in 1709–10 alone, during the War of the Spanish Succession. Yet even a modest military adventure was sufficient to overwhelm Charles II's financial system. To understand why, it is necessary to consider how public revenues and borrowing could match increased spending.

PUBLIC REVENUES IN THE 1670s

Public revenue consisted of ordinary and extraordinary revenues. The three major ordinary revenues were the customs taxes, the excise taxes, and the hearth tax.[17] Customs revenues were politically the most palatable to Parliament, and economically the most variable (depending on foreign trade). Revenue considerations and trade policy both helped set tariff levels (witness the famous Navigation Act of 1660). New customs duties were typically proposed in Parliament and opposed by the Court. At the Restoration, customs revenues were collected directly by the government following the system used during the Interregnum. The shortfall in revenues was substantial, almost £100,000 less than the expected £400,000 per annum total. To improve administration and revenues, the system of collection reverted back to tax farming in 1662.

Compared to customs, excise duties on domestic manufactures were a recent innovation.[18] Excises had been established in the Interregnum period, and were abolished at the Restoration. However, to compensate Charles for the loss of some feudal revenues a new excise was granted on liquor, which promised high revenues and a financial penalty on sinful behavior. There was much more political opposition to excise duties than to customs because the former were considered an overly intrusive form of taxation. Hence, excise duties were usually proposed by the Court and opposed in Parliament. Excise taxes posed far greater administrative problems than the other taxes, for complex duties had to be levied on a scale which strained government administrative capacities.[19] Like the customs, excise revenues were at first collected directly by the government, but large revenue shortfalls forced a switch back to a tax farm in 1662.

By 1662, it was apparent that the revenues granted to Charles II were not going to generate the £1.2 million per annum that Parliament intended him to have. To provide more money, in 1662 Parliament granted the Hearth Tax to the Crown in perpetuity, charging 2 shillings annually for each hearth and stove in a taxpayer's dwelling. It did not generate as much revenue as the customs or excise but it provided a considerable, stable income.[20] For taxpayers, it was the most intrusive and unpopular of the major taxes.[21] Administratively, the levying of the hearth tax relied heavily upon local government officials. The government collected this tax directly until 1666, when the financial straits of the Second Dutch War forced a switch to tax farming.

Rather than administer its revenues directly, for most of the 1660s the Treasury used tax farms to collect the three main revenues. Tax-farming meant contracting out revenue collection to a syndicate for a period of time. At the end of a tax farm, competitive bidding determined which syndicate would get the next contract. Bids typically involved both an annual payment and an advance. The latter, a lump-sum loan to the government, constituted one of the main benefits of tax farming. The winning syndicate would advance money to the Crown and undertake the entire process of revenue collection. Since the administrative problems involved with collection were substantial and the loans were large, no single person could run a tax farm. All consisted of syndicates of wealthy individuals. Profits to the syndicate came from the residual income remaining after all revenues had been collected, administrative costs paid, and the advance and annual payments to the Crown made.

At the outset of the 1660s, the government collected ordinary revenues directly because of the economic uncertainties that accompanied large-scale political change. It was unclear to anyone how substantial government revenues would be and hence what the various tax farms might be worth. Such uncertainty made tax farming unattractive and discouraged lively bidding between rival syndicates. Yet tax farming gave the Crown the advantage of a loan at the start of each farm and ensured a stable revenue. It also reduced the administrative burden of public finance by externalizing the task of revenue collection.[22] In the long run, however, these advantages were offset by the near total absence of central control over public revenues.

Furthermore, the system was vulnerable to the kind of problem that arose in the early 1670s, when one syndicate gained control over too much of public revenue.

Sir William Bucknall headed the syndicate that farmed most of the excise revenues from 1668 to 1671. His group also won the contract to farm the customs starting in 1671. This would have given them control over about two-thirds of the total revenue, and hence a strong bargaining position vis-à-vis the Crown. The syndicate tried to use its leverage to gain greater financial advantage, but the customs contract was canceled five days before its commencement as Treasury officials responded to the danger.[23]

Even if a formal tax farm was not used, there were other arrangements which mirrored the farming principle. The most obvious involved reliance upon the personal credit of government officials in funding departmental expenses.[24] For example, the Paymaster to the King's Guards, Sir Stephen Fox, loaned personal funds to ensure that the Guards were paid regularly, and was later repaid from excise revenues.[25] The personal credit of the Navy Treasurer was often used to shore up navy finances.[26] In all such instances, government finances depended upon intermediaries, using the personal resources of officials to obtain credit, or relying upon private syndicates to collect revenues.

From time to time (typically during war), Parliament would supplement ordinary revenues with special grants. At the Restoration, Parliament had two models of direct taxation to work with: the Subsidy and the Monthly Assessment.[27] Both were general property taxes, in principle taxing both real estate and individuals' personalty.[28] The Subsidy would stipulate a uniform Pound Rate (i.e., so many shillings or pence per pound of assessed value), with the total revenue yield depending upon the rate. The Monthly Assessment involved specifying first the total yield per month, then dividing this among the counties in proportion to their estimated wealth. County commissioners for the Assessment would then set a pound rate sufficient to generate that county's share of the total amount.

The Subsidy imposed a higher tax rate on personalty than did the Assessment (which fell largely on real property). However, given the aversion of taxpayers to having their wealth valued, the Assessment had the advantage of providing a more certain flow of revenue. Its disadvantage to the taxpayer was that it undertaxed personalty, and so amounted in practice to a land tax. Revenue considerations meant that the Assessment was the most common direct tax voted by Parliament under Charles II.

Both of these taxes had roughly the same administrative structure. Direct taxes were not farmed out to syndicates, nor were they directly collected by Crown agents. Instead, collection was entrusted to commissioners appointed by Parliament. Each county or administrative area had its own set

TABLE 3.1

Revenue Inflows from Parliamentary Subsidy (22 & 23
Charles II, c.3), Given Royal Assent March 3, 1671

Time Period	Amount (£)
Easter 1671–Michaelmas 1671	76,572
Michaelmas 1671–Easter 1672	145,593
Easter 1672–Michaelmas 1672	87,956
Michaelmas 1672–Easter 1673	22,378
Easter 1673–Michaelmas 1673	6,038
Michaelmas 1673–Easter 1674	4,444
Easter 1674–Michaelmas 1674	812
Michaelmas 1674–Easter 1675	1,037
Easter 1675–Michaelmas 1675	307
Michaelmas 1675–Easter 1676	0
Easter 1676–Michaelmas 1676	3,395
Michaelmas 1676–Easter 1677	843
Easter 1677–Michaelmas 1677	925
Michaelmas 1677–Easter 1678	180
Easter 1678–Michaelmas 1678	254
Easter 1687–Michaelmas 1687	133
Total	£350,867

Source: Chandaman, 353–57.

of commissioners. The commissioners appointed assessors to determine the
liability of individual taxpayers, and collectors to gather the money. Assessments were inaccurate, partly because of resistance to valuations of wealth
and partly because the commissioners in charge were agents of Parliament
rather than the Crown.[29] The absence of Crown involvement reduced the
incentive to extract maximum revenues.

Although intended to help meet extraordinary expenses, special Parliamentary grants of money were still problematic. Table 3.1 shows a typical
situation. It sets out the revenue stream resulting from the Subsidy granted
by Parliament in 1671 (22 & 23 Charles II, c.3) to cover expenses associated
with the Third Dutch War.

The first problem with the Subsidy was that revenue collection took a long
time, even though the expenses were immediate. Payments were still trick-
ling in as late as 1687, sixteen years later. It took until Michaelmas of the
year *after* the Subsidy was granted for more than 80% of the revenues to
arrive.[30] Second, Parliament grossly overestimated the yield of the Subsidy.
The target was between £750,000 and £800,000, but the final total was less
than half that amount. Such delays and shortfalls made it necessary for the
Crown to borrow.

THE TREASURY IN THE 1670s

The Treasury was the center of public financial machinery, although in the Restoration period it did not provide much centralized control. It was often circumvented as Crown revenues went directly from source to Crown creditors without going into the Exchequer.[31] To make matters worse, offices in the Exchequer and Treasury were generally held by officials enjoying life tenure, and so even the most incompetent could not be turned out. Crown borrowing was heavily dependent upon a small number of London goldsmith-bankers charging high interest rates, and there were no facilities for long-term borrowing.

The affable but ineffectual Earl of Southampton was the Lord Treasurer from 1660 to 1667 and did nothing to improve Treasury operations. After his departure, the Treasury was put into commission, and a number of vigorous junior politicians took over. The new Secretary of the Treasury, Sir George Downing, was familiar with the public financial systems of the Dutch. "Dutch finance" was acknowledged to be superior, providing larger sums to the public fisc at lower rates of interest.[32] The contrast was striking, for the Dutch government could borrow at 4% while Charles II had to pay up to 12% interest. Given the perpetual shortage of money, a number of measures were taken to improve fiancial administration.

First, the Treasury increased its control over expenditures and personnel. Through a series of Orders in Council the Treasury gained a measure of oversight over departmental spending.[33] Switching the terms under which offices were held from tenure for life to tenure "at the King's pleasure" (*durante bene placito*) strengthened control over Exchequer personnel.[34] Incompetent officeholders could now be removed on short notice.[35] Furthermore, Treasury accounting methods were improved and Treasury records in general systematized.[36] Downing proved to be a much better bureaucrat than his predecessor.[37]

At the best of times, revenues came into the Exchequer at a much slower rate than expenditures went out. Rather than postpone spending until the funds arrived, the government usually depended on anticipatory short-term borrowing from a number of sources. Tax-farming syndicates loaned sums at the outset of their contracts. The Crown borrowed from individuals, usually goldsmith-bankers, and from organizations such as the City of London and the East India Company.[38] For short-term loans, both principal and interest had to be repaid quickly. There were no arrangements for the government to borrow over the long term.

To improve the government's position as a borrower, the Treasury tried to circumvent the goldsmith-bankers and obtain loans directly from the public. At the time, many individuals deposited money with the goldsmith-bankers who in turn loaned it to the Crown. The bankers were paying 6% interest on their deposits while receiving much more on their loans to the Crown. One innovation instituted by Downing was "payment in course."[39] Public creditors were to be repaid in the order in which they loaned funds to the Exchequer. The Additional Aid of 1665 (17 Charles II, c.1), one of the extraordinary grants of money given to fund the Second Dutch War, introduced this new system. Downing pushed it through despite the opposition of other ministers, including Clarendon, who disliked the measure because it reduced the Crown's financial discretion. Charles recognized the need to improve his financial system and so backed Downing's proposal.[40] Downing was able to gather support for the measure in the Commons since it was aimed at reducing the profits of goldsmith-bankers, a group unpopular with a House of debtors.

"Payment in course" had a very specific meaning. The Additional Aid granted a sum of £1.25 million and had both appropriation and borrowing clauses. All of the monies were directed to pay for the war effort, and could not be diverted to any other use. The monies were paid first into the Exchequer, so there was no diversion at the revenue source. Receipts and issues of money associated with the act were recorded in two registers at the Exchequer which were open for public inspection. Persons advancing money to the Crown on the security of this Aid received sequentially numbered Treasury Orders, which were, in effect, interest-bearing promissory notes.[41] As the Aid revenues flowed in, Treasury Orders were repaid in numerical sequence. Persons who loaned money early on would be repaid first, and there would be none of the political discretion that allowed well-connected creditors to be paid ahead of the less well connected. Additionally, Treasury Orders were transferable from Crown creditors to third parties. All of this assured a more fair and orderly system of repayment which Downing hoped would encourage potential creditors to bypass financial middlemen and loan money directly to the government.[42]

The Stop of the Exchequer

Downing's administrative changes were important for the future but they were too late to prevent the Stop of the Exchequer. Charles was still beholden to the goldsmith-bankers, and in the absence of any system for long-term borrowing remained dependent on short-term credit. Those with money refused to lend it directly to the Crown, still preferring to deposit it with Lombard Street goldsmith-bankers, who would then loan it to the Crown. Hence, the Treasury Orders created by Downing's innovations of 1665 were mostly bought by goldsmith-bankers.[43] Greater liquidity was one reason why investors continued to prefer goldsmith-bankers over the Treasury. Goldsmith-banker deposits were similar to what we now call demand-deposits, for they could be withdrawn on short notice at any time. Such was not the case for funds lodged with the Treasury.[44] Treasury Orders were transferable in principle, but without a developed secondary capital market, legal transferability did not produce liquidity. In addition, the offices of the Exchequer were at an inconvenient distance from Lombard Street, the center of London's financial district.[45]

The Treaty of Dover committed Charles to join France in an attack on the Dutch, and so by 1671 another war with the Dutch was in the works. Crown finances were in disarray because the debts incurred during the Second Dutch War were still not paid off. The severe economic dislocations caused by the Great Plague and Great Fire of London made matters even worse.[46] Moreover, the new Treasury Order system had been abused when it was extended in 1667–68 to the permanent ordinary revenue. Since Treasury Orders were no longer tied to a specific revenue, there was no automatic limit to the number that could be issued.[47] The government over-borrowed, and the reduction in discretion associated with the Treasury Order system made it difficult to adjust or reschedule the government's loans. A sizable proportion of the public revenue was locked into debt repayment.[48]

To launch the war required cash, and to obtain that cash, repayment of all outstanding Treasury Orders was suspended for a year on 2 January 1672.[49] The monies earmarked to redeem Treasury Orders were now available for the war effort. Most but not all Treasury Orders were affected by the Stop, about £1.2 million worth.[50] Goldsmith-bankers who had invested heavily in Treasury Orders were hardest hit by the Stop as they were squeezed between creditors, who wanted to withdraw their deposits, and the Exchequer, from which no money was forthcoming.

The Stop of the Exchequer confirmed the shortcomings of Charles II's fiscal system, but by revealing who loaned money to Charles it also affords a deeper understanding of the sociology of public credit. What was the social basis of his financial support? The Stop involved the unilateral suspension of debt repayments but it was not an outright repudiation. In subsequent years, Charles asked Parliament for additional money to satisfy his creditors, and he had his accountants determine the exact amount owed to each one. The list of those directly affected by the Stop was short, but because the goldsmiths acted as financial intermediaries—borrowing many small sums from a large number of depositors and loaning large sums to a single sovereign debtor—the number indirectly affected was much greater. In order to understand public borrowing, both direct and indirect creditors must be examined. Table 3.2 gives the final 1677 listing of creditors directly affected by the Stop, ranked by size of debts.

The table shows how concentrated Charles's borrowing was and how much he depended specifically on goldsmith-bankers. The twelve biggest creditors (Sir Robert Viner through George Snell) were all goldsmith-bankers and the amount owed just to goldsmith-bankers was £1,282,144, or about

TABLE 3.2

Sums and Annual Payments Owed to Creditors Affected by the Stop of
the Exchequer, 1677

Name	Total Debt (nearest £)	Annual Interest Payment (nearest £)
1. Sir Robert Viner	416,725	25,003
2. Edward Backwell	295,995	17,760
3. Gilbert Whitehall	248,866	14,931
4. John Lindsey	85,833	5,150
5. John Portman	76,761	4,606
6. Jeremiah Snow	59,781	3,587
7. Joseph Hornby	22,548	1,353
8. Thomas Rowe	17,616	1,057
9. Robert Ryves	16,368	982
10. Bernard Turnor	16,275	977
11. Robert Welsted	11,308	678
12. George Snell	10,895	654
13. Sir John Shaw	9,356	561
14. Isaac la Gouche	5,370	322
15. John Thruston, Esq.	5,208	313
16. Sir Edmond Turner	4,593	276
17. William Gomeldon	2,157	130
18. Richard Lant	1,844	111
19. Isaac Collier	1,784	107
20. Isaac Alvarez	1,581	95
21. Henry Johnson, Esq.	1,389	83
22. Francis Millington	1,285	77
23. Dr. Edward Chamberlaine	706	42
24. Robert Winne	567	34
25. George Toriano	130	8
Total	£1,314,941	£78,897

Source: Calender of Treasury Books, vol. III: xlviii.

97.5% of the total debt.[51] The top six creditors alone were owed 90% of the
total. The direct social base of royal credit was a narrow one.

When payments stopped, both the goldsmith-bankers and their depositors were affected. Normally, depositors could expect to retrieve their
money on fourteen- or thirty-days' notice, but with Exchequer payments at
a standstill, there was no way the goldsmith-bankers could satisfy all or even
most of their depositors. Many sued their bankers in an attempt to get their
money back.[52]

Among the goldsmith-bankers, only the account books of Edward Backwell survive and it is not possible to construct a realistic picture of the
banker's depositors from Backwell's books alone.[53] However, one of the

provisions of the settlement reached in 1677 was that the bankers could assign a portion of their interest payments directly to their creditors (who were mostly former depositors). The banker would be relieved of his financial obligation and creditors would get their money directly from the Exchequer. Such assignments were recorded in a series of volumes called the Bankers' Assignments.[54] These records provide information on the depositors of all of the goldsmith-bankers. They name the assignor (the goldsmith-banker), the assignee (and sometimes their location and occupation), the amount of the original debt, and the date of the assignment.

Using the Assignment Books, Roseveare (1962) examined the clientele of the biggest of the goldsmiths affected by the Stop, Sir Robert Viner. Analyzing the first six hundred of Viner's assignments, Roseveare concluded that

> the gentry and some peers account for rather more than half the sample, merchants and tradesmen for another third, but they leave room for a good percentage of widows and spinsters, together with handfuls of clergy, yeomen and mariners . . . the most significant element here is a solid, wealthy backbone drawn from what, for want of a better word, must be called "the gentry." (Roseveare 1962: 242)

Roseveare also noted that a considerable proportion of Viner's clients came from outside London and Middlesex county (about 31%). Creditors from the countryside were almost always gentry, while business creditors were mostly from London, and included many members of liveried companies.[55] A total of 76 (12.7%) of Viner's clientele were women, mostly widows. Forty-five (or 7.5%) were peers, knights, or baronets and they tended to have larger claims. Almost a third were either merchants or tradesmen, but Viner's clientele were most commonly from the gentry: being referred to in the records as either "Esq." or "Gent."[56]

Viner was the biggest Crown creditor and one should not assume that Roseveare's results apply to the other creditors. If we examine all of the assignments, and not just those of Sir Robert Viner, it appears that each banker worked independently. Out of a total of 1,613 assignments recorded in the first six volumes of the Assignment Books,[57] only five were from one direct Crown creditor to another (from Viner to Backwell and Snell, from Welstead to Turnor, and twice from Whitehall to Backwell). The financial interconnections among the bankers are undoubtedly underestimated by the assignment books because we know from Edward Backwell's account books that most of the other important goldsmith-bankers had a direct financial connection with Backwell.[58]

The distribution of assignments across the goldsmiths is presented in table 3.3. As the table indicates, Sir Robert Viner made the most assignments, followed by Gilbert Whitehall and John Portman. Only one of the assignors, Sir John Shaw, was not a goldsmith-banker, and he made only one

TABLE 3.3
Number of Goldsmiths' Assignments, 1677–1683

Name	Frequency	Percent
Edward Backwell	111	6.9
John Lindsey	156	9.7
John Portman	229	14.2
Thomas Rowe	17	1.1
Robert Ryves	7	0.4
Sir John Shaw	1	0.1
George Snell	39	2.4
Jeremiah Snow	10	0.6
Bernard Turnor	2	0.1
Sir Robert Viner	628	38.9
Robert Welsted	21	1.3
Gilbert Whitehall	392	24.3
Total	1,613	100.0

Source: PRO E/406/27–32.

assignment. The correlation coefficient between the total debt owed each banker (as set forth in table 3.2) and the number of assignments was equal to 0.86, so it seems that assignments were used by the goldsmith-bankers to satisfy their obligations to their creditors.

The records note the size of the original debt owed by the assignor to his assignee. The average debt owed by a goldsmith-banker to an assignee was about £475 (the median was £264), and debts ranged from £36 to £12,942 (the standard deviation was roughly £764). The total amount assigned by the bankers was significant: £767,128 out of the £1,265,779 owed by the Crown to these twelve individuals. In other words, between 1677 and 1683 these bankers assigned about 60% of the interest owed them by the Crown to their own creditors. An analysis of the assignees' characteristics ought to give a fairly accurate picture of the bankers' depositors as a whole.

As noted above, the Assignment Books recorded the names of the assignees and frequently information about where they lived and their occupation. Table 3.4 presents some of the characteristics of these assignees.[59]

Panel I of the table shows that the bankers' assignees were mostly men, although the proportion of women (14.6%) was not insignificant. Similar to Roseveare's findings, the majority of women assignees were widows. According to panel III, most of the assignees (about 70%) came from the London region, either from London itself or Middlesex county. As well, panel II shows that about 25% of the assignees were from the gentry class (i.e., were entitled to use the title "Esquire") or higher. The proportion of peers and baronets was only 3.2%, suggesting that the aristocracy were not significant as indirect public creditors.

TABLE 3.4

Sex, Social Rank, Location, Occupation, and Average Debts of
Bankers' Assignees, 1677–1683

I. Sex of Assignee	Frequency	Percent	Average Debt
Male	1,324	82.1	£493
Female	236	14.6	£294
Widow	173	10.7	£304
Spinster	42	2.6	£272
Other women	21	1.3	£258
Other	53	3.3	£852
Total	1,613	100.0	£475.6

II. Social Rank	Frequency	Percent	Average Debt
Esquire	257	15.9	£691
Knight	62	3.8	£709
Baronet	43	2.7	£973
Peer	8	0.5	£1,424
Lady/Dame	21	1.3	£383
Other Ranks	1,222	75.8	£396
Total	1,613	100.0	£475.6

III. Location	Frequency	Percent	Average Debt
London/Westminster	883	54.7	£457
Middlesex	258	16.0	£456
Other Locations	408	25.3	£524
Unknown	64	4.0	£505
Total	1,613	100.0	£475.6

IV. Occupation	Frequency	Percent	Average Debt
Merchant	174	10.8	£666
Lawyer/Judge	97	6.0	£462
Alderman/MP	29	1.8	£947
Guildmember	319	19.8	£400
Goldsmith	22	1.4	£1,461
Grocer	35	2.2	£477
Merchant-Taylor	28	1.7	£318
Church	15	0.9	£469
Other Occupations	92	5.7	£205
Unknown	887	55.0	£480
Total	1,613	100.0	£475.6

Source: PRO E/406/27–32.

It was possible to learn the occupations of a subset of assignees.[60] The occupation of most assignees (887) is unknown, but of the remaining 726 in panel IV of table 3.4, almost a quarter were merchants, and about half were guild members (the most common guilds were the drapers, goldsmiths, grocers, haberdashers, merchant-taylors, and vintners). A small number of assignees, twenty-nine, were either aldermen or members of parliament. The overlap between active politicians and depositors appears to have been rather small, suggesting that depositors had little political power.

The wealth of the assignees is roughly indicated by the size of the debts the goldsmith-bankers owed to them. In table 3.4, we can also see some of the differences in the amounts owed to different groups of assignees. The average debt for men is much higher than that for women. Furthermore, there is a remarkable coincidence between debts and social rank. As we go up the social scale in panel II, from "Other" to "Esquire" and then on to "Peer," the average debt increases monotonically. There are fewer measurable social gradations among the women, but even there the Dames and Ladies have a higher average than women as a whole. Among the different occupations, it is striking how much larger the debts are for the merchants than for other groups. Merchants were important numerically but this importance increases if we also consider the larger debts due to them. The biggest debts of all were owed to other goldsmiths (who were not necessarily goldsmith-bankers). Although infrequent, assignments to other goldsmiths were large, implying that the financial interconnections among goldsmiths were more substantial than it may appear.

Overall, the evidence from the bankers' assignments suggests that those indirectly lending to the Crown were mostly from the London region. Despite the efforts of Crown officers like Sir George Downing to circumvent the bankers and borrow directly from the public, goldsmith-bankers were intermediaries, funneling money from an investing public to the Crown. Prominent within this investing public were the guild members and especially the merchants of London. These two groups were willing and able to invest substantial sums in a relatively new form of property: an interest-bearing account with a goldsmith-banker. They were unwilling, however, to loan directly to the Crown. Although in the aggregate the great bulk of the wealth of England was in the hands of the landed classes, little landed wealth was invested in this kind of financial asset. The Stop evidently justified their caution.

In the Parliamentary sessions that followed the Stop, Charles pointedly asked for additional money to repay his suspended debts.[61] Few in the Commons, however, were eager to help the goldsmith-bankers or give Charles more money beyond what had already been advanced for the war.[62] Parliamentary inaction reflected the unpopularity of goldsmith-bankers and the

political weakness of bankers' creditors. The one-year suspension was extended, first to May 1673 and then to January 1674. Charles tried to assist
the bankers by slowing down the legal suits that their depositors filed against
them.[63] More significantly, he arranged in 1674 to pay £140,000 in interest
on the debt to his creditors. Pending exact calculation of who was owed how
much, this sum was to be paid annually to the King's creditors. Finally, on
30 April 1677 letters patent were issued that set aside revenues from the
hereditary excise to pay 6% interest on the debt owed to the goldsmith-
bankers. Charles's decision was supported by his Lord Treasurer, Danby,
who happened to be a personal friend of Sir Robert Viner, one of the bankers
affected by the Stop.[64] The terms of the letters patent allowed the goldsmith-
bankers to assign some portion of their total interest payment directly to
their creditors.

The Stop demonstrated the weakness of English government finances.
When revenues failed to match expenditures, borrowing was necessary.
Lacking any machinery for long-term borrowing, indeed, lacking any clear
distinction between short-term and long-term debt, accumulating deficits
soon overwhelmed the public financial system. The documentary trail left by
the Stop also reveals something about the social structure of public credit.
The deposits of numerous creditors were channeled through a small number
of goldsmith-bankers and into public coffers. Banker's assignees were mostly
from the London region, but a significant proportion lived in the country.
Almost 40% of the assignees with the title of "esq." were from outside the
London/Middlesex County area, which bolsters Roseveare's claim that the
country gentry were important as depositors.

Apart from Viner's personal connection with Danby, there appears to
have been no strong relationship between the goldsmith-bankers or their
depositors, and the political factions at Court or in Parliament. There was no
political party or organization to protect the interests of the bankers and
their assignees, however much they suffered financially.[65] Charles pleaded
the cause of the victims of the Stop, but Parliament would not listen. Even
when the victims pleaded their own cause, there was little sympathy.

The financial sector, such as it was, lacked political clout. Those with a
financial interest in Crown debts couldn't effectively pressure Parliament to
repay them. In this respect, the Stop seems to bear out the arguments of
North and Weingast (1989), Levi (1988), and Root (1994) that representative
institutions can reduce the likelihood that sovereigns default on their debts.
Parliament did not represent the bankers and so did little to protect their
interests. Charles could default without fear of retribution from the Commons. Yet there was more than just indifference in Parliament to the plight
of the bankers. Some members of Parliament were actively hostile because
they recognized that the bankers provided one more way for the king to

reduce his dependency on Parliament.[66] If Charles could raise money by borrowing rather than taxing, he could undercut Parliament's control over government purse strings. A financial sector that loaned Charles the money he needed was a threat to parliamentary power. This animosity between financiers and Parliament continued for many decades, and formed the core of conflict between the landed and monied interests.

The Stop was a financial low point. Finances improved later in Charles II's reign, in part due to changes in how public revenues were collected. By 1684, all three of the major revenues had been taken out of farm and were collected directly (the customs tax in 1671, the excise tax in 1683, and the hearth tax in 1684). This meant more centralized control over revenues, greater administrative efficiency, and higher net revenues.[67] Customs farming was abandoned largely because the Bucknall syndicate was rejected at the last moment, and no replacement could be found. But in the cases of the excise and hearth taxes, the switch was more deliberate. After considerable experience with farming it was clear that direct collection could bring in higher net revenues. Finances also improved in the early 1680s because Charles undertook no more expensive wars and because foreign trade flourished. Increased trade meant higher customs revenues, and a peaceful foreign policy meant low expenses.

PUBLIC REVENUES AFTER THE GLORIOUS REVOLUTION

More developments in public finance occurred after the Glorious Revolution, and were associated with the constitutional changes that shifted power from the Crown to Parliament. Not only did Parliament's role in public finance expand but additionally, both the system of borrowing and public revenues changed. Improvements in revenues allowed for increased borrowing, and together they underwrote higher expenditures and a successful war effort.

A succession of Commissions of Public Accounts embodied Parliament's increased role in public finance. The first was set up after the Revolution in 1691 and consisted of members of the House of Commons charged with the task of examining the public accounts and reporting back to the Commons. Parliament was dissatisfied with official accounts of government spending, and sought to conduct its own detailed examination.[68] The Commission became a platform for the opposition to launch attacks on ministry policy, but it also educated members of Parliament about the financial workings of government.[69] Parliament also exerted more control by earmarking funds for particular uses. Rather than granting a sum of money to be used at the Crown's discretion, supply measures included clauses appropriating the monies to specific purposes. Money from Parliament came with strings attached that linked revenues to expenditures and thus constrained what the Crown could do with it.

After the Revolution, William abolished the much-hated Hearth Tax in a vain attempt to speed parliamentary deliberations on the financial settlement. This left only the Customs and Excise taxes as the main sources of public revenue. Starting in 1693, a new Land Tax supplemented the other two and made a crucial contribution to revenues. In most years between 1693 and 1713, it generated more money than any other single revenue source. Granted on an annual basis, land and assessed taxes poured an average of over £1.8 million per year into the exchequer. During the Nine Years' War, the Land Tax contributed 42% of total revenues while during the War of the Spanish Succession, the proportion declined slightly to 37%.[70] This tax was a successful fiscal instrument because the rates were set by Parliament and therefore with the consent of the political nation. Furthermore, tax assessment and collection was the duty of commissioners who were appointed by local elites.[71] There was no central government apparatus controlling the Land Tax, and its administration was undertaken with the cooperation of the gentry. This helped to make the tax more politically acceptable.[72] Not surprisingly, underassessment was a problem, but even so it raised large sums on a regular basis.

The Excise Tax expanded, both in the number of items taxed and the number of excise personnel. Collection of this tax always posed formidable administrative problems because taxpayers generally regarded it as intrusive and illegitimate.[73] Furthermore, complex duties on a wide variety of commodities had to be applied on a nationwide scale. Solving these problems required manpower, and the number of full-time excise employees increased from 1,211 in 1690 to 2,778 in 1716.[74] Consequently, excise and associated revenues went from an annual average of £0.5 million in the mid-1670s to £1.8 million in the mid-1700s.

Customs revenues expanded at a comparable rate, going from an annual average of £0.5 million in the mid-1670s to £1.3 million in the 1710s.[75] The number of customs officials also increased, although not as much as the excise (between 1690 and 1716 the number of customs employees grew by 33%). Growth in foreign trade accounted for most of the increase in revenues. London gradually supplanted Amsterdam as the central entrepôt for international commerce, and even though trade declined in wartime, the total value of English imports rose from £3.3 million in 1697, at the end of the Nine Years' War, to £5.8 million at the end of the War of the Spanish Succession in 1713.[76]

Taken together, improvements in the old revenues combined with the addition of a new land tax to produce higher public revenues. Pushed by wartime necessity, the government became much better at extracting large sums of money. Tax receipts roughly tripled from the mid-1670s to the mid-

1700s, but their impressive growth was still not enough to match the expansion of public expenditures. Patrick O'Brien has estimated that of the extra revenue raised to finance the War of the Spanish Succession, tax receipts accounted for only 26%.[77] The rest had to come from borrowing.

BORROWING AFTER THE GLORIOUS REVOLUTION

Constrained by inflexible revenue systems, early modern states like seventeenth-century England were better at spending money than raising it. Even when taxes could generate adequate sums, short-term borrowing was still necessary to fund spending until the new monies came in. But short-term borrowing could only solve the problem of revenues and expenses that were not in sync. If taxes were chronically deficient, short-term loans would simply accumulate and overwhelm the system, and it became necessary to borrow on a long-term basis. Of course, if the situation became completely unmanageable, sovereigns sometimes just stopped payment on their loans, as Charles II did in 1672.

Before the early modern era, the sources of funds that the English Crown could borrow were limited. Fourteenth-century kings like Edward III borrowed from Italian bankers,[78] while during the sixteenth century Henry VIII had to look to Antwerp for loans.[79] In the early seventeenth century, there were still only a few domestic sources, including the City of London, tax farmers, goldsmith-bankers, and large organizations like the East India Company and Merchant Adventurers. The sums borrowed were rarely substantial, at least by late seventeenth-century standards. Improvements in the system of public borrowing were important in explaining the growing financial strength of the English state, and the changes were dramatic enough to be called a "Financial Revolution."[80] England was able to borrow more money from more sources at lower rates of interest. The borrowing was mostly from domestic sources, and there was little reliance on money raised abroad.[81]

Thanks to the development of trade and commerce, there was in England a growing pool of available capital. Statutory measures like the Navigation Acts gave a great impetus to English shipping, while the Staple Act completed a framework requiring English colonies to purchase all their European goods in England.[82] Trade with southern Europe, the Levant, the Americas, and India grew rapidly, expanding the commercial and mercantile sector of the English economy.[83] It was here that the government could look for potential creditors. Getting them voluntarily to loan their money was, of course, another matter.

Figure 3.1 illustrates the fiscal effects of war.[84] Military expenses accounted for much of public spending between 1692 and 1730 and so the graph shows two lines moving in parallel, with peaks reached during the

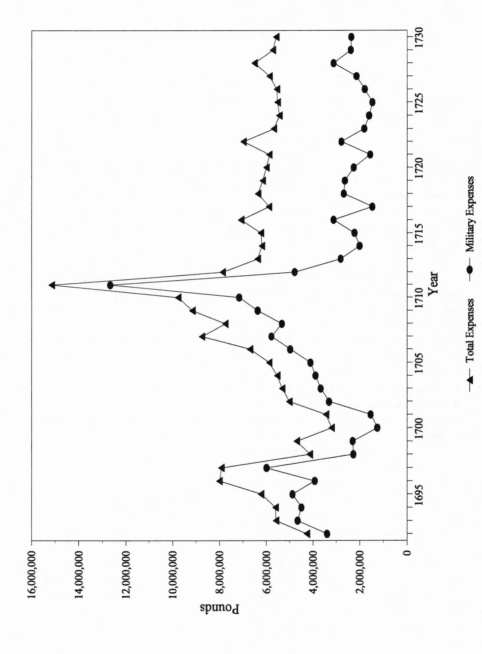

Fig. 3.1. Total and Military Expenses, 1692–1730.

heights of the two wars. Figure 3.2 compares total income with total expenditures over the same period. The national "budget" was at its worst, and the deficit largest, in 1697 and 1711, during the Nine Years' War and War of the Spanish Succession, respectively.

At the start of the 1690s, war-inflated expenses rapidly outstripped revenues, and England had to borrow extensively. The only facilities available were the traditional ones for short-term borrowing.[85] Tallies, Navy Bills, and Ordnance Bills were issued to creditors in anticipation of annual tax revenues. When the money came in, creditors would cash their promissory notes and be repaid their principal and any accrued interest. Revenues failed to keep pace with expenses, short-term debts piled up, and financial markets were soon clogged with heavily discounted bills. Taxes were simply not producing adequate revenue. By 1693, short-term debts had climbed to almost £6 million and were threatening to overwhelm the government's credit system.[86] Short-term credit was expensive and repayment hard to defer, and so financially the government was hard pressed.

England did not invent long-term public borrowing. The sale of life-annuities, for example, was a well-known technique originally developed for towns.[87] Lenders would pay a sum to a town government in exchange for future interest payments that would continue for the duration of the lender's lifetime. What England did was to import and adapt financial techniques developed elsewhere, particularly by the Dutch. In fact, these innovations for the English were known as "Dutch finance," and it was no coincidence that William brought with him the wisdom of his Dutch financial advisors.[88] For some time, English writers and commentators had noted the public financial system of the United Provinces, and suggested that it offered valuable lessons for England.[89]

In 1693, Parliament moved in the direction of long-term borrowing when it set aside additional excise duties for ninety-nine years to encourage individuals to loan £1 million to the government in the form of a Tontine (4 William & Mary, c.3).[90] Long-term borrowing had several distinctive features: subscribers to the loan would be paid interest annually but would not receive back their principal; interest payments would extend for a long period of time but at a lower rate than for a comparable short-term loan; the loan was *funded* in the sense that Parliament set aside specific revenues to meet the loan payments; and the loan was guaranteed by Parliament. Parliamentary guarantees distinguished these loans from earlier Crown debts in that the debt obliged the nation, not just the monarch. Such features were new to English public finance but familiar to the Dutch. The adequacy of future taxes was an important part of the success of long-term borrowing, for revenues had to be able to cover interest payments.[91] In 1713, for example, about 45% of total expenditures were going to debt payments, which under-

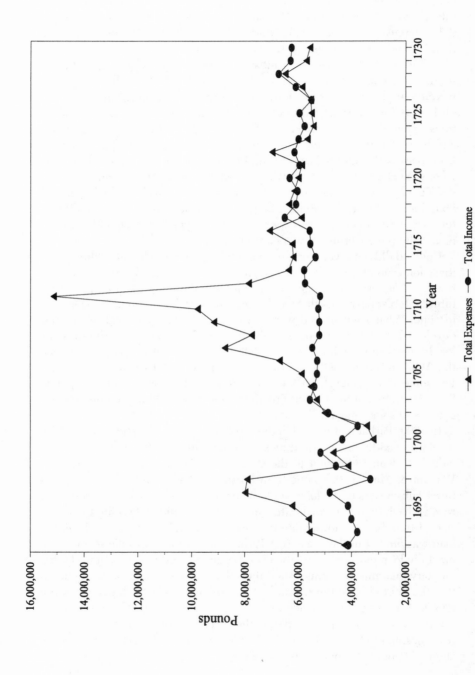

● Fig. 3.2. Total Income and Expenses, 1692–1730.

scores not only how much debt the British government had accrued, but how necessary higher taxes were to service that debt.

The Tontine was unfamiliar to English investors, who subscribed only £108,100, far short of the desired £1 million. This colossal failure ensured that there would be no more Tontines for another seventy years. But the act also provided for life annuities, an alternative devised just in case such a shortfall occurred. Paying 14% interest, the life annuities proved to be very popular, and in the end the full amount was subscribed.[92] This loan marked the establishment of the permanent national debt. Sales of annuities continued for many years and were an important source of funds.[93] A total of £891,900 was raised in 1693 and 1694 to make up for the Tontine. The government borrowed another £300,000 in 1694 through the sale of annuities on one, two, or three lives, and then raised an additional £669,604 by allowing annuity holders to convert life annuities into ninety-six-year terminable annuities. During Anne's reign, the state borrowed a total of £10,403,738 through the sale of various types of annuities.

By the early eighteenth century, annuities were a highly developed financial instrument.[94] They involved the exchange of a sum of capital, paid from creditor to debtor, for a future income stream from debtor back to creditor, but there were many different forms. One important feature concerned the duration of the income stream. An annuity for a life meant that interest would be paid by the debtor so long as the person nominated by the purchaser of the annuity continued to live (the nominee need not have been the purchaser). An annuity for two lives meant interest payments continued so long as either of two persons nominated by the purchaser were still living. Annuities could also be for years, guaranteeing interest payments for a fixed number of years, or they could be in perpetuity. Interest rates were another important feature. Debtors obviously preferred lower rates but if they were set too low it was hard to sell the annuities. Redeemability was another significant attribute because it gave the debtor the option of paying back the principal and thus terminating interest payments at any time. With redeemable annuities, the debtor could take advantage of a drop in market interest rates by paying off the annuities issued at the older higher rate and issuing new ones at the lower prevailing rate, in effect refinancing the debt. Irredeemable debt locked in the interest rate for the entire term of the loan.

In general, annuities stayed in the hands of those who purchased them (or their heirs). Unlike a company share or other financial instrument, it was difficult to transfer these assets to a third party. This was particularly true of annuities for lives, where the value of the annuity (how long payments could be expected to continue) depended on the life-expectancy of persons whose health might be hard for a potential buyer to ascertain.[95] More important, the actual procedure for transferring title to annuity payments, which involved registration with the Exchequer, was exceedingly cumbersome and mistake-prone. As Dickson described it: "... transfers of annuities resembled in length and complexity a conveyance of land" (Dickson 1967: 459). Annuities were attractive in many respects but their illiquidity was a problem. Having loaned capital to the government, purchasers of annuities had difficulty getting their money back. Third-party sales might have solved the problem but practical difficulties made such transfers inconvenient and problematic.

The government exploited the public's interest in gambling when it borrowed using lottery loans.[96] Lottery tickets were sold in small denominations (£10 or £100), and then winning tickets were drawn. Prize payments stretched out over a period of years, and every ticket typically paid something.[97] The Million Lottery of 1694, for example, entitled every ticket holder to £1 per annum for the next sixteen years. If the ticket was a winner, then the annual sum increased to £10, and up to the grand prize of £1,000.[98] The Million Lottery successfully raised £1 million for the government but the Malt Lottery Loan of 1697 failed, and lotteries were not tried again until 1710. Four more lotteries were used to raise an additional £7.1 million in 1711 and 1712.[99] Lotteries were an expensive way for the government to borrow, and their heavy use in 1711 and 1712 was a sign of financial desperation. The Million Lottery loan, for example, cost the government over £2,375,000 in payouts between 1695 and 1711.[100] Like annuities, lottery tickets were illiquid in that it was hard for ticket holders to transfer them to other persons.

Government annuities and lotteries raised money directly from the general public and so fulfilled the change Sir George Downing tried to institute in the 1660s. Through the end of the War of the Spanish Succession, the government borrowed a total of £12,140,030 through annuities, and another £11,500,000 through lottery loans.[101] But the government also continued its traditional practice of borrowing from organizations and so raised money from the major joint-stock companies. In the same period, a total of £16,754,167 was procured from companies, more than from any other source. Joint-stock companies enjoyed special privileges and monopoly powers granted by the state, and in exchange for these they customarily made a financial contribution.[102] What distinguished this period from earlier ones was the sheer volume of borrowing from companies, and the fact that company shares could be easily traded on the London stock market. In contrast with annuities and lottery loans, and unlike shares in earlier times, by the late seventeenth century company equity was easily transferrable to third parties. Through joint-stock companies, public finance became linked to private finance and to the London stock market.

The importance of the Bank of England went far beyond the £1.2 million it loaned to the government at the Bank's establishment in 1694 (5 & 6

William & Mary, c.20). Not only did the government get a substantial permanent loan but it acquired an institution providing many useful financial services. For example, the Bank made numerous short-term loans to the government and assisted with England's remittance problems.[103] The Bank was the brainchild of a Scottish entrepreneur, William Paterson.[104] The support of the Huguenot financier Michael Godfrey, with his connections in the capital market to other investors, was crucial to the success of Paterson's proposal, as was the support of the Whig Chancellor of the Exchequer, Charles Montagu.[105] The government's troubled financial position motivated Montagu's interest in the project. Investors subscribed to the initial £1.2 million issue of Bank stock. The Bank in turn loaned this sum to the government at 8% interest, and certain customs and excise revenues were earmarked by Parliament to fund the interest payments. Investors got Bank stock and dividends, the government got a loan and an institution that helped manage short-term finances, and the Bank got 8% interest, plus an annual £4,000 management fee, plus a corporate charter giving it the right to issue paper money and to take deposits. The term of the Bank's life was until 1705. Thereafter, upon one year's notice and repayment of the loan, the Bank could be dissolved. The entire subscription of stock sold out in twelve days.

War continued after 1694, England's financial situation deteriorated further, and short-term debts again piled up. In 1697 the Bank provided additional help by enlarging its capital (8 & 9, William III, c.20). Those holding short-term government promissory notes (tallies or orders) were allowed to exchange them for Bank stock. Over £1 million was subscribed and "engrafted" onto the original capital stock.[106] The engraftment was partly a response to Tory efforts to establish a Land Bank that would rival the Bank of England.[107] For its part, the Bank was granted an extension of its charter (until 1711) and a statutory monopoly on banking, and was allowed to issue additional Bank notes up to the total of the newly subscribed stock. In effect, the operation converted short-term debt into long-term debt.

The Bank continued to provide important services to the government during the War of the Spanish Succession. It helped manage the short-term debt, and in 1709 added to its long-term loan to the government by extending another £400,000 at no interest and incorporating into its capital an additional subscription of £2,531,347. This enlarged capital was used to fund £2.5 million worth of newly circulating Exchequer Bills. The Bank's charter was extended to 1732, and its monopoly on banking services strengthened.[108]

Other joint-stock companies besides the Bank of England played a role in public finance. The East India Company was originally chartered in 1600 and given a monopoly on trade with the East Indies. The Company routinely made cash gifts and short-term loans to the government during

Charles II's reign.[109] This practice continued under James II, and reached such proportions that the Company became publicly aligned with the regime and with the Tory party. Initially an advantage, this connection became a severe liability after 1688. The association with James made the Company politically vulnerable, and the Company's opponents within the mercantile community exploited the situation.

The monopoly privileges and high profits of the East India Company fostered opposition at the end of the 1670s, partly because the Company stock was limited and ownership was restricted.[110] Outsiders wanting to invest and join in the profits had little opportunity to do so.[111] A small group of individuals owned a disproportionate amount of the shares and exerted almost total control over the company.[112] Those excluded from the lucrative trade were further angered by the Company's decision to allow foreign merchants to trade with the East Indies on their own account, upon payment of a commission to the Company.[113] Foreigners were allowed to circumvent the company's monopoly even though fellow Englishmen were not. The Company opposition allied itself with the Whig party, and included several prominent Whig merchants (e.g., Michael Godfrey and Gilbert Heathcote).[114]

The East India Company and its opponents fought in the House of Commons during the 1690s, and their conflict ended with victory for the Company opposition. With the encouragement of the government (always eager for more money), a bidding war broke out between the two sides for the privilege of trading with the East Indies. The Company opposition outbid the Company and with the political support of Whig ministers (including the Treasury Lord Charles Montagu), an act passed in 1698 approving the formation of a new company to trade with the East Indies (9 & 10 William III, c.44). For this, the subscribers to the new company loaned £2 million to the government at 8%, and so in September 1698 the English Company trading to the East Indies was officially incorporated.[115] The New East India Company did not supplant the old, for both carried on a trade with the East Indies simultaneously. The political support that both companies enjoyed made it unlikely that either could be completely dissolved, and so some kind of merger became the only realistic option. The process of amalgamation was slow and long. The two sides negotiated a deal in 1701, but complete unification wasn't realized until 1709.[116] Thereafter, there was only one East India Company. An additional £1.2 million loan secured government support for the merger.

The third joint-stock company involved in public finance was the South Sea Company. Established in 1711, this company modified the Bank and New East India Company pattern, in which a company was incorporated out of a fresh loan to the government. The South Sea Company was a joint-stock incorporated out of old loans to the government. It was engineered by

Robert Harley, Queen Anne's Tory minister and a former supporter of the failed Land Bank.

During the War of the Spanish Succession, short-term debt piled up once more. Navy and Ordnance Bills, the short-term financial instruments used to pay military suppliers, were at a heavy discount in 1709 and 1710. Following the Tory electoral victory of 1710, a group of financiers approached Robert Harley with a proposal to solve the problem of the short-term debt. The details of the undertaking were fairly simple. At the time, there was over £9 million worth of short-term debt floating in the financial markets.[117] These instruments were selling at a heavy discount, reflecting rather pessimistic expectations about how soon and how completely they would be paid off. By the terms of the South Sea Act (9 Anne, c.21) they could be exchanged for stock in a newly incorporated South Sea Company. The Company was granted a monopoly on trade with the South Seas (a monopoly of dubious value, since there was little actual trade), and received 6% interest on the £9 million capital. Through this Company, Harley managed a refinancing operation that converted short-term unfunded public debt into long-term funded debt.

The three joint-stock companies were an important component of the long-term debt but they were only one component. Together with annuities and lottery loans, they helped to raise very large sums of money on a long-term basis. A related development was the emergence during the 1690s and 1700s of a system for short-term borrowing and a clearer distinction between short- and long-term borrowing.

Traditionally, government creditors were paid in tallies, which would be redeemable later at the Exchequer.[118] Tallies were used to anticipate annual tax revenues, and were employed by the Army, Navy, and Ordnance departments to provide themselves with the equivalent of working cash. The venerable tally was gradually replaced by the Exchequer Bill. Exchequer bills were short-term, interest-bearing bills that were first issued in the wake of the failed Land Bank scheme in 1696, and they circulated much like modern bank notes.[119] Like the tally, the bill was mostly used to satisfy the short-term requirements of the military. The Bank of England agreed to assist in their circulation, and so eventually assumed responsibility for much of the government's short-term borrowing needs.

Long-term debt differed from short-term debt in a number of ways. Most important, long-term debt was easier to manage and so Treasurers preferred it to short-term borrowing. During the 1690s a high proportion of total borrowing was on a short-term basis, which worsened the financial problems of the government. During his tenure as Lord Treasurer in the 1700s, Godolphin improved the situation by putting more emphasis on long-term borrowing. When an accumulation of short-term debts threatened Harley's ministry, his solution was to convert them into long-term debt (hence, the South Sea Company).

Parliament funded long-term debt by setting aside specific revenues to cover the interest payments but short-term debt was not funded. In addition, much of the long-term debt was in effect perpetual debt. The principal of the loan from the Bank of England, for example, was never repaid. Debts which do not have to be amortized, when only the interest but not the principal is repaid to the creditor, are cheaper to service.[120] Much of the debt was also redeemable, which meant that the government could refinance its loans to take advantage of subsequent declines in market interest rates.

Figure 3.3 shows how quickly public borrowing shifted from unfunded to funded debt.[121] The proportion of unfunded debt fell steadily during this period. In 1692, total debt stood at roughly £3.3 million, all of which was unfunded, short-term debt. In 1700 the total debt had risen to £14.2 million, of which £4.7 million, or 33%, was funded. By 1712, the debt was up to £34.9 million with £25.6 million or 73.4% of the total funded. As the overall debt increased, so did the proportion that was funded. Funded debt was not only more manageable, it was cheaper. Annual debt charges, as a percent of total debt, went from 6.0% in 1692 up to 8.8% in 1700, then to 6.8% in 1712, and down to 5.1% by 1720.[122] More money was being borrowed at cheaper rates.

The extent of Britain's financial accomplishment is most obvious when compared to the Stop of the Exchequer. Instead of being financially overwhelmed by a small war with the Dutch, Britain mustered its resources and successfully checked France, a country with a much larger economy and population. Financially, Britain made great strides at the end of the seventeenth century. The importance of long-term borrowing was clear, for taxes could never rise fast enough or high enough to fund a war, and short-term borrowing was simply inadequate. The elements of successful long-term borrowing from both individuals and joint-stock companies included earmarking adequate revenues, the efficient collection and administration of funds, and the creation of a perpetual debt that obligated Parliament, not just the monarch. Such measures assured public creditors that the government would live up to its obligations.[123]

The London stock market played a major role in the development of public finance. The same institutions that contributed so much to the long-term debt were also the most important companies in the stock market. The Bank of England, the East India Company, and the South Sea Company spanned private and public capital markets. Their corporate capital constituted a sizable proportion of the national debt, and their shares dominated trading activity in the London stock exchange.[124] Indeed, the success with which the government borrowed long term depended upon the liquidity that only an active stock market could offer.

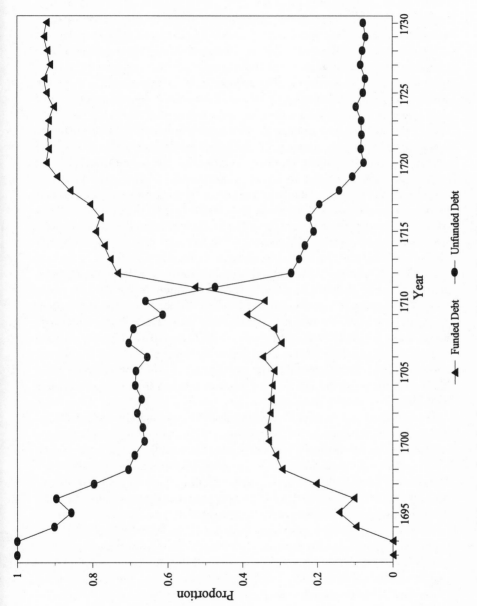

Fig. 3.3. Funded and Unfunded Debt as a Proportion of Total Debt, 1692–1730.

Funded Debt ▲   Unfunded Debt ●

Perhaps the biggest disadvantage facing long-term lenders is that their capital is tied up for a long time. Their debtor-creditor relationships are durable and so it is some time before they can recover their money. Ownership of Bank of England shares was indirectly a long-term loan, for the capital of the Bank had simply been passed on to the government in exchange for interest payments. However, the fact that company shares could be sold easily on the stock market meant that what was for the government a long-term loan could be for the creditor as long or short term a loan as he or she wished. A creditor's capital could be recovered simply by selling shares to a third party, with no need for the government to repay the loan. Liquidity, that is, the ease with which a claim on the government could be transferred to another party, removed what was from the creditor's perspective the chief disadvantage of long-term lending.[125] The government could borrow long term at the same time that its creditors were lending short term. Liquidity was one of the great advantages of lending to the government through company stock rather than through annuities and lottery loans, for the latter were hard to transfer and hence illiquid by comparison. The existence of a secondary capital market for company shares improved the government's position as a debtor in the primary capital market.

In 1672, investors also preferred liquidity and so put their money with goldsmith-bankers rather than into the Exchequer. Although they were more liquid than Treasury Orders, Bankers' deposits (and running cash notes) did not have the liquidity of company shares. Partly this was because in 1672 Exchange Alley was still just an alley, and not yet an active capital market. It was also because bankers' deposits represented claims on individuals, whereas shares were claims on organizations, which were much more likely to remain solvent. Possessing a more certain value, company shares could be more easily sold to third parties.

The Dutch Republic served as an example for how such financial machinery could work and what it could accomplish. The annuities of the province of Holland paid 8.3% in the 1590s, 4% by the middle of the seventeenth century, and between 2.5 and 3% for most of the eighteenth century.[126] Thanks to its highly liquid capital markets and developed financial institutions, the Dutch government could borrow at extraordinarily cheap rates, as English observers jealously noted.[127] The value of liquidity was recognized in a well-known tract on Dutch markets which explained why Dutch East India Company shares sold for more in Amsterdam than elsewhere: "The possibility of quick sales increases the value of the stocks in such a manner that the shares of the Amsterdam chamber command a higher price than those of all other chambers" (De La Vega 1957 [1688]: 13).[128]

By Anne's reign, the Lord Treasurer was the most important political minister. This office was more powerful than any other and gave the Lord

Treasurer the ability to monitor and control government finances. Both Godolphin and Harley worked hard to protect the Treasury from the worst ravages of party conflict. Shifts in party strength and changes of government did not lead to purges of the Treasury, which was an important first step toward the development of an apolitical civil service.[129] Financial expertise accumulated in the Treasury, and this centralized expertise, embodied in expanded Excise and Customs bureaucracies, exerted control over most aspects of public finance.[130]

The financial system that developed in Britain at the end of the seventeenth century proved very effective. As figure 3.4 shows, the total public debt and the funded debt soared between 1692 and 1720.[131] With its new system of borrowing, the public financial machinery creaked but did not break. Through two long wars, Britain was able to fund and deploy unprecedented military forces, and on a per capita basis its efforts outstripped those of the other major combatants.[132] All of Europe was impressed when the additional subscription of over £2 million worth of Bank of England stock sold out in only four hours in 1709.[133] In the 1700s, Britain flexed both its military and financial muscles.

DOMESTIC POLITICS AND THE FISCAL MILITARY STATE

The Financial Revolution, as Dickson termed it, laid the foundation for Britain's "fiscal-military" state: a state capable of fighting large wars and raising the resources necessary to pay for them. The public fisc was the basis for state expansion and empire building. Yet these changes had two faces, an outward one and an inward one. Outwardly, the Financial Revolution gave Great Britain the means to become a great power. Inwardly, however, the domestic consequences were less straightforward as this new financial machinery was drawn into the conflict between Whig and Tory. Several features of public finance became politically salient: who loaned money to the government, what kind of relationship public creditors had to the government and how it affected the balance of power between Crown and Parliament, and the challenge to England's traditional landed ruling class.

Perceptions of who loaned money to the government may have been more consequential than the reality. In this case, however, the two were reasonably close. The number of public creditors increased steadily, although only rough approximations are available. Dickson estimates that the total number of owners of government and related stock started at about 5,000 in 1694, rose to 10,000 by 1709, increased further to about 40,000 in 1719, and reached 60,000 in 1752.[134] Consistent with this trend, the number of Bank shareholders increased from 1,272 for the initial subscription in 1694, to 1,903 in 1701, and then to 4,419 shareholders in 1712.[135] More and more

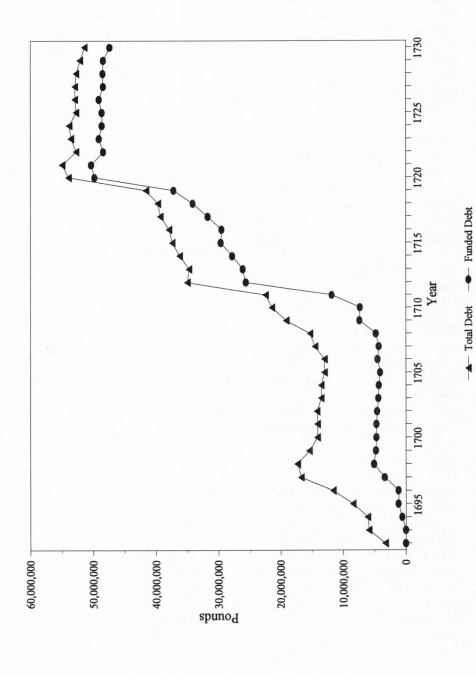

Fig. 3.4. Funded and Total Debt, 1692–1730.

Year

Pounds

▲ Total Debt   ● Funded Debt

60,000,000
50,000,000
40,000,000
30,000,000
20,000,000
10,000,000
0

1695   1700   1705   1710   1715   1720   1725   1730

people were becoming involved in public finance as creditors. However numerous, participants were not drawn uniformly from all walks of English life. Investors in company stocks and government debt were regionally concentrated, and in many respects followed the pattern of 1672. Most of them lived in London or the surrounding counties. Roughly 70% of the subscribers to the Tontine of 1693, for example, and 88% of the subscribers to the Bank of England in 1694 were from London or the home counties.[136] This regional concentration persisted, and so the bulk of Bank and East India Company shareholders in 1709 were from the London region, and this still was true at the time of the South Sea Bubble in 1720.[137]

Socially, investors were disproportionately drawn from the mercantile, financial, and commercial classes of London. Peter Earle found that members of the London middle class invested increasingly in government debt and joint-stock companies as the Financial Revolution unfolded.[138] Other wealthy segments of British society, such as the country gentry, members of Parliament, or the aristocracy, had only a small presence in the stock market. Those members of Parliament that did invest tended to be lawyers, merchants, or officeholders rather than landed gentry. Involvement in government debt was clearly a London mercantile phenomenon.[139]

Jews, Huguenots, and foreigners were especially conspicuous within the investing mercantile community. These groups were most evident among the really big investors and active traders. Huguenots, including many who fled France after the revocation of the Edict of Nantes in 1685, figured prominently among the shareholders and directors of the Bank of England.[140] A number of the biggest shareholders and traders in company stock were Jewish.[141] Both the Huguenots and the Jews involved in the market came from larger international mercantile communities that spanned many countries. Alongside them were a smattering of Dutch and Swiss investors.[142] In addition to the Jews and Huguenots, many of the other prominent government creditors were Dissenters or non–Church of England Protestants.

The relative novelty of financial wealth made investment a questionable and morally suspect activity. Financial assets lacked the tangible and familiar qualities of more traditional kinds of wealth, particularly land. The dubious nature of financial assets combined with the social marginality of those who invested in them to provoke a strong reaction from conservatives. Tories were deeply suspicious of a market filled with such persons. Not only were country gentlemen unaccustomed to such debt instruments but it was easy for them to believe that fortunes were being made at the expense of the government and, ultimately, the land taxpayer.[143] Numerous pamphlets railed against the evils of stockjobbing and financial speculation. For example, one pamphlet from 1711 declared that

the Pernicious Practice of Stock-Jobbing, and the Number of Stock-Jobbers and
pretended Brokers, grew so very Excessive in the beginning of King William's
Reign, that by their Confedracies, Combinations and other Ill Practices to Raise
or Fall Tallies, Parliamentary Funds, Stocks . . . did very often by their dexter-
ous Management Raise or Fall them Fifteen or Twenty per Cent. as it suited
their private Gain; By these Wicked and Dangerous Practices, the Publick
Credit was Exposed to Extream Hazard, and Trade not only weakened, but
great Numbers of Considerable Traders utterly Ruin'd and Undone. (*Reasons
for Passing the Bill,* . . . 1711)

Others blamed the stock market for the decline of civic-mindedness and the
spread of narrowly self-interested behavior. In a 1702 pamphlet, Charles
Davenant argued that "these gimcracks and new devices of funds, stocks,
exchequer bills, malt and lottery tickets, have turned the brains of a great
part of the city: there is not such a thing left as publick spirit, and in its
room we have set up knavery, extortion, and self-interest" (Davenant 1771,
vol. 4: 217).[144] The sheer novelty of the market made conservatives deeply
apprehensive.

The Tory reaction was also colored by the fact that social groups they
found especially distasteful were involved in public finance and the stock
market, particularly Jews, foreigners, dissenters, and Whigs. Whenever the
religion question arose, it called attention to the heavy concentration of nonconforming Protestants in the London mercantile community.[145] The presence of prominent wealthy foreigners further lowered the stock of the financial market in Tory eyes because of Tory xenophobia.[146]

Critics objected to long-term borrowing on other grounds as well. Such
borrowing ensured that the effects of the two wars would last for many years,
which was problematic for Tories eager to minimize the long-term financial
consequences.[147] Tories also opposed long-term borrowing because of its
perceived political ramifications. Some argued that the national debt was not
so much a financial as a political device intended to bind people to the new
regime of William III. The national debt was a means to create a group of
investors with a substantial vested interest in William's regime. The ever-
growing numbers of public creditors seemed a testament to the success of
this strategy. In *The Examiner* No. 14, Jonathan Swift argued that its main
purpose was to ". . . fasten wealthy People to the New Government" (Ellis
1985: 6).[148] In his 1711 pamphlet *The Conduct of the Allies*, Swift also
claimed that ". . . the true Reason for embracing this Expedient [long-term
public borrowing], was the Security of the new Prince, not firmly settled on
the Throne: People were tempted to lend, by great Premiums and large
Interest, and it concerned them nearly to preserve that Government, which
they trusted with their Money" (p. 10).[149]

Swift, Bolingbroke, and Davenant argued that the national debt was part of a strategy by William III's regime to cultivate political support by creating a constituency with a vested financial interest in the new regime. In effect, they accused the regime of emulating Eumenes of Cardia, the Greek general. Their argument assumed that a government deeply indebted to its creditors nevertheless gained a measure of influence over them, for their interests were joined to its survival. The national debt was being expanded as rapidly as possible, not because of financial necessity but in order to enlarge the number of supporters.[150] If money was actually needed to pay for war with France, so the Tory argument went, it was only because the Whigs prosecuted the war with excessive zeal.

Given the danger posed by Louis XIV and the possible return of James II (or his son James III), William's claim to the throne could not be taken for granted. The Jacobite threat was not an empty one, for in 1708, 1715, and 1745, Jacobite military forces landed in Scotland with the intent of restoring the Stuarts to the throne.[151] Furthermore, it was obvious that if James or his heirs were to recapture the throne, the public debts accrued under William, and later Anne, would be repudiated.[152] The expenses sustained in fighting Louis XIV (sponsor and protector of James II and James III) and in keeping William on the throne made such large-scale borrowing necessary. It is highly unlikely that James II or III would have repaid debts when the money was used to keep them off their own throne.[153] Were the Pretender ever to retake the Crown, the property rights of government creditors would certainly be endangered.[154] Later in the eighteenth century, David Hume observed that "the first visible eruption, or even immediate danger, of public disorders must alarm all the stockholders, whose property is the most precarious of any; and will make them fly to the support of government, whether menaced by Jacobitish violence or democratical frenzy" (Hume 1955: 95).

With the joint-stock companies acting as intermediaries, large numbers of shareholders became, in effect, public creditors. They subscribed to shares, and the companies loaned the money to the government. The companies received interest on their loans and paid this to shareholders in the form of dividends. A regime that might default on the loans, or abolish the companies, would threaten the interests of public creditors. The personal finances of shareholders, annuity holders, and lottery loan holders were therefore joined to those of the post-1688 regime and they acquired an interest in the stability of that regime. The state's financial system was more than just an extractive machine, an engine of state, because it also helped build up a political constituency in support of the post-1688 Protestant regime.

Whose interests were financially aligned with the regime's? This central question concerns which social groups invested in public financial assets. The people who invested, and who therefore were long-term state creditors, came from a narrow segment of English society. Mercantile, commercial, and financial elites, and members of the middle class from the London region were eager investors. Traditional landed elites were generally uninterested or unwilling to invest.

The strongest reaction against the new public financial system came from the threatened traditional elites of Britain. In a few short decades, a new and powerful interest group had arisen, the "monied interest." The traditional dependence of the government upon landed elites, the "landed interest," was usurped as the government came to rely increasingly on the financial support of a financial elite. This new interest was gaining in power and wealth at the expense of the old.[155] The stock market boomed even as landed estates were burdened by low rents, high interest rates, and heavy taxes.[156] In 1711, Tories secured passage of a property qualifications Act for members of Parliament in order to prevent monied men from getting into the House of Commons.[157] But given the exorbitant demands of twenty years of warfare between 1689 and 1713, the government could not help but turn to "monied men" for that which they were best qualified to supply, namely, money.

Britain's traditional landed elites continued to control institutions of local government and to dominate both Houses of Parliament.[158] It was not through a takeover of the House of Commons that the new monied interest was going to supplant Britain's traditional rulers but rather through the war-induced financial dependency of government. As creditors of a debtor government, the monied interest seemed to gain disproportionate and illicit power over public policy.[159] In this argument, the presumption was that debtors were generally under the control of creditors. As Broughton expressed it in his criticism of the Bank of England: "The Banks withholding their Money or Credit from the Government, is not the only Case wherein it may nearly affect us in our Constitution; for the Power of that Stock may be too easily employ'd another way, even to the Destruction of the Government" (Broughton 1705: 29–30). Since the monied interest generally sided with the Whig party, this financial power translated into pro-Whig interventions. However, Tory analyses of the national debt were inconsistent on the balance of power between public creditors and the debtor government. To argue that public debt was used by the new regime to "capture" and co-opt public creditors suggests that the debtor had the upper hand, but this went against the idea that debtors were beholden to creditors.

The monied interest gained political influence through its financial control over government but it also gained financially. As compared to other forms of investment such as land or mortgages, government debt was extremely profitable. The vast sums of money flowing into and out of the state were like a river of patronage to which the monied interest had privileged access. Government loans, fees, and contracts all bolstered the earnings of the monied interest. Through the land tax, the burden of all this spending was thought to fall disproportionately on the shoulders of the landed interest. The distributional consequences of government spending, taxing, and borrowing seemed consistently to favor one side over the other.

The final domestic political issue raised by the new financial system concerned the relationship between Crown and Parliament. In the post-1688 era, Parliament's role in public finance increased substantially. Parliamentarians were mindful of the chief lesson of James II's reign: namely, that a financially independent sovereign could be a political threat to the liberties, property rights, and religion of Englishmen. Reducing the fiscal discretion of the Crown forced frequent Parliaments, and gave Parliament more control over government policy. What the national debt offered was a nonparliamentary source of money, a way for the Crown to spend without conceding Parliament oversight over finances. Even during the mid-1660s, when borrowing was on a much smaller scale, men in the Commons were suspicious of the political latitude that Crown debt could give to a sovereign.[160] Large-scale public borrowing certainly did not erase Parliament's role in public finance, but it threatened to reduce it.

CONCLUSION

Public finances changed enormously in the forty years between 1672 and 1712. Tax revenues were greatly expanded and more effectively controlled by a central Treasury. Direct collection superseded tax farms, and sizable bureaucracies grew up to deal with customs and excise revenues. The distinction between ordinary and extraordinary revenues disappeared as the King was no longer expected to "live of his own."

Changes in borrowing accompanied changes in taxation. When revenues were insufficient to cover expenses, the government now had an effective means to deal with the situation. The Bank of England was available to assist with short-term borrowing, and long-term loans were put on an entirely different footing. Annuities, lottery loans, and especially loans from the joint-stock companies provided a means for the government to undertake long-term borrowing. All of these changes were shaped by the increased involvement of Parliament. Public finance was no longer just the business of the Crown, it was the business of the Crown-in-Parliament.

As the state sector expanded, it created new opportunities for the pursuit of power and wealth. The rewards to political power increased even as Parliament itself appeared to be threatened by the growth of the monied interest. Parliament was indisputably at the center of national politics, and successful political careers now led through the House of Commons. But the government's reliance on loans from the financial sector increased the power of a new elite. Tories in particular worried that these financial masters would call the government's tune.

Many of these political concerns crystallized around the joint-stock companies. As unprecedentedly large agglomerations of organizational size and wealth, they were bound to attract attention. But their involvement in public finance thrust them firmly into the political limelight. It was too obvious that joint-stock companies helped to expand the national debt and fund an aggressive and expensive foreign policy. They were at the center of a financial community populated by socially marginal and politically suspect foreigners, dissenters, Huguenots, and Jews. Consequently, the political conflict between Whigs and Tories eventually engulfed the joint-stock companies.

The military conflict that sapped the strength of the French and permanently crippled the Netherlands, also marked Britain's climb in geopolitical status. After the Military Revolution of the sixteenth and seventeenth centuries, "War had become as much a test of financial strength as of military power."[161] On a per capita basis, England in 1709–10 was outspending France by a ratio of more than two to one.[162] England had the equivalent of roughly 5.4% of its total population under arms, as compared to 2.1% for France.[163] Whether we consider troops, money, or ships, the increase was impressive. In 1685, for example, James II's army numbered 8,865 men. By contrast, William III had an army in Flanders that numbered 50,349 in 1697, and about 170,000 troops fought for Britain in various theaters in 1710–11. In 1673, during the Third Dutch War, Charles II's army cost £451,975 to fund. In the middle of the Nine Years' War, William III's army cost £2,881,194 for the 1694–95 fiscal year. The navy increased from 173 ships in 1689 to 323 ships in 1697.[164] England's armies and navies grew enough to make it a serious contender on the world scene.

England's expanded international role was not unrelated to domestic politics. Quite the contrary, how to fight the war and how to pay for it were both controversial issues. Feeling themselves to be bearing the costs of the war, but excluded from its benefits, Tories wanted to minimize the war effort, to seek peace with France sooner rather than later, and to shift strategy away from land warfare to a naval contest.[165] More than that, however, there was a direct connection between war with France and the domestic status of the post-1688 Protestant regime. A defeat by France would doubtless mean the demise of William III, and later Anne, and their replacement by a Catholic regime beholden to France.[166]

England's experience in this period bears out the close connection between state-building and war-making recently underscored by Charles Tilly. According to his analysis, England followed the "capitalized coercion" path of state growth. This mixed mode of state-building combined resource extraction from domestic populations with alliances between the state and capitalists. The capitalists provided crucial help with state borrowing.[167] In many of Europe's emerging nation-states, the buildup of military resources and extractive capacities were mutually reinforcing processes. Taxes paid for troops, but troops also helped to extract taxes, and so the financial and military strength of states grew together. A growing martial establishment could be used both externally and internally. Yet, in England's case, external strength combined with internal weakness. There were no large standing armies to suppress domestic populations and aggrandize an absolutist state. However envious Charles II was of Louis XIV, and despite James II's attempts to emulate the Sun King, there would be in England no massive state-bureaucratic intrusion into social life. To the extent that there was one, it was primarily fiscal, exemplified by the expanded excise bureaucracy. But by French standards, such a bureaucracy was unimpressively small.[168] The English trajectory was idiosyncratic if not unique.

Chapter Four

BRITAIN IN COMPARATIVE PERSPECTIVE

Always be in debt to someone. That person will constantly
pray God to give you a long and happy life.
—François Rabelais

BRITISH POLITICS shaped the capital market which undergirded the buildup
of Britain's fiscal-military state. Yet the significance of Britain's financial development and the consequences for national state formation can only be
assessed in a comparative context. How can we gauge the extent of these
financial achievements? Was the buildup a common seventeenth-century
experience? Were there similar relationships between politics and public
borrowing in other European countries?

To answer these questions and to gain the full measure of the Financial
Revolution, I compare Britain with four other early modern European countries: France, the United Provinces, Sweden, and Spain. Obviously, I cannot
go into the same level of detail but even a summary analysis of the other
cases will shed some light on the significance of Britain's experience. It will
also reveal the varied ways that public financial systems established political
relationships between rulers and constituents, and show the prevalence of
the "Eumenes effect."

No random sampling process lies behind the selection of these countries.
Quite deliberately, I focus on Britain's primary geopolitical and commercial
adversaries: France and the Netherlands. Imitation is a form of flattery, and
early modern states scrutinized their competitors assiduously, always noting
and sometimes emulating advantageous features and characteristics. The
economic prowess of the Dutch, for example, generated endless commentary among the English, who were eager to learn the secret of their success.
Similarly, English kings like Charles II and James II tried, albeit unsuccess-
fully, to reproduce the absolutist monarchy they enviously beheld across the
English Channel.

Sweden and Spain are included for different reasons. As compared to
Britain, France, and the Netherlands, these two were economically backward countries, sorely lacking the kind of robust monetarized economy that
facilitated resource extraction by the state. Despite this fundamental liability, both Sweden and Spain enjoyed a period of national military glory in the
early modern era. Under Habsburg kings like Charles V and Philip II, Spain

controlled an empire that encompassed the Iberian peninsula, much of the Low Countries, parts of Italy, and vast territories in the New World. Yet by the middle of the seventeenth century, Spain was in decline, unable to prevent the secession of the United Provinces and eclipsed by France as the major European power. Similarly, Swedish armies carved out an empire around the Baltic Sea even though the Swedish economy was even smaller and more undeveloped than Spain's. The apogee of Swedish geopolitical stature came after that of Spain, but by the end of the seventeenth century Sweden too was weakening. If the rise of Britain as a great power is instructive for understanding state-building, so are instances of national decline. Both success and failure mark out this historical process.

All of these countries fought throughout the seventeenth century (for all the reasons why, see Tilly [1990: 183–87]). England fought with France and with the Netherlands, France fought with Spain, England, and also with the Netherlands, Sweden fought the Danes, the Austrian Habsburgs, the Russians, the Poles, and the Germans, and the Spanish fought just about everyone. Extensive warfare posed for these states the same fiscal challenge: How to fund military adventures that were on an unparalleled scale? They were all under pressure to extract enough resources to fund their armies and navies. As we will see, the responses to this common fiscal problem were highly variable.

In making summary comparisons among these four countries, I intend to focus on a small number of characteristics. The first is the economy: Was it advanced or backward? Large or small? Growing or shrinking? The domestic economy was the first place a ruler wishing to build up a military-bureaucratic apparatus will look for resources. A large and growing economy provides a better resource base than a small or shrinking one. Furthermore, within the domestic economy, the size of the mercantile or commercial sector is particularly important. As the British case illustrates, rulers looking for pools of liquid capital to tax or borrow will often find them among urban merchants and bankers. The bigger the commercial and financial sectors of the economy, the easier it was for states to acquire funding.

The significance of post-1688 parliamentary involvement in British public finance points out another key feature. All across Europe, representative institutions like parlements, estates, and diets often played an important role in negotiating taxes and loans with rulers, often in exchange for political concessions. A powerful national representative body could almost be an equal partner in public finance, forcing rulers to negotiate with them but making tax collection easier once agreement had been reached, and providing credible assurances that loans would be repaid.[1] The more powerful the representative body, the more its internal political divisions and conflicts would affect public finance.

Another major feature concerns the public financial system itself. How were taxes raised? Were there long-term loans? Who were the government creditors? I will also consider how well the financial system dealt with the fiscal strains induced by warfare. Whose financial machinery was up to the task? In this regard, the fiscal outcomes ranged from one extreme to the other. An effective financial system meant that tax revenues could fund the military and repay loans but an inadequate system would result in outright defaults on state loans, the equivalent of bankruptcy, as the state declared itself incapable of meeting all its obligations. Obviously, adequacy is a relative term, so one must be mindful of the burden which the financial system had to bear. But in all of these countries during the seventeenth century, the public fisc had to deal with warfare, the biggest financial burden of all.

FAILING POWERS: SWEDEN AND SPAIN

How to fund a national state and a significant military is a question best answered not only by looking at countries that were successful but also at those that weren't. Neither Spain nor Sweden were simple failures, however, for both attained great power status for a time. Yet by the end of the seventeenth century, both were in decline, unable to match the financial and military achievements of England or France.

During the Thirty Years' War (which ended in 1648), Sweden became a great power and built up an empire around the Baltic littoral.[2] This was a remarkable achievement considering the limited nature of Sweden's human, financial, and economic resources. Sweden was a sparsely populated, rural country. The whole of Scandinavia contained only about 2.6 million people in 1650, and marginally more (2.9 million) fifty years later.[3] Few lived in urban areas and the percentage of the total Scandinavian population living in cities larger than 10,000 people was 2.4% in 1650, and 4.0% in 1700.[4] Stockholm's population, for example, numbered around 45,000 in 1700. Consistent with the overwhelmingly rural character of Swedish society, about 95% of all Swedes were peasants.[5]

Sweden had an agrarian economy and small-scale peasant agricultural production satisfied domestic consumption needs. The only significant industry was in mining and metals (mostly copper and iron), and foreign merchants dominated much of Sweden's overseas trade.[6] Sweden's capitalists were few and far between, and there was no developed financial system or capital markets. The fact that most of the revenues paid to the Swedish crown were in kind, rather than in cash, was a testament to Sweden's backwardness.[7] Of course, Swedish rulers were well aware of these problems but despite their attempts to create a more dynamic urban sector, there was little change.[8]

If Sweden's domestic economy was not conducive to military prowess, in some respects neither was its polity. Sweden possessed a remarkably inclusive national parliament, the *riksdag*. Four estates were represented, the nobility, clergy, burghers, and the peasantry, and it was possibly the most democratic national political institution in seventeenth-century Europe.[9] According to the Swedish constitution or Land Law the consent of the *riksdag* was necessary for the passage of new taxes or the levying of troops, and so it wielded significant political power.[10] Taxing the peasantry, a favorite device of many early modern states, was harder to do in Sweden because the peasantry had a political voice. It was not so easy for a Swedish king to extract domestic resources, and parliamentary consent could not be taken for granted.[11]

Sweden's simple fiscal system was based primarily on a land tax.[12] Land worked by peasants was taxed at different rates, depending on whether it was owned by the Crown, the nobility, or by the peasants themselves.[13] Aristocratic land was frequently exempt from taxes levied against the other two categories. Taxes were generally collected in kind, so it was an ongoing struggle for the state to secure assets in cash (armies had to be paid with money, not butter and tar).[14] Sweden used tax farming during the 1620s as a way to generate cash, since the task of converting commodities into money became the tax farmer's problem, not the crown's. But political resistance to tax farming forced a resumption of collection by the Crown, and by 1635 all tax farms for direct taxes had been abolished.[15] In the 1620s, the *riksdag* also passed three extraordinary taxes which permanently enhanced the crown's income, although these were not sufficient to cover military expenditures.

Sweden was short of fiscal alternatives. Unlike Spain or France, the Swedish state had no venal offices, and so could not sell them off to raise money. The crown occasionally forced civil servants to loan money to the government by failing to pay their salaries but there were obvious limits to this fiscal strategy, especially given the small size of the state bureaucracy.[16] The crown also tried, without great success, to encourage mining and industry in order to raise more money.

Crown debts were often satisfied by alienating crown lands or using them as security for loans. When this happened, the land often ended up in the hands of the Swedish nobility.[17] As the fiscal pressure continued, more and more crown land became owned by the aristocracy. In the latter part of the seventeenth century, and with the consent of the *riksdag*, the Crown took back these lands in what was called the "*reduktion.*" The first move came in 1650, when the three commoner estates called for a resumption of crown land, a measure that would mostly hurt the nobility. Although nothing happened, this laid the groundwork for similar resolutions in 1680 and 1682, again proposed by the three commoner estates. Internal divisions among the nobility undercut their ability to oppose the policy, and so it eventually passed.[18] According to Åström (1973), the proportion of assessed lands under noble ownership went from about two-thirds in 1655 to about one-fourth at the end of the century. Concomitantly, the national debt went from over 40 million *riksdaler* in 1681 down to about 10 million in 1697.[19] The *reduktion* was largely responsible for these dramatic declines, and it increased the financial autonomy of the crown by enlarging its independent income. Thenceforth, the Swedish king was less reliant on the *riksdag* for money.

As the functional equivalent of a repudiation of public debt, the legality of the *reduktion* was questionable. After all, the lands were alienated to cover expenses and repay debts, and thanks to the *reduktion* they were returned to the crown. At first glance, therefore, the *reduktion* appears to be the kind of sovereign violation of property rights that North (1981, 1990) is concerned with. Two additional facts correct this impression, however.[20] First, the crown did not act alone but in conjunction with the *riksdag*, Sweden's national legislature. However unhappy it made the nobility who lost their property, the *reduktion* was not an illegal, extra-parliamentary act.[21] In addition, Sweden's fourteenth-century constitution prohibited the alienation of Crown lands.[22] Even though such alienations occurred from the sixteenth century on, there were constitutional grounds to revert the land back to the crown.

One shouldn't make too much of the *reduktion*, for although it generated a substantial financial windfall, it was also a one-time event. Thereafter, Crown creditors were wary of accepting Crown land as compensation. Furthermore, it came long after Sweden's intense period of military activity during the 1620s and 1630s. The *reduktion* may have helped Swedish finances in the 1680s, but not earlier in the century.

Despite serious economic, fiscal, and political shortcomings, Sweden nevertheless raised a huge army and built an empire. In 1632, the armies commanded by Gustavus Adolphus numbered 149,000 men, at an annual cost of 4.4 million *riksdaler*.[23] Given how difficult it was in 1613 for Sweden to raise 1 million *riksdaler* over four years (to ransom the fortress of Älvsborg from the Danes) how could it maintain such a massive army? The answer, put most simply, is that Sweden managed to externalize the financial and manpower costs of warfare. Rather than tackle the almost insurmountable problem of raising sufficient domestic resources, Sweden extracted resources externally. Rather than tax at home, it in effect taxed abroad. This strategy was crucially dependent on military success.

Gustavus Adolphus followed the principle that war ought to pay for itself. This meant that the financial burden of war should fall upon the territories occupied by the army, rather than on the homeland.[24] Since Swedish armies in the early seventeenth century spent most of their time fighting on German soil, they were able to survive off the resource-rich German economy. Swedish armies established a regular fiscal administration over occupied territory (the "contribution"), and refrained from arbitrary plunder.[25] For example, after 1629 Sweden levied a toll in Prussian harbors, including Danzig, and was therefore able to tax the lucrative Baltic trade. The success of this strategy meant that the amount of money sent from Sweden and Finland to pay for the German wars declined, going from 2,368,000 *riksdalers* in 1630 down to only 128,573 *riksdalers* in 1633.[26] So long as the Swedish army was lodged on someone else's land, almost the full cost of maintaining it could be externalized. But this required Sweden to be the military aggressor, and to be successful. Should Sweden have to fight a defensive war, the cost would devolve on its own territories.

Large armies were also a drain on Sweden's scarce manpower resources. Since Sweden was a small country, manning an army was difficult. Although the Swedish male population felt the impact of mobilization, most of the manpower burden was also externalized as Sweden made heavy use of foreign mercenaries.[27] The elite corps of the army was composed of Swedish natives, but the number of foreign troops was impressive. In 1632, about 90% of the 149,000 men in the Swedish army were mercenaries.[28] Of course, mercenaries fight for money not national glory, and so the greater the reliance on them, the more important it was to have sufficient financial resources.

Sweden's age of military greatness came to an abrupt close in the early eighteenth century, at the inglorious end of the Great Northern War. After its defeat, Sweden's Baltic territories were much reduced and it ceased to be a great power. Forced to rely on its own resources, Sweden was unable to maintain its position. Yet the Swedish experience shows that neither a profusion of domestic resources, nor an elaborate tax structure, nor even a developed system of public debt, was necessary for military strength. Although British state strength depended on these things, Swedish strength did not. But the Swedish experience also suggests that lacking this fiscal and economic foundation, its success was historically precarious, the unrobust result of a string of military victories which didn't require Sweden to rely on its own resources. A single defeat was enough to knock Sweden out of contention as a great power.

If Sweden had its moment of glory in the seventeenth century, Spain was well past its pinnacle and declined steadily throughout the century.[29] In the latter sixteenth century, during the reign of Philip II, Spain was arguably the greatest power in Europe, with an empire much larger than Sweden's at its height.[30] Over the long run, however, Spain was unable to sustain the empire it had acquired through inheritance. Dynastic good fortune, not military prowess, created the Spanish empire.[31]

Spain was a bigger country to begin with, although its population actually shrank in the first part of the seventeenth century. The total Spanish population numbered about 8.1 million in 1600, 7.1 million in 1650, and 7.5 million in 1700.[32] Part of the decline was intentional, as Spain expelled some 275,000 moriscos (converted Muslims) in the 1610s.[33] Although it was a more urbanized country than Sweden, in comparison to Britain and Holland, Spain was still largely rural. Madrid and Seville were the two biggest cities, with 130,000 and 60,000 inhabitants, respectively, in 1650.[34] That same year, urban inhabitants accounted for 9.5% of Spain's total population (as compared to 2.4% in Scandinavia).

In Spain's agrarian economy, peasants cultivated land they seldom owned, as vassals of either the crown or nobility.[35] For most of the early modern period, Spain exported raw materials and imported manufactured goods, and consequently faced an adverse balance of payments. Wool and silk were the two most important export textiles, and Spain produced and exported iron-ore and mercury as well.[36] Spanish industry was generally unable to match the foreign competition, and it got progressively weaker as time passed. There was no domestic capitalist class to speak of, and trade and other entrepreneurial activities were dominated by foreigners.[37] Even when the empire was at its height, Spain lacked industrial capacity. Furthermore, financial markets were undeveloped and Spanish banking was dominated by the Genoese, and later by Portuguese Jews.[38]

The economy was much more developed in the Burgundian lands inherited by Charles V. Even in the sixteenth century, the region of northwest Europe which now comprises Holland and Belgium was a highly urbanized center for trade, with advanced agricultural production in the surrounding countryside. Yet, for political and logistical reasons, the distant Spanish Crown was unable to tap into this wealth.

With its stagnant rural economy, Spain did not provide its rulers with an impressive tax base. It did, however, enjoy privileged access to New World silver and gold through its colonies in Peru and Mexico. Important though this source of revenue was, even at its highest point American silver never produced more than about 20% of Spanish revenues.[39] The flow of silver via the treasure fleets was generally reliable but insufficient to solve Spain's financial problems. Much of it went directly to other European countries to pay for imports of manufactured goods.

These economic and demographic limitations might not have been such a problem but for Spain's onerous diplomatic and military commitments. During the sixteenth and seventeenth centuries, Spain's twofold strategic situation involved interests in both the Netherlands and the Mediterranean. Events in either place would have tested a military power, but in combination they created a particularly formidable challenge.

Philip II is considered the picture of an absolutist monarch, but in actuality the Spanish polity was an agglomeration of independent provinces, each with its own special rights and privileges.[40] The Spanish crown combined the leadership of Castile, Aragon, Portugal, parts of the Netherlands, the kingdom of Naples (which included most of southern Italy), Sicily, and Sardinia, but there was no unitary centralized government over all these territories. Each was governed separately, according to its own set of rules. Castile was the core of the empire, and there the power of the Spanish Crown was greatest. Yet, even in Castile, royal power was constrained by the *cortes*, the Spanish Parliament.[41] The *cortes*, which represented eighteen Castilian cities, had the right to approve extraordinary taxes (and to seek redress of grievances), and so could use the power of the purse to influence royal policy.[42]

Obtaining the cooperation of local elites was more difficult outside of Castile. The province of Aragon, for example, was extremely protective of its traditional rights (*fueros*) and institutions, and seldom paid much money into the royal coffers.[43] The relationship between the Spanish Crown and the other territories in the empire was close to a contractual one, with each side making commitments to the other. Thus, the task of raising money outside of Castile was politically difficult, even for a king. Neither Portugal, nor the Italian territories, nor even the Spanish Netherlands contributed much to royal expenses. Taxes collected in the Netherlands, for instance, never covered the cost of the Army of Flanders.[44]

If provincial political institutions could hinder the exercise of royal power, so could the Spanish aristocracy. Spanish monarchs lacked a substantial, centralized bureaucratic apparatus to help govern and had to rely heavily on local elites.[45] The king was the "absolute" ruler at the political center but the nobility dominated local government and the king could only reach the local level with their cooperation. Many of Spain's peasants were not under direct royal jurisdiction, and most towns, villages, and hamlets were *in señorío*, that is, fiscal and legal jurisdiction was in the hands of a noble, rather than the king.[46] This situation worsened as jurisdictions were alienated, and new *señoríos* created, to raise money for the Crown. By the sixteenth century, most civil municipal governors (*corregimientos*) were appointed by local oligarchs, not by the crown. Thus, even though Spanish government was unequivocally monarchical, in practice the king's power was dissipated and constrained by local elites and institutions.[47]

Spanish state revenues came from a number of different sources. The customs and the *alcabala*, a type of sales tax, were the most important of the ordinary revenues.[48] These were supplemented from time to time by extraordinary revenues voted by the *cortes*, for example, the *millones*, a tax on basic foodstuffs. The church contributed three extraordinary revenues (the *cruzada*, the *subsidio*, and the *excusado*) that were earmarked for specific military purposes.[49] The flow of New World specie augmented these ordinary and extraordinary revenues. Because the Council of Finance had no organization of its own, revenue collection was usually undertaken by tax farmers (many of whom were non-Castilian) and local elites.[50]

To compensate for inadequate revenues, the crown borrowed money using *asientos* (short-term loans) and *juros* (long-term loans). *Asientos* were contracts that anticipated future tax revenues, running between five and ten years in duration.[51] The lenders (*asientistas*) were mostly foreign bankers, and provided a sum to the Crown in exchange for a claim on the future revenue of a specific tax. As negotiated, the repayments were sufficient to cover both the principal and the interest of the loan, and each contract presumed that the crown had adequate revenues to pledge to the lenders.[52] Extraordinary revenues, those which were collected with the prior agreement of the *cortes* or church, tended to be more predictable than ordinary revenues, and so *asientistas* preferred to have their loans secured by extraordinary revenues. When all revenues had been anticipated for years into the future, *asientistas* became reluctant to loan more money to the Crown. *Juros* were the financial instrument used for long-term borrowing. They were akin to annuities, paying a lower interest rate than the *asiento* but doing so for a longer period of time.[53] Typically, they were secured on the ordinary revenues of the Crown.

The Crown also raised money through the sale of patents of nobility (which conferred aristocratic status on the purchaser) and venal offices.[54] Venality was strictly a response to financial problems.[55] In fact, practically all offices (legal, financial, and military) in Spain could be purchased, although most of those sold were municipal or local offices.[56] Once sold, an office became private property, heritable and alienable at the discretion of the owner. Venal offices necessitated the devolution and dilution of sovereign power and so exacerbated the administrative weaknesses of the crown, but they did generate cash.[57]

One other strategy was used to try to manage the Crown's recurrent financial problems. Since warfare was the major cause of budgetary deficits, Spain organized its military apparatus around subcontractors. Reliance on military subcontractors varied from reign to reign but whenever financial problems got out of hand, their use increased.[58] Military subcontracting meant, for example, that the galleys in Spain's Mediterranean fleet were independently owned and operated for profit. In the 1630s, subcontracting was at a high point, and so the naval fleet, the arms industry, the victualling of galleys and garrisons, and even recruitment into the military was in the hands of private contractors.[59] Subcontracting diminished the effectiveness of the Spanish military, but was financially advantageous because the contractors extended credit to the Crown, and they could often provide services to the Crown more cheaply than the Crown could do them itself.[60]

Despite all these measures (extraordinary revenues, venal offices, tax farming, and military subcontracting), the Spanish Crown was unable to cover its massive expenses. Sixteenth- and seventeenth-century Spain simply fought too many wars too much of the time. Troops in the Low Countries often went unpaid, and consequently mutinied.[61] Debts piled up, and the proportion of crown revenue devoted to servicing them grew.[62] The inevitable outcome was bankruptcy, and the inevitable occurred with alarming frequency.

Bankruptcies resulted in 1557, 1560, 1575, 1596, 1607, 1627, 1647, 1653, and 1662, and followed the same basic pattern.[63] High-interest, short-term debt, in which the principal of the loan was repaid, was forcibly converted into low-interest, long-term debt, where the principal was never repaid.[64] In other words, *asientistas* were forced to accept *juros* to satisfy their claims. The crown unilaterally broke its financial agreements with its creditors but did not repudiate its debts completely.

Bankruptcy may have provided short-term relief by forcibly refinancing loans, but in the long run the Spanish Crown acquired a richly deserved reputation as a poor credit risk. Bankruptcy was the strategy of last resort to which the Crown resorted too many times. *Asientistas* understandably insisted on high interest rates to compensate for the substantial risk of default and so the Spanish crown was paying 17.6% interest on its short-term loans in the 1520s, and an incredible 48.8% interest by the 1550s.[65]

The growth in Spanish state debt had an important political dimension that illustrates the Eumenes effect. Although *asientistas* were mostly foreign bankers (at first Genoese, and later Portuguese Jews), much of the long-term debt, made up of *juros*, was held domestically.[66] Rentier status was highly desirable in Spanish society, and many were eager to buy up *juros*.[67] The incomes of the aristocracy, for example, became increasingly dependent on investments in public and private loans.[68] Kamen's analysis of the 1681 income of the third Marquis of Leganes, Don Diego Felipez de Guzman, shows that 45% of the nearly 30,000 ducats total came from government annuities (Kamen 1980: 230). In general, Spain's social elites had a strong financial interest in the viability of the Spanish state.[69]

Spain's military adventures and costs were on a much greater scale than Sweden's so it is improbable that the Swedish "contribution" system would have worked for Spain. Given the particular political circumstances of the war in the Netherlands, however, such an option was completely out of the question. The Dutch were fighting a war of independence, and so for political reasons the Spanish territories in the Netherlands could simply not be taxed heavily enough to cover the expenses of war. If they were to be taxed at such a level, the rebellion would very likely have spread. Thus, the Swedish strategy of "externalization" was not an option for the Spanish.

Forced to rely on resources extracted from a backward domestic economy (albeit supplemented by New World specie and bullion), and working from a relatively weak political position, the Spanish Crown was unable to hang on to the empire it inherited. Widespread geopolitical interests forced Spain to fight more wars than it could afford, even given a variety of fiscal-political measures (tax farming, venal offices, military subcontracting, bargaining with *cortes* for extraordinary revenues, and bankruptcy, the strategy of last resort).

Taken together, the cases of Sweden and Spain show how useful a thriving mercantile-capitalist economy was for a state to sustain high levels of military activity.[70] Commerce created a large tax base and a pool of lendable capital, and both the Spanish and Swedish states were hobbled by low levels of national economic development.[71] Furthermore, the crowns of both countries had to deal with representative institutions (the *cortes* and *riksdag*) that had some control over the public purse. Despite ongoing attempts to reduce financial dependence on parliament, rulers were forced to compromise and accommodate their policies. The process of resource extraction was politically constrained, just as it was in Britain. However, neither the *cortes* nor the *riksdag* was organized along party lines. There was no party competition, no conflict between Whigs and Tories, that might shape public finances.

BRITAIN'S RIVALS: THE UNITED PROVINCES AND FRANCE

In many respects, the rise of the Netherlands was the flip side of the decline of Spain. The Dutch were equal to the same fiscal challenge that overwhelmed Spain, and so the war that drained the Spanish Treasury also earned the United Provinces its freedom from Spanish rule. The connection with Britain is equally important, for in the matter of public finance the United Provinces were the pacesetters. The Financial Revolution that occurred in Britain at the turn of the century was old hat in Holland.

In terms of urbanization and economic development, the United Provinces were the opposite from Sweden. The Netherlands had a small population (about 1.9 million in 1650) that was the most highly urbanized in all of Europe: 31.7% lived in urban areas in 1650.[72] By the middle of the seventeenth century, for instance, Amsterdam had over 200,000 inhabitants.[73] The United Provinces also had a highly advanced, commercial economy based on a very productive agricultural sector. It had virtually no natural resources but nevertheless Amsterdam was the center for world trade and international finance, at the very core of the world capitalist system.[74] Politically, it had a federated polity, run by urban oligarchs rather than the usual monarch or aristocracy.[75]

Seventeenth-century Amsterdam was the world's entrepôt, and the Dutch dominated the shipping industry, particularly in the movement of bulk goods.[76] To give but one example, during the 1660s Finland was under Swedish rule. Yet from 1661 to 1670 exactly one Swedish merchant ship sailed westward from Finland, as compared to 167 Dutch ships.[77] The Dutch expanded their command over the Baltic trade in grain, salt, and herring to take a strong position in commerce with Iberia, the East and West Indies, and the Mediterranean.[78] Spanish oranges, for example, were cheaper in the Netherlands than they were in Spain![79] Commodities, capital, and foreign exchange all funneled through Amsterdam and provided the Dutch state with voluminous material flows and numerous economic transactions that could be easily monitored and taxed. The United Provinces also benefited from having a developed textile industry, especially after thousands of textile workers moved from Flanders and Brabant in the late sixteenth century.[80]

Dutch predominance as a center for trade helped it develop as a center for finance, banking, and insurance.[81] This shift was helped by the establishment in 1609 of the *wisselbank*, Amsterdam's exchange bank.[82] Innovative contracts like commodity futures were traded on the Amsterdam exchange, as were joint-stock company shares. Capital could be borrowed at low interest rates, and foreign exchange transactions were easy to perform.[83] Dutch financiers were sophisticated and willing to invest in a variety of debt instruments.[84] Developed capital markets in turn bolstered Dutch trade.[85]

Since the advanced Dutch economy facilitated intensive resource extraction, we might expect to see a highly developed national state. But in fact, the peculiar structure of the Dutch polity stood in the way.[86] Since the Union of Utrecht in 1579, the separate provinces that comprised the United Provinces retained a great deal of political power and autonomy. The Dutch polity was highly decentralized, with a federal structure and consensus decision-making procedures that were prone to paralysis and prevarication.[87] The States General, the national governing body, was a permanent assembly whose members were selected by the different provinces. The delegates were answerable to their respective provincial assemblies, and often had to refer back to them for instructions. On important national issues, such as the approval of foreign treaties, unanimous agreement among the provincial assemblies was necessary, so decisions were not easily reached. Even when national policy was set, the central state had little ability to implement it for the central state apparatus was minuscule.[88] Urban elites possessed the most power within this unwieldy political structure. There was no hereditary monarch, no strong rural landed class, and the Dutch aristocracy was weak and declining.[89] A small group of urban merchant oligarchs, the regents, held most of the important political offices and were dominant well into the eighteenth century.[90]

Public revenues reflected the decentralized nature of political power. The United Provinces had no unified tax system and the provinces were fiscally autonomous. Money was raised at the provincial level, and then handed over to the generality, but the latter possessed almost no fiscal machinery of its own.[91] Quotas were set for the proportion of monies coming from each province, but how that money was raised was up to the province. Holland, being the richest province, naturally paid more than the others. Its quota for ordinary war expenses was 57.7% in the mid-seventeenth century. Friesland, which had the next-highest quota, paid only 11.6%.[92]

The United Provinces had the unenviable reputation of being the most heavily taxed country in Europe.[93] Certain taxes were earmarked for specific purposes. Customs revenues, for example, were used to cover admiralty expenditures, but because of the importance of trade to the Dutch economy, customs taxes were kept at a relatively low level. In Holland, the biggest and wealthiest of the provinces, indirect taxes carried the fiscal burden, particularly the excise taxes. In 1640, indirect taxes provided over 70% of Holland's revenue, and included levies on beer, grain, meat, and peat. Direct taxes, including the property tax, generated only 22% of revenues.[94] Although taxes were administered at the provincial level, and thus varied from region to region, they frequently were collected using tax farms. Holland's numerous excises, for example, were farmed out.[95] Contracts were usually for a single year, and the districts that were farmed out could be as small as a single rural village. The Dutch tax system was complex and varied, but it reliably generated enormous revenues.

As compared with the fiscal systems of other countries, certain features were notably absent. The Dutch did not rely on venal offices to raise money, although the sale of offices in the army was not uncommon.[96] As a fiscal device, venal offices were simply unnecessary. Furthermore, although tax farming was convenient administratively, tax farmers were not a major source of loans to the provincial or central governments. Government borrowing was successfully placed on a very different footing. Finally, public borrowing was done with the consent of the lenders, and so "forced loans" were a rarity.

The Dutch fought throughout the seventeenth century. Hemmed in by multiple rivals, at different times they fought the Spanish, the English, the Danes, and the French. All of this fighting, of course, cost money. Despite the ability of the Dutch tax system to obtain large sums from the Dutch economy, deficits were common and as a result borrowing was necessary. The debt of the province of Holland went from less than 5 million guilders before 1620 up to between 125 and 147 million guilders at the end of the Eighty Years' War (1648).[97] By the end of the War of the Spanish Succession, after three wars with France, the United Provinces were very deeply in debt (250 million guilders' worth) and in a state of fiscal near collapse.[98]

For several reasons, the Dutch found long-term borrowing to be an attractive alternative. The techniques had already been developed by Dutch cities in the sixteenth century so in many respects it was simply a matter of transferring the method from the municipal level up to the provincial, and then to the national level.[99] In addition, public debtors could turn to Holland's highly developed capital markets for funds. The supply of lendable capital was substantial, and just as capital markets benefited Dutch traders by granting them cheap credit, they also allowed public debtors to borrow large amounts at low interest rates.[100] High levels of taxation ensured that debts could be serviced, and the reliability with which Dutch governments repaid their debts made them extremely attractive as borrowers (in contrast, for example, to the Spanish Crown). They could borrow at interest rates half those charged other sovereign debtors.[101]

Sovereign creditors were mostly domestic. Unlike many other early modern states, the United Provinces did not have to borrow from foreign bankers or capitalists. Lending money to the government was not, however, simply an economic decision. An examination of who provided loans to the Dutch state reveals the very political texture of public debt. Loans were obtained only with the consent of the provincial estates. Dutch provinces borrowed by issuing three different types of long-term bonds: obligations, *lijfrenten* (a type of life annuity), and *losrenten* (akin to a perpetual annuity).[102] All of these instruments were traded on the Amsterdam exchange, although some were more easily transferable than others. Ownership of government bonds was widespread, and they found their way into the hands of many small investors. It is hard to estimate the total number of public creditors with any accuracy (Temple put it at around 65,000 during the 1660s), but it is clear that many of the inhabitants of the United Provinces had a direct financial interest in the solvency of their own government.[103]

Members of the regent class were especially likely to be heavy investors.[104] One study estimates that the Amsterdam elite invested about 50% of its wealth in public bonds, and 32% in joint-stock company shares.[105] Those who controlled the Dutch state politically also tended to be its biggest creditors.[106] Not surprisingly, public debts were reliably repaid because they were owed, in large measure, to the same class of people who controlled the state. In this regard, the aristocracy provided a telling contrast with the regents. Not only were they absent from political office but despite their wealth, aristocrats did not invest in public bonds.[107] A political role in government, and a financial role in public debt, went hand in hand.

The political pattern of investment in government loans was established early on. In the sixteenth century, ownership of Dutch provincial *renten* (annuities) was associated with occupancy of public office.[108] In fact, office-holding was a very good predictor of whether a wealthy person purchased *renten*. Even though no organized political parties existed in the Netherlands, there is some evidence that beyond simple office-holding, partisanship affected investment in public debt. Tracy explains: "The sharpest difference between the groups [the magistrates and their political opponents] lies in their interest in Holland renten, high among elected officials, and very low among the Doleanten" (Tracy 1985: 167). The political import of public debt continued from the sixteenth century into the seventeenth.

Through widespread domestic ownership of government bonds, many
Dutch citizens had their individual financial interests joined to those of the
state. This was particularly true for Holland's ruling elite.[109]

If the United Provinces were Britain's greatest commercial competitor,
France, by comparison, was the great political and military rival. Britain's
financial revolution was modeled after Holland's but it was necessitated by
the wars with France. France had many of the ingredients necessary for
great power status. First and foremost, it was a populous country, with almost twenty million inhabitants in 1700, or about four times as many people
as England. France had large cities but overall it was about as urbanized as
Spain, and most of its inhabitants were peasants.[110] France's internal economy was large but fragmented. Internal customs duties and provincial and
municipal privileges inhibited the movement of goods within the country.[111]
Agriculture was not as developed as in Britain or the Netherlands, making
France vulnerable to subsistence crises. Nevertheless, the French economy
was large and advanced enough to provide a substantial tax base. It did not
have, however, the kind of developed financial markets that London or Amsterdam possessed.

Louis XIV was the exemplary absolutist monarch, the embodiment of in-
divisible sovereignty.[112] As the holder of the highest judicial, executive, and
legislative powers in France, it seems obvious that the crown could easily
extract whatever resources were necessary to fund France's foreign policy.[113] After all, in comparison with other political institutions like England's
parliament, the Swedish *riksdag*, or the Dutch estates, France's General
Estates were moribund.[114] Who could rival the king? In addition, as compared with many other contemporary states, French officialdom was substantial. There were many officers, functionaries, and bureaucrats to do the
king's bidding.

Louis XIV was absolutist in theory, but not in practice.[115] There was no
single national political institution to counterbalance his power, but there
were many local and provincial institutions (estates, parlements, sovereign
courts, etc.). France's large size was advantageous except that it was hard for
Parisian ministers to control distant provinces, so the national government
had to gain the cooperation of local elites to help run the country. Furthermore, there was no single, unified system of government. Administration
was a patchwork because different regions were incorporated into the nation-state at different times and under a variety of political circumstances, so
many of them kept their traditional political structures and provincial privileges.[116] Legal, political, and fiscal privileges were so basic to the *ancien
régime* that it was virtually impossible to systematize and unify the highly
variegated political-legal system.[117] In addition, for financial reasons explained below, there were massive numbers of venal offices at all levels of
government. Such offices were owned privately (they were a form of prop-

erty), and this greatly reduced the Crown's ability to discipline the officer or reform the office. In sum, the structure of French government was complex and unwieldy, and highly resistant to reform.

The crown followed two basic strategies to overcome its de facto political weaknesses.[118] One involved the appointment of intendants directly answerable to Paris to circumvent local government and give the central government more control. Intendants were appointed through revocable commissions and had no property rights in their own offices.[119] These were not, in other words, venal offices. This strategy almost inevitably resulted in conflict between holders of traditional political offices, and the newer intendants.

The second strategy complemented the first, and involved the cultivation and use of informal patron-client networks. Parisian ministers created client networks out in the provinces, and dispensed patronage through them, in order to exert more control. The goal was also to reduce the amount of patronage going through provincial governors and thus diminish their autonomous power. These networks operated within, across, and outside formal political institutions.[120] As Kettering explains: "Richelieu asserted ministerial control over the distribution of royal patronage in the provinces and used it to create reliable administrative clienteles of his own to help him in governing, particularly in distant frontier provinces with unreliable governors, and to control traditional tax-granting assemblies in the pays d'Etat" (Kettering 1986: 174).

The structure of French government forced the king to compromise with his subjects. The picture of absolutism suggests that the king merely had to wave his hand to have his coffers filled. In fact, however, raising money required protracted political negotiations with regional political institutions and elites, and even with the royal bureaucracy itself. Extracting resources out of the large French tax base was no easy matter.

The tax system reflected these political and administrative compromises. French revenues derived from a complex combination of direct taxes, indirect taxes, and extraordinary revenues. The most important of the direct taxes was the *taille*, a land tax which fell disproportionately on the peasantry and from which many groups (including the clergy and aristocracy) were exempt.[121] It made up between 25% and 30% of total royal revenues and was supplemented by other direct taxes like the *capitation*, levied in 1695, and the *dixieme*, levied in 1710.[122] It was no coincidence that the additional direct taxes were introduced during the war with Britain, and also that there were fewer exemptions as compared to the older *taille*.

Indirect taxes were many and their incidence varied. There were taxes on salt (the *gabelles*) and on tobacco (the *tabacs*). There were duties on commerce (the *traites*), a sales tax and stamp duty (the *aides*), and a tax on legal documents (the *domaines*). The *gabelles*, to take one example, were not uniformly applied throughout France. Different regions paid different salt taxes

that were assessed and collected using different tax organizations.[123] Like
the *tailles*, the *gabelles* hit the peasantry hard but many of these indirect
taxes fell upon cities, and in particular the urban poor.[124] Indirect taxes were
mostly collected through tax farms, which also provided the Crown with an
important source of short-term loans. Tax farms were let for a period of
years, and at the beginning of each new contract the winning bidder was
expected to provide a substantial loan to the crown.[125] Although direct collection of these revenues may have been more efficient than relying on tax
farms, the latter's role in royal credit ensured their continuance.

France suffered from the same problem as other early modern states—it
was impossible to pay military expenses using tax revenues alone. In theory,
the French Crown wielded more domestic power than the British Crown
but the latter proved much better at raising money (e.g., the per capita incidence of taxes was much heavier in eighteenth-century Britain than in
France).[126] Frequent war meant frequent deficits and borrowing became
necessary to cover the shortfall.[127] The inadequacies of the revenue system
made the need to borrow even more pressing. Money raised this way fell
under the category of extraordinary revenues but even when added to ordinary revenues there was still not enough.[128]

Absolutist monarchs had serious problems when it came to borrowing. It
was difficult to imagine what recourse sovereign creditors had when the
king was the fount of all political and legal authority and therefore, in effect,
above the law. Crown creditors were involved in a very risky business.[129]
Such difficulties were not just theoretical, for the French Crown had a history of insolvency. Sovereign debts were rescheduled in 1559, 1598, 1648,
and 1661, and unlike the Spanish bankruptcies, involved much more than
the simple conversion of short-term debt into long-term debt.[130] Furthermore, bankers to the Crown always operated under the shadow of a *chambre
de justice* (a financial tribunal), which could be used retroactively by the
Crown to alter the terms of loans and tax the profits of Crown creditors.[131]
Although it might bring short-term benefits, over the long term use of the
chambre de justice had the effect of encouraging financiers to keep their
government dealings as secret and obscure as possible.[132] State finance was
enshrouded in mystery, making it hard for anyone to know what was really
going on.

Since the French Crown was an untrustworthy borrower, much of the
public debt was underwritten by lower-level political bodies. The money
was borrowed for national purposes and it ended up in the hands of the
Crown, but should a default occur the liable party was not the Crown and
hence not "above the law." The best example of this involved annuities issued by the Paris corporation. Since the sixteenth century, the king assigned
certain revenues to the corporation, and on the security of these, the corpo-

ration issued annuities known as *rentes sur l'Hôtel de Ville de Paris*. Proceeds still went to the king, but the Paris corporation, not the king, was the indebted party.[133] In 1713, for instance, the capital of long-term government loans totaled 1.36 billion *livres*, most of which (almost 95%) was administered through the *Hôtel de Ville de Paris*.[134]

What truly distinguished the French Crown as a debtor was its reliance on venal offices. Not even the Spanish came close in the sale of public offices. Thousands of offices were put up for sale, including those centrally involved in public finance.[135] Venal offices included court clerks, ushers, tipstaffs, salt-fish counters, wigmakers, as well as the offices of the general receiver and financial receiver.[136] The price varied with the stature of the office. New offices were created for the sole purpose of raising money, old offices were split into two or three new ones, and so over time the total number of offices rose. From about four thousand in 1515, the number of public offices increased to more than forty-six thousand in 1665.[137]

Venal offices raised money for the crown because the purchaser paid a sum for the office (the *finance*). The government then paid annual interest on this sum (the *gages*) and so the office constituted a kind of long-term loan.[138] Additional money was occasionally extracted through the use of the *augmentation de gages*, wherein existing officeholders were required to invest more money in their offices and receive in exchange additional interest.[139] Given the inequities of the tax system, venal offices provided a way for the crown to tap into the wealth of the under-taxed upper and middle classes.[140] To dissolve a venal office, the government would have to repay the principal but with so many offices the total capital tied up was extraordinary. In the 1660s, forty-six thousand offices embodied a sum worth about 419 million *livres*, or about four or five times the annual revenue of the crown.[141] For financial reasons, large-scale reform of the system was virtually impossible. For administrative reasons, however, such reform was highly desirable. The king had a difficult time controlling his own officials when they owned their offices.[142]

Venal offices were attractive to French investors for a variety of reasons.[143] First, they provided financial benefits to their owners through the *gages* paid by the crown, and the fees and receipts paid by the office's clientele. The purely financial compensation was not enough, however, for it often compared unfavorably with other investments.[144] Many venal offices also involved privileges. Some of the rights were highly valuable, as in offices which would ennoble their owner/occupant. Others conferred smaller increments of social status, or involved other kinds of fiscal, legal, or political privileges.[145] Offices also entailed a public function, a set of duties, and powers. Sometimes this function was substantial, as in the case of receiver generals and magistrates, but other times it was not.

Venal offices were also valuable because they were heritable and alienable forms of property. As a perpetual loan, the capital invested in a venal
office was immobilized until such time as the crown decided to repay the
principal, which was almost never. However, because venal offices were
freely alienable, the owner could recover the principal by selling it to someone else. In addition, after the institution of the *paulette* in 1604, venal offices were heritable and so could be passed down through the generations,
along with other valuable property such as land and *rentes*, as part of the
family patrimony.[146] Heritability increased the value of an office and hence
allowed the crown to charge more money when selling one.[147] Finally, financial offices in particular were valuable because they offered easy access to
tax revenues and cash flow.[148]

An almost insurmountable tension lay at the heart of the old regime fiscal
system. With its complex, heterogeneous revenue system, large-scale rationalization and reform was necessary to improve government finances. This
would have entailed sweeping away many of the cumbrous exceptions, exemptions, and privileges that interfered with revenue collection. Yet it was
these very privileges that formed the basis for royal credit. Venal offices in
the revenue apparatus itself as well as in other departments of government
blocked administrative reform. More generally, the crown relied upon privileged corporate bodies such as the General Farms, the *Hôtel de Ville de
Paris*, and other cities to borrow money. The incidence of taxes was highly
uneven because of the many rights and exemptions held by particular social
groups (such as the nobility) or by particular regions. In sum, as Bossenga
observes: "This irreconcilable contradiction—privilege in return for loans,
but greater equality as the basis for taxation—prevented the monarchy from
rationalizing and creating a more equitable [and effectual] tax structure"
(Bossenga 1987: 125).[149]

France's public financial system looks unimpressive as compared with
Britain's. Over the course of the eighteenth century, British governments
were able to tax their citizenry at a higher level, and borrow more money at
lower rates of interest than could the French government.[150] Weighed down
by venal offices, the French system was resistant to change, however desirable change may have been.[151] Yet, the French fiscal structure should not be
condemned for its inefficiency at revenue extraction. There was an important political purpose which it served more ably. Like long-term debt in the
cases of England, Spain, and Holland, France's fiscal system was used to
build alliances and create domestic supporters for the regime.

Through financial and other venal offices, the French Crown was not only
able to bolster its finances (however unsatisfactorily), but it established political connections with local and national elites. In the province of Languedoc,
for example, taxes constituted one of the largest sources of liquid wealth, and
access to this flow of resources conferred substantial benefits. Taxes in-

volved the extraction of resources out of the province (and off to Paris), but also the redistribution of resources within it. Through the state financial machinery the Crown incorporated local Languedocian elites into the state apparatus.[152] The tax system became the foundation for common interests between the crown and local elites.[153]

At the national level, venal offices were an effective way to tap the resources of undertaxed groups. Mercantile capitalists and the aristocracy paid few taxes, but as they purchased offices or became involved in the administration of state finances the state gained access to their personal wealth.[154] Doing so brought obvious financial benefits but it also helped the Crown politically. France was a regionally diverse country and the absolutism of the French Crown was in practice quite constrained. There were numerous revolts and rebellions in the course of the seventeenth century, and the rule of the French monarch was often challenged and contested.[155] In the early seventeenth century, the opposition consisted of popular groups led by dissatisfied aristocrats. Expanding the number of state offices created a way to incorporate these elites and inhibit domestic resistance. Merging the financial interests of elites with those of the state gave them a stake in the success of the absolutist regime.[156] A political alliance between crown and elites was forged out of venal offices that gave those elites a vested interest in the viability of the crown, and the use of state offices as a political tool was recognized by one of Louis XIV's advisors who, commenting on the 1688 English revolution, stated that "if England had as many officials supported by the king as France does, the revolution would never have occurred. For it is certain that so many officials means so many committed people attached to the maintenance of royal authority. Without that authority they would be naught. If it were destroyed they would instantly lose the large sums of money with which they bought their positions" (quoted in Tilly, 1986: 161).[157]

The fiscal system went unreformed until the time of the French Revolution, and so one might well ask how effective it was in cultivating supporters with a vested interest in the regime. Did officeholders and rentiers rally to the side of Louis XVI in defiance of revolutionary forces? One cannot be sure, of course, but the fact that venal officeholders and other government creditors were compensated for their losses after the revolution is extremely revealing. Although debts and venal offices can create a financial interest in the continuation of a regime, that interest can be severed if the regime's opponents live up to the regime's obligations.[158] Venal offices were abolished in 1789, but their owners were to be compensated and the debts of the old regime settled.[159] By contrast, holders of British debt were bound more firmly to the post-1688 regime because of their belief that their claims would be repudiated if the Pretender were to take the throne.

CONCLUSION

These four cases set in clear relief the nature of Britain's financial revolution. Throughout the seventeenth century and into the eighteenth, all five countries were subject to the same intense fiscal pressures. How they resolved their financial problems was, however, highly varied, as was the degree of success. The Swedish solution required certain preconditions in order to work but when they were satisfied, even a small poor country could project disproportionate military power. Sweden externalized the financial and manpower costs of war but could only do so when fighting a successful offensive war in someone else's country. The United Provinces were also a small country but not a poor one. Although hampered by a decentralized polity that made decisive action almost impossible, the Dutch nevertheless exploited their domestic capital markets and through public borrowing managed to fund a substantial and ongoing military effort. The financial techniques they developed were appropriated by the British in the next century.

Spain was a larger country but, like Sweden, was economically backward. It was unable to externalize its costs, and had no domestic capital market to exploit. Furthermore, the monarchy was politically weak (being highly dependent on provincial elites for government) and the state apparatus was largely farmed out. Over the course of the century, Spain lurched from one military and financial disaster to the next, continually shedding its empire and losing its great power status. Spain was a lesson in how not to build up a state.

France was the largest and wealthiest of the five countries, and in theory had the strongest crown. Yet for a variety of political and administrative reasons, French government was unable to exploit fully France's domestic wealth, and could not follow the fiscal path set out by the Netherlands and Britain. France could have stood head and shoulders above the other great powers but instead was only first among equals.

Bankruptcies were common among early modern sovereign debtors. Spain and France rescheduled their debts numerous times, Sweden undertook the *reduktion*, and England had its Stop of the Exchequer. All of these events adversely affected government credit, however beneficial they were in the short run. The Spanish Crown in particular had to pay very high interest rates to compensate its creditors for the risk of default. The Netherlands, in contrast, lived up to its obligations, repaid its debts, and consequently enjoyed the highest creditworthiness. After the reform of the public financial system and the adoption of "Dutch finance," Britain also became a reliable debtor.

Across all the cases, it is obvious what a difference a thriving economy made. Capitalist economic development created the base upon which a state structure could be erected. Given sufficient market activity, even a "weak" state could deploy substantial military power, as the examples of Britain and the Netherlands attest. A backward economy was a substantial impediment that hurt Spain and which Sweden was able to overcome only because of its unique situation. Thus we witness in this period an early version of a relationship called the "structural dependence of the state." Rulers depend on economic activity for their revenues, and so almost regardless of their ideological perspective or political preferences, they are compelled to some extent to encourage capitalist economic development.[160]

By the end of the seventeenth century, Britain and France were the two main contenders for dominance in western Europe. Sweden and Spain were in decline, and the Dutch were so debt-laden as to be forced into a largely passive (and pacifist) stance. France was much the larger of the two but Britain's fiscal-military state made more efficient use of domestic economic resources. It seems clear why Britain's tax system worked better than France's but tax revenues were only part of the story. States raise money through taxing and through borrowing, so the system of public credit must also be considered. And it is not so obvious why a combination of annuities and venal offices could not have been as effective as one of annuities and joint-stock company shares.

There are many similarities between a venal office and a debt instrument issued by a public treasury. Both involved the exchange of a lump sum (paid by the creditor or officeholder) for a series of future interest payments (to be paid by the sovereign debtor). As well, both venal offices and debt instruments could be bought and sold on secondary markets and could be inherited like other forms of private property. Financially, there was little to distinguish them, at least in principle. The key difference was that venal offices involved financial, administrative, and social rights and privileges, whereas a debt instrument involved only financial claims. The owner of a government bond was entitled to cash interest payments, but no more. He or she had no other formal claims over the government, and so the vested interests of the bondholder qua bondholder in the government were strictly financial. The owner of a venal office, in contrast, possessed a richer set of rights and claims that extended beyond cash into social status (in the case of ennobling offices), and administrative power (when the office entailed public duties). It was the nonfinancial rights attached to venal offices which interfered with the ruler's ability to control or modify his own public bureaucracy. Reform of an organization built around venal offices wasn't possible unless the office owners were bought out first. This fundamental constraint applied as much to Louis XIV as to the post-revolutionary government a century later. Privilege, which made a venal office an attractive asset in the first place, was precisely what stopped the French Crown from tapping into all pools of wealth. Offices had to include privileges in order to be sold, but those privileges subsequently protected the wealth of the owner from further fiscal intrusions.

In addition to its fiscal mission, the public financial system served a political purpose as well. Whether through annuities, *renten*, joint-stock company shares, or venal offices, it aligned together the economic interests of the Crown (or the governing regime) with other elites and so established political relationships between them. As clever Eumenes recognized, creditors have an interest in the well-being of their debtor, for otherwise they lose their investment.[161] And so the more numerous the creditors become, the bigger the support group for the debtor; and the more substantial the debts, the stronger the support. Property was the substance out of which such political alliances were built, property in the form of financial obligations and venal offices. Brenner's (1993) notion of "politically constituted property rights" must be broadened to take account of the political nature of common forms of property (not just particular monopoly privileges, one-time concessions, or other "sweetheart" deals). To build a state is not just a process of constructing an extractive apparatus, it also involves forging political relationships with social and economic elites, and aligning their interests with those of the ruler. In different forms, property proved to be a remarkably effective device for this end.[162]

Chapter Five

FINANCIAL PROPERTY RIGHTS
AND THE STATE

We may boast of large fortunes, and quantities of money in
the funds. But where does this money exist? It exists only
in name, in paper, in public faith, in parliamentary
security: and that is undoubtedly sufficient for the
creditors of the public to rely on.
—Sir William Blackstone

. . . experience hath shewn, that property best answers
the purposes of civil life, especially in commercial
countries, when it's transfer and circulation are totally
free and unrestrained.
—Sir William Blackstone

Commerce and manufactures can seldom flourish long in
any state which does not enjoy a regular administration of
justice, in which the people do not feel themselves secure
in the possession of their property, in which the faith
of contracts is not supported by law, and in which the
authority of the state is not supposed to be regularly
employed in enforcing the payment of debts from all
those who are able to pay.
—Adam Smith

BRITISH public and private finance changed dramatically at the end of the
seventeenth century. The state's fiscal machinery developed, its ability to
borrow expanded, a London stock market emerged, and the number of joint-
stock companies grew. This newfound financial strength propelled Britain
ahead of Spain and Holland and into rough parity with the much larger
France. Yet, beneath the details and events it is not clear what caused
these changes, however consequential they were. It is not obvious why, for
example, this financial transformation did not happen fifty years earlier, or
fifty years later. Was it the inevitable culmination of long-term trends, or
the idiosyncratic outcome of a conjuncture of forces? What produced
Britain's market-based "weak" state? What caused the stock market to grow
so fast?

There are many factors to consider in explaining these financial developments but for simplicity's sake they can be grouped into two categories. The "demand" side is perhaps the most straightforward. The financial needs of the military led to increased government demand for tax revenues and borrowed money. The "supply side," in contrast, is not so simple: where did all the extra money come from? Among the most basic supply-related factors was the capacity of the domestic economy: How did the English economic base become large enough to support a massive fiscal structure? Where did the taxable income and wealth come from? Why did people loan their money?

England's economic base expanded in the late seventeenth century because of sustained growth in English overseas trade.[1] Much of the growth came from the importation of goods (sugar and tobacco from the Americas and textiles from India) that were re-exported to European markets. In addition, the new American colonies provided a protected market for English manufactures. A great deal of overseas trade occurred through joint-stock companies like the East India Company, or through such regulated companies as the Levant, Eastland, and Hamburg Companies. The accumulation of mercantile wealth provided a pool of capital that was available for investment, inasmuch as wealthy traders and capitalists, more than owners of landed wealth, were willing to consider nontraditional financial ventures.[2]

Economic capacity may have been necessary, but it was not sufficient to ensure an adequate supply of money to the government. Not all taxable wealth gets taxed, and not all lendable funds are loaned. How willingly a population tolerates taxation depends on the burden and legitimacy of the taxes, and the purposes for which tax revenues are used. In the latter respect, war was a traditional activity for which monarchs could call upon their subjects for financial support.[3] Thus, both William III and Anne expected a measure of cooperation with higher taxes to pay for their wars with France. If fighting dragged on, however, or if the war was especially expensive, that political support would diminish.

If the consent of taxpayers is important for tax revenues, it is absolutely critical for loans. Loans are by choice and so absent sufficient inducements, people will not lend their money.[4] Potential creditors can be swayed by the purposes for which the loan is sought—the more that they support the goal, the more likely they are to lend their money.[5] Loans create an opportunity for creditors to put their money "where their mouths are." Of course, they will also be influenced by the financial terms of the loan: the interest rate paid, and the chances of repayment. As the likelihood of repayment decreases, lenders will demand a higher rate of interest on their loans.[6] If the probability seems too small, lenders may not be willing to loan anything at all. There are, however, other aspects of a loan that may encourage people to lend.

Debts which are assignable are much more attractive to investors.[7] Assignability means that the debt can be transferred or alienated from the original creditor to a third party, and that the third party has as strong and complete a claim on the debtor as the original creditor (including the right to assign the debt to yet another person). Assignability can give to loans a highly desirable measure of liquidity. It confers upon debts a moneylike quality that allows them to be used in satisfaction of the creditor's own debts. Liquidity also lets lenders recover their capital, without requiring the borrower to repay it. Furthermore, since inalienable property rights cannot be exchanged, alienability is a necessary condition for a market. Like other property rights, alienability can be restricted in various ways.[8]

Increased stock market activity and expanded government borrowing both represented changes in economic behavior. People and institutions were doing something that they weren't doing before. Again, the change was mostly on the "supply" side, for in the early modern period there was nothing unusual about an expensive war. The central question is how to explain the development of a financial market, and the concomitant willingness of people with capital to invest in government debt. Economic theory provides several answers to this question, but is generally reluctant to use changing preferences as an explanation.[9] Most economists would not want to argue that people refused to loan money to the government in the 1660s because they preferred not to loan money to governments but that later on they acquired a "taste" for loans.

One of the best known of the New Economic Institutionalists, Douglass North, offers an explanation of this period. He argues for the importance of changing political and legal institutions to account for the growth in government borrowing. A shift in the institutional framework led to the development of what North and Weingast call an "impersonal capital market."[10] Their elegant analysis focuses on the property rights of public creditors (and makes no mention of changing preferences), but raises the more general issue of the financial property rights of all creditors, public and private. Property rights are defined and enforced by a legal system, so changes in the law can alter the rules of the economic game, redefining the meaning of ownership and reshaping people's behavior.[11] During the seventeenth century, increasing commercial litigation reflected both the importance of the legal system for commercial life and the growth of commerce. Economic actors were using the courts to enforce their contracts and protect their property rights.[12]

To understand the importance of law, I address three issues in this chapter. The first grows out of a discussion of North's analysis, and considers the enforcement and assignability of the property rights of public creditors. As a borrower, the monarch (or government) is in the unique position of having to enforce the legal rules that bind his or her own behavior. Potentially, this means the monarch is unlike other debtors in not being subject to the same set of rules. Second, because of the connection between public and private finance, I also consider the enforcement and assignability of private financial property rights. People's familiarity and experience with private debt instruments can have significant spillover effects for public finance, and the two sets of legal rules (one for debtor-creditor relationships that involve the sovereign, and another for those which don't) can influence one another. Finally, given the importance of joint-stock companies for public and private finance, I address the legal status of corporations in the seventeenth century. The discussion of law is brought to a close with a reconsideration of how well the political and legal changes identified by North can explain the financial changes discussed in chapter 3.

Financial instruments embody credit relationships: they specify a debtor, a creditor, and the extent and nature of the obligation between them. In this sense, they directly embody social relationships. Unlike other forms of property, a debt represents a partially consummated transaction. A creditor has given money to a debtor and has received in exchange a promise to repay the loan. The exchange is not completed on the spot, for when the loan is negotiated only one-half occurs—the lender gives money to the borrower. The other half is to occur sometime in the future, and what the creditor has is a commitment from the debtor to repay. The credibility of the commitment and how easily a creditor can enforce it, is therefore an essential and inescapable aspect of credit relationships and financial property rights. Furthermore, the creditor has an interest in the ability of the debtor to live up to the commitment, for anything that undercuts that ability goes against the creditor's interests.

INSTITUTIONALIST ANALYSIS OF ENGLISH FINANCIAL MARKETS

The New Economic Institutionalists, as this group has been labeled (Eggertsson 1990), point out that many markets have not enjoyed perfectly functioning contract law, costless information, or enforceable private property rights. The costs of transacting are frequently positive.[13] This affects how traders behave, for being rational they take into account the fact that their contracts will be imperfectly binding, that the information they have may be incomplete, inaccurate, or unevenly distributed, or that they may possess only partial or attenuated property rights. Institutionalists also point out that the provision of the framework for markets is itself a costly undertaking. Resources must be expended if contracts are to be enforced and property rights protected. Hence, the same kind of cost-benefit calculus that motivates behavior within the market also constrains the provision of the market framework itself. If it is too costly to acquire information, for example, then a certain amount of ignorance may be rational. It may be too expensive to anticipate and close all the loopholes in a contract, so some contracts remain incomplete. There may be an optimal level of contractual ambiguity. Or if it is too costly to specify fully private property rights, then a measure of unspecificity is also rational. With the application of economic tools of analysis to the framework for markets, institutionalists can explain various features of contracts, information, and property rights.

Douglass North (1981, 1990) cautions that efficiency explanations of the market framework can be too simplistic, and notes that there have been many historical instances of persistently inefficient property rights. If efficient property rights drive out inefficient ones, how could the latter survive for so long? North's answer takes into account the important role played by the state in the creation and enforcement of property rights. With the addition of the state (and its quest for revenues), the processes that affect property rights become more complicated. It is no longer simply that market forces shift communal property rights in the direction of private property rights.

According to North and Weingast (1989), North (1991, 1990), Levi (1988), and Root (1994), the political events of late seventeenth-century England played a significant role in improving public finances. The primary effect of constitutional shifts was to improve the property rights enjoyed by public creditors and thus encourage more lending to the government. North and Weingast focus especially upon the events of the Glorious Revolution that altered the balance of power between the English Crown and Parliament. Changes in public finance are attributed in large part to this shift in political power.

By contrasting early modern England with France, Margaret Levi argues that the weakness of the English Crown in relation to representative institutions like Parliament ultimately led to higher revenues for the English state.[14] The Crown had to make concessions to its constituents and grant them a greater voice in setting public revenues and expenditures. Citizens tolerated higher taxes in exchange for more control over spending, and their involvement in public finance reduced resistance to fiscal measures. Less resistance made it easier to extract revenues, and so net revenue (gross revenue minus the cost of revenue extraction) was higher. Levi's general point is that sovereign weakness (in relation to a parliament or other representative institution) led, in a somewhat ironic fashion, to fiscal strength.

North and Weingast give a more detailed analysis of English public finance. They are concerned with the legal rules that underpin markets and economic growth, and address the ways in which a state can credibly commit to comply with those rules. As the institution that establishes and maintains property rights, a state can easily alter or violate the rules to its own advantage.[15] States can back out of their agreements with constituents, or fail to honor commitments. Whether or not they do depends on the incentives they face, and these are structured by political institutions.

The Glorious Revolution produced a set of institutional arrangements that enabled the English state to make more credible commitments. Before the Revolution, the argument goes, public creditors demanded high interest rates to compensate for the substantial possibility that the King would default on his loans, and in effect confiscate lender wealth. Sovereign immunity left creditors with little hope of recovering their money since the normal legal recourse was unavailable to them.[16] But after 1688–89, commitments became more credible and the risks declined. This meant that the state was able to borrow more money at lower rates of interest. Institutional changes enhanced the willingness of potential lenders to supply money to the state.

North and Weingast argue that in the early seventeenth century the English Crown had to undertake "forced loans" to raise money because of its poor financial situation. These loans were seldom repaid fully or in a timely manner.[17] The Crown also raised money by granting economic monopolies to favored individuals but did so in a way that hurt existing economic interests. When it suited its short-term financial interests, the Crown used its prerogative powers and institutions to circumvent the property rights of citizens.[18] Although the Civil War altered the position of the Crown, most of its powers were reinstated at the time of the Restoration in 1660, and so potentially at least, its ability to abuse the property rights of Crown subjects was undiminished.[19]

Not until the Glorious Revolution did the Crown's position change enough to curtail its ability to interfere with creditors' and citizens' property rights. William and Mary wielded considerable power but the role of Parliament was much greater than it had been under James II. The Crown was now financially dependent upon Parliament. Since Parliament represented the upper and upper-middle classes of English society, these groups indirectly gained a measure of control over the workings of public finance.[20] Additionally, the common-law courts became more independent of the Crown, and more resistant to political pressures from above.[21] Legal rights were henceforth less likely to change depending on how political winds were blowing, and however much the Crown might wish to violate property rights, its ability to do so was sharply curtailed.

North and Weingast examine the consequences of these political changes. They point to the tremendous increase in public borrowing as evidence that lenders were now willing to extend funds to the government, knowing that their loans enjoyed the security of Parliament. Not only did the size of the public debt increase but the interest rate on the debt declined.[22] They conclude that change in property rights brought about this growth in the market for public debt, and in effect endorse the viewpoint expressed earlier by Sir William Blackstone.

The War of the Spanish Succession provides a telling contrast with the Third Dutch War. During both, financial pressures created a temptation to default on loans. During the Third Dutch War, Charles II succumbed to that temptation and stopped the Exchequer, whereas later on Anne did not. The difference lay not in the personal morality or probity of the two sovereigns, nor in Anne's greater fondness for investors, but rather in the constitutional limits that constrained Anne far more than Charles. Investors had better reason to suppose that debts incurred under Anne would be repaid. This politically induced change in the rules of the market affected not only public finance, although that is for North and Weingast the best measure of change.[23] The development of a market for public debt ". . . provided a large and positive externality for the parallel development of a market for private debt" (North and Weingast 1989: 825). Credible commitments not to interfere with property rights led to the development of both public and private financial markets.

North and Weingast's account has several noteworthy features. As an intangible form of property, the property rights for financial instruments preceded the market for them—property rights had priority over the market.[24] North and Weingast's political focus is exclusively on constitutional matters such as the separation of powers, the autonomy of the judiciary, and the balance of power between Crown and Parliament. Partisan politics, particularly the conflict between Whigs and Tories, is deemed to be largely irrelevant. Moreover, they emphasize the *enforceability* of the property rights of public creditors rather than the *assignability* of such rights. These are separate dimensions which both affect the willingness of creditors to loan money. Insofar as North and Weingast attend to the enforcement of property rights, they fail to detail what those property rights were. They do not consider how the content of property rights, as opposed to the strength of their protection, affected market growth. Finally, their explanation focuses on the institutional framework of the financial market, not upon the motives or preferences of the individuals who inhabited that market. They follow the standard assumption that investors are concerned with risk and rate of return and do not consider other goals. For example, despite its centrality in English social and political life, North and Weingast do not explore the role of religion either in financial markets or in the constitutional changes that are crucial for their argument.[25]

The Stop of the Exchequer appears at first glance simply to illustrate many of the shortcomings North and Weingast attribute to pre–Glorious Revolution public finance. Yet its legal ramifications continued to unfold into the eighteenth century, thirty years after the event itself and fully a

decade after the Glorious Revolution. The Stop does much more than affirm
North and Weingast, it affords the opportunity to understand in detail the
legal options available to sovereign creditors in the pre–Glorious Revolution
era when their property rights were violated. It also sheds light on the importance of assignability of debts, and more generally on the content of public creditors' property rights.

THE STOP OF THE EXCHEQUER

The pressure of immanent war with the Dutch led in 1672 to the Stop of the
Exchequer, a unilateral suspension of debt repayment which when finally
calculated in 1677 totaled over £1.3 million.[26] At a time when annual Crown
income was usually less than £2 million, this was a huge sum. Crown revenues were tied up servicing older debts, and the Stop freed them up to fund
military expenditures.[27] Charles II's foreign policy shifted in 1670 as he
joined with France to be able to pursue war with Holland without fear that
Louis XIV would intervene on the side of the Dutch, as happened during
the Second Dutch War (1665–67). Domestically, Charles and his advisors
hoped that war with the Dutch would make him less beholden to Parliament.[28] Recalling the successes of the First Dutch War, which included the
capture of many Dutch commercial vessels and payment of a substantial
war indemnity by the losers, Charles expected that this war would also produce a short-term financial windfall.[29] A defeat of England's main commercial rival would also mean more trade, and hence higher customs revenues
in the long run.[30]

In the early 1670s, Charles II was heavily indebted to a small group of
London goldsmith-bankers. Goldsmith-bankers held the bulk of the Treasury Orders that, ironically, had been designed and implemented to reduce
the Crown's reliance on its small circle of creditors. The system of finance
instituted in 1667 to circumvent the goldsmith-bankers and borrow directly
from the public had failed.[31] Goldsmith-bankers took deposits from the
general public, for which they paid 6% interest, and then loaned the money
to the Crown, earning approximately 10% interest. Much of the borrowing
arose out of the simultaneous decline in public revenues and increase in
spending brought about by the London Fire, the Plague, and the Second
Dutch War. Thomas Clifford, one of Charles II's five chief ministers, was
primarily responsible for the decision to institute the Stop in early 1672.

The Stop was timed to occur when Parliament was not in session. It was
part of an overall strategy to present Parliament with a successful war that
would greatly strengthen Charles II's political and financial position. When
Lord Keeper Bridgeman, the chief legal officer of the Crown, hesitated to
support the legality of the Stop, he was quickly dismissed and replaced by
the then more cooperative Shaftesbury.[32] Goldsmith-bankers had been

openly criticized in the Commons for charging excessive interest on their loans to the Crown,[33] and so it is perhaps not too surprising that when Parliament reconvened in 1673 there was little concern for those hurt by the Stop.[34] Instead, the Commons brought its critical attention to bear on the Declaration of Indulgence issued by Charles II shortly after the Stop. The purpose of the Declaration was to grant some measure of religious tolerance to dissenting Protestants. On this occasion, therefore, Parliament showed more concern for religious policy than for the protection of property rights.

Initially, repayments were suspended for a single year, until 31 December 1672 but the suspension was extended to May 1673, and then to January 1674, as Charles urged Parliament to supply the money necessary to begin repayment.[35] Parliament was unmoved and so outside appeals were made to redress the situation. In a legal and political analysis, replete with erudite references to historical precedent, Turnor (1674) took the bankers' side, posing arguments both practical and principled. The Stop, according to him, was an unambiguous violation of property rights.[36] Turnor argued that the protection of private property from the depredations of the sovereign had long been a principle of the common law.[37] Furthermore, this principle should not be compromised, even under wartime conditions.[38] Not only did the Stop violate common-law tradition, it also contradicted the explicit promises of the King. Turnor noted in addition that the number of people indirectly affected was much larger than the small number of goldsmith-bankers directly hurt by the Stop.[39] The Stop resulted in financial losses for many people, not just for an unfortunate few. Turnor also foresaw dire consequences for future credit. Having violated the trust of creditors, it was likely that future borrowing would be difficult: "I am afraid that when men shall be importuned to lend money upon any future Occasion, they will be apt enough to discourse within themselves, That that which hath been done may be done again."[40]

Perhaps in answer to such entreaties, starting in June 1674 the Exchequer paid out £140,000 annually to creditors as interest on their debt, pending final determination of the exact amount owed.[41] By 1677 the sums had been calculated exactly, and so on 30 April 1677, letters patent were issued that set aside revenues from the hereditary excise to pay 6% interest on the debt, payable in quarterly installments.[42] The letters patent also gave the goldsmith-bankers the option of assigning some or all of their interest payment directly to their creditors.[43] The bankers' creditors, most of whom were former depositors, could then receive their money directly from the Exchequer. Additionally, the bankers were protected from being sued by their creditors. There was no provision to repay the principle of the loans but nevertheless bankers (and their creditors) welcomed the decision.[44] The property rights of sovereign creditors had been violated but now a measure of compensation was forthcoming.

For the rest of Charles II's reign, creditors received regular interest payments but only a few were made under James II. By the accession of William and Mary, the payments were in considerable arrears, for only about six years' worth of interest payments were made from 1677 to 1689. Attempts by the bankers to gain satisfaction from Parliament failed, and Parliament used the hereditary excise as backing for a £250,000 war loan without making any provision for the debt to the bankers (2 William & Mary, c.3). Their inadequacy notwithstanding, the revenues that had been earmarked to pay the bankers' debt were being diverted to another use, and so it was clear that some kind of action was necessary.[45]

One possibility was to take legal action but the alternatives available to a Crown creditor were not impressive. If the Crown defaulted on its debts, either canceling them outright or postponing repayment, there was traditionally only one avenue open: the petition of right. Sovereign immunity meant that a Crown creditor could not sue the King in the King's own courts, for the Crown was above the law.[46] The petition of right was one of a larger class of petitions of grace. The petitioner would make his case directly to the Crown, establishing and documenting his claims as if in a court of law. Procedurally, however, all the advantages lay with the Crown. Proceedings were complex, lengthy, and could be suspended at any point. The burden of proof lay on the petitioner and even if he or she could prove the case it was still up to the Crown whether or not to grant the request.[47] Obviously, if the Crown defaulted on loans, the creditors affected were in a very difficult position, and their chances of recovery were slim indeed.[48]

Faced with the unhappy necessity of legal proceedings, in 1691 the bankers and their assignees brought a suit of *monstrans de droit* in the Court of Exchequer (the court with jurisdiction over cases involving Crown revenue) for payment of the arrears. They did not present a petition of right directly to William and Mary. The validity of their claim to the interest payments was easy to establish, and so the outcome rested primarily on a procedural question: had they followed the correct procedure?[49]

With only one dissenting opinion, the Court of Exchequer affirmed that they had used the right procedure, and so ruled in the bankers' favor. Since the government didn't want to repay the debt, the Attorney General appealed the decision to the Court of Exchequer Chamber. This court of appeal consisted of the Lord Treasurer and the Lord Chancellor (or Lord Keeper), assisted by the judges of the King's Bench and Common Pleas. The offices of Lord Treasurer and Lord Chancellor were both political appointments, and the office of Lord Treasurer was in commission. Thus, when the Whig Sir John Somers was appointed Lord Keeper in 1693, the case came before him.[50] All of the advising judges argued that the debt continued to exist, and all but two argued that *monstrans de droit* was the appropriate legal action for the creditors. However, Somers rejected their counsel and ruled in 1696 that a petition of right was the correct procedure, and that a *monstrans de droit* was not.[51] He also asked for a ruling from the advising judges on whether or not he could override their advice. On this question, the judges ruled seven to three in his favor.[52] Somers's decision was widely regarded as a political rather than a legal one, since at that point the government could ill afford additional debts.[53]

With this ruling going against them, the final option for the bankers and their assignees was an appeal to the House of Lords, which they brought in 1699. Hearings in the Lords took place in early 1700 and the Lords reversed the decision of the Court of Exchequer Chamber and ruled in favor of the bankers.[54] This final decision recognized an action of *monstrans de droit* brought in the Court of Exchequer as a legal alternative to the petition of right. The bankers were vindicated. However, the decision did not provide for actual repayment of the debt. Since Parliament had already used the hereditary excise to provide for the Civil List and as security for loans,[55] it wasn't until a statute of 1701 (12, 13 William III, c.12) that provision was actually made for payment of the accrued interest. By the final settlement, the capital of creditors had been reduced by about one-half, but after almost thirty years something was better than nothing.[56]

The Stop made little impression when it occurred. Parliament, for example, was more concerned about religion than property. Yet as the years passed, it remained in the public consciousness, perceived as a violation of the property rights of public creditors. Subsequent discussions of public credit often mentioned the Stop (and invariably blamed it on evil counselors rather than Charles II). From the beginning, advocates for the bankers argued that the Stop was an unambiguous breach of property rights,[57] and it was invoked for years to warn against the abuse of public creditors.[58] With the additional security offered by Parliamentary involvement in public credit,[59] a recurrence of a Stop became less likely and so, it was argued, allowed the government to borrow at lower interest rates.[60]

The Bankers' Case established a more satisfactory procedure for sovereign creditors than the petition of right. It gave creditors greater security, and more easily enforceable property rights. Ironically, the case concluded only after the public financial system had changed so as to make sovereign defaults less likely in the first place. Should a default occur, the Bankers' Case established a precedent that was favorable to public creditors, but such a default was much less likely.

Some features of the Stop are consistent with the North-Weingast argument.[61] Before the Glorious Revolution, legal claims against the Crown were not easily enforceable and the Crown abused the property rights of its creditors. When these creditors sought redress, they were defeated by a politically controlled court system until they reached the House of Lords, the highest court. Whether the eventual success of the bankers and their assignees was due to the constitutional changes associated with the Glorious Revolution is not obvious. On the one hand, greater autonomy of the judiciary, a factor stressed by North and Weingast, did not play a major role in the Stop. On the other hand, and consistent with North-Weingast, it was Parliament, rather than the Crown (or Crown ministers) which finally affirmed the property rights of the aggrieved creditors. Sufficient parliamentary power vis-à-vis the Crown would ensure the protection of those rights. Yet, the politics of the case were not simply constitutional, for party conflict appears to have played a role in the Lords' reversal of Somers's ruling. A Tory majority in the Lords was responsible for overturning Somers the Whig, and Somers' own legal ruling was used against him when he was later impeached by his Tory enemies.[62] A Whig majority in the Lords could well have sustained Somers, and so the final affirmation of sovereign creditors' property rights was not simply a function of constitutional structures but also a product of the Whig-Tory conflict.

The enforceability of the property rights of sovereign creditors was the key question raised by the Stop of the Exchequer. The assignability of public debts was a less central issue, although it was important for the development of financial markets more generally. Bankers' debts were made assignable in recognition of the perilous financial situation which the Stop put them in but the letters patent only applied to these particular debts, not to sovereign debts in general.

The assignability of private debts was highly problematic under common law, but the assignability of sovereign debts was a different matter. In the twelfth and thirteenth centuries, when most lending involved Jewish bankers, English kings could assign the debts they acquired from Jews. Rather than paying his own debts in coin, the king would try to transfer to his creditors the obligations owed him.[63] Often, the assignee (the person to whom the king assigned a debt) did not receive the right to assign that debt to yet another person. In other words, such debts were not generally transferable.[64] Tallies, the notched wooden sticks used by the Exchequer as a kind of receipt of payment, were also assignable.[65] Later on, as Crown ministers tried to reform the Exchequer and update its medieval procedures and devices, assignability remained an important characteristic. For example, the Treasury Orders introduced by Sir George Downing in 1665 could be transferred from one person to another upon written endorsement on the order, and notice to the Exchequer.[66] But it is important to recognize the difference between de facto and de jure assignability. In the early eighteenth century, government annuities, government lottery loans, and company shares were all legally assignable. As a practical matter, however, it was much easier to transfer title in company shares than the other two. The actual procedure was more cumbersome when dealing with the Exchequer (for annuities and lottery loans) than with a joint-stock company. Furthermore, the Exchequer offices were in Westminster and so at some distance from London's financial district. Hence, in practice, company shares were a much more liquid asset than annuities or lottery loans.

PRIVATE FINANCIAL INSTRUMENTS

The growth of the national debt was influenced not only by the changing relationship between the government and its creditors but also by changes that affected all debtor-creditor relationships. In particular, the emergence of an active London capital market at the end of the seventeenth century facilitated public borrowing. Public trading of joint-stock companies contributed to the emergence of this capital market, but legal developments also played a role. Changes in the law pertaining to financial instruments affected the general depth and liquidity of the market.

What is especially interesting about debts as a form of property is that they directly embodied social *relationships* between one person, as debtor, and another, as creditor. Debtor-creditor law therefore directly affects how people relate to one another. Legal change occurred as part of a general process through which the "law merchant" (or *lex mercatoria*) was "incorporated" into the common law.[67] Historically, the common law did not recognize many of the relationships and legal devices that merchants used in commerce, and so it was hard, for example, to construct and enforce complex debtor-creditor relationships using the common-law framework.[68]

Liquidity and negotiability are closely connected aspects of debtor-creditor relations. The modern definition of negotiability (as in "negotiable securities") encompasses several features. A negotiable financial instrument is one which is transferable or assignable by delivery, which can be sued upon by the transferee, and which is held in good title by the transferee if taken in good faith and for value, even if the title of the transferor was defective.[69] Many of the essential elements of the doctrine of negotiability in English law developed in the latter part of the seventeenth century.[70] The legal characteristics of specific instruments such as promissory notes, inland bills of exchange, and outland bills of exchange took shape during this period.

Negotiability is important for the development of financial markets because it allows creditors to transfer their claims on a debtor to third parties. A relationship that was dyadic (involving only debtor and creditor) can become triadic (or even more distant if a fourth or fifth person becomes involved). Depending upon the period of the loan, a relationship that was of medium or long-term duration could become almost ephemeral, since creditors would be able to recover their capital and terminate the relationship as soon as they transferred title to a third party. Negotiability confers liquidity, which makes a loan a much more attractive investment. By turning to what is now called the secondary capital market, a creditor can recover his or her capital when needed. The more active the secondary market, the greater the liquidity and flexibility.[71]

In addition, negotiability leads to debtor-creditor relationships that are more distant and anonymous.[72] With no assignment of debts, the two parties who originally enter into a relationship are still bound together when the debt is finally repaid and the relationship extinguished. With assignment to a third, fourth, or higher-order party, a debtor may have no idea who he or she owes money to. Furthermore, liquidity means that creditors are more willing to lend money to people they are unfamiliar with.[73] Both the debtor and the creditor may know very little about each other, and the social distance between them can be very great.

Formal debtor-creditor relationships in the seventeenth century were constructed using financial instruments like the promissory note (also called the "bill obligatory") and the bill of exchange (both inland and outland). The promissory note was a domestic instrument and became prominent in England as mid-seventeenth-century goldsmith-bankers issued receipts for the deposits they received from the public.[74] The receipt constituted a claim on money in the possession of the goldsmith banker and represented a bankers' debt or promissory note.[75] Bankers' notes began to circulate as depositors used them to satisfy their own debts (depending on whether the promise to pay was to "X," to "X or order," or to "X or bearer"). A key legal question concerned whether or not the transferee had as good title to the money as did the original depositor (the transferor). In other words, were promissory notes assignable? To the extent that they were, they could function as a form of paper money whose value would then depend on the solvency of the banker.[76]

Bills of exchange were much older than promissory notes. Since the Middle Ages, they had been used by merchants engaged in long-distance trade for international and interregional payments.[77] In their most elaborate form, bills of exchange involved four parties: W (the purchaser of the bill), X (the drawer), Y (the drawee), and Z (the payee). W wishes to make a payment to Z, and so W pays X, who draws a bill on Y, to ensure that Y makes the sum available to Z. W would obtain the bill from X, and send it to Z, who would present it for payment to Y. Usually, W and Z would be in different cities or countries, and because the physical transfer of specie was very difficult, bills of exchange were extremely useful. The issue of negotiability concerned the ability of Y to transfer the bill to some other party, YY, and whether YY would have as good a title as Y. The difference between inland and outland bills of exchange consisted only in whether the bill involved an international payment (outland) or a domestic payment (inland).

Merchants were familiar with both financial instruments, particularly the bill of exchange. Disputes concerning bills of exchange were traditionally settled according to a loose body of international and mercantile law and custom called the law merchant.[78] The origins of the law merchant were quite distinct from those of the common law, with its primary concern with rights over land.[79] The law merchant was administered in local courts in port towns or at commercial fairs, and later in the Admiralty Courts.[80]

The law merchant had its problems. As a specific law for merchants, the remedies it offered were not available generally and the law merchant did not enjoy the full backing of the state.[81] The legal remedies for commercial disputes available under common law before the end of the seventeenth century were not very satisfactory. A third party in possession of a bill of exchange or promissory note was in a weak legal position since persons who were not the original parties to a contract were not entitled to demand the performance of any duties specified by the contract.[82] This meant that transferees did not have the same legal rights as the original creditor if a debtor defaulted on a loan. *Assumpsit*, the legal action usually used to enforce a contract under common law, could not be applied easily to bills of exchange.[83] Financial instruments that were not readily transferable, and hence not negotiable, made for less liquid capital markets. This fact was readily appreciated by Josiah Child when he contrasted English and Dutch law:

> The law that is in use among them [the Dutch] for transferrence of Bills for Debt from one man to another: This is of extraordinary advantage to them in their Commerce; by means whereof, they can turn their Stocks twice or thrice in Trade, for once that we can in England. (Child 1668: 6)[84]

Financial instruments could not be easily transferred under common law because they were regarded as "choses in action": a form of property that was enforceable by a legal action and not by possession.[85] A legal action was personal, involving a particular plaintiff and defendant. Hence the right to an action was not assignable.[86] A plaintiff could not transfer his or her right to an action to someone else. "Choses in action" originally included various actions (on contracts, debts, torts, etc.) and was later extended to cover the documents which evidenced the rights to those actions, including bills, notes, and company shares.[87]

During the seventeenth century, the common-law and Admiralty courts disputed jurisdiction over commercial litigation in England.[88] Traditionally, this litigation was conducted in the Admiralty Courts, where merchants could resolve their disputes quickly and cheaply.[89] With the expansion of international trade, commercial litigation became an increasingly valuable (and lucrative) jurisdiction.[90] Attempts by the common-law courts to wrest it away from the Admiralty Courts were especially vigorous when Sir Edward

Coke became a Common Pleas judge in 1606.[91] Using writs of prohibition,[92] the common-law judges halted proceedings for cases before the Admiralty Courts. After Coke's departure from the bench, the Admiralty judges responded to these attacks by calling upon Charles I to adjudicate the jurisdictional dispute. A kind of "cease-fire" was arranged in 1633 but this did not halt common-law poaching for long.[93]

Through much of the seventeenth century, merchants could litigate in one or both of these court systems. The Admiralty Courts were better-suited to dealing with the kinds of problems faced by merchants: judicial rulings (if not justice itself) could be obtained there more easily, cheaply, and expeditiously. These courts were being severely challenged by the common-law courts, although the latter provided less satisfactory procedures for mercantile cases. The existence of two overlapping jurisdictions added uncertainty to all commercial litigation since a dispute resolved in one forum could be reopened in the other.

During the seventeenth century, the law merchant gradually merged into the common law.[94] This process took place in several stages, and the tenure of Sir John Holt as Chief Justice on the King's Bench (1689–1710) was especially important. First, mercantile customs were recognized as providing the basis for a legal duty under common law. This was only a limited change because a custom, to serve as the basis for law, had to have existed "since time immemorial," and could apply only to certain groups of persons or in particular locations. The custom also had to be established in each and every court case.[95] But through a series of precedents, these restrictions were lifted by the end of the seventeenth century.[96]

Bills of exchange payable to "X or order" were already recognized by mercantile custom as assignable by endorsement and delivery. With the incorporation of the law merchant, this also became true under common law.[97] In the case of a default on a bill of exchange, the last endorsee (the holder of the bill) could sue any prior endorser. Bills of exchange payable to "X or bearer," however, were still not transferable under common law.[98]

The situation for promissory notes was different. Promissory notes were a new instrument and there was no place for them in the traditional law merchant. Promissory notes were also considered quite different from bills of exchange, and consequently the mercantile customs that pertained to the latter did not necessarily apply to them.[99] The distinction between the two instruments was drawn sharply when Chief Justice Holt ruled in Clerke v. Martin (1702) that a promissory note payable to "X or order" was not a bill of exchange, and hence not negotiable.[100] This ruling was upheld in three subsequent cases and so it remained for the Promissory Notes Act of 1704 (3 & 4 Anne, c.9) to settle the matter. By that act, all notes, whether payable to "X," or to "X or order," or to "X or bearer," were made negotiable.[101]

The establishment of negotiability for bills of exchange and promissory notes altered property rights under common law for private debtor-creditor relationships. These changes did not involve public creditors and so did not directly influence public finance. Yet by enhancing the general liquidity of the London capital market, they had an important indirect effect. The presence of a more liquid market made it easier for the British government to borrow money.

One consequence of these legal changes was that debtor-creditor relationships became less personal. With negotiability, such relationships conjoined abstract social roles into which any number of different persons might enter. A debt, as a chose in action, could not traditionally be assigned under common law because it was considered a personal relationship between two specific parties.[102] In contrast, negotiability meant that debts could be assigned to third parties, and therefore that the debt obliged the debtor, no matter who the creditor was. Legal change created the potential for a much more anonymous and impersonal market.

JOINT-STOCK COMPANIES

Joint-stock companies, particularly the Bank of England, the South Sea Company, and the East India Company, played important roles in English public finance. In this period, there were no major developments in the laws for joint-stock companies until the Bubble Act of 1720 (6 George I, c.18).[103] There was, however, a large increase in the number of companies and in trading activity on the London stock market.[104] An institutional account of London financial markets must therefore consider the legal framework within which such companies operated. In particular, sovereign creditor property rights were as much influenced by the law governing joint-stock companies as by the outcome of the Stop of the Exchequer, for many creditors loaned money to the government using the companies as intermediaries. People invested in Bank of England stock, for example, and the money was subsequently loaned to the government. Only annuity holders and purchasers of lottery tickets loaned directly to the government.

People in seventeenth-century England wishing to mobilize capital for a large commercial undertaking had two available organizational forms: the joint-stock company and the partnership. For those who wanted powers of self-government or monopoly control over a trade, there were also two options: the joint-stock company and the regulated company. These different alternatives possessed very different legal characteristics. A major difference between the joint-stock company and the partnership was "perpetual succession."[105] On the death of a partner, a partnership was legally dissolved. In contrast, the death of a shareholder in a joint-stock company did not threaten the existence of the company, although it raised the issue of who got the deceased's shares. Company owners could come and go, but the company they owned could continue on, potentially forever.

Joint-stock companies and regulated companies frequently enjoyed monopoly rights over trade with some part of the world. The difference between the two was that each member of a regulated company traded using his own capital (subject to the rules of the company) while members of a joint-stock company pooled their capital and traded as a single unit.[106] If pooling capital was important, then the joint-stock was clearly the superior option.[107]

There were no general laws of incorporation and so the establishment of a joint-stock company required either a royal charter or a parliamentary statute. Joint-stock companies were therefore exceptional entities. Royal charters were most common before the Revolution of 1688 but parliamentary statutes became necessary after. Such charters and statutes typically granted the right of perpetual succession, the right to sue and be sued, to have a common seal, and to own property. Companies were also restricted and empowered in more particular ways. The East India Company, for example, received a monopoly on trade with the East Indies. The Bank of England could own property, but was prohibited from purchasing Crown lands or from trading in goods. Joint-stock companies were typically headed by a governor, a deputy-governor, and a number of assistants or directors, all of whom were elected by the shareholders for year-long terms. Except in unusual circumstances, company ownership was separated from control, and generally shareholders had little direct influence over company policy.

As mentioned earlier, shares in a company, like financial bills and promissory notes, were "choses in action," a form of property that was not assignable under common law and which therefore could not be easily traded on a market.[108] Not only is liquidity an attractive characteristic for a financial asset but without some way to transfer ownership of shares, perpetual succession becomes impossible.[109] The inclusion of specific articles in company charters stating that the shares of the company were to be freely and legally transferable and assignable helped to resolve the problem.[110] Assignability de jure was enhanced by the fact that the actual bureaucratic procedure for transferring company shares was relatively easy, especially as compared with annuities and lottery loan tickets.[111] Merchants, among others, valued liquidity, and consequently had a strong preference for company shares over annuities and lottery tickets.[112] In a similar fashion, company shares were explicitly granted the status of personal, not real property (which had important implications for the inheritance of shares).[113]

Another set of constraints on the transferability of shares derived from the historical antecedents of the joint-stock company form. Joint-stock companies (as well as regulated companies) inherited a number of features from guilds, a much older form of corporate organization.[114] Early companies, including the East India Company, were considered to be a kind of brother-hood. Shareholders were also members, and as such had to take an oath upon entry into the company. They could be fined if absent from company meetings or if they engaged in improper conduct.[115] The similarity with fraternal societies extended to the feasts and other social events that companies would occasionally stage.

The guild form of organization influenced the transfer of shares and how individuals could gain the freedom of the company. Two traditional ways to obtain membership in a privileged group such as a guild were to be the son of a member, or to be a member's apprentice. The East India Company, which for most of the seventeenth century was the largest of the joint-stock companies, acknowledged both as ways to gain company membership.[116] To purchase company shares on a market was not the only way to become a member.[117] Privileged groups had a right to be selective about new members, and this meant that company shares were not freely assignable.[118] The East India Company, for example, could exert some control over its membership (at first foreigners were excluded), and the right to alienate shares was not unconditional.[119]

The legal rights, privileges, and obligations of shareholders were not entirely clear. Limited liability, which restricts shareholder liability to the money invested in shares, was not a fully developed doctrine. Those who subscribed to company shares might be subject to subsequent assessments if the company tried to increase its capital. In addition, it was uncertain whether such assessments were limited, and it was also not obvious that the liability for assessment was transferred along with the shares. An original subscriber could still be liable long after he had sold his shares,[120] and in one case a court ruled that company shareholders could be assessed more money in order to satisfy the debts of their company.[121]

Ownership of joint-stock company shares was proven by registration with the company. Each of the three major companies kept a stock ledger which detailed the accounts of all shareholders, as well as any transfers of shares among them. Ownership was evidenced by an entry in the ledger, not by a piece of paper held by the shareowner.[122] This is why all share transfers had to be registered with the company, for otherwise the purchaser would not have a legally secure title.[123] Since their property depended on it, shareowners had considerable incentive to register with the company. Once a year the company's books would be closed and everyone's account calculated in order to determine who could participate in the annual elections and vote for company directors.

By the end of the seventeenth century, joint-stock companies were an increasingly common way to mobilize capital. Shares were sold to gather from many sources money to pursue some commercial undertaking. Since only a small number of shareholders possessed decision-making power (those who were elected governor, deputy-governor, or assistant), joint-stock shares were mainly a passive investment. Being "choses in action," company shares were subject to restrictions on their transferability that had to be circumvented explicitly in company charters. Additional constraints on the transfer of shares followed from the guildlike organization which many companies inherited. Although there was no sudden event or discrete legal change equivalent to the Bankers' Case or the Promissory Notes Act of 1704, these restrictions disappeared during the latter part of the seventeenth century.[124] Their disappearance, however, had little to do with the Glorious Revolution.

LIMITS OF NORTH AND WEINGAST

Changes in property rights helped to develop London's capital markets and consequently enhance the strength of Britain's "weak" state. The evolution of property rights influenced the willingness of people with capital to lend it to the government and to private borrowers. That willingness was a direct function of the security and assignability of financial property rights. Lenders who can legally enforce their property rights, or who can freely assign them to others, are more likely to loan their money. Secure but unassignable claims are certainly better than insecure claims but they still suffer the considerable defect of illiquidity. In this sense, the emphasis North and Weingast put upon the legal framework for capital markets is well placed. But the stock market was also affected at a very basic level by politics, and in the early eighteenth century this meant party conflict.

North and Weingast argue for the importance of the shift in political power from Crown to Parliament. In their analysis, the sovereign creditor led the way for general capital market development—externalities were substantial enough that improvements in the property rights of sovereign creditors affected private debtor-creditor relationships. Their focus is on the security or enforceability of sovereign creditor property rights, and they note how this security increased after the Glorious Revolution. Yet, North and Weingast address only a subset of property rights. The assignability of public debts was not really affected by the Glorious Revolution, for it had been in place since the late Middle Ages. Indeed, the debt instruments involved in the Stop of the Exchequer, an event which problematized in dramatic fashion sovereign creditors' property rights, were legally freely assignable. Furthermore, both the security and assignability of private debts were influenced by the incorporation of the law merchant into common law, which had little to do with the Glorious Revolution. Even if the sovereign creditor led the way for the enforceability of financial property rights (via "externalities"), it certainly did not do so for their assignability. Finally, North and Weingast discuss public indebtedness as if it consisted mostly of a direct relationship between the sovereign and his or her creditors. Some of the debt was direct, but much of it was indirect, mediated by the joint-stock companies. No adequate account of the national debt can fail to give them careful scrutiny.

North and Weingast's analysis is accurate as far as it goes but it does not go far enough. They neglect other changes in financial property rights that were as relevant to public finance as constitutional politics. They fail to consider adequately the importance of joint-stock companies for public finance. They overlook the improvements in public revenues (such as the switch from tax farming to direct collection) that helped public borrowing but which predate 1689.[125] Finally, having argued for the importance of shifts in power (from Crown to Parliament), they completely disregard how political power in Parliament was organized. To their credit, North and Weingast stress the importance of institutions, but they fail to consider political parties. Power in Parliament was now run along party lines, and party strife directly influenced public finance. Partisan conflict even shaped the enforceability of sovereign creditors' property rights, as the final outcome of the Stop of the Exchequer attested. The Whig minister Somers tried to help the government reduce its obligations to the Bankers' assignees, but was defeated by Tories in the House of Lords who were happy to see Somers fail.

Legal changes created the possibility for more anonymous, impersonal, and abstract debtor-creditor relationships. Public debts were no longer the personal debts of the king, and most private debts became freely alienable. The debtor-creditor relationship did not permanently bind two individuals, for upon assignment of the debt, the role of creditor could be passed from one person to the next. A debt became more like an alienable object than a stable binding relationship. With free assignment of debts, debtors no longer knew who their creditors were, and as the social distance between debtors and creditors expanded, creditors knew less and less about debtors. A face-to-face relationship was transformed into a more anonymous obligation. Agnew observed that in market exchange more generally,

> buyers and sellers transacted their business along principles and with instruments that rendered the participants conveniently yet distressingly opaque to one another. Whether consolidated in a bourse or exchange or dispersed throughout a network of petty traders, commodity exchange was gravitating during the sixteenth and seventeenth centuries toward a set of operative rules that fostered a formal and instrumental indifference among buyers and sellers. (Agnew 1986: 67–68)

It is important to keep in mind that legal change created the *possibility* of greater anonymity and impersonality but not its *necessity*. Law created only a potential. Any discussion of property rights must recognize the difference between formal rights and actual practices. To take effect, rights must be used and laws must be applied.[126] When considering late seventeenth-century developments in formal property rights, one must not assume that these were automatically translated into changes in market practices. Thanks to legal changes, financial relationships and financial markets could be much more anonymous and impersonal. As I will argue in chapter 7, however, financial property rights had a distinctly political aspect in their application within the stock market. This political dimension can help explain trading patterns in the stock market, and returns us to the Whig-Tory conflict that North and Weingast overlook in their analysis. As commodities, company shares might be perfectly interchangeable and freely assignable, but the social characteristics of the people trading them and the political implications of ownership continued to matter. A company share is a financial asset, providing a rate of return, but financial considerations were not the only thing that people cared about. To understand why, it is necessary to consider how closely intertwined the joint-stock companies were with party politics and public finance.

Chapter Six

POLITICS AND THE JOINT-STOCK COMPANIES

... the Gross of the Cash is with the Whigs.
—Daniel Defoe

JOINT-STOCK COMPANIES such as the Bank of England, East India Company, and the South Sea Company were both political institutions and financial commodities. As institutions, they were pillars of public finance and thus directly implicated in the very political process of helping to pay for two expensive and controversial wars. Since there were no general laws of incorporation, the establishment of each company required a distinct political act on the part of the sovereign or legislature. They enjoyed special rights and powers that were delegated to them and no one else, and in return provided loans and other kinds of support. In this way, an exchange took place between joint-stock companies and the political powers that created them. On the institutional side, joint-stock companies were partisan battlegrounds, highly centralized and strategic locations from which political leverage could be exerted and political support provided. The magnitude of their contribution to the national debt makes North and Weingast's neglect of joint-stock companies even more problematic.

On the other hand, a joint-stock company was an economic asset that could be bought and sold. Joint-stock company shares embodied legal rights of ownership over the company, divided proportionately into as many shares as were issued. Company shares were simply a financial commodity that merchants could trade freely in the stock market. According to Chaudhuri, shares represented an important change: "The most powerful and revolutionary impact of the companies lay in the public acceptance of the notion that the corporate financial liabilities were someone else's assets" (Chaudhuri 1985: 95). Companies were composed of shares whose exact disposition was the result of thousands of independent decisions by traders about whether to buy, sell, or hold.

This and the next chapter show how political conflict between Whigs and Tories influenced joint-stock companies at both levels, the institutional-organizational, and the individual-economic. The two lines of influence were not separate, for how politics influenced trading in company shares depended on the way that politics affected companies as institutions. It was precisely because of the political consequences at the institutional level that trading in shares itself became politicized. Even as commodities, company shares included the "political" right to elect governors and directors. When company leaders became politicized, so did company elections, voting rights, and ultimately share ownership. This imbued the market with a political as well as an economic logic, and made it much less "impersonal" than North and Weingast claim it was.[1]

The three major joint-stock companies were easily the most salient landmarks within the new monied interest. Annuities, lottery loans, excise and land taxes, goldsmith-bankers, insurance companies, and other companies traded on the stock market were all part of an expanding financial sector but none gained the prominence of the Bank of England, East India Company, and South Sea Company. The Bank and South Sea Company were newly established, which was enough to put them in the spotlight. However, the pattern in which joint-stock companies had a relationship to a political regime was much older. The exchange of economic rights and privileges for some measure of financial support (either in the form of taxes, loans, or gifts) had been going on for a long time.

Robert Brenner (1993) has shown how in early seventeenth-century England, merchant involvement in joint-stock companies influenced the role that they played in national politics.[2] The English Crown granted economic privileges to particular groups of merchants, mainly through incorporation as a joint-stock, or regulated company.[3] Such an arrangement could be extremely profitable for the merchants, and the Crown benefited in two ways. First, it received loans, taxes, and gifts in return. But because the fate of the merchants was now joined to the ruler, merchants acquired a vested interest in the political stability of the regime. Only the East India Company dated from the early seventeenth century but its financial ties to the Crown made it a core royalist supporter within the merchant community.[4]

Given the contingent nature of the rights enjoyed by joint-stock companies (what the King gives, the King can also take away), their relationship with the Crown was a crucial and problematic one of mutual dependence. The balance of power obviously favored the King but at times he had to lean very heavily on his merchant constituents for crucial monetary and political support. It was also a very public relationship, easily visible to rivals in the merchant community as well as opponents of the Crown. For these reasons, joint-stock companies played a political role, whether it was during the early seventeenth century or the early eighteenth century.

In the late seventeenth century, joint-stock companies became particularly controversial because of their connection with religious issues. Those participating in such companies were disproportionately dissenters and nonconformists (Protestants who were not members of the Church of England). Most investors in the joint-stocks were from the London region, and London was notorious for its large numbers of dissenters. De Krey estimates that some 100,000 Londoners, or about 15–20% of the greater London population, were nonconformists.[5] Furthermore, dissent was common within the occupational groups that invested most heavily in the joint-stocks. Merchants, for example, were big investors and contained a high proportion of dissenters, which reached almost 40% in the case of colonial traders and 30% of Iberian and Levant traders. Nearly half of the merchants trading with Turkey who invested in company stocks were from dissenting backgrounds.[6]

The result was a high involvement of dissenters in the joint-stock companies. De Krey has identified 158 (or about 12%) of the original 1,272 investors in the Bank of England as belonging to the "dissenting interest." These 158 dissenters provided almost one-fifth of the total capital. At the upper reaches of the joint-stock companies, dissenters were even more prominent. Forty-three percent of Bank of England directors, and 33% of New East India Company directors were dissenters.[7] At a time when there was no separation of Church and State and when a good deal of politics was about religion, the strong association with dissent and religious unorthodoxy made the monied interest particularly suspect in the eyes of the Anglican majority.[8] The spread of dissenting congregations in the wake of the Toleration Act of 1689 only served to make Anglicans feel even more threatened.

Joint-stock companies became politicized because of their religious associations and their close relation to the state. There were, however, some important variations among them. With two competing political parties, a politicized company could be either Whig or Tory, or torn between the two. The three main companies were each established at a different time and in a different political context. The original East India Company was established long before there were Whigs and Tories, the Bank of England was created in 1694 when William III was shifting his government from the Tories to the Whigs, and the South Sea Company was founded in 1711 under a Tory ministry. Political conflict occured between joint-stock companies, such as when the New East India Company tried to supersede the Old, or when a Land Bank was proposed by Tories to supplant the Whiggish Bank of England. Company politics at the institutional level were complex, unfolding over time, and varied depending on the company.

THE BANK OF ENGLAND

An account of the establishment of the Bank of England soon reveals its political connections. Of all the joint-stock companies, the Bank was probably the most "Whiggish." The main reason for the creation of a Bank of England was the government's incessant need for money. As a financial innovation, however, the Bank was but one of several proposed options. Why the bank was chosen had partly to do with general admiration for the Bank of Amsterdam—English commentators had long known of the advantages which the Bank of Amsterdam gave to the Dutch. Sir William Temple observed that "in this City of Amsterdam is the famous Bank, which is the greatest Treasure, either real or imaginary, that is known any where in the World" (Temple 1972 [1673]: 56).[9] William Paterson had been advocating bank projects for several years and in early 1694 banks were once again on the political agenda.[10] What distinguished the successful proposal from previous ones was that Paterson had some new and influential backers, including the Huguenot merchant Michael Godfrey (and some other opponents of the East India Company), and Charles Montagu, a Whig member of the Treasury Board and after 1694 the Chancellor of the Exchequer.

Partisan controversy surrounded the parliamentary act which established the Bank (5 & 6 William & Mary, c.20). In order to protect Parliament's financial leverage over the Crown, the act was amended in the Commons to prevent the Bank from lending money to the Crown or purchasing Crown lands without parliamentary consent. When the bill went to the House of Lords, several prominent Tories opposed it on the grounds that banks were suitable only for republics and thus would undermine royal authority, and also that a bank would monopolize capital and make mortgages for landowners harder to obtain.[11] The Bank was attacked again by the Tory Nottingham in the House of Lords in early 1695 and in general continued to be surrounded by controversy.[12] Little of the political rhetoric was aimed at Paterson himself, for he was clearly not the main force behind the bank. In fact, Paterson was removed from the directorate after only seven months. Those truly in charge included wealthy merchants like Michael Godfrey, the Houblon brothers, Sir William Scawen, Sir Gilbert Heathcote, and Theodore Janssen.

Subscriptions to the initial offering of bank stock sold well and the bank was successfully established.[13] However, Bank opposition continued unabated. One frequently stated objection rested upon the connection between land prices, interest rates, and the effect of the Bank's operations. By absorbing so much capital, the argument went, the Bank made money scare and forced up interest rates, adversely affecting both trade and the price of land.[14] Land was a productive asset, and its market price was determined by the capitalized value of future revenues. As interest rates went up, its price went down.[15] Higher interest rates also made it harder for landowners to borrow against the security of their land and obtain a mortgage. Between high interest rates, high taxes, fallen rents, and declining land values, the landed gentry were being squeezed, and the Bank made an inviting target.[16]

Opponents also argued that the Bank was affecting trade.[17] By absorbing capital and raising interest rates, the Bank made credit scarce, and, given how much trade depended on credit, this restrained commerce.[18] In the 1690s capital was removed from trade and invested in the stock market, including Bank of England shares, at the same time that trade shrank, so it was easy to conclude that the Bank indirectly caused the fall in trade.[19] Such charges, however, did not go unanswered. Michael Godfrey, for example, responded that the Bank would actually lower interest rates, raise the price of land, and financially strengthen the monarchy. He also denied that it would serve private Whiggish interests.[20]

Goldsmith-bankers generally opposed the Bank because they were competitors and the Bank had driven a number of them out of business. At first they undermined the Bank by refusing to accept its notes, and then in May 1696 city goldsmiths accumulated a stockpile and tried to cash them all at once, in effect organizing a run.[21] Some of the Bank's opponents recognized that given the size of its loan to the government, the Bank was not going to disappear anytime soon. This suggested that rather than try to eliminate the Bank, the best strategy might be to create a rival to check its power and influence. Thus, during the mid-1690s, much of the Bank's opposition rallied behind the idea of a Land Bank.

Various Land Bank schemes were proposed in the 1690s, mostly by Dr. Hugh Chamberlen and Robert Briscoe.[22] The basic idea paralleled that of the Bank of England but whereas the Bank only invested its stock in government debt, a Land Bank would invest in land or mortgages on land, thus providing direct financial relief to landowners. Land prices would rise and mortgage costs would decline. Supporters also hoped that a Land Bank would counterbalance the Bank of England. John Briscoe argued that "a Monopoly of the Money and Credit of the Kingdom . . . it is most certain, if no other Bank be set up by Authority, the Bank of England will soon be Masters of both" (Briscoe 1695: 1).[23]

John Asgill and Dr. Nicholas Barbon proposed the particular Land Bank scheme that gained parliamentary sanction. The Bank would take in subscriptions totaling £2,564,000 in coin and loan this sum to the government at 7% interest, secured against certain tax revenues. Conveniently, this amount exactly equaled the projected size of the government's budget deficit for 1696. The Bank would provide mortgage loans to its shareholders on favorable terms, and offer an additional £500,000 for mortgage loans to qualified borrowers. The scheme enjoyed the support of the government (since it meant more money) and was clearly aimed at bolstering the situation of landowners.[24] The Earl of Sunderland pushed for it as a way to encourage the landed interest to support the government.[25]

In 1696 the enabling bill passed in the Commons (7 & 8 William III, c.31) with the strong support of those former Whigs who were in the process of moving over to the Tory side.[26] Both the Bank of England and the Whig Junto strenuously opposed the Land Bank.[27] The Bank, for example, moved quickly to respond to the Land Bank while it was still in the proposal stage.[28] The Bank mobilized Bank directors who were also MPs, and replied with a counteroffer to loan the same amount to the government as the Land Bank, at only 5%.[29] In February of 1696 a delegation from the Bank met with some MPs to get advice and present the Bank's counterproposal.[30] Whig ministers expressed their concern about this new bank but the Commons rejected the Bank of England's offer and proceeded with the plan.[31]

To protect the Land Bank from capture by its rival, all persons connected with the Bank of England were explicitly excluded from the venture. The Land Bank was given about three months in which to raise its subscription but, unfortunately, the scheme did not gain the support of investors. This may have been because of the political nature of the Land Bank, or because 7% interest was insufficient financial incentive. It was certainly also due to the fact that subscriptions had to be in coin at the very moment when England was going through a recoinage. Thanks to the reminting of England's silver coin, cash was extremely scarce in 1696.[32] Very little money was subscribed (only £2,100), and the Land Bank failed completely.[33] The political consequence was a general discrediting of the project's Tory supporters, and reinforcement of the idea that only the Whig party could successfully engineer large government loans.[34] Failure also set the stage for the "ingraftment" of 1697, in which the Bank of England absorbed into its capital a large number of short-term government obligations, in exchange for monopoly privileges.[35] The contrast between the ability of Whigs and Tories to generate money for the government was further accentuated when the Bank enlarged its capital in 1709 by over £2.5 million, and the entire subscription sold out in only two hours.[36]

The Bank was quick to attack its rivals. Both the Land Bank and the Hollow Sword Blade Company (which, its name notwithstanding, tried to offer financial services in the early 1700s) felt its wrath.[37] But even in its relations to companies with which it did not compete, the Bank was mindful of the political ramifications. For example, it provided financial services to many departments of government, private individuals, and to both the new and old East India Companies.[38] When it came to making loans, however, the Bank favored the Whiggish new East India Company over the old Tory-connected company,[39] and relations with the latter were sometimes overtly hostile. In February 1701, for example, the old East India Company organized a run on the Bank. The Bank had to raise its discount rate from 4.5 to 6% in order to maintain its liquidity but in the end it successfully defended itself.[40] After the two East India Companies merged, conflict with the Bank declined.

Even after the disappearance of its rivals and the settlement of the East India Company, the Bank of England continued to be embroiled in politics. During the highly charged trial of Dr. Henry Sacheverell in 1710, rioting broke out in London and pro-Sacheverell rioters at one point targeted the Bank's headquarters.[41] Sacheverell's trial marked a huge swing in electoral sentiment toward the Tories, and it was certain that the next general election would see a Tory ministry replacing the Whig government. Before the election, Queen Anne reconfigured her ministry and shifted it toward the Tories. Till then, Godolphin, as Lord Treasurer, and Marlborough, as Captain General, had been her two chief ministers within a largely Whig government. Her first big change was to replace the Earl of Sunderland (Marlborough's son-in-law and a member of the Whig Junto) with Lord Dartmouth (a Tory) as Secretary of State on 14 June 1710. This was widely interpreted as a sign of more radical changes to come in the ministry, and in general such alterations indicated the monarch's own preferences about whom the electorate should support in the next election. Anne was sending an unambiguous signal in favor of the Tories. The following evening, a delegation from the Bank of England led by Sir Gilbert Heathcote, the Bank's Governor and a prominent Whig, visited the Queen. The delegation cautioned her to make no more changes in the ministry, claiming that this would endanger public credit. They argued that only Godolphin as Lord Treasurer enjoyed the confidence of the monied interest, and thus that only he could raise the large loans that the government still needed.[42] With the Treasury hoping to borrow another £120,000 from the Bank, Anne tried to placate them with various assurances. Later that summer, the Bank refused to discount bills of exchange for military pay officers, something that was part of its normal service to the government.[43] It did so on the grounds that government credit was declining, and sought further assurances from Godolphin that Parliament would not be dissolved anytime soon (and thus that the Tories would not be able to exploit their favorable political circumstances with an election).[44] When Godolphin relayed these concerns to the Queen, Anne simply dismissed him and replaced Godolphin by a Treasury Commission, with the Tory Robert Harley as the head.[45]

The failure of the Bank delegation to save Godolphin was only the start, for news of the Bank's attempt to pressure Anne spread and was not well received.[46] For the politically resurgent Tories, such action confirmed their worst fears of an overly powerful Bank attempting to dictate policy to the monarch.[47] The Bank was clearly stepping beyond its proper role, and its behavior was considered both insolent and a threat to government.[48]

> In order to that, their [the Whigs'] Emissaries propagated a wild Notion, That the Publick Credit of England wholly depended on the late Lord Treasurer [Godolphin]; and the Continuation of the last Parliament; so that the whole Confederacy seemed to be concern'd in their Preservation, some Members of the Bank of England, and some of the Allies were unwarily drawn in to interpose in their behalf with her Majesty: Than which, a greater Affront was, perhaps, never offer'd to the Crown of England. (*An Essay Towards the History of the Last Ministry and Parliament* 1710: 20–21)

Besides discrediting both the Bank and the Whigs, these events embold-ened the Tories. Outraged at the Bank's actions, the Tories made a con-certed effort to capture the directorate at the next election for Bank direc-tors, held in April 1711. For similar reasons, they also tried to seize the East India Company. As with today's large corporations, early eighteenth-cen-tury joint-stock companies were effectively controlled by their directors, although they were owned by the shareholders.[49] Tories offered their own slate of candidates to oppose the Whig slate. Shareholders with £500 or more of Bank stock could vote in the director's elections, and so die-hard opponents of the monied interest like Dr. Sacheverell purchased Bank stock in order to be eligible. The primary resource in the contest for control of the directorate was, of course, votes in the company election. The number of votes a shareholder could cast was determined by the size of his or her shareholding, and so who owned shares determined who controlled the company.[50] For evidence on how hotly contested the 1711 elections were in relation to other elections, consider table 6.1.

The minute books of the Bank and East India Company list only the elec-tion winners but the number of votes received by elected candidates shows how contested the election was.[51] When voter interest is high, more voters participate and so more votes are needed to win. Table 6.1 gives the average, minimum, and maximum number of votes for winning candidates for the years 1707–13, and each measure shows that the number of votes cast in the Bank elections reached a peak in 1711. In the case of the East India Com-pany, there was a similar rise in 1711, although it was not as dramatic as the Bank's. More shareholders participated in the 1711 election than in any of the others, indicating a high level of voter interest. To put these results in perspective, consider that in 1725 only 131 Bank shareholders voted, and each of the candidates received 131 votes.[52] In 1725 there was very little interest in the election and no disagreement about whom to vote for.

Whigs mustered their company votes and so despite their best efforts the Tories failed to take either company.[53] Partisan interest in directors' elec-tions waned, although it did not disappear altogether. Episodes like the at-tempt in 1710 to pressure the Queen, and the 1711 Bank elections, only confirmed the partisan qualities of the Bank itself. At the time it was widely viewed as a Whig institution, created by the Whigs for the benefit of a Whig constituency (the monied interest). Further examination of the evidence bears this perception out.

Table 6.2 presents the political composition of the Bank of England and the East India Company directorates. All Bank directors from 1694 until 1712 were included, and all directors of the United East India Company from 1709 (the first year they were elected for the united company) until 1712.[54] Although political information was not available for all Bank direc-tors, it is clear that the great majority of them were Whigs.[55] Since directors

TABLE 6.1

Average, Minimum, and Maximum Votes for Winning Candidates in Annual Bank of England Directors' Elections, 1707–1713, and East India Company Directors' Elections, 1709–1712

Year	Bank of England Number of Votes:			East India Company Number of Votes:			Adjusted Average
	Average	Minimum	Maximum	Average	Minimum	Maximum	
1707	83.8	82	85	—	—	—	—
1708	82.2	77	83	—	—	—	—
1709	223.3	138	248	511.4	372	710	911.2
1710	755.1	477	871	528.0	420	799	940.7
1711	1,197.5	950	1,473	744.2	655	1,071	1,325.9
1712	383.8	378	385	464.1	424	475	826.9
1713	296.9	292	298	—	—	—	—

Sources: India Office Library B/255, Bank of England Archives G7/2.

TABLE 6.2

Political Affiliations of Bank of England and United East India Company Directors, 1712

	Bank of England Directors	
	Frequency	Percent
Tory	2	4.4
Whig	37	82.2
Unknown	6	13.3
Total	45	100.0
	East India Company Directors	
	Frequency	Percent
Tory	14	33.3
Whig	22	52.4
Unknown	6	14.3
Total	42	100.0

Sources: India Office Library B/255, Acres 1940, and appendix.

actually ran the Bank, having Whig directors might not surprisingly lead to Whiggish policies. At the very least, it created the appearance of a very Whiggish institution.

There was also a strong pattern in the religious affiliations of Bank directors. De Krey examined the directorates of seven joint-stock companies and found that there were more dissenters, both absolutely and proportionately, among the Bank's directors than for any other company.[56] Forty-three percent of the Bank's directors were dissenters, as compared with the New East India Company, which was the next highest at 33%.[57]

The Bank's political stance went beyond what was implied by its financial relationship to the government, or by the general religious character of the monied interest. The Bank's ongoing connections with politics showed in the way that the price of Bank stock reflected political events. Favorable war news produced rising share prices, while a bad turn of events invariably saw a drop in prices.[58] More than that, however, by virtue of who founded the Bank, who defended it, who ran it, and what the Bank did, the Bank played a prominent role in domestic politics, consistently taking a Whig position. At times the Bank's partisanship was blatant and extreme, as when it tried to defend the Whig ministry in 1710. At other times its Whiggishness was more moderate, as when, for example, the Bank reached an accommodation with Harley's ministry.[59] In the main, however, the Bank belonged to the Whigs.

THE EAST INDIA COMPANY

The East India Company provides an important contrast with the Bank for the simple reason that it preceded the arrival of Whigs and Tories. Rather than being born into the Whig-Tory conflict, as the Bank was, the East India Company became caught up in it.[60] The Old East India Company's partisan entanglements began during the latter 1680s, when the company became closely tied to James II's monarchy.[61] Merchants who were unhappy with the East India Company for a variety of reasons sought support from the Whigs.

The East India Company enjoyed lucrative trading privileges that provoked the jealousy of other merchants and companies. In the 1670s and 1680s, the Company was the largest of the joint-stocks but nevertheless its capital structure was quite restricted. The Company raised money through stocks and bonds but mostly relied upon the latter and was therefore highly leveraged. Shareholders enjoyed dividends and capital gains, while bondholders were paid only a fixed rate of interest. Despite a substantial increase in trade, the Company's capital was not enlarged between 1657 and 1693. Thus, even though it was the biggest joint-stock company until the Bank of England appeared, the number of shareholders remained relatively small.[62] This meant that profits went into only a few hands and that shares became extremely valuable.[63] Furthermore, even among shareholders, shareholdings were increasingly concentrated in a few hands. Peter Lougheed reports that in 1675 the ten largest shareholders held 15% of the total stock but that by 1689, the top ten had increased their share to 23%, led by Sir Josiah Child with £51,000 worth.[64] Since shares came with voting rights, this meant that control of the company was in only a few hands.

Many merchants wanted to buy into the East India Company but were unable to do so. The years after the Third Dutch War and before the Glorious Revolution were generally very good for the Company, and it earned high profits and paid large dividends.[65] Given the Company's monopolistic privileges, however, and the restricted number of shares, only a select few could enjoy the bounty. This led to some forceful attacks, but the Company was defended against its critics. One pamphlet argued that because the stock market was open and anyone could buy stock, the claim that the company excluded people was baseless.

> What should be the reason, that the present East-India-Company hath so many Enemies? Is it because some persons that would not subscribe at the beginning of the Stock, nor yet afterwards, when the Books were laid open, are filled with Envy at the Companies prosperity, and would ruine all, because they are excluded by their own default? There may be much in this, and yet any that will, may buy Stock, according to the Market-price when they please. (Papillon 1677: 26)[66]

Despite such denials, events suggested that the company was too dependent on debt, and that there was not enough equity.[67] Unlike modern corporate bonds, seventeenth-century company bonds were repayable on short notice, so if large numbers of bondholders tried to cash them in at the same time, the company could experience a liquidity crisis. This happened in 1682, when a series of bank runs forced London financiers to acquire as much cash as they could. The East India Company was unable to come up with enough cash, and so had to suspend bond payments for three months.[68] More use of equity would have solved the problem.

Other merchants criticized the East India Company on different grounds. In particular, members of the Levant Company, which traded with Turkey, felt that their business suffered from competition from the East India Company. Both companies imported similar goods from the East, but the Levant Company was not as prosperous as the East India Company. In 1680, the Levant Company petitioned parliament to break the East India Company's monopoly and open its restricted share capital.[69] The Company's credibility weakened when it permitted private foreign merchants to trade with India on their own account, so long as they paid a percentage to the East India Company.[70] English weavers were another source of opposition because the East India Company imported cheap Indian textiles that competed with domestically produced cloth.[71]

In addition to launching political attacks on the company, some opponents challenged East India Company privileges more directly by sending ships to trade with India in violation of the Company's monopoly. In this undertaking, interlopers could exploit the strains that persistently afflicted relations between the East India Company directors in London, and their staff in India. Given the impeded and sluggish nature of communication between company headquarters and company servants (as the employees were called), it was very difficult to monitor and control the latter.[72] Servants were susceptible to bribes and kickbacks from Indian suppliers.[73] The company tried to make a virtue out of necessity by allowing its servants in India to trade on their own account, which created conflicts of interest. The company nevertheless tried to curtail such activities by prohibiting all trade with England, without permission from the Court of Directors in London. Thus, although company servants could accrue profits in India, they could not easily patriate their earnings. This problem the interlopers were happy to solve by circumventing the East India Company's monopoly and dealing directly with dissatisfied company servants.[74]

The general response of the East India Company to all these attacks was to bind itself ever more closely to the Crown. Loans and gifts were regularly extended from the Company to the reigning monarch.[75] The close ties between Crown and Company were tightened when James II became a shareholder in 1686, and the Company's identification with James's regime strengthened.[76] The specific response to the interlopers was twofold. The company prosecuted interlopers in court, and it also increased its imports from India in order to reduce the economic rewards to interloping.[77] These countermoves brought mixed success in protecting the Company, but the entire context for the conflict was radically altered by the Glorious Revolution. The East India Company's close relationship with James II and the Tory party changed overnight from a political asset to a liability.[78]

The controversy over the East India Company had constitutional implications since one key question was whether a company could legitimately possess monopolistic trading privileges on the basis of a royal charter alone, or if it needed parliamentary sanction. As power shifted to the Commons in the aftermath of the Glorious Revolution, it became clear that the old East India Company needed to consolidate its position with an Act of Parliament. Opponents of the old company quickly lobbied Parliament and were able to use its close association with James II to good effect.[79] Former interlopers and Levant company merchants figured prominently among the company opponents.[80] Although the company was weakened, it was not without political resources and could not be defeated easily. The split in the mercantile community between the old East India Company and its opponents made Parliament reluctant to act. Furthermore, to dissolve the old company outright would endanger trade with India at a time when customs revenues made an important contribution to government coffers. Neither group could gain a decisive advantage over the other, and so the company continued to trade without a parliamentary charter.[81] In 1693, William granted a new twenty-one-year royal charter to the company so that the India trade would not be interrupted but the company continued to pursue parliamentary sanction just as vigorously as the opposition tried to block it.

A chronic shortage of money during the Nine Years' War offered to the company and its opposition their greatest opportunity to earn government favor. It was a new version of the old exchange of commercial privileges for loans and money. In March 1694, after consultation with the company, the Commons resolved to negotiate a £600,000 interest-free loan from the old East India Company in exchange for a twenty-year parliamentary confirmation of its royal charter. Shortly after, however, the deal was rejected by the Commons because the company's opponents suggested that they could raise even more money for the government. Instead, the Commons approved the establishment of the Bank of England, which came with a £1.2 million loan.[82] The company continued to lobby Parliament and other loan proposals were considered.[83] In 1697, the company directors discussed lending £400,000 to the government for two years in exchange for a parliamentary charter.[84] The directors called a shareholders meeting and recommended this proposal to the "generality" (as the shareholders were called), but it was rejected. Instead, the shareholders were willing to loan only £40,000.[85] The old company also used more devious methods. It tried to co-opt key members of the opposition by secretly giving them company stock, and engaged in widespread bribery of politicians. The latter strategy backfired when it came to light in 1695 and was fully exploited by the Whigs to create a public scandal.[86]

Another financial proposal was made in March 1698. It was again suggested that the East India Company loan £600,000 to the government in exchange for a parliamentary charter. Internal discussions within the company raised the sum by another £100,000.[87] This time, however, the opposition was ready with a substantial counteroffer and secured the political backing of Charles Montagu and the other Whig Treasury Lords. Thus, when Sir John Fleet, speaking on behalf of the old East India Company, announced its willingness to loan £700,000 at 4% to the government, Montagu responded that the interlopers could loan £2 million at 8%.[88] Given the state of government finances, a larger sum at a higher interest rate was preferable to a smaller amount at a lower rate. At first, William III was skeptical of the interlopers' ability to raise such a sum but preliminary subscriptions were so successful that his doubts soon vanished.[89] The old company responded with an offer to restructure its capital and loan an additional £200,000 to the government, but Parliament accepted the interlopers' proposal.[90] The full £2 million was raised in only three days, and provided a marked contrast with failure of the Tory Land Bank scheme. The old East India Company was the biggest investor in the new one, subscribing to £315,000 worth of stock.[91] The old company was then given three-years' notice of its dissolution in October 1698.[92]

Thus there came to be two East India Companies, the old and the new. The old was strongly associated with the Tory party, and the new with the Whigs. De Krey's analysis of London City leaders shows that two-thirds of the leaders who were also directors of the old East India Company were Tories, while over 80% of the leaders who were directors of the new East India Company took the Whig side.[93] There was a similar contrast with respect to religion. Seventeen percent of the directors of the old East India Company were dissenters, as compared with 33% of the new East India Company directors.[94] Consistent with these partisan associations, the Bank of England favored the new company over the old, and in order to undercut the new company's chief financial supporter, the old company organized a run on the Bank in 1701.[95]

Fairly soon the two companies were negotiating a merger, an alternative made more compelling perhaps by the fact that the old company was the single biggest shareholder in the new one.[96] Yet even as negotiations were underway, the partisan connections of the two companies meant that shifts in Parliament affected relations between them. The results of the general election of 1698 gave hope to hardliners within the old company, and, for example, the new company experienced a setback in early 1700 when Parliament passed a bill incorporating the old company for the remainder of the twenty-one years left on its 1693 charter.[97] This victory pushed up the market price of old East India Company stock. The emboldened old East India Company then offered to loan £2 million at 5% to the government, and in effect to take over at a reduced rate the new company's loan. Then the new company lost its strongest ally in the House of Commons when Montagu was granted a peerage in December 1700, and moved to the Lords. In the general election of 1700–1701, both companies mobilized their political connections to try to get supporters elected into the House of Commons.[98] Despite several setbacks, the new company fared better in its electioneering than the old.

In the meantime, the economic rivalry between the two companies accelerated their investments in the East Indies. Competition forced them to construct or acquire duplicate trading facilities. These investments provided unintended benefits during the War of the Spanish Succession by contributing to Britain's balance of payments. The lack of foreign currency and resulting remittance problems that so plagued the war effort in the 1690s was easier to resolve in the 1700s thanks to this overinvestment.[99]

A merger of the two East India Companies was finally negotiated in 1701 and settled with an Indenture Tripartite, signed in January 1702.[100] The process of amalgamation was slow, with a complete merger not coming until 1709. Parliament approved the deal in exchange for another loan of £1.2 million paid in 1708. Just as the United East India Company was a combination of the new and old companies, so was the political complexion of the

United Company. Table 6.2 above shows that when compared with the Bank of England, the directorate of the United Company included a mixture of Whigs and Tories. Whigs were in the majority but there was a significant Tory minority.

The Tory offensive in the elections of 1710–11 made the Bank of England a direct target, but it also swept up the East India Company. Like the Bank, the 1711 directors' elections for the East India Company witnessed a deliberate Tory attempt to capture the directorate. An examination of table 6.1 above shows that, like the Bank, the 1711 election was more heavily contested than those either before or after. Robert Harley sponsored a ticket of alternative candidates to challenge the incumbent Whig directors. As with the Bank, however, the Tory challengers lost.[101]

Although the East India Company elections followed the same pattern as the Bank elections, there was an important difference between them. Table 6.1 shows that if vote counts are adjusted for the fact that there were more Bank than East India Company shareholders, East India Company elections were *always more contested* than Bank elections. East India Company vote counts have to be multiplied by 1.78 to make them comparable to the Bank (2,530 Bank and 1,420 East India Company shareholders were eligible to vote in 1712). When this is done, then for any year the number of East India votes exceeds those of the Bank (compare the adjusted East India averages in table 6.1 with the Bank averages). Only in 1711 do the numbers get close, a year when the Tories made a special effort to capture the Bank.

The events of 1711 showed that higher partisanship in company elections led to more contested elections. The fact that East India Company elections were always more contested than Bank elections suggests that partisan conflict was sharper within the East India Company. Given the institutional history of the United Company, this is perhaps not surprising. The United Company was a fusion of a largely Whig new East India Company and a Tory old East India Company. The partisan conflict between the two companies was internalized within the United Company, but evidently not extinguished.[102] As compared to the Bank of England, whose Whiggish qualities were unimpaired from the beginning, the United East India Company was contested terrain, a corporate battleground for Whigs and Tories.

The East India Company's heavy involvement in politics was not an aberration, for it continued to play a role throughout most of the eighteenth century. The government usually managed to obtain a fresh loan or a reduction in interest payments whenever the company's charter was up for renewal, and company directors and large shareholders continued to sit in Parliament. Whenever directors' elections were contested, the turnout was heavier, and there was a noticeable increase in the turnover of £500 blocks of shares (the minimum amount necessary to be qualified to vote) just before company elections.[103]

THE SOUTH SEA COMPANY

The South Sea Company, later to be made infamous by the South Sea Bubble of 1720, was the youngest of the three great monied companies. The political circumstances of its birth were different from the other two for it was launched in 1711 at the height of Robert Harley's Tory ministry. It was something of a curiosity, for within the mostly Whig monied interest, Tories were able to cultivate enough support to establish another joint-stock company. The dismal failure of the Land Bank proved that Tories could not take such support for granted.

As with the Bank of England, the financial needs of the government set the context for the South Sea Company. When Harley's Tory government took over in 1710, the War of the Spanish Succession had been underway for eight years. Despite several successful lottery loans, deficits continued and the short-term debt instruments used by government departments accumulated and were at a heavy discount. One prominent naval contractor, Ambrose Crowley, was discounting Naval bills and tallies by 19.5% in December 1709 and by 27% in July 1710. The bills owed him by the Navy were running three and four years in arrears.[104] Crowley's problems exemplified the general situation: the system of short-term borrowing was sinking under the weight of unpaid debts.

As a Tory, Harley's relations with the Bank and East India Company were not very good, although things improved after Sir Gilbert Heathcote's term as governor of the Bank came to a close.[105] Upon taking power, Harley rejected the remittance contractor long used by Godolphin and awarded the lucrative contract to a syndicate of his own choosing (comprising three financiers: Lambert, Hoare, and Gibbon).[106] The explicit attempt by Tories to capture the Bank and East India Company in the directors' elections of spring 1711 did not endear the Tories to the monied interest. And even if relations with these two companies had been more amicable, it is unlikely that together they could have absorbed into their capital the vast sum of unpaid short-term debts that were then floating in the market.

George Caswall, a London financier and merchant, first proposed the idea of a South Sea Company in a letter to Robert Harley in October 1710. The following spring Harley worked on the proposal with a group of financiers that included Caswall, and brought it before Parliament in May 1711. The idea was to incorporate a new joint-stock company to trade with the South Seas and encourage holders of short-term government tallies and bills to exchange them for company stock. It was a huge debt-for-equity swap that would put a large amount of short-term debt on a long-term funded basis. The government's system for short-term borrowing would be relieved of its burden, and debt-holders would have stock in a company receiving 6% interest on its loan to the government, as well as earnings generated using its trading privileges.

All of the main promoters of the scheme—George Caswall, John Blunt, Jacob Sawbridge, and Elias Turner—had previously been directors of the Hollow Sword Blade Company, that misleadingly named organization which during the early 1700s tried to compete directly with the Bank of England in several financial undertakings.[107] The Hollow Sword Blade Company almost went bankrupt, and its financial troubles were blamed on the Bank. What these ex-Sword Blade Company directors offered to Harley was a means to challenge the Bank as the main buttress of government finance. Harley could simultaneously resolve the government's financial problem and create a Tory constituency in a financial community that was overwhelmingly Whig.[108] The defeat of Tory candidates in the Bank and East India Company elections that very spring was a strong reminder of Whig dominance within the monied interest. The combination of financial necessity and political expediency was irresistible, and so Harley backed the project.

A bill proposing the South Sea Company was introduced into Parliament on 17 May 1711 and received its second reading the very next day. With a large Tory majority in the House of Commons, Harley could be confident of eventual passage. For obvious reasons, the two other major companies were concerned about the impact this new company might have on their own interests. By the 15th of May, and undoubtedly before then, the directors of the East India Company knew that a new trading company was in the offing.[109] The day after the South Sea bill was introduced, the East India Company directors were discussing a petition to Parliament, and the day after that they were devising amendments that would protect their company.[110] Similarly, the directors of the Bank of England discussed the potential impact of a South Sea Company upon the Bank, and formulated amendments to secure their position.[111] Both companies were successful in obtaining clauses that maintained their privileges. The failure of the Land Bank taught its supporters, including Robert Harley, that it was dangerous to antagonize the monied interest. In the Commons, the strongest opposition to the new company was organized by Robert Walpole, a zealous Whig, but it was easily defeated by the overwhelming numbers of the Tories.[112]

One notable feature of the new company was that the power to appoint the first court of directors was vested in the Queen. In effect, this meant that Harley would choose the directors. Having directors appointed instead of elected by the shareholders was a way to prevent Whigs from gaining control of the Company, even if they subscribed to its stock.[113] Once again, Tory failure during the 1711 Bank and East India Company elections was an important motive. The list of directors, headed by Harley himself as

governor, were listed in the South Sea Company charter and thirteen of
them were chosen from among the unsuccessful Tory candidates for the
Bank and East India elections.[114] Furthermore, anyone who was a director,
governor, or deputy-governor of either the Bank or the East India Company
was prohibited from having a similar position with the South Sea Company.
Harley was going to ensure that this joint-stock company would remain
under his control. Even after the first year, when a number of company
directors were replaced, Harley and all the political appointees retained
their positions.[115]

A total of £9,177,967 in the form of Navy bills, Army and Transport debentures, seamen's wages and other debts were subscribed. Parliament earmarked tax revenues from duties on wine, vinegar, tobacco, and various other
goods to pay 6% interest on the loan. The immediate effect of the South Sea
scheme was to raise the price of Navy bills by 20%, although this may have
been only temporary.[116] The operation was a success and preserved public
creditworthiness. It served more than just financial ends, however, for Harley was able to reward his supporters in the financial community,[117] and satisfy Tory clamoring for an anti-Whig financial institution.[118]

Harley wanted to establish a Tory-controlled monied company without
completely antagonizing the Whig monied interest, for as Lord Treasurer
he had to ensure that the government could continue to borrow on a large
scale. Thus, provisions were added to protect the other major joint-stock
companies. Nevertheless, the political orientation of the South Sea Company differed sharply from the other two. Dissenters were much less prominent among South Sea Company directors than they were among Bank and
United East India Company directors.[119] Among London City leaders who
were company directors, there was a much higher proportion of Tory directors in the South Sea Company than either the Bank or the United East
India Company.[120] It was no coincidence that the South Sea Company chose
as its banker the Hollow Sword Blade Company, former rival to the Bank
of England.[121]

POLITICS AND THE COMPANIES

All of the major joint-stock companies were politically salient. The Bank of
England, the New East India Company, and to a lesser extent the United
East India Company, had connections with the Whigs. The Old East India
Company, South Sea Company, and failed Land Bank had strong connections with the Tory party. Partisan loyalties shaped intercorporate relations
and so, for example, commercial rivalries between the New and Old East
India Companies, or between the Bank of England and Land Bank, were
overlaid and reinforced by political rivalries. Annuities and lotteries were
less politically controversial ways to borrow money and perhaps this is

why after the South Sea Bubble (1720) government ministers tried to broaden the base of the national debt and become less reliant on joint-stock companies.[122] But during Anne's reign, much of the long-term borrowing was done through the joint-stock companies. By 1712, the three monied companies had in effect loaned £15.8 million to the government, which was approximately 62% of the total funded debt, and 35% of the total debt (funded and unfunded).

Joint-stock companies cannot be understood only as devices for resource extraction by a needy government. Both the goals they served (helping to fund the war) and the means they used were highly controversial. Furthermore, the companies were important sources of financial power and patronage, leading to recurrent conflict for control over them. Strong connections were built between company directors and courts of directors, on the one hand, and political parties, on the other. Thus, parties sponsored candidates in directors' elections, substantial numbers of directors were also politicians,[123] and company leaders on occasion used their position for partisan purposes. The companies monitored Parliament as much as Parliament watched the companies, and the political complexion of the court of directors was noted carefully. Consider that after the Hanoverian Succession, South Sea Company shareholders showed their loyalty to the new regime by purging prominent Tory politicians from the company court.[124]

How the public perceived company shareholders also fueled partisanship. Tory conservatives were convinced that Whiggish merchant-dissenters, Jews, and foreigners dominated the monied interest as a whole and not just company directors. Table 6.3 presents a breakdown of Bank of England and East India Company shareholders by their political affiliations.[125] For each political group, it also gives the average (nominal) value of their shareholdings, and the average number of stock transactions they undertook during 1712. Among the shareholders of both companies, there were many persons whose political allegiances were impossible to determine.[126] However, among the others there were some striking patterns.

In both companies, Whig shareholders outnumbered Tory shareholders by more than two to one (1,107 Whigs to 497 Tories in the Bank, 674 Whigs to 272 Tories within the East India Company). Popular beliefs are sometimes overly simplistic but the general impression that Whigs dominated within the monied interest is certainly born out here. Furthermore, if we consider wealth and activity, Whig dominance is magnified even further. In both companies, Whig shareholdings were significantly larger than Tory holdings. In addition, Whigs traded more frequently, with Whig Bank shareholders trading on average 2.4 times per year versus 1.5 trades for Tory shareholders. Combining numbers, wealth, and activity together accentuates the difference between the two political groups. Not only were there many more of them but the average Whig owned more

TABLE 6.3

Political Affiliations and Financial Characteristics of Bank of England and United
East India Company Shareholders, 1712

Bank of England Shareholders:

	Frequency	Percent	Average Shareholdings	Average Transactions
Tory	497	11.2	£1,251.3	1.5
Whig	1,107	25.1	£2,242.4	2.4
Split Support	7	0.2	£1,100.7	1.4
Unknown	2,808	63.6	£841.1	0.9
Total	4,419	100.0	£1,239.6	1.4

East India Company Shareholders:

	Frequency	Percent	Average Shareholdings	Average Transactions
Tory	272	12.0	£1,534.2	1.6
Whig	674	29.8	£2,315.9	2.9
Split Support	4	0.2	£875.0	6.0
Unknown	1,311	58.0	£927.1	0.9
Total	2,261	100.0	£1,414.5	1.6

Sources: See appendix.

shares and was more active in the market than the average Tory. No wonder
Jonathan Swift declared that "the great Traders in Mony were wholly devoted to the Whigs, who had first raised them" (Swift 1711: 42), and no
wonder that Harley wanted to create his own monied company for the Tory
interest.[127]

Partisanship was not the only social distinction among shareholders.
Tables 6.4 and 6.5 present the breakdown of Bank and East India Company
shareholders from 1712 along the lines of gender, social background, and
social status.

The monied interest was a predominantly male interest.[128] Although
women were not altogether excluded, most shareholders were men, men's
shareholdings were larger, and men were more active as traders in the market.[129] As evidenced by the Bank and East India Company shareholders, the
monied interest was not an aristocratic interest. Traditional landed elites
were numerically almost insignificant as shareholders. Peers and baronets
were wealthier than others, as the size of their holdings indicates, but they
were no more active in trading. The total number of shares in aristocratic
hands was very small.[130]

The popular perception was also that people from unorthodox social backgrounds dominated the stock market, much to its discredit. When added
together, foreigners, naturalized persons, Huguenots, Quakers, and Jews ac-

TABLE 6.4
Selected Social and Financial Characteristics of Bank of England
Shareholders, 1712

Sex:	Frequency	Percent	Average Shareholdings	Average Transactions
Male	3,610	81.7	£1,364.1	1.6
Female	795	18.0	£680.3	0.5
Other	14	.3	£756.8	2.2
Total	4,419	100.0	£1,239.6	1.4

Social Background:	Frequency	Percent	Average Shareholdings	Average Transactions
Orthodox*	4,139	93.7	£1,112.0	1.3
Unorthodox**	280	6.3	£3,118.5	3.4
Total	4,419	100.0	£1,239.6	1.4

Social Status:	Frequency	Percent	Average Shareholdings	Average Transactions
Commoner	4,282	96.9	£1,170.3	1.4
Baronet or Peer	137	3.1	£3,396.8	1.0
Total	4,419	100.0	£1,239.6	1.4

* Native English. ** Foreigner, Naturalized, Huguenot, Quaker, or Jewish.
Sources: See appendix.

counted for only 6% of Bank shareholders and 10% of East India Company shareholders. These few unorthodox people, however, called attention to themselves by being among the wealthiest and most active of shareholders. Average shareholdings and numbers of trades for unorthodox shareholders were significantly higher than for the majority. A few unorthodox shareholders captured the political imagination far more than the numerous small, inactive shareholders.

Tory conservatives were convinced that Whigs, dissenters, Jews, and foreigners dominated the monied interest, and they were partly correct. As indicated by Bank and East India Company shareholders, Whigs outnumbered Tories, although dissenters, Jews, and foreigners were very much in the minority. Political perceptions were likely shaped by the most prominent features of the monied interest. Within such salient groups as the wealthiest shareholders, most active traders, and company directors, there was plenty of evidence to confirm Tory prejudices. Whigs, dissenters, Jews, and foreigners were numerous among these highly visible sections of the monied interest.

TABLE 6.5

Selected Social and Financial Characteristics of United East India Company
Shareholders, 1712

Sex:	Frequency	Percent	Average Shareholdings	Average Transactions
Male	1,926	85.2	£1,548.6	1.8
Female	331	14.6	£643.0	0.4
Other	4	0.2	£595.0	0.5
Total	2,261	100.0	£1,414.5	1.6

Social Background:	Frequency	Percent	Average Shareholdings	Average Transactions
Orthodox*	2,016	89.2	£1,180.4	1.3
Unorthodox**	245	10.8	£3,309.0	4.3
Total	2,261	100.0	£1,414.5	1.6

Social Status:	Frequency	Percent	Average Shareholdings	Average Transactions
Commoner	2,212	97.8	£1,348.0	1.6
Baronet or Peer	49	2.2	£4,409.5	1.7
Total	2,261	100.0	£1,414.5	1.6

* Native English. ** Foreigner, Naturalized, Huguenot, Quaker, or Jewish.
Sources: See appendix.

CONCLUSION

New financial institutions were established in a highly politicized context.
International conflict played a role because war-related expenses necessitated financial innovation. Yet, domestic politics was also important. The
conflict between the two parties found expression in the rivalries between
the New and Old East India Companies, the Bank of England and the Land
Bank, and the South Sea Company. Commercial rivalries and political rivalries mirrored and reinforced each other. For instance, political rivalry between Whigs and Tories enhanced commercial rivalry between different
groups of merchants, and as a result a bidding war broke out between the
New and Old East India Companies. Political rivalries also affected commercial ones. Tory challengers like the Land Bank and South Sea Company
forced the Whiggish Bank of England to offer better terms to the government by enlarging its loans or lowering its interest rates.

The institutional side of the joint-stock companies was undeniably partisan in this period. For many reasons, what these companies did, who owned
them, who ran them, their relations among themselves and with the government, altogether inserted joint-stock companies into the conflict between

Whigs and Tories. Yet joint-stock companies were more than just institutions. The property rights embodied in company stock were a liquid asset, a form of property that could easily be bought and sold on the active London market. As institutions, companies were massive concentrations of economic power and political control. But as innocuous commodities, company shares were subject to the highly decentralized profit-maximizing considerations of the market. Did the politics that unfolded at the institutional level affect how traders dealt with these financial commodities? Just how anonymous and apolitical was the stock market? That is the central issue of the next chapter.

Chapter Seven

TRADING ON THE LONDON STOCK MARKET

> You know that the price of public bonds and of money, and
> the rate of exchange, are the pulse of the body politic, and
> show clearly its state of health or its illness.
> —Voltaire

THE CHIEF INSIGHT of the New Institutional Economics was that the institutional setting of markets affected economic behavior. Markets emerge from a set of legal and political institutions, not out of thin air. The North-Weingast analysis of this period is incomplete in some important ways but the general point that institutions matter remains true. The key explanatory task is to figure out which institutions matter and how.

Joint-stock companies were deeply involved both in party competition and public borrowing but politics at the institutional level need not engender politics in the market. As a type of property, joint-stock company shares provided the opportunity for passive investment and were a way for someone with capital to earn dividends without having to manage the business actively. From the perspective of an individual investor, company shares could be no more than financial assets, apolitical commodities to be bought and sold on an anonymous market. The task of this chapter is to examine individual action in the London stock market and see if it was influenced by the political conflict that unfolded at the institutional level. Thus, we return to the central questions about the embeddedness of economic action. Is economic behavior embedded in other social structures, and if so, how?

There are three general factors that can influence individual economic behavior. In addition to institutions, which North and Weingast (and many others) stress, there are the characteristics of the commodity being traded and the preferences of the traders. Market behavior depends on what it is that people are buying and selling. A commodity of uncertain quality, for example, can generate the "market for lemons."[1] Markets for highly standardized commodities will differ from those for idiosyncratic or variable commodities.[2] The preferences of traders also affects what happens, although economists have generally sidestepped the issue either by ignoring them (keeping preferences exogenous) or by assuming a very simple set of preferences (e.g., profit maximization). In economics and sociology, these three factors are combined to construct different pictures of what individual economic behavior looks like. Each picture has important implications for whether politics could, or could not, affect market behavior.

The most common approach supposes that people behave rationally in markets. They are profit-maximizers who evaluate their alternatives and choose the best one. Such *homines economici* are not distracted in their decision-making by irrelevant details and they focus on only a few key economic variables like price and quantity. They are indifferent about whom they trade with, *ceteris paribus*.

The economist W. Stanley Jevons elaborated this view in his *Law of Indifference*. Jevons considered exchange under ideal market conditions: the goods were perfectly homogeneous, the institutional framework provided enforceable contracts and property rights, and traders were knowledgeable profit-maximizers. When these conditions obtain, people buying and selling are indifferent about which specific commodities they purchase or sell, or with whom they transact (Jevons 1931: 90–92). Economically rational traders pay attention only to quantity and price and do not respond to any other traits.[3] Such traders are indifferent about whom they trade with, so all traders are equally likely to be involved in any given transaction.[4] Trading is done anonymously and pairs of transactors form at random. Thus, social group boundaries are ignored and consequently transgressed. In an active market, randomly joined pairs will gather into a single interconnected network.[5] The Law of Indifference leads to a single interconnected network with no sub-cliques.

Real markets seldom comply with this theoretical ideal, although some come closer than others. Alfred Marshall stressed that goods have varying degrees of homogeneity and the more homogeneous the good, the more likely it was that traders would be indifferent. The best example of a market with homogeneous goods was the stock exchange, for: "Any one share or bond of a public company, or any bond of a government is of exactly the same value as any other of the same issue: it can make no difference to any purchaser which of the two he buys" (Marshall 1938: 326–27).[6] This suggests that the Law of Indifference applies particularly to trading in financial securities. In a modern restatement of Jevons, Telser and Higinbotham argue that

> in an organized market the participants trade a standardized contract such that each unit of the contract is a perfect substitute for any other unit. The identities of the parties in any mutually agreeable transaction do not affect the terms of exchange. The organized market itself or some other institution deliberately creates a homogeneous good that can be traded anonymously by the participants or their agents. (Telser and Higinbotham 1977: 997)

Among traders who know each other personally or who transact frequently, exchange is often influenced by the identity of the traders. In contrast: "An organized market facilitates trade among strangers" (Telser and Higin-botham 1977: 998).[7] It allows the market to expand and include friends, acquaintances, and strangers. Organized markets provide a framework that makes indifferent trade possible.

Economists are not the only ones to subscribe to this view. Max Weber, for example, believed that capitalist markets operated anonymously: "In sharp contrast to all other groups which always presuppose some measure of personal fraternization or even blood kinship, the market is fundamentally alien to any type of fraternal relationship" (Weber 1968: 637). The orienta-tion of market participants was toward the commodity and not toward each other. Consequently, capitalist markets were important for social change: they eroded the fraternal bonds of traditional society and contributed to processes of rationalization.[8] Although he may have been the most influen-tial, Weber was not the only sociologist subscribing to this view.[9] Market relations were considered antithetical to other social relations and, in a sense, threw off their influence. Thus, the emergence of capitalism involved the disembedding of economic relations. As the anthropologist Cyril Belshaw put it: "To be rational (in the economists' sense) and to pursue profit one must ideally put aside all other extraneous considerations of an emotive character which create bonds of social relations which might work against the profit motive" (Belshaw 1965: 79).

The orthodox view suggests that politics would not matter in the stock market. Political loyalties and affiliations are irrelevant features of the social landscape, and economically rational actors are indifferent to them. Further-more, if the stock market is competitive, then market forces will punish those who even try to discriminate politically. Becker's economic theory of discrimination (1971) develops this argument.[10] People with a "taste for discrimination" prefer not to hire minority or women workers, for example, even when they are as productive as white male workers. Discriminating employers concern themselves with features that are economically irrele-vant. Conceived this way, discrimination hurts those who are discriminated against but can also hurt the discriminator. In particular, the Becker model implies that discrimination diminishes in more competitive markets (Becker, 1968: 210).[11] Under conditions of perfect competition, wage dis-parities between black and white workers, for example, converge to zero.[12] Such wage disparities disappear not because discriminating employers have become enlightened, but rather because their prices have been undercut by less discriminatory competitors. Discriminators are less efficient than nondiscriminators because they compromise the pursuit of profit with a concern for racial purity. They refuse to hire qualified workers, and thereby hurt themselves.

An alternative to the orthodox view emerges when one weakens the institutional framework for markets. Jevons's ideal market has a legal framework that allows contracts to be costlessly enforced. What happens if the law is ineffectual or faulty? How can traders enforce their agreements? According to Homogeneous Middleman Group theory, traders compensate by forming clublike arrangements and restricting their transactions so as to exclude nonmembers.[13] Familial or ethnic ties serve as the most common basis for group membership and these reduce contract uncertainty and transaction costs. Social ties among traders mean that informal sanctions can be brought to bear against those who breach agreements, which helps compensate for the unreliability of legal sanctions.[14] Group members will prefer to trade among themselves rather than with nonmembers.[15]

The market structure that emerges in this situation is one with a higher density of transactions within groups than between them. Pairs of transactors do not form at random and overall the market network is structured into cliques as market structure mirrors group structure. Additionally, when contract law improves and the legal uncertainty of contracts diminishes, the incentives for endogamous trading decrease and the cliques become more diffuse.[16] As the legal framework for the market improves, the market increasingly resembles the pattern in which each trader follows the Law of Indifference.

Homogeneous Middleman Group theory gives an economic explanation for market discrimination.[17] The advantages to be gained from enforceable agreements combined with the inability of the formal legal apparatus to provide them, lead traders to devise compensatory schemes. They discriminate amongst themselves, preferring to deal with fellow club members. The clubs are defined along ethnic or kin lines but other social groups could serve this purpose. If political groups can help to reduce transaction costs, then there clearly is a possibility of politics in the market. Such political discrimination would be, however, in the service of economic interests.

If we broaden the preferences of market traders, we can construct yet another picture of market behavior. Economic sociologists have drawn on Polanyi's argument that the market is but one of several institutions for the distribution of goods in a society, and that by privileging the market economists have neglected the others.[18] Furthermore, anthropologists have always known that the economic transactions they studied could not be understood outside of their social contexts, which typically included kinship and other social relations. They have been reluctant to consider the market as an autonomous or "absolutized" social institution but instead note how markets are shaped by culture, kinship, or politics.[19] There are important differences between the kinds of economies that anthropologists and sociologists study but nevertheless much economic anthropology bolsters the idea that economic relationships occur in a social context from which they should not be divorced.[20] Following this line, Granovetter (1985, 1992) has criticized economics for taking an "under-socialized" view of human behavior, and for failing to consider how economics is embedded in other social relations.

Sociologists like Granovetter reject the image of markets as anonymous institutions. Embeddedness means that the social characteristics of traders influence their behavior. How this occurs depends upon which social characteristics are relevant and also upon the ongoing social relations into which traders are entered. In general, ". . . the pursuit of economic goals is normally accompanied by that of such non-economic ones as sociability, approval, status and power" (Granovetter 1992: 4). The plurality of goals is not something that an economist like Gary Becker would find objectionable in principle, although there would be disagreement over how easily actors could pursue noneconomic goals in a competitive market. But the socially situated character of economic action is something that can only be understood in light of the particular context.[21] An embeddedness argument implies that politics could affect trading, depending on how much people in general cared about politics, and how politicized joint-stock companies were.

To determine the actual role of politics in the stock market, it will be necessary to step away from these theoretical approaches and reconsider the three factors mentioned above: the institutional setting of the market, the characteristics of the financial commodities traded in the market, and the preferences of market participants.

The Financial Sector

In early modern England, a variety of financial instruments could be used to complete a transaction. They developed because of the almost permanent shortage of coin and included things like bills of exchange, promissory notes, sealed bills, exchequer bills, and running-cash notes.[22] Bills of exchange were especially important for trade because they were used for international remittances and formed the core of a complex system of international payments.[23] Other instruments were used mostly for domestic payments. How well these functioned as near-monies depended on their negotiability, which was problematic.[24] Nevertheless, because of these alternatives, specie was not always necessary for trade.

If near-monies were useful for transactions, they were hardly appropriate for long-term investment. In the seventeenth century, investors had a range of alternatives.[25] Land was the oldest, most secure investment, and brought with it considerable social and political benefits. Ownership of a landed estate was a sine qua non for elite social status and conferred influence in both national and local politics.[26] As a purely economic investment, however, its rate of return compared unfavorably with most of the other alterna-tives.[27] Furthermore, land was difficult to convey and hence was a relatively illiquid asset.

Loans secured by land were another type of investment.[28] Mortgages brought a higher rate of return than land per se, and were riskier, but were still relatively safe as compared to other alternatives. Mortgages were also illiquid because of legal complexities and the lack of a national land regis-try.[29] Scriveners played an important role in the mortgage market.[30]

Investors could also deposit their money and earn interest. Before the Bank of England there were two places to make deposits: goldsmith-bankers and on a more limited scale, scriveners. Goldsmith-bankers were based mostly in London and took in deposits on a large scale. Before 1672, as the Stop of the Exchequer made clear, a large proportion of these deposits were loaned out to the government, but the goldsmith-bankers also issued "run-ning-cash notes" against their deposits, on a crude fractional-reserve sys-tem.[31] In addition, they made a variety of other loans. Bankers' deposits were a relatively liquid investment since they could be withdrawn on short notice. As depositors discovered in 1672, however, they were also risky.[32]

Trade and commerce provided opportunities for both passive and active investment. Active investment meant becoming personally involved in trade. A large proportion of the active merchant's capital would get absorbed by trade credit (i.e., "circulating," as opposed to "fixed," capital), and without connections and experience it was easy to lose money.[33] For passive invest-ment in trade, people could invest in shipping or in loans secured by ships and their cargo (bottomry loans).[34] The growth in overseas trade provided more opportunities for this kind of investment but it was always very risky.[35]

People could also become involved in trade indirectly. This meant in-vesting in the shares or bonds of joint-stock companies that undertook for-eign trade: the East India Company, the South Seas Company, the Royal Africa Company, or the Hudson's Bay Company. The development of this kind of investment was a very important part of the growth of the London stock market.

Trading companies raised capital through stocks and bonds. Share-owner-ship brought with it the prospect of capital gains (and the danger of losses), dividends, and some influence over company management (through com-pany elections). Bonds brought no ownership rights but paid a steady stream of interest.[36] As compared to other financial instruments, bonds were rela-tively nonspeculative. In part because of legal developments, by the end of the seventeenth century company shares and bonds could be very liquid assets. Liquidity depended not only on the law, however, but also on the level of market activity.

In the 1670s there were few opportunities for investment in joint-stock companies. There weren't many trading companies and the only one of any real size, the East India Company, had a restricted capital.[37] The other joint-stock companies were all much smaller and less established than the East India Company. The Royal Africa Company, chartered in 1672, had a total capital worth approximately £110,000, while the Hudson's Bay Company, chartered in 1670, had only thirty-two shareholders and a total capital of £10,500.[38]

With so few opportunities, it is not surprising that the market for company shares was virtually nonexistent. Over time, however, this situation changed as the level of market activity rose. Table 7.1 shows how trading in East India Company stock grew between 1661 and 1689.

Table 7.1 documents a strong upward trend, peaking in 1682–84, declining, and then rebounding in 1688–89. Over the whole period, trading activity increased more than tenfold, as did the value of shares traded.[39] Trading activity in East India shares continued to rise in the early 1690s after the outbreak of war with France.[40]

Market activity also increased because of the growth in the number of joint-stock companies. Before 1689, only fourteen companies had been established in England.[41] This number soon expanded to over one hundred, as a splurge of company foundings occurred in the early 1690s. The most important proximate cause of the surge in market activity in the early 1690s was probably the outbreak of the Nine Years' War with France, for warfare interfered with foreign trade. French privateers made any overseas journey a dangerous proposition, and the expansion of England's own navy created competing demands on domestic shipping and the nautical workforce.[42] Overseas traders who were not bankrupted by wartime problems had idle capital on their hands, and to put their cash balances to profitable use many invested in the stock market.[43] The flow of money out of trade and into stocks was evident at the time:

> For, as it was observ'd before, the money'd Men have for some Years past, kept their great Sums out of those Channels of our National Trade, in which they were employ'd before; besides, that in Foreign Parts the War has made Trading less secure; so that they now find their Account in Trading another Way, viz. chiefly in lending to the Government, and discounting the Government's Credit. (Broughton 1710: 74)[44]

Shares in the major "monied companies" offered security and a reasonable prospect of dividends. With a sufficiently active market, company shares could also be a very liquid investment. Liquidity came from the ease with which shares could be transferred from one set of hands to another. The legal aspects of share transfers were largely unproblematic but *de jure* assignability is not the same as *de facto* assignability. The latter depended on the specific institutional structure of the stock market, and the bureaucratic procedures used to transfer share ownership. It was not only the law but also

TABLE 7.1
Transactions in East India Company Shares,
1661–1689

Years	Average Number of Transactions	Total Value (nearest £100)
1661–63	44	18,900
1664–66	57	23,900
1667–69	71	32,100
1670–72	126	47,000
1673–75	152	53,800
1676–78	131	55,400
1679–81	172	68,100
1682–84	780	268,300
1685–87	537	191,000
1688–89	655	238,000

Source: Lougheed 1980: 151.

the evolution of a particular set of organizational practices that enhanced the liquidity of the London stock market. We may term this the micro-institutional setting of the market, to distinguish it from the macro-institutional context (law, the Constitution, etc.) discussed by North.

THE MICRO-INSTITUTIONAL SETTING
OF THE STOCK MARKET

The weight of historical opinion is that the London stock market emerged very quickly. In 1688 there was no organized stock market in England, but by the late 1690s there was.[45] The sharp increase in market activity in East India Company shares during the 1680s and 1690s bears this out, as does the growing number of joint-stock companies. Davies also remarks that ". . . before 1690 facilities for buying and selling company stock appear to have been primitive" (Davies 1952: 294).[46] Aside from the sheer increase in market activity, what specific institutional features did the English market so suddenly acquire?

The first concerns the social roles played by market participants. As the market grew in size, it became possible for traders to assume different positions within an emerging division of labor. A key indicator of the growth in the English market was therefore the emergence of brokers and jobbers who specialized in company shares.[47] Playing the market was the primary occupation of these men. There is some evidence of their activity starting in the early 1680s when brokers began to advertise their services in newspapers, and by the 1700s such advertising was commonplace.[48] Brokers were so central to the stock market that they were invariably the scapegoats when the market crashed.[49] An Act of Parliament (8 & 9 William III, c.32) designed to control the numbers and activities of stockbrokers suggests that they were a fact of commercial life by the end of the 1690s.[50] Yet a similar act passed in 1673 to regulate brokers makes no mention of trade in company shares.[51]

A broker was someone active in the market on a daily basis who, if he did not buy or sell directly, could arrange a deal. In order for shares to be transferred between individuals, first, a purchaser and seller had to agree to trade. They could do this directly or use a broker.[52] It is unclear how often transfers were accomplished with the assistance of brokers, but in any case brokers often traded on their own account.[53] Second, the transfer of shares had to be recorded with the company (this required the signatures of both purchaser and seller). At their offices, joint-stock companies kept Transfer Books to record transfers of company stock.[54] Entries would later be posted to the Stock Ledger, which contained all the information about ownership and transfer of company shares. Persons whose purchases of stock were not recorded with the company did not have a secure title, so registration was imperative. The importance of the procedure warranted careful monitoring by the company.[55] As generic or "boilerplate" contracts became common, share transfer procedures became more routine and predictable.[56] For example, John Houghton published generic contracts for the transfer of company stock in his A *Collection for Improvement of Husbandry and Trade* in 1694.

Transactions could either be for immediate delivery (what is known as a "spot transaction") or for future settlement (a futures contract). Options, a more exotic type of contract, consisted of either the right to sell stock at a future date (a "put"), or the right to purchase it (a "refusal"). Sample contract forms for these more complex transactions were also printed by John Houghton.[57] Even as futures and options became more familiar and routine for sophisticated market participants, they remained among the most enigmatic and controversial transactions in the eyes of outsiders.[58]

The publication of generic contracts helped to routinize market transactions. The press influenced the market in other ways, as well. Among the most important was the part newspapers and business publications played in disseminating information about share prices. Because an efficient market is one where prices reflect all available information, information is the key to market efficiency.[59] The more widely information is distributed among traders in a market, the more efficient the market becomes.[60] One of the pieces of information of greatest import concerned share prices. Buyers and sellers wanted to know the market price of a share and how that price had changed over time.[61]

Market prices were first published in the 1680s. Whiston's *The Merchants Remembrancer* started with weekly information, noting when shares were selling at their highest and lowest prices.[62] John Houghton's *A Collection for Improvement of Husbandry and Trade* appeared twice weekly and provided actual share prices starting in 1681. This publication was joined by John Castaing's *The Course of the Exchange*, and eventually by a number of others, all primarily serving a business audience.[63] Castaing had an office in Exchange Alley and so could easily monitor prices by himself. The Company of London Insurers, which published the *British Mercury*, paid their agent (a Mr. Justice) £6 per annum to provide price information for their newspaper.[64] In such endeavors, a premium was placed on precision. Traders wanted accurate and impartial information and in one case at least, the publisher consciously avoided any partisanship or political favoritism. At a meeting in October 1710 of the Company of London Insurers, the directors resolved: "That the account of Elections shall be printed without any reflexions or flourishes upon the Candidates of either side and that no party business shall be inserted in our paper."[65] With all these sources, almost any member of the English reading public had easy access to accurate information on daily share prices.[66]

Physically, the English stock market was highly centralized. It was located in the coffee houses in Exchange Alley, a small area near Lombard Street in central London. Two were of particular importance: Jonathan's Coffeehouse and Garroway's Coffeehouse. According to one contemporary, it was possible to circumambulate Exchange Alley in its entirety in about one and a half minutes.[67] Nearby shopkeepers and residents complained of the crowds and bustle which attended the stock market and there is no evidence of significant amounts of trading going on elsewhere.[68] The use of coffeehouses to do business was not peculiar to stock trading in London. Marine insurance was usually transacted in Edward Lloyd's Coffeehouse and fire insurance in Tom's and Causey's Coffeehouses.[69] Specialist coffeehouses were common, with activities ranging from medicine and literature to commerce.[70]

For anyone interested in trading shares, Exchange Alley was the only place to go. In the coffeehouses one would find a small group of brokers and jobbers ready to buy or sell. It was easy to transact in shares as information was widely available, the market was active, and the process of share transfer was routine. There were few visible barriers to prevent anyone interested in selling from transacting with anyone interested in buying.[71] In fact, by the mid-eighteenth century, stockbrokers were complaining that access to Jonathan's Coffeehouse was *too easy*, for it cost only a sixpence to be in the coffeehouse all day.[72] Overall, the micro-institutional features of the market reduced transaction costs.

Many of these features were derived from Dutch markets. English capitalists had long been familiar with the stock exchange in the Amsterdam Bourse and English writers on trade and commerce frequently analyzed

Dutch mercantile technique, Dutch law, and Dutch finances. They often concluded that England should emulate Dutch methods.[73] De La Vega's description of the Amsterdam stock exchange in 1688 bears a striking resemblance to the London stock exchange two decades later.[74] The use of the terms "bulls" and "bears" to describe certain kinds of traders was common to both markets, and stock trading in Amsterdam was also conducted in coffeehouses.[75]

By the end of the 1690s, more shares of a larger number of joint-stock companies were being traded in an increasingly sophisticated stock market.[76] By historical standards, the appearance of this market was almost an instantaneous event. Although there were other financial investments, none were as easily transferred as a joint-stock company share. Government annuities, which constituted a significant proportion of the total long-term public debt, could only be transferred at the Exchequer. The cumbersome nature of this procedure discouraged buying and selling, and so there were far fewer transactions in annuities than in company stock.[77]

In conjunction with a legal system that was increasingly hospitable to financial instruments, the advanced institutional setting of the London stock market facilitated trade. With accessible information and routine procedures, transacting with other market participants was easy. Furthermore, company shares were indistinguishable from each other. Every £100 worth of Bank of England stock was exactly like every other £100 worth. Finally, the stock market operated in the absence of most of the regulations and controls that twentieth-century governments place on contemporary financial markets. There was a stamp tax on the transfer of shares but there was little of the regulatory machinery or other kinds of taxation that could affect (or "distort") how the market operated.[78]

Putting all these features together, the early eighteenth-century London stock market seems close to the ideal of economic theory. Consequently, the arguments of Jevons, Marshall, and Telser suggest that traders in this market would have been indifferent about whom they traded with. This institutional setting was conducive to the emergence of *homo economicus*. The neoclassical picture is of an atomized market where traders transact anonymously and without regard to social identity. Its preconditions were closely approximated, if not perfectly satisfied, by the early London stock market.

This theoretical picture becomes even more plausible when we realize that contemporaries viewed the stock market in a similar fashion. In *An Essay Upon Loans*, Daniel Defoe paid particular attention to those who traded shares in the stock market: "Men in Trade, more especially than the rest of Mankind, are bound by their Interest; Gain is the end of Commerce" (Defoe 1710a: 14).[79] In the marketplace, people are primarily concerned with making a profit, and not with political questions. Defoe asked rhetorically

... if there is either Whig or Tory in a good Bargain; Churchman or Dissenter in a good Freight; High Church or Low Church in a Good Adventure; if a Shop-keeper sees a good Pennyworth, a Scrivener a good Mortgage, a Money'd Man a good Purchase; Do they ever ask what Party he is of that parts with it? Nay, rather in spite of Party Aversions, do we not Buy, Sell, Lend, Borrow, enter into Companies, Partnerships, and the closest Engagements with one another, nay Marry with one another without any Questions of the Matter? (Defoe, 1710a: 16–17)

His point was that political distinctions did not matter in the marketplace. Profit, not politics, was the central concern and so Defoe's traders complied with the Law of Indifference.[80] During the frenzied height of the South Sea Bubble in 1720, Edward Harley noted in a letter the promiscuous inter-mingling of all social types in the market: "The demon stock jobbing . . . has seized all parties, Whigs, Tories, Jacobites, Papists and all sects" (Murphy 1986: 168).[81]

The Dutch set an important example in this regard. Not only were new techniques of public finance termed "Dutch finance," and the London stock market modeled after the Amsterdam bourse, but the Dutch also set the standard for indifference. For them, neither religion nor politics should interfere with trade and the pursuit of profit. Holland was a remarkably tolerant society, with few restrictions placed on religious minorities. Indeed, religious toleration was considered to be one reason for Dutch economic success.[82] As merchants and bankers, the Dutch cared little about whom they dealt with. Dutch lenders were happy to loan money to both sides in a war and Dutch merchants were even willing to trade with the Netherlands' own enemies.[83] When the French armies invaded Holland during the 1672 war, their gunpowder, match, and lead were supplied by Dutch firms![84]

The picture of market perfection is further buttressed by evidence that the stock market was efficient.[85] Using time-series data on share prices, several economic historians have examined the early London stock market. The basic test for efficiency uses autocorrelations among price changes and if the autocorrelation coefficients are statistically equivalent to zero, then this supports the "weak-version" of efficiency.[86] In an efficient market, the best predictor of share price at time $t+1$ is the price at time t, and no one is able to construct a better predictor of future prices or price changes. Using this test, both Parsons and Neal found strong evidence of market efficiency.[87]

Information costs and transaction costs that are zero are sufficient conditions for the strongest version of market efficiency.[88] Even advocates of the efficient markets model concede that the strongest version is probably false for the simple reason that information and transaction costs are always positive, although they may be very small. When a market experiences a significant decline in these costs, however, the case for efficiency becomes much more plausible. If it cannot be said that the market was perfectly efficient, it is probably true that the market was becoming more efficient. The same process that leads to greater efficiency also leads to greater indifference and anonymity among traders: declining information and transaction costs, and trade in increasingly homogeneous commodities within an increasingly secure legal framework. As Baskin put it: "A prerequisite for strangers trading with each other is that the value of the commodity can be reasonably ascertained by both parties" (Baskin 1988: 206). Thus, the evidence for market efficiency makes indifference seem more plausible (although the two are not the same thing).

For a number of reasons, it seems likely that in the early eighteenth-century London stock market, traders traded for profit and ignored whatever was not relevant to this goal. Yet were such economic rationality to have prevailed, it would have done so in a context of intense political conflict. As organizations, joint-stock companies were caught up in the Whig-Tory struggle, particularly at the level of the directors. At the level of individual company shareholders, economic action took place in a highly developed and competitive market. Over the long run, competitive markets supposedly punish extraneous and economically irrelevant concerns like political partisanship, or other forms of discrimination.[89] In a competitive market, someone who begins to discriminate performs less efficiently than someone who remains indifferent. Indifferent traders make more money than discriminating traders and eventually drive them out. Thus, even traders who wanted to worry about politics, ethnicity, gender, status, or something else, would be forced in the long run to set aside these concerns and focus on the business of making money.

We are thus presented with a puzzle. Financial commodities were traded on an organized and efficient market with low information and transaction costs. This strongly suggests that trading conformed to the Law of Indifference. Furthermore, contemporaries treated market trading as if it were an apolitical activity. And yet, company shares were connected to institutions that were deeply involved in partisan conflict, which suggests that politics may have affected trading. Which of the two possibilities was true?

SHARE PRICES

Prices were the most important piece of information for those trading in company shares. For the researcher, price is a useful measure of the commodity being traded and so is important for understanding market behavior. Following standard econometric methods, an analysis of price changes can be used to estimate the degree of market efficiency. Furthermore, the extent of market integration is measured by correlations among share prices and changes in prices.

Data on share prices can be gotten from the same source traders used: the *Course of the Exchange*, published by John Castaing and later to become the official journal for the stock market. This was a business newsletter, containing information on share prices, exchange rates, and exchequer and lottery loans. The *Course* published daily market prices of Bank of England, East India Company, South Sea Company, Million Bank, Irish Lands, and African stock, as well as Army debentures. The prices given were: "Prices of stocks from Twelve to Two of the Clock," and the data analyzed here start from December 31, 1711 and go through the end of 1712. This is the same year for the transactions data analyzed below (why I chose 1712 is discussed below). Except for holidays, Sundays, and days when the company books were closed, the series is complete and numbers 292 data points. Prices were stated as a proportion of the par or face value of the stock. A market price of 100 meant that market price and nominal price were equal, while higher or lower market prices meant that shares were selling at a premium or a discount.

Table 7.2 provides descriptive statistics for Bank of England shares, East India Company shares, and South Sea Company shares for 1712. The mean values for Bank of England and East India Company shares were 112.04 and 117.19, respectively. This meant that on average one could buy £100 worth of Bank stock for just slightly more than £112. The mean price for South Sea Company shares was 75.83. Obviously, Bank and East India stock was selling at a premium, while South Sea Company shares were selling at a substantial discount. The Bank and East India Company were older established companies, while the South Sea Company dated from only 1711 and had yet to undertake any trading activity.

If we examine the variability of share prices, there are some other significant differences. The two older stocks, Bank and East India Company, were quite distinct. The standard deviation of East India stock was significantly higher than that of Bank stock (3.53 vs. 2.17), as was the coefficient of variation (0.030 vs. 0.019).[90] East India Company stock was a riskier, more speculative, investment.[91] This reflected its status as a trading company whose fortunes were subject to the vagaries of weather, pirates, and Indian politics. By contrast, the Bank's fortune depended primarily on a loan to the government, which year after year reliably paid its interest. The variability in South Sea stock was greater than the other two companies (the coefficient of variation was 0.036, the highest of the three). As a newly established entity with uncertain trading prospects, the South Sea Company was the riskiest of the lot.

The correlations between share prices are presented in Table 7.3. Bank and South Sea Company stock were significantly *positively* correlated with each other and both were uncorrelated with East India Company stock. This was probably because the East India Company was a trading company,

TABLE 7.2
Bank of England, United East India Company, and South Sea Company
Share Prices, 1712

Bank of England:		
Mean 112.04	Standard Deviation 2.17	
Median 112.50	Coefficient of Variation 0.01936	
Minimum 107.75	Maximum 117.00	
East India Company:		
Mean 117.19	Standard Deviation 3.53	
Median 117.50	Coefficient of Variation 0.03012	
Minimum 109.25	Maximum 124.00	
South Sea Company:		
Mean 75.83	Standard Deviation 2.74	
Median 75.00	Coefficient of Variation 0.03613	
Minimum 71.25	Maximum 82.00	

Source: Castaing, *Course of the Exchange.*

TABLE 7.3
Correlations of Bank of England, United
East India Company, and South Sea
Company Share Prices, 1712

	BANK	*EIC*	*SSC*
BANK	1.0000		
EIC	.0329	1.0000	
SSC	.8043**	−.0628	1.0000

** Statistically significant at the 0.001 level.
Source: Castaing, *Course of the Exchange.*

while the values of the other two securities were more directly tied to government finance. Over the entire year, there were two distinct trends for East India stock. During the first seven months, East India stock was declining. Starting in August, however, its price began to climb almost continuously. Bank and South Sea Company stock were rising, in fits and starts, throughout the entire year. Thus, East India Company stock was negatively correlated with the prices of the other two from January until the end of July, and positively correlated for the rest of the year, resulting in a net year-long relationship of close to zero.[92] Figure 7.1 shows the market prices for all three securities over this period.

Correlations among price changes, as distinct from prices, are presented in table 7.4. All daily price changes were significantly and positively correlated with each other, suggesting an integrated market. Short-term price changes for all three were closely linked even though the longer-term trends

TABLE 7.4

Correlations of Changes in Bank of England, United
East India Company, and South Sea Company
Share Prices, 1712

	CH-BANK	CH-EIC	CH-SSC
CH-BANK	1.0000		
CH-EIC	.6668**	1.0000	
CH-SSC	.6440**	.6818**	1.0000

** Statistically significant at the 0.001 level.
Source: Castaing, *Course of the Exchange.*

were quite distinct for the East India Company versus the other two. One instance involved the quick price rise provoked by rumors of a coming peace agreement with France. As these rumors spread during the period between Thursday, 8 May 1712, and Tuesday, 13 May, Bank prices rose from 112.75 to 116.50, East India Company prices from 117 to 119.5, and South Sea Company prices from 75.75 to 79.50. This upward "bump" is visible in all three lines in figure 7.1. After early October, as the prospect of peace became more and more certain, all three shares increased in price. In general, share prices reacted to political events and changing expectations about interest rates and government borrowing, among other things.

There are two conclusions to draw from share prices. First, different company shares possessed different financial characteristics. Owners of capital looking for a safe "blue chip" investment would have preferred Bank stock. People with a higher tolerance for risk would have found East India shares to be a better choice, with South Sea Company shares being even more speculative. Second, their financial differences notwithstanding, all three companies were traded on the same, integrated, market. Based in London, there was a single stock market for company shares.

Social Patterns of Share Ownership and Trading

Transactions are the elementary form of market life, involving the exchange of one commodity for another or for money. An empirical analysis of the stock market must, therefore, focus on transactions. The major practical issue is how to "measure" transactions and where to obtain data.

For several reasons, I have selected 1712 as the best year from this period to gather data. Unlike 1710, 1715, or 1720, there were no economic or financial crises to distort the market.[93] The War of the Spanish Succession was winding down and although it was not yet over, its fiscal demands were diminishing. Furthermore, 1712 was not a year with national parliamentary elections (unlike 1708, 1710, and 1713), so there was no general election to

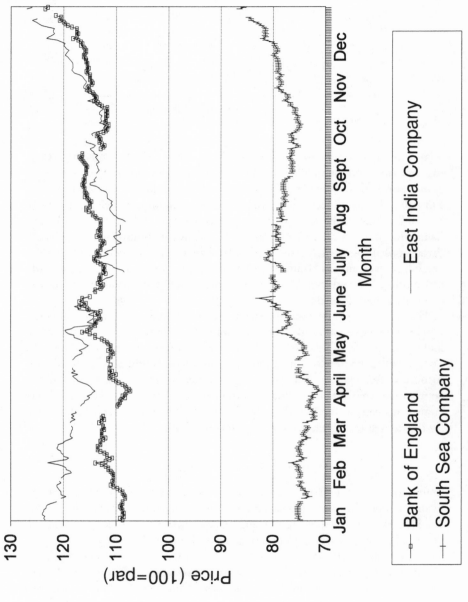

Fig. 7.1. Market Prices of Joint-Stock Company Shares, January 3–December 23, 1712.

inflame partisan feelings. The year 1712 came after the establishment of the
South Sea Company (which occurred in 1711) and after the merger of the
two East India Companies, so there were three major joint-stock companies,
each with a different relationship to extant political forces. Comparisons
among the three companies can provide important analytical leverage. The
year 1712 also preceded the accession of George I (1715), a regnal transition
which resulted in a sea change in political forces as the Tory party was con-
signed to political near-oblivion. Most important, however, 1712 was sufficiently late that one could say the stock market was "up and running." Data
from the 1690s and early 1700s would be open to the objection that the
market was still too undeveloped to provide a fair test of theories of economic action. From both the perspective of economics and politics, market
trading in 1712 was not unduly influenced by national electioneering, financial disasters, company mergers, or the immaturity of the market.

Table 7.5 describes shareholdings and transactions (both purchases
and sales) for the Bank of England and East India Company. From the
numbers of shareholders, it is clear just how much bigger the market for
Bank shares was as compared to East India shares (4,419 vs. 2,261). This
difference carried over into the number of market transactions, which totaled around 3,000 for the Bank and 1,800 for the East India Company, and
the number of shares (5.5 million for the Bank and 3.1 million for the East
India Company).

The variation in holdings among East India Company shareholders was
considerably greater than among Bank shareholders. Although median
shareholdings were the same (£500 worth), the mean for the East India
Company (£1,414.5) was higher than the Bank mean (£1,239.6) because of a
relatively large group of very wealthy shareholders.[94] The difference exists
at the other end of the shareholding spectrum as well: 25% of Bank shareholders held less than £126 worth, while the 25th percentile for the East
India Company was £160. At the time, the Bank was considered to be a more
conservative investment, and hence more attractive to small-time investors.

There were more trades in Bank stock but in terms of *relative* activity it
appears that the East India Company takes precedence. The average number of transactions for East India Company shareholders was 1.62, while for
the Bank it was 1.39. The 99th percentile for East India transactions was 22,
in contrast to only 12 for the Bank. These differences must be taken in context, however, for most shareholders were inactive. Median transactions for
both companies was 0. The majority of shareholders simply hung on to their
investments, although there was a greater tendency for East India shareholders to play the market.[95]

Shares of both the Bank of England and the East India Company were
traded on the London stock market but they were distinct securities, partic-

TABLE 7.5
Shareholdings and Transactions in Bank of England, and
United East India Company Stock, 1712

Bank of England Shares Owned:		Number of Transactions:	
Mean	1,239.62	Mean	1.39
Std Dev	2,762.91	Std Dev	6.72
Median	500.00	Median	0.00
Sum	5,458,055	Sum	3,077
n (no. of shareholders) = 4,419			
East India Company Shares Owned:		Number of Transactions:	
Mean	1,414.49	Mean	1.62
Std Dev	3,497.61	Std Dev	5.40
Median	500.00	Median	0.00
Sum	3,126,016	Sum	1,826
n = 2,261			

Source: See appendix.

ularly in terms of risk. It is valuable to know the degree of overlap between the two "submarkets," and because active traders dominated the total volume of trades, it is sufficient to consider the active traders. Defined as those making seven or more trades, these traders comprised only 3% of the Bank shareholders, and 4.5% of East India Company shareholders, yet as buyers or sellers (or both) they accounted for 40% and 50%, respectively, of all trades. If we shift the threshold down to five or more trades, active traders still constituted only 5% of Bank shareholders and 7% of East India shareholders but accounted for 47% and 58%, respectively, of total trades.

Among active traders, Whigs outnumbered the Tories between three and four to one. They comprised only men, and included no persons living abroad. Naturalized, Huguenot, Quaker, or Jewish individuals constituted a significant proportion (about 20% for the East India Company, and 30% for the Bank). There were no peers in this group, and only two baronets, so England's traditional landed elites were essentially absent.

Bank and East India Company active traders overlapped considerably. Of 192 individuals, more than one-fifth were active traders in both stocks, and these 43 men accounted for a substantial proportion of all trades. There may have been "submarkets" for Bank and East India Company shares but much of the trading in both was accounted for by a single group of individuals. Active traders were a small group that met face-to-face in the same small location, Exchange Alley. They accounted for the bulk of trading in both securities, although some of them specialized in either Bank or East

India shares. The overlap between the two groups of active traders is consistent with the analysis of price movements. Social overlap led to common price changes.

In the previous chapter, we analyzed the Bank and East India Company shareholders in terms of gender, social background, social status, and political affiliations. It was clear that shareholders were a diverse group but with a strong tendency to favor men, merchants, nongentry, and Whigs. There was also a small number of prominent traders who were members of ethnic or religious minority groups. Party differences among shareholders are particularly interesting because of their connection to larger political and economic struggles. The contrast between the numbers of Whigs and Tories is especially striking because the primary sources of political information, the two London poll books, are biased in favor of the Tories. Whig dominance is probably underestimated.

The Whig-Tory distinction loomed large in the composition of the stock market. Whigs dominated, although they did not monopolize, the market. The Whig-Tory distinction was also salient at the level of company directors and the political struggle for control over joint-stock companies. Did compositional differences among shareholders generate behavioral differences, or to put it differently, did political differences at the institutional level produce political differences in the market? When shareholders transacted, did it matter that potential trading partners were Whigs or Tories, Jews or non-Jews, Huguenots or non-Huguenots? Theoretically, our expectations about trading behavior are set by the arguments reviewed earlier. If this is an efficient market for a homogeneous good, then the Law of Indifference ought to hold. Characterizations like Defoe's only reinforce the impression that politics didn't matter in the stock market.

The top part of table 7.6 sets out trading among Tories, Whigs, and political unknowns in East India Company shares and describes the political characteristics of pairs of traders.[96] No distinction is made between buying and selling, we are concerned here only with trading per se. There are six combinations (Whig trading with Whig, Whig with Tory, Whig with Unknown, Tory with Tory, etc.). The upper-right of the table is not filled-in since it is just the mirror image of the lower-left. The table shows that the two most frequent combinations are Whig trading with Whig, and Whig with Unknown. This is to be expected given that Whigs were more numerous and active than the others.[97] To address the predictions for market trading, however, we need more than just raw numbers.

Table 7.6 can be analyzed using log-linear techniques.[98] What makes these methods useful is that one can operationalize Law of Indifference predictions about market trading. The lower panel of table 7.6 presents the results of fitting three different log-linear models. The no-effects model is a baseline model and predicts equal counts in every cell by estimating a single

TABLE 7.6

Party Trading in United East India Company Shares,
and Log-Linear Analysis

	Tories	Whigs	Unknown
Tories	39		
Whigs	221	565	
Unknown	134	610	228

Model	Degrees of Freedom	G^2
1. No effects	5	1,071.20
2. Quasi-independence	3	15.78
3. Endogamy	2	2.14

Source: See appendix.

"propensity to trade" parameter across all political pairings. The likelihood-ratio statistic G^2, which measures how well the model fits the data, is very large, meaning that the model fits poorly. Model 2, the "quasi-independence" model, is the Law of Indifference model.[99] It assumes that each group of traders has a different "propensity to trade" and that they select their trading partners at random, without consideration of politics. It provides a much better fit than the no-effects model, but the predicted and actual counts still diverge considerably.[100] Examination of residuals (not presented here) shows that the Law of Indifference model consistently *underestimates* how much people trade with members of the same party, and *overestimates* how much people from different parties trade with each other.[101] The model most underestimates Tories trading with Tories.

The third model I call the endogamy model because not only does each group have a different "propensity to trade," but there is a parameter measuring the extent to which members of a political group favor trading with other people from the same group. This model uses up another degree of freedom but provides a much better fit than the quasi-independence model. The G^2 statistic drops from 15.78 down to 2.14, a substantial improvement, and there does not appear to be any systematic misfitting of the model. For East India Company stock, there was a strong tendency for party members to favor trading with people from the same party. Contrary to the Law of Indifference (and Daniel Defoe), people did not trade at random: they discriminated on the basis of politics. Whigs traded disproportionately with Whigs, and Tories with Tories.[102]

One can try to explain this pattern, which I term "political endogamy," in a number of ways. Endogamy might be spurious, it might be a rational response to transaction costs (following Homogeneous Middleman Group theory), or it might be a genuinely political phenomenon. The most obvious explanation, that strong political cleavages made it difficult as a practical matter to trade across party lines, is clearly wrong. Trading of shares occurred in the coffeeshops of Exchange Alley, and there were no separate Whig and Tory stock markets. To begin to explain endogamy, however, it is necessary to understand more about it.

One important dimension is that of number of trades, and splitting the table this way distinguishes market specialists from other traders. The distribution of trades is highly skewed, with a small number of traders accounting for a large number of trades. The explanation of financial endogamy depends on which subtable(s) it persists in. If the small number of active traders traded endogamously, there could have been a conscious arrangement (a "conspiracy") at work. One can imagine something like a price cartel, where instead of trying to raise prices, the conspirators restricted between-group trades. If endogamy existed among the large number of inactive traders, however, a conspiracy seems unlikely and endogamy would have to be the result of a sentiment or condition general enough to influence a large number of persons.[103]

Table 7.7 shows trades in East India stock that involved the active traders (anyone trading seven or more times). This group included the professional traders, those who earned their living and sometimes great notoriety on the London stock market (e.g., Moses Hart and John "Vulture" Hopkins). By this criterion, the number of active traders was very small in relation to the total number of East India Company shareholders: only 102 out of 2,261 (roughly 4.5%). It was an extremely wealthy and active group, for on average they owned £5,015 worth of East India shares and traded eighteen times. These individuals were responsible for a disproportionate share of all transactions in East India stock, but it turns out they accounted for virtually none of the endogamy pattern.

Unlike the market as a whole, among active traders the endogamy model performs no better than the quasi-independence model (the G^2 statistics for the two models are virtually the same). The quasi-independence model does a reasonable job fitting the data and there is no systematic underprediction of within-party trades, or overprediction of between-party trades. As far as politics was concerned, the professional brokers at the core of the market did not discriminate, and endogamy cannot be understood as the result of coordinated action on the part of this small group.

If we consider the other subtable, trades that involved only "small," inactive traders, we find endogamy. Table 7.8 presents the trades and the results of the log-linear analysis.

An examination of the fitted values and residuals shows that among inactive traders, there is more within-group trading than one would expect if trading partners were chosen at random. The drop in the G^2 statistic shows the endogamy model to be an improvement over the quasi-independence

TABLE 7.7

Party Trading in United East India Company Shares
Involving Active Traders

	Tories	*Whigs*	*Unknown*
Tories	26		
Whigs	178	496	
Unknown	77	445	93

Model	*Degrees of Freedom*	G^2
1. No effects	5	1,031.10
2. Quasi-independence	3	4.48
3. Endogamy	2	4.32

Source: See appendix.

TABLE 7.8

Party Trading in United East India Company Shares
Involving Inactive Traders

	Tories	*Whigs*	*Unknown*
Tories	13		
Whigs	43	69	
Unknown	57	165	135

Model	*Degrees of Freedom*	G^2
1. No effects	5	240.00
2. Quasi-independence	3	5.53
3. Endogamy	2	1.15

Source: See appendix.

model. It seems that whatever caused political endogamy was general
enough to influence the behavior of a large number of persons.

Another important dimension is wealth, measured here by the size of
shareholding. Table 7.9 shows the distribution of trades after splitting the
sample into trades which involved wealthy shareholders (defined as a shareholding greater than £5,477) and those which did not.[104]

This log-linear analysis shows that the endogamy pattern persisted among
the wealthy shareholders but not among the "poorer" shareholders. The
quasi-independence model underpredicts within-group trading and over-
predicts between-group trading, and according to the G^2 statistic, the endogamy model fits the data much better.

Separating traders according to activity and wealth shows that political
endogamy was not a universal phenomenon. Some traders in East India

TABLE 7.9
Party Trading in United East India Company Shares
That Involved Wealthy Shareholders

	Tories	Whigs	Unknown
Tories	10		
Whigs	62	185	
Unknown	27	65	27

Model	Degrees of Freedom	G^2
1. No effects	5	367.70
2. Quasi-independence	3	26.76
3. Endogamy	2	5.03

Source: See appendix.

Company stock discriminated politically while others did not. In particular, endogamy centered around the wealthy shareholders and those who were inactive traders. This was a group that largely *excluded* the market professionals.

One way to interpret the endogamy pattern is to question whether it really was a political phenomenon, and in effect to explain it away. Perhaps political groups were only a proxy for some other group. If the social groups within which endogamy really transpired were highly correlated with party, then we would get the *appearance* of party endogamy. The strongest candidate for these social groups are the ones that Homogeneous Middleman Group theory focused on: some mixture of family, ethnicity, and religion. If members of the same family or ethnic or religious group had similar political allegiances, then endogamy among them could produce spurious endogamy among parties.[105]

The recent exodus of Huguenots out of France, the salience of religious dissent, and the growing number of Sephardic Jews in England made Huguenots, Quakers, and Jews among the most prominent minorities in 1712. These groups socialized, married, and worshiped among themselves, and were lumped together by the rest of English society because of their religious unorthodoxy. If they traded shares amongst themselves, could it account for the pattern among the parties? Since these groups were part of the Whig constituency, their endogamy would contribute to Whig endogamy.

Examining trades after dividing traders into two groups (Huguenots, Quakers, and Jews, and all the rest) is one way to resolve this question. Table 7.10 sets out trading in East India shares, together with a log-linear analysis. Table 7.10 has only three degrees of freedom, and the quasi-independence model uses two of them. The large G^2 indicates that this model fits poorly,

TABLE 7.10
Ethnic-Religious Trading in United East India
Company Shares, and Log-Linear Analysis

	Others	Hug.-Quaker-Jew
Others	1,013	
Hug.-Quaker-Jew	614	206

Model	Degrees of Freedom	G^2
1. No effects	2	785.83
2. Quasi-independence	1	50.30

Source: See appendix.

and the residuals from the model are those characteristic of endogamy: underestimation of diagonals and overestimation of off-diagonals. It is clear that Huguenot, Quaker, and Jewish traders in East India stock tended to trade among themselves.[106]

To see if endogamy among minorities accounted for endogamy among the Whigs, I redid the analysis of party trading after removing minorities from the Whig party so that only those who explicitly voted for Whigs in the parliamentary elections were classified as Whigs. This reduced the number of Whig-Whig trades but the endogamy pattern persisted. The endogamy model is a substantial improvement over quasi-independence (with a G^2 of 3.11 vs. 11.51), and the latter fails to fit in just the way that it failed before. Evidently, party endogamy cannot be reduced to these other forms of social endogamy.

THE ECONOMIC EXPLANATION OF ENDOGAMY

Party endogamy was not spurious but it may have been undertaken for economic reasons. Although financial property rights were relatively secure, one could generalize Homogeneous Middleman Group theory to argue that there were other economic risks that encouraged traders to trade within groups. For example, purchasers might prefer to deal with someone they could trust when buying a commodity whose value was unpredictable. Or perhaps there were information asymmetries between buyers and sellers. A buyer may wonder "Why does so-and-so want to sell now? Does he know something I don't?" Such suspicions were not uncommon—in his diary entry for April 6, 1713, for example, Sir David Hamilton recorded that "I told Her [Queen Anne] that Stocks rose in the morning, and fell in the Afternoon by the Jews selling out. Which made People Suspicious of their knowing something that might occasion it" (Roberts 1975: 52–53). In a market composed of both sophisticated and unsophisticated traders, waves of buy-

TABLE 7.11
Party Trading in Bank of England Shares, and
Log-Linear Analysis

	Tories	Whigs	Unknown
Tories	52		
Whigs	330	616	
Unknown	341	1,197	605

Model	Degrees of Freedom	G^2
1. No effects	5	1,475.90
2. Quasi-independence	3	0.96
3. Endogamy	2	0.48

Source: See appendix.

ing and selling could always be interpreted as the result of people with inside knowledge, problematizing the trustworthiness of trading partners. For any number of reasons, trading in East India Company shares may have entailed economic risks that traders tried to ameliorate by trading within political parties.

A comparison of Bank and East India stocks allows us to pursue this argument because the latter were riskier. Bank stock was a less speculative investment and so if endogamy was used to deal with economic risks, we could expect less of it in Bank stock. Table 7.11 sets out trading among Whigs, Tories, and Unknowns in Bank of England stock for 1712 and in the lower panel are the log-linear results.

These results show that the level of party endogamy was much lower for the Bank than for the East India Company. With Bank stock, the endogamy model was only marginally better than the quasi-independence model, and the latter fit the data rather well.[107] But one shouldn't rush to conclude that economic risks explain party endogamy, for it is still not clear why traders would discriminate along party lines. Homogeneous Middleman Group theory proposes that traders use ethnic and familial groups because these provide effective substitutes for contract law, but other groups could serve the same purpose. Traders trying to reduce economic risks or transaction costs had much better organizational options than political parties. One obvious choice would have been the London guilds. They were well established in the economic life of London, and since their purpose was to control the products and prices of their membership, they already possessed monitoring and sanctioning mechanisms.[108] Although not as dominant as in the Middle Ages, the guilds still possessed considerable organizational vigor.[109] A trader looking to reduce transaction costs or ameliorate risk would do better to exploit guilds than political parties.[110]

TABLE 7.12
Ethnic-Religious Trading in Bank of England Shares,
and Log-Linear Analysis

	Hug.-Quaker-Jew	Others
Hug.-Quaker-Jew	122	692
Others		2,333

Model	Degrees of Freedom	G^2
1. No effects	2	3,480.20
2. Quasi-independence	1	47.78

Source: See appendix.

Assume for the moment that within-group trades were a rational response to economic risk, and that traders used group solidarities and collective self-monitoring mechanisms to manage risk. If this were the cause of party endogamy, then there ought to have been even more endogamy among the guilds than among the parties. Using the London poll books, I obtained information on the guild membership of 481 East India Company shareholders and 860 Bank shareholders.[111] Log-linear analysis showed that the endogamy model offered no improvement over the quasi-independence model (the G^2 declined only from 52.3 to 52), and the residuals showed that the quasi-independence model did not systematically underestimate within-guild trades or overestimate between-guild trades.[112] The endogamy pattern does not appear among the guilds trading in East India Company shares, nor among guilds trading in Bank shares.

If differences in party endogamy resulted from differences in risk, as an economic argument might suggest, then this ought to show up in trading among guilds. Thus, the absence of guild endogamy is telling. Furthermore, recall that ethnic-religious endogamy existed for trading in East India Company stock. If ethnic-religious groups were used to deal with economic risks, then we would expect less endogamy for ethnic-religious trading in Bank stock.[113] Yet, there was strong evidence of such endogamy in Bank stock trading, as table 7.12 shows.[114] The presence of ethnic-religious endogamy for both the East India Company and the Bank, and the absence of guild endogamy for both the East India Company and the Bank, contradicts the interpretation that endogamy was a strategy to deal with economic risk.[115]

The party endogamy result is a complex one but it represents a challenge to the Law of Indifference and Homogeneous Middleman Group theory. It exists in East India trading but not in Bank trading. It is not just a response to price volatility, nor the product of ethnic-religious endogamy. It appears where guild endogamy does not, and is concentrated among wealthy share-holders and those who were not professional traders. Party endogamy is a market-based form of political discrimination. Why would people do such a thing? The answer is to be found in the political and institutional context for the market and in the political motivations of market participants.

THE POLITICS OF ENDOGAMY

In an era characterized by the "rage of party," political affiliations were a defining social characteristic. How people voted was usually public knowl-edge, and consequently the connection between the joint-stock companies and political parties influenced trading in East India Company stock.[116] Company shares conferred both economic and "political" rights since own-ers enjoyed a claim on profits and a right to vote. A party's voting base in the directors' elections comprised the shares owned by party members. When party members sold shares, that voting base would be eroded if they were sold to a supporter of the other party, or conserved, if sold to a fellow mem-ber. Given the intense contest for control of the East India Company, it seems that traders were choosing the latter option. Whig shareholders were not simply selling shares, they were selling Whig shares and so preferred to sell them to other Whigs. Of course, Whigs would prefer to sell to other Whigs (and conserve the voting base of the party) but would also like to buy from Tories (and expand the base). But for a Whig to buy from a Tory, the Tory must sell, which went against the Tory's political interests. Freely negotiated transactions generally occurred only when in the (perceived) mu-tual interests of both buyer and seller. Self-interest in this context included political and economic components.

Politically, within-party transactions were mutually beneficial. Between-party transactions, in contrast, enlarged the base of one party and dimin-ished that of the other. Since it was not in the interests of both parties, such a transaction was less likely to occur. Of course, cross-party transactions did happen, as can be seen from the tables analyzed above. This could be the result of variation in the strength of partisanship (e.g., lukewarm Tories would be more willing to sell to Whigs than would hardline Tories) but also because of trade-offs between political and economic interests. A Whig could more easily purchase shares from a Tory if he offered a higher price. The Tory would then face a trade-off between his political interests (which would reject the deal) and his economic interests (which would mean acceptance).[117]

It was only in the East India Company that partisan considerations notice-ably influenced trading patterns. This is consistent with Mirowski's finding that only in the case of the East India Company did ". . . share prices have no statistically significant relation to profitability" (Mirowski 1981: 575).

Evidently, something besides profits drove the market for these shares.[118] What distinguished the East India Company from the Bank (and the South Sea Company) was that it was heavily contested. Neither party had firm control over the court of directors and so every trade potentially could shift the political balance from one side to the other.[119]

According to Gary Becker's model of discrimination, if the stock market was perfectly competitive, the party pattern of trading would have involved only a small economic concession to political interest. One would see the "segregation" of shareholdings into Whig and Tory camps but with no significant price differences. To sell shares to a fellow Whig would be easy if the alternative was to sell at the same price to a Tory, the political equivalent of a "free lunch." But in a less than perfect market, a trader who restricted himself to fellow party members was forgoing whatever economic opportunities might be presented by dealing with the other party. Just as a racially discriminating employer hurts him or herself by not hiring qualified minorities, so does a politically discriminating Whig who forgoes dealing with a Tory.

To see how this might happen, consider that a trader wishing to buy shares would be interested in paying the lowest price. He or she would survey the market and collect offer prices, looking for the lowest one. Price dispersion is typical in markets and so the potential buyer will get a range of offers.[120] In general, the larger the sample of sale prices, the lower the expected value of the lowest price.[121] In other words, the more offers the buyer collects, the lower the price he or she will have to pay for the shares. By restricting trading partners to fellow party members, a trader reduced the sample of sale prices and so was likely to pay more for the shares he bought. A similar opportunity cost would be paid by someone looking to sell at the highest price.

Even if this opportunity cost argument were false, and the stock market was perfect and endogamous trading was costless, it would be hard to explain the pattern of political endogamy without concluding that it involved some kind of economic price. If political discrimination were costless, all traders could freely indulge their political whims with no financial penalty. In fact, however, actively trading Whigs and Tories did not let partisanship influence their trades, although many others did. This important difference makes sense if endogamy had a price: active traders were professionals whose livelihood involved trading on the stock market, and so they couldn't afford to let partisanship interfere with profits.[122] Given their level of activity, even a modest cost would mount up when added across multiple trades.

It seems that the indifference of active traders was predicated on political discrimination among the more numerous inactive traders.[123] With politically defined "submarkets," in which political allies traded with each other, indifferent professional traders could make money by trading or arbitraging between them. Opportunities to exploit price differences between the sub-markets would be forgone by discriminating traders, but not by the indifferent. However, without politically discriminating traders, there would be no opportunities for the indifferent to exploit.[124]

It is telling that the East India Company Tories were more endogamous than the Whigs. In the log-linear analysis, even the endogamy model (which assumes that groups are equally endogamous) underestimates the extent to which the Tories traded among themselves. As the minority in a politically hostile environment, Tories were especially likely to seek out other Tories even though the opportunity cost of endogamy was highest for them (by refusing to trade with Whigs, they were ignoring most of the potential trading partners).

As further evidence of politically motivated trades, consider individual-level trading patterns among East India Company shareholders. By focusing on individuals rather than pairs, we lose the dyadic quality of transactions but gain further insight into the political texture of the market. If political considerations led to politicized trading, then we might expect that politically active traders would be more likely to trade along partisan lines. Table 7.13 takes all the people who traded East India Company shares and constructs for each an index of how frequently they traded with fellow party members (a person trading only with fellow members would score one). Using this index, the overall proportion of within-party trades for all 1,100 traders is low (0.1346) because of the large numbers of political unknowns and the frequency of trade between party members and unknowns. That aside, however, there is a striking difference between those who were politically active and those who weren't.[125] Politically active traders were much more likely to trade with members of the same party than those who were politically inactive.

The results in table 7.13 are dampened by the large numbers of political unknowns. If we remove them, and consider outright partisanship, another strong pattern emerges. Table 7.14 includes only trades by East India Company shareholders who were either Whigs or Tories.

Both Whig and Tory partisans tended to trade with Whigs. Among the 530 shareholders in table 7.14, the overall proportion of trades with Tories was 0.31, while that for Whigs was 0.69. This is an unsurprising consequence of the fact that there were many more Whigs than Tories in the market, and the Whigs were more active. If we divide shareholders into Whig and Tory supporters, and consider their propensity to trade with other Whigs or Tories, there is a consistent pattern of partisanship. Tory supporters were more likely to trade with Tories than Whig supporters, and Whig supporters were more likely to trade with Whigs than Tory supporters.

Evidence of politics in the stock market is found primarily among patterns of behavior. To be sure, there is much to suggest why political concerns

TABLE 7.13
East India Company Shareholder Same-Party Partisanship by
Political Status

Political Status	Proportion of all Trades with Same Party	Number of Cases
Politically Active	0.2854	110
Politically Inactive	0.1179	990
All Shareholders	0.1346	1,100

Sources: See appendix.

TABLE 7.14
East India Company Shareholder Partisanship by
Party Support.

Partisanship	Proportion of Party Trades with Tories	Number of Cases
Tory Supporters	0.4304	136
Whig Supporters	0.2690	394
All Shareholders	0.3103	530
	Proportion of Party Trades with Whigs	Number of Cases
Tory Supporters	0.5696	136
Whig Supporters	0.7310	394
All Shareholders	0.6897	530

Sources: See appendix.

mattered in the market: strident conflict in the society at large, the political salience of joint-stock companies, and the connection between the voting rights attached to share-ownership and the political composition of company directorships. There is, alas, very little evidence that directly documents the subjective motivations and intentions of those who traded shares. Merchants and financiers were not given to recorded introspection, and the documents they left behind chronicled debits and credits much more than designs and concerns.[126] In the absence of such evidence, it may still seem implausible to some that traders in a competitive financial market could have been politically motivated, and some readers might be tempted to return to an economic explanation of party endogamy. Yet, the significance of political motivations is not so improbable as it may seem at first.

There are clear instances of investors who were motivated by politics. Sarah Duchess of Marlborough, for example, was a notorious Whig sympathizer, and even though she could not vote in parliamentary elections, her social stature and friendship with Queen Anne made her a powerful political figure. The Duchess consistently favored the Whigs in both her public and private undertakings, including her investments. Thus she invested in the Bank of England and in 1712 held in her own name £5,750 worth of stock. Furthermore, despite her penchant for financial investments, the Duchess refused to have anything to do with the South Sea Company. Its Tory connections were strong enough to earn her disapproval. Only after the South Sea Company joined the Hanoverian interest in 1714 did she begin to buy South Sea stock. With her enormous wealth the Duchess had a substantial economic incentive to invest in a variety of financial securities, but chose not to do so for political reasons.[127]

There are other examples of political investment, including Dr. William Stratford of Christ Church, Oxford, who wrote in a letter of November 1712:

> I am glad to perceive that South Sea rises, I had that faith in my Lord Treasurer [Oxford, the Tory] as to venture all the little ready money that I have in it, I hope it will be at par before the Parliament meets. I expect some strange turn, for the worse I am afraid in my own soul, now I am got into the funds, which I never was before in my life. (H.M.C. Portland, vol. VII: 112)

Stratford was just the kind of neophyte investor who would let his Tory loyalties lead him into a new and unfamiliar financial venture. Many other Tories bought Bank stock in 1710 so that they could vote in the directors' elections, not because they had all suddenly decided that the Bank was a good investment. Among Whigs, Anne Clavering wrote to her father in 1710 that "Mr. Lamberts' other bill becomes due when I must return to town. He remitts mony for the new [Tory] Treasury so I will not putt to much confidence in a Tory" (Dickinson 1967b: 97). Clavering recognized the political loyalties of financiers, and shaped her dealings with them accordingly.

The variegated nature of endogamous trading suggests that different groups had different concerns. In 1712, professional traders were much more likely to conform to the Law of Indifference than others. Whatever their politics, they would leave partisanship at the entrance to Exchange Alley. In a related context, Rabb (1967) noted that early seventeenth-century investors in English joint-stock companies also had varied motives for investment. While professional merchants used profitability as their criterion for investment, the gentry were more easily swayed by political considerations and the chance to pursue national glory. Colonies and dramatic explorations were more attractive to the investing squirearchy and aristocracy than to merchants.[128] Not surprisingly, gentry investors were more likely to lose their money. Furthermore, Brenner (1993) points out the importance of Puritanism as a motivation for certain of the colonial projects undertaken during the 1620s. As he put it: "... the raison d'être of these ventures [e.g., the Massachusetts Bay Company] was primarily religious and political" (Brenner 1993: 272).[129] Nor was the intrusion of politics into business symptomatic of an immature capitalist spirit, for such things happened in the eighteenth century as well. During the Jacobite uprising of 1745, for example, London merchants signing a declaration stating that they would accept Bank Bills were taken to be Whigs.[130] Economic action during the financial crisis was interpreted politically.

Credit relationships were ubiquitous because of the shortage of ready money, and many were constructed without the benefit of formal contracts or debt instruments. Merchants typically bought and sold on credit, and settled accounts at the year's end.[131] Credit relationships would seem to provide a perfect opportunity to witness *homo economicus* unbound, for debtors and creditors could easily gauge their economic interests and act accordingly. When discussed by contemporaries, however, credit relations were interpreted through an ethos of neighborliness, and framed by a language of moral obligation.[132] Such an ethos was more likely to emerge in smaller communities, but it nevertheless shows how noneconomic concerns could enter the early modern market.

These indications are only suggestive, of course, but when joined with economic behavior that is patterned along political lines, the case for political motives in the market becomes much stronger. Even in a competitive market, people were not single-mindedly devoted to profits. They recognized that share-ownership had political and economic consequences.

EMBEDDEDNESS IN POLITICS

Party endogamy makes sense in political terms. It did not serve a narrow economic end, and was not a proxy for some other form of social endogamy. Party endogamy was a reflection of the way that political cleavages penetrated the market and structured trade. It was based on how individuals used their political preferences to organize trading in light of the connection between shares as a financial instrument and control over the joint-stock companies as institutions. For all the liquidity and rationality of the London stock market, it was also a locus for the pursuit of political projects. *Homo economicus* and *homo politicus* were in the market together.

Table 7.15 summarizes the overall trading results. In three of the six cases, there is evidence of endogamy. All three instances of endogamy occur in a setting in which, according to the Law of Indifference, they ought not to, for the stock market was highly organized, centralized, and efficient in 1712.

Endogamy among ethnic-religious groups occurred for both Bank and East India Company stock. Adherents of Homogeneous Middleman Group theory might argue that this was because property rights were not secure for minorities. Jews in particular have throughout Western European history

TABLE 7.15

Patterns of Trading in East India Company and Bank of England Shares
among Political Parties, Ethnic-Religious Groups, and Guilds

	EIC 1712	Bank 1712
1. Political Parties	Endogamy	No Endogamy
2. Ethnic-Religious Groups	Endogamy	Endogamy
3. Guilds	No Endogamy	No Endogamy

been persecuted and had their property rights violated. Jews were banished from England in 1290 by Edward I and only began to return starting in 1656.[133] Could their marginal social and economic position make endogamy a rational response? The evidence is clearcut. There is *no indication* that Jewish property rights were any less secure than those of other English property owners.[134] Jews received virtually the same protections in English courts of law as everyone else.

The explanation for ethnic-religious endogamy lies in the special situation of the Huguenots and Jews (there were so few Quaker shareholders that they are less relevant). The connection between Britain's war with France and investment in the joint-stock companies was clear to contemporaries. Britain's war effort was sustained by the contribution the monied companies made to public borrowing, and without a developed capital market the government could not have borrowed on such a large scale. Financial investments were therefore more than just an opportunity to earn profits, they were a way to support the war (akin to modern war bonds). It is this latter aspect which was important for the Huguenots and Jews.[135]

Following the Revocation of the Edict of Nantes in 1685, Huguenots were a persecuted religious minority in France. Profoundly opposed to Louis XIV, Huguenot refugees formed an international network dedicated to his defeat and used both military and financial means. Huguenot officers and soldiers joined the British army but the Huguenot contribution to wartime finance was equally important.[136] Huguenot money and expertise assisted the development of the national debt which funded Britain's military efforts.[137] And although their situation was not as bad as that of the Huguenots, Jews in France also suffered from Louis XIV's militant Catholicism.[138] Jewish financiers played a similarly important role in funding and supporting the international alliance against Louis XIV.[139] During the War of the Spanish Succession, the Jewish financial and mercantile community in Amsterdam strongly opposed the possibility of having Louis XIV's grandson inherit the Spanish throne.[140]

Investment in the London stock market represented for Huguenots and Jews more than just a financial decision. It was an act of political opposition to Louis XIV. Trading among themselves offered these minorities an opportunity to affirm their solidarity in supporting the effort to defeat France. Ethnic-religious politics were enacted through market interactions and so within-group trading had little to do with property rights.

An economic explanation of party endogamy in East India shares which points to their riskiness is plausible only until one sees that there were no real differences between the two companies for trade among guilds and ethnic-religious groups. The Homogeneous Middleman Group explanation for endogamy is problematic because property rights were secure for traders. A modified Homogeneous Middleman Group explanation in terms of transaction costs founders on the fact that there was no endogamous trading among guilds. Guilds were a much better organizational vehicle for trading than the parties but were never used as such. Furthermore, there are no consistent differences in endogamy between trading in risky East India shares and conservative Bank shares.

Party endogamy was a genuinely political phenomenon, not a strategy to deal with economic problems, and not a reflection of some other form of social endogamy. Political differences penetrated the market and organized trade. Market transactions were embedded in the political system and in the organizational forms into which politics was organized. One would be mistaken, of course, to conclude from this analysis that all other English markets were politically embedded, or that markets in general must be shaped by politics, or even that England's experience was representative of other early modern European countries. The role of party politics in the London stock market arose out of a conjuncture of political, economic, and institutional forces. Its idiosyncracy can only be assessed through the comparisons with other countries done in chapter 4. If the details of Whig and Tory were peculiar to England, however, the generally political nature of public debt was not. Whether done through venal offices or financial instruments, government borrowing frequently involved political relations and was "symptomatic" of the polity.[141]

Chapter Eight

GOVERNMENT BONDS AND POLITICAL BONDS

> But if exchange is thought of as a primary form of inter-
> action, exchange patterns can define group composition,
> the relations between group members, and interaction
> across boundaries. Trade and marketing constitute
> one concrete form of exchange and hence give one
> major indication of social structure.
> —Cyril Belshaw

ANTHROPOLOGISTS have traditionally been more aware than other social scientists that relationships between social groups get enacted and sustained
through the exchange of what appear to be "mere" things. Objects transferred across group boundaries have a symbolism and social life that can
far exceed their utility or use-value.[1] Their movement maps out a social
structure. Yet even anthropologists tend to distinguish "traditional societies"
from "modern market societies."[2] Kula rings, ropes of moka, potlatches,
and other symbol-laden forms of exchange occurred among the native peo-
ples of the South Pacific islands and northwest coast of North America.
Among the tribes of investment bankers who inhabit lower Manhattan Island and the City, however, market exchange supposedly has a much reduced social content. Anthropologists therefore tend to study ceremonial
exchanges more than financial exchanges, although they have not entirely
overlooked the latter.[3]

It is important to recognize that a reduced social content is not the same
thing as no social content at all. Clan relations may not get enacted in rational capital markets but political relations do. They can confer upon economic action a political logic that is distinct from the logic of the market. In
posing this argument, one must resist concluding that such a political logic
is only an external force, interfering with what would otherwise be a pris-
tine, self-sustaining social institution. To adhere to a laissez-faire picture of
markets is to miss the point, for in the case of early modern England, political differences were part of the foundation upon which the stock market was
built. Politics was not external to the market; it helped provide the social
material out of which the market was fashioned.

England underwent two parallel developments in the latter seventeenth
and early eighteenth centuries. The shift in political power from Crown to

Parliament and the formation of two parties transformed English politics. Parliament's newly acquired power became organized around its internal conflict for control. At the same time, the English financial system was transformed by the emergence of an organized capital market in London. This new market affected both public and private finance. Here, I have undertaken to describe the connections between these two important developments.

Political parties did not exist in 1672. Evidence at many levels points to their emergence during the Exclusion Crisis at the end of the 1670s: political commentary and popular consciousness both recognized the formation of two competing political groups; records of voting in Parliament by members of the Houses of Commons and Lords reveal stable political coalitions across a number of different issue areas; and voting by the general electorate also shows how it was ordered by the two political parties. The emergence of Whig and Tory organizations gave a consistency and coherence to political conflict as the same two groups took the opposite sides of a whole set of political questions.

A comparison of 1672 with 1712 shows the importance of parties. The same general issues of war, religion, and public finance were at the center of politics, whether it was war with the Dutch, anti-Catholic sentiment, and the Stop of the Exchequer in 1672, or war with France, anti-dissenter controversies, and the national debt in 1712. But similar issues were pursued, debated, and contested through very different political institutions. The *form* of political conflict, as well as its *content*, was significant. By 1712, the partisanship of individuals was a key organizing principle in politics as well as an important fact of social life.

Politics influenced finance in a number of ways. The most obvious is underscored by North and Weingast and concerned the Glorious Revolution. This political event marked a substantial increase in Parliament's power and one of the main levers of parliamentary influence was its control over public finances.[4] Most public policies had a budgetary side and so could be shaped by those who controlled the public fisc. British monarchs needed the consent of parliament to fund their policies, and the financial demands of war ensured that parliament was called frequently. The rise of Parliament also changed the terms of public borrowing, for after 1689 public loans enjoyed parliamentary sanction, and no longer depended solely on the credit of the sovereign. Parliamentary consent gave greater security to public creditors, and improved the terms on which the government could borrow. Consent also helped lower resistance to taxes.

There were more linkages between politics and finance than North and Weingast recognized. Parliamentary power mattered, to be sure, but so did the forms into which that power was organized. Partisan politics influenced how and when institutions like the Bank of England, New East India Company, and South Sea Company were established. Political competition accelerated the development of public finance by marrying political interests to economic ones. Politics also influenced the progress of the war policy that so much of the new financial machinery was devoted to supporting. In the case of the East India Company, partisan considerations even shaped how shares were traded on the London stock market.

Again, a comparison with 1672 is instructive. Although much of public borrowing was done through intermediaries in both periods, using goldsmith-bankers in 1672 and joint-stock companies in 1712, the political context was strikingly different. Hence, however politically contentious bankers were in 1672, they could not compare with joint-stock companies in 1712. The latter were much more deeply and controversially inserted into organized conflict.

Throughout the entire period, party competition was a fact of life that made people uneasy. Institutionalized political conflict was anathema to the received vision of politics, which idealized a consensual parliament advising an enlightened sovereign.[5] Among political elites, there were too many memories of the civil war period and of the dire social consequences that followed from an elite at war with itself. Yet the perceived illegitimacy of party struggle only sharpened the conflict, for there was no conception of a "loyal opposition." It was hard for Tories to believe that Whigs could differ from them on so many basic issues and still remain a legitimate part of the body politic (and vice versa for Whigs). For Tories, Whigs did not simply differ over policy, their very existence as an organized group was an affront to the Church and Monarchy.

However uncomfortable it was to live with, partisan politics had a beneficial effect on public finances. Political competition was reproduced in the market as Whig and Tory institutions struggled to outbid each other and receive parliamentary approval. The government got better terms when, for example, New and Old East India Companies improved the offers they made for the right to trade with the East Indies, or when the threat of a Land Bank forced the Bank of England to do more financially. The conflict intensified because it was not simply a matter of rival groups of merchants bidding for a concession from the government, but Whig merchants versus Tory merchants. Political and economic competition reinforced each other, and so it is a mistake to attribute the improvements in public finance solely to the increased power of Parliament, as North and Weingast do. It is also not sufficient to point to improvements in tax revenues as the basis for government borrowing.[6] Without a doubt, creditor confidence in the future of British public revenues encouraged people to loan money to the government but such a loan was not just an economic decision. It was also a political one and as such was influenced by political considerations and loyalties.

The historical evidence consistently underscores the vigorous nature of the conflict between Whigs and Tories and the deep divisions among British elites in this period. Political identities mattered outside of formal politics as issues, rivalries, and institutions received a partisan cast: there were Whig and Tory social clubs, hospitals, newspapers, coffeehouses, and so on.[7] Many other spheres of British social life were politicized. The analyses of chapters 2, 3, 5, and 6 show that the stock market also became politicized, precisely along Whig and Tory lines. Notwithstanding the high levels of market centralization, organization, and efficiency, it too became a political arena. In the case of the East India Company, it was political at the most basic level, with partisan identities influencing individual decisions about whom to trade with.

One might concede that political conflict mattered in the stock market and yet still insist that economic interests lay behind politics: political interests were only second-order economic interests, as it were.[8] There is, of course, something to this argument. Economic interests figured into the conflict between Whigs and Tories, especially given the tendency for the monied interest to support one party, and the landed interest to support the other. Tories who were concerned about their economic situation became unhappy with the burdensome land tax and the fact that Whigs enjoyed more government patronage than they. To the extent that this was true in general, the pursuit of political goals in the market could be seen as an indirect way of pursuing economic goals. Such an argument would restore the picture of the market as a place to pursue economic goals. Yet any attempt to view Whig and Tory parties as simply economic interest groups founders on the content of political conflict, particularly the importance of religion.[9] Disagreements over the Church, toleration, and nonconformity were at the heart of the Whig-Tory split, and these disputes were not about economics. Political conflict cannot be reduced simply to economic interests.

Ethnicity rather than party mediated other connections between politics and finance. International politics was partly behind the role that Jews and Huguenots played in the British financial markets. Both groups were persecuted in France and so they provided financial support and expertise to the alliance arrayed against Louis XIV. Their commitments were expressed when ethnic and religious identities influenced individual decisions about trading in Bank and East India Company stock.

The line of influence between finance and politics ran both ways. Financial developments raised a new set of political questions because the power of traditional landed elites was threatened by a rising group of financiers and merchants whose wealth came from entirely different sources. Government ministers had to maintain the cooperation of the monied interest in order to finance wartime deficits, and since most members of the monied interest were Whigs, this gave Whig ministries an advantage. Whig governments were generally more effective in funding the war. When the Tories came to power, as in 1710, they had to gain the cooperation of a community whose natural sympathies lay elsewhere. Robert Harley's solution involved a two-fold strategy: control the excesses of the Tory right-wing (the October Club), and cultivate and reward a Tory constituency in the financial market.

With these connections between politics and finance in mind, property rights can be set in their proper perspective. Various changes between 1672 and 1712 affected the property rights that investors and public creditors possessed. Some were narrowly legal, like the Bankers' Case. Others represented broader legal trends, like the incorporation of the Law Merchant into Common Law, and still others were constitutional, as in the increase of Parliament's power.

Property rights theory, including North and Weingast (1989), argues that changes in property rights explain the development of English public finance and the rise of a capital market. After reviewing the relevant legal and political developments, it is clear that these corresponded with the financial developments and also that the state was important for market formation. Changes in property rights occurred between 1672 and 1712, and potentially can help explain financial changes over time.

In the abstract, property rights are rules specifying the rights that individuals possess with respect to property. As rules, they are no more than intangible forms, legally enforceable possibilities, until they are used in practice. Their full significance doesn't unfold until the rules get applied. An economic market involves the application of rights in action, and so one needs to understand how rights are exercised. Depending on the owner's motivation, property rights can be applied in a variety of ways, although most economists and many sociologists assume that profit-maximization is the primary, and even sole, purpose for economic behavior. In the British case, the practical application of financial property rights was infused by a set of extra-economic concerns. Freely alienable financial commodities were not alienated freely. The formal property rights so emphasized by North, Levi, and others were at best a necessary but not sufficient condition for the emergence of a market and the development of public financial machinery. Property rights created a legal possibility, which when suitably animated became an economic actuality. Self-interest activated their use but it was a broad self-interest that encompassed both political and economic interests.

The overlap between politics and finance becomes clearer if we recall how property rights, especially financial ones, embody social relationships. To borrow money is not simply to undertake a brief transaction. Debtors and creditors have more than a fleeting connection, for their relationship endures into the future. Debtors are obliged to their creditors and hence

dependent on them but at the same time creditors acquire an interest in
their debtors. When the debtor is the political sovereign, these mutual de-
pendencies invariably acquire a political meaning. The creditor wants the
debtor to be financially and politically capable of repaying the debt. A loan
to the government becomes more than a financial investment, for it is also a
political gesture. Even with joint-stock companies acting as intermediaries
between the investing English public and the sovereign debtor, the political
significance of a loan was apparent. In general, public debt constructed relationships between Spanish, Dutch, French, and English investors, and their
respective sovereign borrowers.

The 1672–1712 period also marked a quantum increase in the military
capacity of the English state.[10] Starting with a weaker state, a smaller economy, and a relatively small population, by the War of the Spanish Succession
Britain had easily outstripped France in per capita levels of mobilization.
This was an extremely successful episode in state-building, for even as
power shifted within the British state, its ability to project military force
outward expanded dramatically. Changes in the public financial system accounted for much of the increase, for the cultivation of a capital market
allowed the British state to finance its military expenditures in a timely fashion and at a reasonable rate of interest. With its expanded tax revenues the
British state could service its enlarged debt. The state was able to tap into
the pools of capital held by the British mercantile class, which loaned its
money willingly.

On the financial side, the contrast with France's experience is noteworthy. French financial officials had to work with a fiscal system that routinely
undertaxed wealthy social groups like the nobility and the clergy, and over-
taxed the peasantry.[11] France relied heavily on tax farms, and rarely were
revenues collected directly. In contrast, Britain stopped using tax farms
even before the Glorious Revolution. To tap into the wealth of the mercantile classes, France followed a very different fiscal strategy when it came to
borrowing. Through the sale of offices and annuities, the middle classes
were both incorporated into the state and encouraged to loan their capital to
it. To potential buyers, financial offices were an attractive commodity since
they offered the prospect of access to tax funds, but the use of venal offices
was simultaneously a political and a fiscal strategy. As officers of the French
state, individuals shared the political interests of the monarch, and by purchasing their offices these same individuals became a source of capital. Officials had a vested interest in the political success of their monarch.

Much of the borrowing done by French monarchs was from incumbent
financial officials who also had the task of collecting and administering
public finances.[12] When finances reached the crisis point (and they did so
frequently in the seventeenth century), the King would unilaterally alter the
terms of loans obtained from his own financial officials and in effect go

through with a partial default.[13] A bad situation would worsen since not only did venality of offices prevent any large-scale rationalization of the French financial bureaucracy, but in a default the monarch's own financial officials were among the suffering creditors.

In contrast to England, France had no centralized capital market to exploit and gain access to middle-class wealth. England possessed a far better system for borrowing funds, and French public finances were in a state of chaos by the end of the War of the Spanish Succession.[14] An active capital market was an important resource for the English state, just as its absence was a hindrance for France.

The social composition of English public creditors was similar in 1672 and 1712. Merchants, the middle class, and people from the London area predominated.[15] Yet, improvements in the process of intermediation brought in much more money. Joint-stock companies replaced goldsmith-bankers as the intermediaries through which middle-class and mercantile wealth was brought into the state. In this regard, England emulated the success of the Dutch.

The Amsterdam market provided a large pool of capital from which the Dutch government could finance its spending at very low interest rates. Widespread domestic borrowing gave a large number of Dutch citizens a personal financial interest in the state, and public office was closely connected to public lending.[16] Although Holland's public financial machinery was more advanced than that of England, its political structure was insufficiently centralized to permit the kind of state-building that occurred in England. The United Provinces possessed a federated political structure, with considerable power remaining in the hands of the separate provinces.[17] The provinces were loath to surrender control to a central authority, and this made decisive and coordinated policy difficult to achieve.

Despite deep internal divisions, British political and economic elites cooperated in the buildup of state power. Partly this was because the buildup was in response to France, a much detested enemy. But it was also because these elites acquired a dual vested interest in the state. Through the institution of Parliament, traditional political elites gained a hand in governance and in the direction of public policy.[18] Through the marketplace, British economic elites gained a vested interest in the financial stability of the nouveau regime.[19]

Hilton Root's recent analysis (1994) downplays and even ignores these important divisions among English elites. He argues that Parliament represented the interests of government creditors and hence the post-1688 increase in the power of Parliament produced the financial success of eighteenth-century England.[20] According to Root, English elites used their newly expanded political powers to protect their economic interests as public creditors. In fact, however, those who occupied Parliament were quite distinct from those who loaned money. The landed gentry and aristocracy, England's traditional ruling class, dominated Parliament until well into the nineteenth century but played only a minor role as government creditors. The merchants and financiers of London, who did not dominate Parliament, were the main source of money for government borrowing. Furthermore, there was little sympathy within the landed interest for the monied interest, so one cannot assume that members of the former would "represent" and protect the interests of the latter. The tension between economic and political elites, between the landed and monied interests, was a driving force in politics, and only through a dual process of incorporation did both groups acquire a vested interest in the post-1688 regime.

Early modern public finance proved to be much more than just a problem in resource extraction. State-building involved the erection of a fiscal apparatus capable of delivering large sums into the public fisc, but a fiscal apparatus served a political mission as well: to build alliances, establish relationships, co-opt elites, and create a constituency with an interest in the regime. For Britain, as for the other cases with substantial borrowing from domestic sources (Spain, the United Provinces, and France), public finance shored up the regime both politically and financially. Enlarging the class of public creditors, or of venal officeholders, was one way to cultivate support for the ruler.[21] In countries like Britain and the United Provinces, where lending by public creditors was voluntary and where government debt was a lucrative investment, public borrowing was almost a form of political patronage. Whigs reaped the financial rewards of lending to the government, while those creditors whom the Dutch government chose to repay received their money "with tears."

The political texture of public borrowing varied from country to country, depending on the particular financial vehicle and on the structure of politics. Venal offices in France, for example, were effective at creating vested interests but they overlapped with public administration and made reform of the state apparatus difficult, if not impossible. They created general interests in the regime but also specific interests in a particularly inefficient state structure.[22] Long-term borrowing through bonds, annuities, or company shares also created vested interests but without the administrative side effects. Debt instruments were a more purely financial, rather than financial-administrative, form of property. But both were political.

Underlying venal offices, bonds, annuities, and shares lay the same principle: the creation of property by the government and its distribution into the hands of subjects. There is a deep connection between polity and property. People whose property is protected by government are more likely to protect that government. As Tocqueville observed, property owners as stake holders are less likely to foment revolution: ". . . the more widely personal property is distributed and increased and the greater the number of those enjoying it, the less is a nation inclined to revolution" (Tocqueville 1969: 637). They have something to lose, and so are reluctant to challenge the regime which created the property they enjoy.

The "fiscal-political" variant of the Eumenes strategy has been pursued in other historical settings besides early modern France, Holland, and Britain. During the American Civil War, for example, Union government borrowing yielded more than money, for quite deliberately its intended fruits included political supporters. In his annual report, then Secretary of the Treasury Salmon Chase proposed to sell government bonds to banks, who could use the bonds as the backing for the issue of bank notes. Bond sales would raise money but would also serve a political end, according to the Secretary:

> The proposed plan is recommended, finally, by the firm anchorage it will sup-
> ply to the union of the States. Every banking association whose bonds are de-
> posited in the treasury of the Union; every individual who holds a dollar of the
> circulation secured by such deposit; every merchant, every manufacturer,
> every farmer, every mechanic, interested in transactions dependent for success
> on the credit of that circulation, *will feel as an injury every attempt to rend the
> national unity, with the permanence and stability of which all their interests are
> so closely and vitally connected*. Had the system been possible, and had it actu-
> ally existed two years ago, can it be doubted that the national interests and
> sentiments enlisted by it for the Union would have so strengthened the motives
> for adhesion derived from other sources that the wild treason of secession
> would have been impossible? (Chase 1862: 20, my emphasis)

In this instance, government bonds were used to build political bonds, and might even, the Secretary suggested, have prevented secession in the first place.[23] British politicians were never as explicit as this but commentary on the national debt went along similar lines.[24]

Given its dual role, it is perhaps inevitable that public debt both reflected and reinforced the structure of political relationships. In the United Provinces, public debt helped cement the hold which the regents had over the state and polity. In France, financial offices played an important role in the construction and management of patron-client networks. In Britain, where elites were divided along party lines, public debt proved to be a surprisingly subtle instrument for the pursuit of partisan ends. Party conflict was reproduced in the stock market as partisan loyalties influenced share trading and share holding. The development of public debt also produced change, for the rise of the "monied interest," a new financial elite whose power began to threaten the traditional ruling elite, transformed domestic politics.

Others have noted the political role of public debt. In the *German Ideology*, Marx and Engels argued that public debt was a vehicle through which the bourgeoisie controlled the state:

To this modern private property corresponds the modern State, which, purchased gradually by the owners of property by means of taxation, has fallen
entirely into their hands through the national debt, and its existence has become wholly dependent on the commercial credit which the owners of property, the bourgeois, extend to it, as reflected in the rise and fall of State funds
on the stock exchange.[25]

Tory critics of the monied interest would almost certainly have agreed with
this analysis but the balance of power is neither so simple nor so one-sided
as Marx and Engels suppose it to be. A governing regime is beholden to
those it must borrow from, but once the money has been lent, creditors have
a vested interest in the well-being of that regime.

It is ironic that liquidity was one of the major attractions offered by the
capital market.[26] Liquidity meant that shares could be bought or sold freely
and easily to anyone. Creditors could recover their capital by selling shares
on the stock market. Long-term loans did not require long-term lending,
which made long-term debt an attractive investment. This formal freedom
increased as trading in East India Company shares shed the constraints of its
early guildlike structure. The veto power which East India shareholders
held over potential shareholders disappeared, and shares became thor-
oughly alienable and anonymous. Yet, as the analyses of share trading attest,
such freedom was not fully utilized. For various reasons, trading was patterned along political and ethnic lines. This was not because of externally
imposed institutional constraints but rather because of the way in which
individual traders chose to trade. In practice, noneconomic motivations
shaped the formal freedom to trade shares. As political partisans, investors
relinquished some of that freedom in order to benefit their party and pursue
their political goals.

Increased liquidity in the capital market resulted from the transformation
of debtor-creditor *relationships* (in legal terms, *choses in action*) into alienable *commodities* like promissory notes, bills of exchange, and company
shares. In the classic Marxist sense, a social relationship acquired the form
and appearance of a thing or object, and legally became defined as a commodity that could be bought and sold freely.[27] In Marx's argument, this
transformation caused people to misperceive systematically the reality of
their situation.[28] The underlying relationship became obscured or forgotten,
and people saw in its place only commodities. Yet in the case of early modern England, those who bought and sold financial commodities did not treat
them fetishistically. Even as freely alienable and homogeneous commodities, company shares retained enough social meaning to induce distinct
patterns of trading. People were cognizant of the social and political import
of the financial commodities they traded. Whigs and Tories alike knew that
investment in company shares was ultimately a political investment in the

post-1689 regime. When the partisan consequences were substantial, as in the case of the East India Company, people modified their economic behavior accordingly.

Liquidity, negotiability, and alienability all point to the crucial feature that distinguishes economic markets from what Coleman (1990) terms "social markets." In a social market, an obligation which person A has toward person B cannot, in general, be traded by B to a third person. Coleman (1990: 126) suggests that this is because the value of the obligation: ". . . depends on the particular relation and is intrinsically connected to the identities of the two parties involved."[29] Whatever its significance, the boundary separating economic from social markets is a permeable one, for debts in English law went from being *choses in action* to being negotiable securities, from inalienable relations to alienable things. Their personal particularity evolved into an anonymous generality which nevertheless retained an important measure of social meaning.

The development of capitalist markets is frequently interpreted as a process of social differentiation in which a purely economic sphere emerges as a distinct subsystem of society.[30] In "traditional societies," kinship, economic production, and politics are all bound up together. In the Middle Ages, religion and economy were intertwined, and so the religious prohibition against usury constrained lending. Later, in the early modern period, moral regulations against usury weakened and then were discarded as religion and economy became distinct and separate spheres. Moral economies disappeared as free markets in land, labor, and foodstuffs emerged.[31] Overall, differentiation had the effect of making monetary obligations less particularistic by removing them from a social and moral context and creating one in which they were purely economic.

The transition from a social market (in Coleman's sense) to an economic market, from *choses in action* to full negotiability, sets the stage for the Law of Indifference. As anonymous homogeneous commodities in an asocial market, we expect that company shares would be traded indifferently. But they were not. In three of the six instances reported in table 7.15 in chapter 7, there was strong evidence of nonrandom trading: party and ethnic-religious trading in East India Company stock, and ethnic-religious trading in Bank of England stock. The results are especially problematic since they date from a time when the stock market closely resembled the kind of market to which Jevons's Law of Indifference applies.

For political reasons, party trading in East India shares, and ethnic-religious trading in East India and Bank shares manifested the pattern of financial endogamy. The fact that there was no party endogamy among active East India Company traders further suggests a kind of trade-off between political and economic goals. Among active traders, the economic costs of endogamy may have been too high. As a group, active traders were the market experts, the ones most attuned to "market rationality," and politically biased trading was a luxury they could not afford.

Another relevant theory from economics, Homogeneous Middleman Group theory, explains trading within ethnic groups in terms of imperfect property rights. There is evidence of endogamous trading within ethnic-religious groups but the timing of their occurrence was wrong. Endogamous trading ought to have happened before imperfect property rights were "perfected," not after, and by 1712 the legal framework for financial property was mostly settled. One might generalize Homogeneous Middleman Group theory and propose that while endogamous trading had little to do with formal property rights, it served some other economic purpose, perhaps having to do with transaction costs or uncertainty. Yet, were this true, it remains unclear why there was no endogamy among the London guilds. They would have been a much better vehicle than a political party for economic goals that required an organization capable of monitoring and sanctioning its members.

When economic historians have studied the capital markets of the past, they have focused mostly upon efficiency and analyzed the movement of share prices. They have found strong evidence of efficiency in the markets for Bank and East India Company shares. Although the extent of efficiency is certainly an important question, we find that many other things go on in markets. In the early eighteenth-century London capital market, political cleavages, political competition, and ethnic-religious groups all figured prominently, and to focus solely on efficiency is to overlook all these other aspects of market phenomena.

To understand how trades occurred in the London stock market, it is necessary to realize that market transactions were not purely economic phenomena. They were *embedded* in a highly politicized social context. The influence of politics was especially powerful because it worked simultaneously at the individual and institutional levels and in a setting which is purportedly "apolitical." These two levels are frequently decoupled, and it is easy to imagine a shareholder who supported his political party and cared about government policy but who nevertheless did not let partisan considerations interfere with his economic goals. Yet because of the politicization of British society these two levels were "coupled." Government creditors became political supporters because of their financial interest in the regime. Furthermore, because their claims on the government were tradeable on the stock market, politics affected trading activity. Partisan institutions set a context in which individuals sometimes did and sometimes did not engage in individually partisan trading. But even the variation made sense in political terms, since it was driven by the closeness of the contest over the East India Company and the near-futility of Tory attempts to capture the Bank of England.

The appearance of politics in the early modern London stock market should not be dismissed as a sign of the market's immaturity, for there are many other contemporary examples of political influence in the marketplace. An individual who divested the shares of a company because it did business with apartheid South Africa was not simply making a financial decision but a political statement in protest of South African race relations. Many American university faculty can invest their pension funds in "politically acceptable" companies (using, e.g., the CREF Social Choice Account). Chilean wine, California grapes, Coloradan tourism, and Nike athletic shoes have all been boycotted because some political interest group objected to domestic Chilean politics, labor practices in California agriculture, lifestyle politics in Colorado, and the minority employment record of Nike Corporation. Boycotts are certainly not the specialty of "progressive" or "liberal" political activists, for during the 1920s, for example, the Ku Klux Klan in Indiana organized "successful" boycotts of Catholic and Jewish firms, and drove many of them out of business.[32] "Buy American" campaigns try to invoke nationalistic sentiment to encourage the purchase of domestically produced commodities.

Behind all of these practices is the realization that markets can be an effective tool to pursue political goals. Sometimes, the purchasing decision is narrowly focused on the utilitarian value of a commodity, but at other times it may encompass broader concerns, such as the environment, animal rights, patriotism, foreign policy, and labor relations. The insertion of politics into the market is not just an eighteenth-century phenomena.

Such practices remind us that markets possess a sociological richness that economists have ignored but which sociologists have also failed to appreciate. This is partly because of the way in which disciplinary boundaries mark out the division of labor in social science research. Markets are what economists are supposed to study while sociologists labor at other sites. If disciplinary boundaries are transgressed, it is mostly because economists are moving into sociological territory. The interest classical sociologists like Marx and Weber had in economics and political economy serves as a continuing reminder that markets have been, and will remain, quintessentially social institutions.

APPENDIX

SEVERAL DIFFERENT kinds of evidence have been brought together to "measure" transactions and ownership in the London stock market. The core evidence is financial, consisting of data on shareholders and transactions for the Bank of England and the East India Company in 1712. For both companies, this information came from the company stock ledgers, used by the companies to keep track of who owned how much of their stock. Such records were necessary for company officials to know who was eligible for dividend payments, and who could vote in company elections. They were also necessary for shareholders to have secure title to their property, so both the company and the shareholder had an incentive to ensure accurate and complete information. The records usually gave the name of the shareholder, the shareholder's title (if any), sometimes information on where the shareholder lived, and the balance of the shareholder's account carried forward from the previous ledger.[1]

Transfers of stock were recorded according to the double-entry method.[2] Each shareholder had a separate account, and a purchase or sale of stock was recorded as a transfer between accounts. Someone who sold one thousand pounds' worth of stock would have that amount deducted from their account while the purchaser's account would be credited for the same. Hence, each transaction was recorded twice: in the seller's account and in the purchaser's account (which provided an internal check on the accuracy of the records). The date of transfer was recorded, and the amount of stock transferred, but not the price paid by the buyer.

From the name of the shareholder, it was possible to find out the shareholder's gender, and social status (knight, lord, lady, baronet, duchess, etc.).[3] From information on the shareholder's residence, it was possible to determine whether he or she lived in a foreign country. Using the name together with other records, it was possible to learn a good deal more.

The most significant of these other records were the London poll books for the 1710 and 1713 Parliamentary elections. Both were used because these were the closest elections in time to the 1712 financial data and because most of the persons involved in the stock market came from the London region.[4] As we know from chapter 2, parliamentary elections that went to a poll were not conducted by secret ballot. A voter's choices were public knowledge, and with the production of a poll book, those choices became published knowledge as well. A poll book listed the voters in a constituency by name and gave their votes. In the case of the London parliamentary elections of 1710 and 1713, the poll books list the voter's name, the liveried company (guild) they were a member of, and whom they voted for. The 1713 poll book has been published (see Speck and Gray 1981), and the 1710 poll book was transcribed from a copy at the London Guildhall Library.[5] Men who were "free of the city" (i.e., who were members of a liveried company) could vote for up to four MPs. In both elections, there was a total of eight candidates: four Whigs and four Tories. Usually, voters used all four of their votes, but some voted for fewer than four candidates. By matching names from the two poll books with names from the list of shareholders, it is possible to determine which shareholders were Whig supporters, and which were Tory supporters.[6]

Of course, matching names can lead to mistaken identifications, as when two separate individuals have the same name. Errors in the use of the two poll books will probably not be random because both of the elections resulted in big Tory victories. If anything, errors in the matching of names from the list of shareholders with names from the poll book would probably inflate the estimated number of Tories among shareholders.

The major restriction of poll books is that only men who were free of the city could vote. Shareholders who were not citizens, either because they did not live in London or because they did not belong to a guild, will not be found in the London poll books (neither will any of the women who owned shares). Other sources of political data were therefore used to supplement the two poll books. Some of the individuals had been, were, or came to be members of Parliament. The published volumes of the History of Parliament project as well as the notes for the forthcoming 1690–1715 volumes provide information on all MPs, including their party affiliations.[7] Additionally, there are various published division lists recording how MPs and Lords voted on particular issues. Given the strong party line taken on most issues, how someone voted in parliament could be used to infer his party affiliation. The party affiliations of especially prominent individuals required no specific documentation. For example, the Duke of Leeds was a large holder of Bank stock, and anyone familiar with the political history of the period would know him to be a Tory supporter.

There were other nonparliamentary elections that were conducted along party lines, including aldermanic and other municipal elections. The great advantage of these is that to vote, people did not have to be citizens. A London ward election of 1711 was used to determine the political affiliations of additional shareholders whose names did not show up on the other voting and electoral lists.[8]

Political affiliations are one major additional piece of information, but using a shareholder's name, there were other things one could learn. We already know that foreigners, foreign-born individuals, and particular ethnic groups played a prominent role in the stock market.[9] Jews and Huguenots are the two most important of these groups. Using previous research, it was possible to ascertain who the Jewish shareholders were in Bank and East India stock.[10] To determine the Huguenots (French Protestants who left France because of religious persecution) among the shareholders and traders, I matched names with the published lists of aliens naturalized or denized.[11] These lists gave information on when an individual was denized or naturalized, and frequently identified persons as "French Protestants."

For reasons outlined in chapter 2, Jews, Huguenots, and Quakers were considered part of the Whig constituency, even if they could not participate in parliamentary elections. Tory supporters were xenophobic and strongly opposed to non–Church of England Protestants (which included the Quakers and Huguenots). The Tory party supported legislation that made it difficult for non–Church of England Protestants to practice their religion and also legislation that prevented foreigners from becoming naturalized. Additionally, when nonparliamentary voting lists are examined, Huguenot support for the Whigs was very strong. For example, those Huguenots and Jews who voted in the London aldermanic election mentioned earlier gave their support to the Whig candidate. Huguenots and Jews were politically active in other contexts as well. They frequently acted as scrutineers for the annual elections that selected the directors for the Bank and East India Company, or were themselves directors. One cannot consider them apolitical merely because they couldn't vote for MPs.

By consulting various published and unpublished lists, we can also learn who was a member of the Court of Directors. Acres (1940) lists all of the Bank directors from 1694 on. I included in my analysis of directors anyone who had been a director at some point between 1700 and 1712. For the East India Company, the Minutes of the General Court of Proprietors were used.[12] The General Court was akin to a modern meeting of the shareholders, in which directors were elected on an annual basis. I included those elected as a director of the United Company between 1709 and 1712 (the 1709 election was the first one for directors of the United Company). As with modern corporations, actual control over the company was much more in the hands of the directors than the general shareholders.[13]

NOTES

1. See also Minowitz 1993: 80.

2. For more on the argument that free markets erode discrimination, see Hampsher-Monk 1991 and Sunstein 1991.

3. "I am infinitely delighted in mixing with these several Ministers of Commerce, as they are distinguished by their different Walks and different Languages: Sometimes I am justled among a Body of *Armenians*: Sometimes I am lost in a Crowd of *Jews*; and sometimes make one in a Groupe of *Dutch-men*" (Ross 1982: 437). Voltaire also commented on the social and religious diversity of London's markets (Voltaire 1926 [1733]: 34). Michael Walzer summarizes the social openness of markets by saying that "the market is open to all comers" (Walzer 1983: 10).

4. Sir Josiah Child also remarked that: "Shop-Keepers are, like all other men, led by their profit" (Child 1740: 116).

5. See Hirschman 1970.

6. Some use this idea to explain the absence of economic development in the contemporary third world: states and governments are too corrupt, and there is too much political interference in markets. See, for example, Sandbrook 1986.

7. The outstanding exemplar is Coleman 1990, but also see Hechter 1987.

8. See Becker 1968, 1971, 1981; Brenner 1980; Schotter 1981; Cooter and Ulen 1988; Downs 1957; Jones 1984; and Wolfe 1989: 32, 35.

9. See Baron and Hannan 1994.

10. Neal (1990) believes it to be very useful for testing theories from financial economics.

11. See DiMaggio 1990.

12. Friedman goes on to argue that criteria which have no bearing on productivity, efficiency, or profitability are excluded from markets by the forces of competition: "A businessman or an entrepreneur who expresses preferences in his business activities that are not related to productive efficiency is at a disadvantage compared to other individuals who do not" (Friedman 1962: 109). In the long run, those who pursue their noneconomic preferences will be outcompeted by those who stay focused on the bottom line. See also Alchian 1950.

13. See Sunstein 1991.

14. For more on this idea in its early modern context, see Hirschman 1977.

15. As Joseph Schumpeter put it: "Taxes not only helped to create the state. They helped to form it. The tax system was the organ the development of which entailed the other organs" (Schumpeter 1991: 108).

16. Co-optation can be a double-edged sword. See Selznick's famous analysis (1949).

17. See Veitch 1986, and Barzel 1992.

18. As an example, consider the worthlessness of Imperial Russian bonds after 1919, or Confederate bonds in the postbellum period. The Communist regime was not going to take on Tzarist financial debts, and the victorious Union refused to repay Confederate creditors. Of course, not all political revolutions result in debt repudiation, particularly if the new regime wants to borrow from the same creditors as the old one did.

19. Colley states that ". . . members of the landed elite made up over 75 per cent of the Commons' membership as late as 1867. Peers of the realm, who formed the bulk of every British cabinet until the early twentieth century, were also, almost invariably, men with landed estates to their name" (Colley 1992: 61).

20. As Colley puts it: "Government creditors, and those embroiled in the nets of private credit arrangements, worried about the security of their investments and about recovering what was owed to them in the event of a civil war" (Colley 1992: 76–77). See also Cain and Hopkins 1986.

21. These estimates are from Dickson 1967.

22. On the magnitude of the French threat, see Bosher 1994.

23. See, e.g., Holton 1985; Lachmann 1987; Brenner 1976; and Hilton 1976.

24. See Inikori 1990; and Roseveare 1991: 73.

25. Consider, for example, Alfred Marshall's and Léon Walras's discussions of stock markets (Marshall 1938: 326; Walras 1954: 83–84).

26. The economic literature on these topics is vast and ably surveyed in Sheffrin 1983; Fama 1970; and Fama 1991.

27. See, e.g., North 1981, 1990; Libecap 1989; Eggertsson 1990; and Posner 1986.

28. See Landes 1969; Lachmann 1987; and Brenner 1976.

29. In the feudal period, economic goods were distributed in a number of ways, including market exchange. But in the early Middle Ages, market exchange was less important than unilateral transfers of property that were either voluntary (in the case of gifts) or involuntary (theft). These other modes were actually preferred over market exchange because of their superior ability to construct and sustain social relations of dominance and subordination. Gifts, for example, created an obligation in the recipient toward the gift-giver. Theft, or the exaction of tribute, was proof of the superiority of the despoiler over his victim. In contrast, market exchange cultivated no such social asymmetry. See Grierson 1959; Geary 1986; and Jones 1993.

30. "Market thinking could be relied upon only after the variety of forces influencing personal preferences in the use of time and wealth had been ruthlessly narrowed to one—the likelihood of gain" (Appleby 1976: 514).

31. See Lougheed 1980: 151.

32. See Neal 1990 for a recent and thorough study.

33. See North 1981; North 1990; Libecap 1989; Ensminger 1992; Jones; 1993; and Basu, Jones, and Schlicht 1987.

34. This contrasts with the usual image of politics "interfering," "corrupting," or "crippling" the operations of the market. Cf. North 1990: 117.

35. See Fligstein 1990.

36. For example, see Anderson 1974: 113; Tilly 1975: 35; Braun 1975: 289; and Dibble 1965: 907.

37. Consider Benjamin and Duvall 1985; and Mann 1984.

38. See Lachmann 1987: 148–49.

39. According to North (1981), this explains why the state plays such an important role in the specification and enforcement of property rights: coercive power is necessary to protect property.

40. This process is discussed in Tilly 1985: 169, 183; Hintze 1975: 174, 181; and Lane 1958. See Ertman (1994b) for an insightful discussion of the entire literature on state-building.

41. See also Rasler and Thompson 1985.

42. Aylmer 1961: 7.

43. See Mousnier 1979: 665–67. Of course, while absolutism in theory was one thing, absolutism in practice was something else, as Beik's (1985) and Kettering's (1986) work on France shows. See also Mettam 1990.

44. Aylmer 1961: 440.

45. Miller 1984: 187; Speck 1988: 8,125; and Holmes 1993: 86.

46. See Childs 1976.

47. Jones 1987: 8, 81.

48. See Goubert 1970: 72–73. Earlier, England and France were compared unfavorably by French politicians. At the time of the English Civil War, Mazarin wanted to ensure that "France did not follow the trend across the Channel where the independent financial powers of the crown had been drastically curtailed" (Bonney 1981: 211).

49. See Jones 1988: 29.

50. Lossky 1970: 155.

51. Wallerstein 1980: 288.

52. As Levi points out (1988: 32–33), however, rulers would confiscate wealth if their discount rates were high enough, i.e., if they oriented toward the extreme short run.

53. These include the potential for mass mobilization and elite mobility or competition.

54. See, e.g., Brewer 1989; North and Weingast 1989; Levi 1988; and Root 1994.

55. See Parker 1988.

56. So-called "forced borrowing" is really taxation by another name.

57. Earle points out that the return on investment in land "compared unfavourably with almost any other form of investment" (Earle 1989: 152).

58. There are no surviving South Sea Company financial records for this period.

59. For example: "Money as always was mobile and its exchange transcended political frontiers even during the big European wars. Huguenot money was lent to Louis XIV by Protestant bankers based in Amsterdam and Geneva, notwithstanding the impecunious Sun King's persecution of their coreligionists who had remained in France. Similarly, the British government probably did not deem it politic to examine the religious beliefs or political backgrounds of bankers prepared to lend it money and enable it to use their credit facilities on the European continent" (Murphy 1986: 26).

60. As I am using the term, discrimination does not mean "price discrimination."

61. See Goldin 1990: 88–89, 214.

62. See Landa 1981, and Cooter and Landa 1984.

63. Joseph Addison claimed in 1711 that the "rage of party" gave rise to all sorts of problems: "A furious Party-Spirit, when it rages in its full Violence, exerts it self in

Civil War and Bloodshed; . . . It fills a Nation with Spleen and Rancour, and extinguishes all the Seeds of Good-Nature, Compassion and Humanity" (Ross 1982: 444). The political ideal remained that of a unified parliament advising the Crown.

64. In a tax farm, independent subcontractors collect tax revenues and make negotiated payments to the government, keeping the difference for themselves as profit.

65. See Riley 1980: 60, and 't Hart 1993: 101.

66. In his famous *Fable of the Bees*, Mandeville said: "The Dutch may ascribe their present Grandeur to the Virtue and Frugality of their Ancestors as they please; but what made that contemptible spot of Ground so considerable among the principal Powers of Europe, has been their Political Wisdom in postponing every thing to Merchandize and Navigation, the unlimited Liberty of Conscience that is enjoy'd among them, and the unwearied Application with which they have always made use of the most effectual means to encourage and increase Trade in general" (Mandeville 1970 [1723]: 202). See also Child 1740: 6.

67. Mann 1986: 479.

68. In fact, they were too political, and so after the South Sea Bubble of 1720, the British government reduced its reliance upon joint-stock companies as a source of loans.

69. Concomitantly, the macro-historical sample of one becomes two data sets with information on over 6,600 individuals.

70. Most political-economic analyses rely upon the stated interests of the actors, or upon interests imputed to them by the researcher. In contrast, my data measure the *actual* political and economic behavior of individuals, and is based on records of voting in parliamentary elections, and joint-stock company ledgers.

71. For this reason, what political scientists call the "voter's paradox" (Mueller 1989, chap. 18) was less applicable to East India Company elections. As compared to a Bank election, it was far more likely in an East India Company election that a voter would cast a consequential vote.

72. See, for example, Greif's analyses of medieval Maghribi traders (Greif 1989, 1993).

73. To borrow the title of Stigler and Becker's well-known paper about preferences and economic explanations (1977).

74. See Baker 1984.

CHAPTER TWO
BRITISH POLITICS FROM 1672 TO 1712

1. For an unsuccessful attempt to reduce early eighteenth-century party politics to family-based patronage factions, see Walcott 1956a.

2. For a recent statement of this "institutionalist" perspective, see Skocpol 1992.

3. See Harris 1993: 1, 6, 74.

4. Swift's tongue-in-cheek analysis in *The Examiner* number 31, exaggerated only slightly: "Where Parties are pretty equal in a State, no Man can perceive one bad Quality in his own, or good one in his Adversaries. . . . so the Women among us have got the distinguishing Marks of Party in their Muffs, their Fans, and their Furbelows. The Whig Ladies put on their Patches in a different Manner from the Tories. They

have made some Schisms in the Play-House, and each have their particular Sides at the Opera: And when a Man changeth his Party, he must infallibly count upon the Loss of his Mistress" (Davis 1940: 102).

5. See, e.g., Root 1994.

6. This is not an original definition. See Schattschneider 1942: 35, 37; Epstein 1967: 9–10; and La Palombara 1966: 6.

7. The electorate in the seventeenth and eighteenth centuries was, by modern standards, highly restricted. However, it encompassed a significant proportion of the total adult male population. For the later seventeenth century, estimates range from 15% (Plumb 1969) to 40% (Hirst 1975).

8. During, for example, the Glorious Revolution and the Hanoverian Succession.

9. Although there were no formal restrictions on the prerogative power to create new peerages, it had to be used sparingly if other peers were not to be alienated by too many new creations. See Jones 1978: 30.

10. In seventeenth-century England, "division lists," which recorded how members of parliament voted, illustrate the influence of parties on voting. Hoadley's study of the emergence of political parties in the U.S. Congress at the end of the eighteenth century also uses this kind of evidence. The emergence of stable coalitions of legislators voting together marks the formation of political parties (Hoadley 1980: 760).

11. There are no poll books from the early seventeenth century. The earliest, according to a recent catalogue, is for the Essex by-election of 1694 (see Sims 1984: 47). Kishlansky (1986: 186) claims that the use of poll books began in the 1660s.

12. See Russell 1983: 124–25.

13. Parliamentary members could also do their own business through the passage of private bills.

14. This was the power of *plena potestas*, and characterized parliament since the reign of Edward I. See Russell 1983: 127.

15. See Lambert 1990: 61; Sharpe 1986: 324; and Hirst 1975: 158.

16. There was an increase in the period leading up to the Civil War.

17. See Hirst 1975: 111, and appendix IV.

18. Kishlansky 1986: 17.

19. Contests threatened to unleash conflict in a society greatly concerned with the preservation of hierarchical social order. See Hirst 1975: 15, and Kishlansky 1986: 48, 71.

20. This was literally a "voice vote." The electorate would assemble in one spot and be asked to call out the name of their favored candidate. The candidate with the most supporters (or the loudest) would win.

21. Supporters for different candidates would be assembled in different locations, and the size of the crowds compared.

22. Of course, this normally meant adult males only, but occasionally women tried to vote. See Hirst 1975: 18–19.

23. See Hirst 1975: 29–30.

24. See the general discussion of franchises in Henning 1983: 104–7.

25. See Hirst 1975, appendix V, for estimated sizes of early seventeenth-century electorates.

26. This was the result of Goodwin's case, involving the Buckinghamshire election of 1604. See Plumb 1969: 95, and Kenyon 1966: 25, 27, 37–38.

27. Kishlansky (1986: 38) points out the bilateral relationship between boroughs and magnates. It was not simply that the magnates dominated the borough, for they were expected to provide services and connections in return.

28. According to Plumb and Hirst, fears of an increasingly powerful Crown caused parliamentarians in the 1620s to expand the size of electorates. Larger electorates were less susceptible to Crown or aristocratic control, and helped maintain the independence of Parliament (Plumb 1969: 96–98; Hirst 1975: 67–68). Kishlansky has argued that the strict size of the electorate was less important than the willingness of elites to tolerate an electoral contest, and sees the revolutionary period as being more important for the transformation of politics than the 1620s. See Kishlansky 1986: 31, 108.

29. See Kishlansky 1986: 21, 106, 111.

30. Not everything, however, was reinstated. Certain prerogative courts were abolished (e.g., Star Chamber and the Courts of the Duchy of Lancaster) and feudal rights of the Crown terminated. See Carter 1979: 84–85.

31. See Jones 1978: 52, and Witcombe 1966: 78.

32. According to Seaward (1988: 17, 78–79), Clarendon's method for parliamentary management was strictly Elizabethan.

33. See Browning 1951: 56.

34. See Seaward 1988: 96–98.

35. Ibid.: 84.

36. The first letters of the ministers' five names form the acronym CABAL (Clifford, Arlington, Buckingham, Ashley-Cooper, and Lauderdale).

37. Jones 1987: 6–7, 80.

38. See Haley 1953: 3, and Ogg 1955: 344.

39. See Witcombe 1966: 104, 127. Clifford's efforts at creating a group of court supporters also helped. See Holmes 1993: 90, 133–34.

40. The Declaration also satisfied Charles's personal desire for greater toleration. The Lord Keeper, Sir Orlando Bridgeman, had his doubts about the legality of both the Stop and the Declaration. As the Crown's chief legal officer, the Lord Keeper's support was crucial, so Bridgeman was quickly sacked and replaced by Lord Ashley, now the Earl of Shaftesbury.

41. Jones 1987: 81, 93.

42. Miller 1973: 107.

43. Lee 1965: 159; Witcombe 1966: 134.

44. Ogg 1955: 368; Miller 1973: 55–56.

45. Osborne started out originally as a follower of Buckingham, but soon gained an independent stature. See Browning 1951: 111.

46. James Duke of York was among those who pressured Charles to sack Shaftesbury. See Haley 1968: 336.

47. Jones 1978: 176–77.

48. Jones 1987: 110.

49. See Browning 1948: 23, and Henning 1983: 34. For lists of the members of this Court group, see de Beer 1933–34: 4–23.

50. Haley 1968: 347.

51. Jones 1978: 181.

52. See Miller 1984: 187, and Bosher 1994. A pamphlet from 1680 illustrates in

lurid prose anti-Catholic sentiment: "Yourselves forced to fly destitute of bread and harbour, your wives prostituted to the lust of every savage bog-trotter, your daughters ravished by goatish monks, your smaller children tossed upon pikes, or torn limb from limb, whilst you have your own bowels ripped up . . . or else murdered with some other exquisite tortures and holy candles made of your grease (which was done within our memory in Ireland), your dearest friends flaiming in Smithfield, foreigners rendering your poor babes that can escape everlasting slaves, never more to see a Bible, nor hear again the joyful sounds of Liberty and Property. This, this gentlemen is Popery" (quoted in Miller 1973: 75).

53. The Reverend Titus Oates claimed that there was a plot among Catholics to assassinate the king and massacre English Protestants. See Ogg 1955: 559, 565–69, and Harris 1993: 80.

54. Jones 1961: 6, 40.

55. Henning 1983: 37, 106.

56. Glassey 1979: 49, 57.

57. Jones 1961: 134–39.

58. On the origins of the terms "Whig" and "Tory," see Willman 1974.

59. Jones 1978: 219.

60. Miller 1973: 176–77; Jones 1961: 180.

61. Allen 1976: 564–66; Haley 1970.

62. Jones 1979: 58.

63. Jones 1987: 162, 174.

64. Speck 1988: 43.

65. Harris 1993: 124; de Beer 1970: 197.

66. Glassey 1979: 72–75.

67. See Chandaman 1975: 261. Whatever its virtues for other periods of English history, Goldstone's model of political stress fails to work for the reign of James II. Goldstone argues that public financial difficulties led to political upheaval, *ceteris paribus*. His political-stress indicator posits a monotonically increasing relationship between financial and political stress (Goldstone 1986: 280–85, 302). Yet the political reaction against James was brought about by his ability to follow pro-Catholic policies. This ability was based on the independence from Parliament that a rosy financial situation gave him. In other words, political stress followed from the *absence*, not the presence, of financial stress.

68. Speck 1988: 66.

69. Glassey 1979: 78–79; Harris 1993: 126.

70. Plumb 1967: 54,60; Speck 1988: 134.

71. Speck 1988: 144.

72. Schwoerer 1977: 843, 845.

73. Only a monarch could call a regular Parliament, and there was at this point no acknowledged monarch. Hence, it was a Convention rather than a Parliament that debated and selected the terms under which the Crown would be offered to William and Mary.

74. See Harris 1993: 138.

75. See Horwitz 1968: 71; Hill 1976: 30; and Speck 1988: 98. For obvious reasons, William was also eager for a quick settlement.

76. See the discussions in Bennett 1969: 161–62, and Horwitz 1977: 24–28.

77. Bennett 1969: 163; Holmes 1973: 37.

78. Horwitz 1977: 26.

79. Ibid.: 27.

80. William was disillusioned with the Whigs, partly because he overestimated their strength, and partly because they failed to satisfy him over the question of the financial settlement (Horwitz 1977: 17, 44).

81. Revenues would have been higher had William not renounced the Hearth Tax, which brought in roughly £200,000 per annum. See Roberts 1977: 63.

82. Roberts 1977: 62–65; Reitan 1970: 582.

83. This was the Harley-Foley group.

84. For a useful discussion of the Country outlook, see Brooks 1984, and Hayton 1990.

85. Hill 1976: 51.

86. Partly, this was because the Whigs were better organized and hence more capable at passing the legislation William wanted. It was also because the Tory party harbored a number of Jacobites, persons who continued to support the deposed James, and who sought his return to the throne.

87. Snyder 1972: 40.

88. Plumb 1967: 71.

89. Carter 1969: 55. The parliamentary Commissions of Public Accounts were the major vehicle for this growing expertise and oversight. For a useful discussion of the development of these commissions and their role in the Court-Country split, see Downie 1976.

90. A Jacobite was someone who supported the return to the throne of James II, or, after he died in 1701, his son James Francis Edward (the Pretender) or his grandson Charles Edward Stuart.

91. De Krey's work analyzes the transposition of Whigs and Tories within London. He shows how the Whigs started out during the Exclusion Crisis as the populist opposition and became by the mid-1690s the oligarchic establishment. City Tories simultaneously moved in the opposite direction (De Krey 1983: 590; De Krey 1985, chap. 5).

92. This is Jones's (1988: 16) term.

93. Most of the fighting done by English armies occurred in Flanders, a heavily populated region between France and the Dutch republic. The major architect of the land war was John Churchill, the Duke of Marlborough. As general, Marlborough led the allied armies to great victories at Blenheim (1704) and Ramillies (1706). The battle of Malplaquet (1709) was nominally a victory, but casualties were so heavy that it did little to advance the allied cause. The allied armies did not fare as well in Spain, losing battles at Almanza (1707) and Brihuega (1710).

94. Pitt 1970: 453.

95. Gregg 1980: 289.

96. The German prince who later became King George I was the grandson of Charles I's older sister.

97. Gregg 1980: 130–31. In part, this was because Jacobite sentiment remained strong in Scotland: the Pretender could always count on the Scots for some support.

98. For various reasons, Scottish members of the Commons and Lords were vulnerable to court influence. Whatever the political complexion of the government, it

could count on many of the votes of the Scots, especially in the House of Lords. See Holmes 1967: 392–93.

99. Richards 1972: 83.

100. Flanders was dotted with fortifications, and it was necessary to lay siege to each one before advancing.

101. See Veenendaal 1970: 430, and Gregg 1980: 347. Britain's allies certainly wanted to continue the war. The Elector of Hanover, for example, was opposed to peace since a war with France was one way to ensure the Hanoverian Succession. So long as Britain was fighting the Pretender's host, France, there would be little opportunity for the Pretender to seize the throne after the death of Anne.

102. As Swift put it in *The Examiner* number 23, "It is not obvious to conceive what could move Men who sate at Home . . . to be so utterly averse from putting an End to a long expensive War, which the victorious, as well as the conquered Side, were heartily weary of. . . . But, they well knew by what Tenure they held their Power; that the Queen saw through their Designs; that they had utterly lost the Hearts of the Clergy; that the Landed Men were against them; that they were detested by the Body of the People; and that nothing bore them up but their Credit with the Bank and other Stocks, which would be neither formidable nor necessary when the War was at an End. For these Reasons they resolved to disappoint all Overtures of a Peace" (Davis 1940: 62–63). See also Jones 1994: 85, and MacLachlan 1969: 200.

103. Holmes 1973: 47.

104. Sacheverell's speech was also published as a pamphlet. See Holmes 1973: 64, 68, and Jones 1976: 763.

105. To make matters worse, Sacheverell's pamphlet, *The Perils of False Brethren*, became a best-seller.

106. Richards 1972: 106.

107. Hill 1988: 128.

108. See Holmes 1967: 226, and Speck 1970, appendix D.

109. McInnes 1970: 102–3.

110. Holmes 1967: 251; Szechi 1986: 3.

111. See Dickinson 1970: 155. A contemporary pamphlet suggests the kind of difficulties faced by Harley in attempting to manage the October Club: "Why, the very nature of an October-Club-Man is to be Mad, Precipitant, Hot as Sulphur, Flashy as Gunpowder, Noisy, Wild, and Ungovernable" (*The Secret History of the October Club*, 1711).

112. Glassey 1979: 203.

113. Gregg 1980: 336–37; Szechi 1984: 95.

114. This measure required all MPs to be worth at least £600 per annum in real estate, if they sat for a county seat, and at least £300 p.a. if they sat for a borough seat. The idea was to ensure that only landed men were eligible to sit in Parliament.

115. The Naturalization Act of 1709 (7 Anne, c.5), passed by the Whigs, made it easier for foreign-born protestants to become naturalized British subjects. To the xenophobic Tories, naturalized foreigners were doubly anathema: they were not followers of the Church of England, and they usually supported the Whig party.

116. Dickinson 1970: 164.

117. Plumb 1956: 178–80.

118. Szechi 1986: 4.

119. Hill 1988: 166.

120. See Speck 1970, appendix E.

121. A politically biased sheriff could exert influence at this point.

122. After passage of an Act for Regulating Elections (7 & 8 William III, c.25) in 1696, sheriffs were required to write down the names and votes of the electorate.

123. The partisan nature of some of the newspapers was public knowledge. The *Post-Boy*, for example, was a well-known Tory paper. The *Observator* was a Whig paper. One issue of *The Medley* (No. XX, May 5–9, 1712) even identified the various Whig (*Protestant Post-Boy, Flying-Post, Observator, Medley*) and Tory (*Post-Boy, Supplement, Abel's Letter, Dyer's Letter, Review, Examiner*) papers.

124. Speck 1972: 18–19.

125. See Speck and Gray 1970: 111, and Speck et al. 1975: 84–86.

126. Landau 1979: 574.

127. There are many other similar examples, both Whig and Tory: Henry St. John (later Viscount Bolingbroke); Sir John Somers (later Baron Somers); Charles Montagu (Earl of Halifax); and Sidney Godolphin (Earl of Godolphin), to name but a few.

128. Thus, even though Lord Somers had held high office under William, Anne excluded him from office for as long as she could on account of his extreme Whiggery (Sachse 1975: 262).

129. For example, in 1679 Shaftesbury drew up several lists of MPs he thought were likely to support an Exclusion Bill.

130. Divisions were so called because in practice those voting divided into two groups and were counted separately.

131. See Hayton and Jones 1979: 66.

132. In Holmes 1967, appendix A; Snyder 1972, appendixes A, B, C; Burton et al. 1968, appendixes A, B; Horwitz 1977, appendixes B, C; and Newman 1970.

133. See Horwitz 1977: 318–19.

134. See Holmes (1967: 45) for a discussion of issues that could produce cross-voting.

135. This discussion owes a great deal to Holmes 1967, chapters 9 and 10.

136. Getting members to attend parliamentary sessions was a frequent problem, especially for the minority party. Traveling to London was an arduous task for many of the country members, and residence in London was expensive. The Tories relied on regional "whips" to ensure that attendance was good, but in both parties the independent country gentleman MP was notoriously unreliable. Attendance in the House of Lords was less crucial since the Lords could use proxy votes. See Holmes 1967: 306.

137. The Whig Kit-Cat Club was the most famous example of a social-political club. See Harris 1993: 151–52.

138. See Holmes 1967: 323.

139. One must be careful not to overestimate the power of kinship. For there are enough examples of families split into Whig and Tory sides to realize that kinship did not automatically guarantee political solidarity (Holmes 1967: 333).

140. Marlborough's extensive military patronage was put to good use in the Commons.

141. The importance of these connections raises the possibility that they, and not parties, were the fundamental political units in this period. Such an argument, inspired by Namier's analysis of mid-eighteenth-century British politics, has been made by Robert Walcott (1956a). His analysis has been soundly refuted by numerous authors, including Plumb, Holmes, Speck, and others.

142. The members of the Junto were, at various times, Lords Somers, Wharton, Halifax, Sunderland, and Orford.

143. Holmes 1969: 216; Holmes 1967: 235–37.

144. This is what made the October Club such a significant and singular group: for the first time the Tory backbenchers possessed an autonomous organization.

145. Holmes 1967: 248–49, 252.

146. As Jonathan Swift put it: "Besides, the Whigs themselves have always confessed, that the Bulk of Landed Men in England are generally of Tories" (Ellis 1985: 182).

147. See Statt 1990: 49.

148. Holmes 1973: 29.

149. See De Krey 1985: 214.

150. Holmes 1973: 156–76; Harris 1993: 13.

151. Harris 1987: 164, 188.

152. See Beckett 1986: 10, 128, 404–6.

153. See Harris 1993: 188, and Langford 1991: 121. Anne Clavering described in a letter to her father of December 1710 how politicized Eton had become: "Jacky is come and proves a bully on the Whig side. . . . Att Eaton the school is devided W[hig] and To[ry]. Jacky one day ingaged fighting a Tory boy and Lady Oglethorp came and bid him give over. Jacky pursued his quarrel so she call'd him names. . . ." (Dickinson 1967b: 106).

154. This may have been simply a "homophily" effect, an expression of the desire among people to associate with similar persons.

CHAPTER THREE
FINANCE AND STATE-FORMATION

1. Mann's distinction between despotic and infrastructural power (1984) is relevant here.

2. See Schofield 1988: 227.

3. These figures are from Mitchell 1988: 575, 578, and Chandaman 1975: 332–33, 350–55.

4. See O'Brien 1985: 776.

5. During the Civil War period, of course, English government broke down and English politicians were primarily concerned with domestic affairs.

6. The Military Revolution consisted of three changes: the new use of firepower, new types of fortifications, and larger armies (Parker 1988: 43). All three made war more expensive.

7. See also Stone 1994.

8. In truly desperate situations, there was recourse to outright confiscation of property.

9. This summary is based on Schofield 1988, and Fryde and Fryde 1963.

10. See Veitch 1986; Barzel 1992; and Root's discussion (1994) of France.

11. Charles V of Spain, for example, was paying annual interest rates of almost 49% during the 1550s. See Parker 1988: 63.

12. See Hutton 1985: 148. The permanent, ordinary revenue consisted of the customs taxes, excise taxes, and hearth taxes, with some additional minor revenue sources.

13. This is Chandaman's (1975: 263) estimate.

14. See Aylmer 1961: 58. In England, excise revenues generally funded the army, while customs revenues funded the navy. The unpopularity of standing armies was transferred to the means used to pay for them, and so excises engendered more opposition than customs (Hughes 1934: 122).

15. See Haley 1953: 30, and Horsefield 1982: 515–16.

16. See Chandaman 1975: 224, 228.

17. These were supplemented by lesser revenues from Crown lands, First Fruits and Tenths, and other sources. Income from these was erratic but at times made an important contribution to Crown revenues. See Chandaman 1975: 136–37.

18. This discussion is based on Chandaman 1975: 38, 49, 51.

19. In contrast, the collection of customs revenues took place in a small number of port towns, with a single location, London, accounting for the bulk of revenues.

20. See Meekings 1969: 556.

21. See Chandaman 1975: 85. This was true notwithstanding the fact that under-assessment was almost guaranteed since homeowners themselves certified the number of hearths they possessed (Hutton 1985: 158).

22. See Harper 1929: 64.

23. See Chandaman 1975: 27, 61, and Hughes 1934: 141.

24. In this regard, the system was similar to that of France, in which financial officers both administered public finances and were the sources of loans.

25. See Clay 1978: 33–36, 93, 109, and Nichols 1987: 33.

26. Roseveare 1973: 53; Seaward 1988: 125.

27. This discussion of direct taxes is based on Chandaman 1975, chapter 5.

28. Personalty, as distinguished from realty (land), is a class of property consisting of intangible property, moveable property, and personal property.

29. See Chandaman 1975: 173–74, and Braddick 1994.

30. Michaelmas is the 29th of September, celebrated as the feast of St. Michael the Archangel.

31. See Roseveare 1973: 23; Tomlinson 1979: 95; and 't Hart 1991.

32. The superiority of Dutch finance was well recognized at the time. See Tracy 1985; Roseveare 1969: 59–60, and Parker 1973: 51.

33. Roseveare (1973: 27, 37), discusses these.

34. Institutionally, the Exchequer was older than the Treasury and was divided into two parts: Upper and Lower Exchequer. The Upper Exchequer was one of the Courts of Law, hearing cases that pertained to the King's revenue. It also audited accounts. The Lower Exchequer dealt with the nitty-gritty of receiving and paying out money. See Baxter 1957: 109–10, 122.

35. See Sainty 1965: 465–67.

36. Tomlinson 1979: 97–99.

37. See *Calender of Treasury Books*, vol.1: xliii–xliv.

38. See Nichols 1971: 84. Sharpe mentions numerous occasions when the city extended loans to the Crown. See Sharpe 1894: 385–86, 389, 399, 403, 406, 414, 437, 443, 455–56.

39. See Roseveare 1991: 14–15.

40. See Hutton 1985: 234, and Roseveare 1962: 46.

41. The traditional instrument for short-term credit was a notched wooden stick called a tally. For a discussion of how they were used, see Chandaman 1975: 287–95, and Robert 1952.

42. Roseveare 1973: 23–25.

43. See Roseveare 1962: iii.

44. Ibid.: 260, and Roseveare 1987: 117.

45. See Roseveare 1991: 18.

46. See Holmes 1993: 89.

47. See Horsefield 1982: 511. Since the original Additional Aid had been for £1.25 million, at most that amount worth of Treasury Orders could be issued. But the permanent ordinary revenue did not consist of discrete sums. The more orders that were issued against it, the further into the future that revenues would have to go to debt repayments.

48. Chandaman estimates that the disposable income of the government was reduced to only £400,000 by 1672 because of the number of outstanding Treasury Orders (Chandaman 1975: 226).

49. As Charles Davenant argued in his 1695 pamphlet, *An Essay upon Ways and Means*: ". . . now the whole art of war is a manner reduced to money; and now-a-days, that prince, who can best find money to feed, cloath, and pay his army, not he that has the most valiant troops, is surest of success and conquest (Davenant 1771: vol. 1:16).

50. See Chandaman 1975: 227, and Horsefield 1982: 513.

51. Isaac Collier and Henry Johnson, Esq. were also goldsmith-bankers. The rest of the creditors were an assortment of merchants, former customs farmers, and others.

52. See Horsefield 1982: 514.

53. These are kept at the Royal Bank of Scotland in London. A brief examination of ledger S, for 1670–71, shows that many of the other goldsmith-bankers had an account with Backwell, including Bernard Turnor, Jeremiah Snow, John Colville, George Snell, John Lindsey, Thomas Rowe, Joseph Hornby, John Portman, Henry Johnson, and Robert Welsted.

54. E/406/27–32 at the Public Record Office cover assignments between 1677 and 1683.

55. See Roseveare 1962: 242–43.

56. Ibid., appendix VII.

57. PRO E.406/27–32.

58. See above, note 53.

59. The unit of analysis here is the assignment of interest payments from a goldsmith-banker to a creditor. If the same individual receives assignments from two goldsmith-bankers, then that person is included twice. However, an examination of the source shows that such multiple counts are not a significant problem, and so the results in the table are representative.

60. Persons were coded as merchants, Aldermen, or MPs if they were identified as such (as in "John Doe, Merchant"), or if I was able to identify them using standard sources like Henning and Woodhead. They were coded as having a legal career if they were identified as legal officers (e.g., Sergeants at law), or, more frequently, if one of the Inns of Court was given as their residence (e.g., Lincoln's Inn, Inner Temple, Middle Temple). They were coded as having a church career if they were Doctors of Divinity (e.g., John Doe DD) or if they were identified as Bishops, Church Wardens, or Rectors.

61. See Witcombe 1966: 145. In his diary, Sir Edward Dering notes that Charles mentioned the plight of the bankers in his address to Parliament (Henning 1940: 151, 157).

62. See Roseveare 1991: 22. In conversation, Henry Roseveare has suggested that a clue for the reason for the apparent lack of concern in Parliament over the financial consequences of the Stop lies in Melton's analysis of the firm of Clayton & Morris. Goldsmith-bankers were not the only persons supplying financial services. Melton's work indicates the size of the financial operations of scriveners, particularly in the area of mortgages (Melton 1986: 12, 33, 94). Freezing the deposits of the goldsmith-bankers may not have been as great a trauma to the financial system as formerly was thought.

63. See Roseveare 1962: 235.

64. Browning 1951: 138, 211.

65. As a consequence of the Stop, credit conditions tightened, goldsmith-bankers' notes became unacceptable as a means of payment, and several of the bankers became bankrupt. Losses to the bankers' depositors were also substantial, although the magnitude was not apparent for many years.

66. See Jones 1994: 70–72.

67. Tomlinson 1979: 100–101.

68. Horwitz 1977: 88.

69. See Downie 1976: 33, 51, and Horwitz 1977: 202.

70. These figures are from Brewer 1988: 341, 346–47.

71. Brooks 1974: 291–93; Ward 1953: 22, 31.

72. See Beckett 1985: 301, and Brewer 1988: 348.

73. See Chandaman 1975: 51.

74. See Brewer 1988, table 1.

75. The revenue estimates are from O'Brien 1988, table 4.

76. See the figures in Mitchell 1988: 448.

77. O'Brien 1988, table 3.

78. See Fryde and Fryde 1963: 455–63, and Kindleberger 1984: 43.

79. See Clay 1984: 269.

80. This is P.G.M. Dickson's term (1967), but one should heed Roseveare's (1991) caution not to overemphasize the discontinuous nature of the changes.

81. £150,000 was borrowed in Berne in 1710, and two short-term loans, for £220,000 and £280,000 were raised in Holland in 1695 and 1697, respectively (see Dickson and Sperling 1970: 288). By the standards of the time, these were modest sums.

82. See Holmes 1993: 58–60.

83. See Davis 1954.

84. Figures 3.1 and 3.2 are based on information from Mitchell 1988.

85. See Dickson and Sperling 1970: 286.

86. See Dickson 1967: 343, 348, and Jones 1988: 11.

87. See Van Der Wee 1977: 361.

88. See Brewer 1989: 133, and Tracy 1985: 7–27. The Dutch connection was not always welcome, and Jonathan Swift was sure that it was a serious mistake: ". . . the pernicious councels of borrowing money upon publick funds of interest, as well as some other state-lessons, were taken indigested from the like practices among the Dutch, without allowing in the least for any differences in government, religion, law, custom, extent of country, or manners and dispositions of the people" (Swift 1738: 160–61).

89. The ease with which Dutch government could borrow on good terms is clear from Sir William Temple's observation that "besides the Debt of the Generality, the Province of Holland owes about Sixty five Millions, for which they pay Interest at Four in the Hundred; But with so great ease and exactness both in Principal and Interest, That no man ever demands it twice; They might take up whatever money they desired. Whoever is admitted to bring in his money, takes it for a great deal of favour; And when they pay off any part of the Principal, Those it belongs to, receive it with tears, Not knowing how to dispose of it to Interest with such safety and ease" (Temple 1972 [1673]: 130). For more on Dutch finance, see 't Hart 1993, chapter 6.

90. For a description of this type of loan, a collective annuity, see Jennings and Trout 1982: 1, 30, and Weir 1989: 102.

91. See Reitan 1970: 571, and Brewer 1989: 88.

92. See King's *History of the Earlier Years of the Funded Debt*: 3.

93. The following figures are based on King 1898: 5–6, and Dickson 1967: 48–49, 60–61, 63.

94. The rulers of Holland were the first to use annuities for their own purposes. In the eyes of the Church, annuities did not violate the prohibition on usury, which explains their early origins and longevity. For a discussion of annuities, see Alter and Riley 1986; Fryde and Fryde 1963: 496, 529–31; Parker 1973: 45–46; and Riley 1980: 36–37.

95. The original buyer of an annuity for life would nominate a person (typically a young relative) whose lifespan determined how long annuity payments continued. A buyer who didn't know the nominee would have a hard time assessing the economic value of the annuity, and so might be reluctant to buy.

96. See Dickson 1967: 45, and Cohen 1953.

97. Because of the structure of payouts, lotteries were considered as much an investment as a form of gambling. Lottery tickets were a conservative enough investment that even insurance companies bought them (using the premiums paid by their customers). London's Sun Insurance Office, for example, instructed its Treasurer to buy more lottery tickets in April and October 1712. See Guildhall Library Mss 11,931, ff. 77, 91.

98. The details are in Ewen 1932: 127–29.

99. See King 1898: 6, 14–16.

100. This total is based on the figures in King 1898: 47.

101. These totals are based on the figures in King 1898, and House of Commons, *Return of the Whole Amount of the National Debt of Great Britain and Ireland* 1858.

102. See Brenner 1993, and Ashton 1960.

103. The latter involved the payments remitted to Flanders to pay for the army and by 1694 these exceeded £1 million annually. See Clapham 1945: 26, and Jones 1988: 18–21, 38.

104. He did not invent his scheme out of thin air, but drew considerable inspiration from the Dutch and their public banks. See Clapham 1945: 2.

105. See Horsefield 1960: 128, and Richards 1934: 201–2. Montagu was titled Baron Halifax in 1700, and was one of the Whig Junto.

106. See King 1898: 67.

107. The Whiggish connections of the Bank were obvious from the beginning and Tory members of Parliament found the Bank objectionable on several grounds. The connections with partisan politics will be discussed at greater length in chapter 6.

108. See Acres 1931: 100.

109. For a yearly listing of the loans made by the company to Charles II's government, see Lougheed 1980: 97, 122–23.

110. Opposition of a different sort came from the Levant Company, which competed with the East India Company and attacked it politically in the early 1680s. See Wood 1935: 102.

111. The Company would raise additional necessary capital through debt rather than equity, i.e., through the issuance of bonds rather than shares. Hence, at times it was highly leveraged. See Jones 1988: 286–87.

112. See Lougheed 1980: 314–15.

113. See Jones 1988: 295.

114. There was a significant degree of overlap between those opposed to the East India Company and those later involved in the Bank of England. See De Krey 1978: 17, and Horwitz 1978: 6–7.

115. In an interesting twist, the old East India Company subscribed £315,000 to the new company whose establishment it had so strongly opposed.

116. See Horwitz 1978: 17.

117. See the *Calender of Treasury Books*, vol. XXV, part 1: l–li. Over half of this debt was comprised of Navy bills.

118. A tally was a wooden stick with cut notches representing a particular sum, and then split with one part kept by the Exchequer and the other going to the payee.

119. See Dickson 1967: 372.

120. On this point, see Riley 1980: 74–75.

121. Figure 3.3 is based on data from Mitchell 1988.

122. These calculations are based on figures from Mitchell 1988: 578, 600.

123. Punctuality and reliability were foremost in establishing public credit, as Defoe argued: "Publick Credit is the Consequences of honourable, just, and punctual Management in the Matter of Funds and Taxes, or Loans upon them" (Defoe *An Essay Upon Publick Credit* 1710: 21). Elsewhere, it was argued that "the Apostolick Chamber, and Bank of Amsterdam, have Mony cheaper than others can have on private Security; which plainly shews, that the truest, as well as the most honest way of supplying the Publick at a cheaper rate, and thereby lessening the Taxes, is, not by the little tricking Arts of these infamous Projectors, but by punctual and steady dealing" (*The Importance of Public Credit* 1699: 6). This pamphlet goes on to tell the story

of Philip II of Spain, and the consequences of his many bankruptcies: "In his Wars of Flanders he had been often supplyed with Mony by the Merchants of Antwerp, to the great advantage of his Affairs; but a piece of such good Husbandry as we are advised, came into his head: Those Tally-jobbing Merchants of Antwerp he thought had got too much by lending him Mony, therefore his profound Wisdom thought it convenient to break his Faith with them, in moderating their Gains . . . by which he seemed perhaps to have saved forty or fifty thousand Pounds. But what followed? In the next line we are told, that neither they, nor any other, would trust him any more, which in few days was the occasion of his losing the then great City of Amiens, and after of infinite Desertions and Mutinies of his Armies for want of Pay, by which his Affairs were wonderfully retarded, and those of his Enemies much advanced" (p. 7). Defaulting on loans might be advantageous in the short run, but it was detrimental in the long run because of the effects on credit.

124. In 1717, the share capital of the Bank, East India Company, and South Sea Company totaled over 90% of all the share capital of all English companies in existence. See Scott 1912: vol. 1, 394.

125. As MacNeil observes: ". . . the ability to transfer wealth, particularly by exchange, typically enhances its value" (MacNeil 1974: 790).

126. These figures are from Riley 1980: 72.

127. See Haley 1988: 162.

128. Josiah Child also noted: "The great advantage that would accrue to this Kingdom by a Law for Transferring Bills of Debt, from one person to another, is sufficiently understood by most men, especially by Merchants" (Child 1740: 135).

129. William Lowndes, Secretary to the Treasury from 1695 until his death in 1724, was left undisturbed by the changes in party fortunes to acquire much bureaucratic wisdom and experience.

130. It was a testament to the rise of Treasury expertise that the public financial projects proposed by private entrepreneurs, which were so characteristic of the 1690s, became less frequent. With its own experts, the Treasury did not have to look outward for new ideas.

131. The data for figure 3.4 are from Mitchell 1988.

132. See Jones 1988: 29, and Jones 1991: 389.

133. See Sperling 1955: vi.

134. Dickson 1967: 254, 260, 273, 285.

135. Clapham 1945: 273, 279.

136. See Dickson 1967: 256.

137. Ibid.: 267, 276. A more detailed analysis of the social and political composition of Bank and East India Company shareholders will be done in chapters 6 and 7.

138. In his sample of 211 estates from the 1665–89 period, Earle found that 27.4% of all investment was in government debt and company stocks and bonds. For the 1690–1720 period, this increased sharply to 47.6%. See Earle 1989: 143–52.

139. See Dickson 1967: 258, 267, 302, and Beckett 1986: 86.

140. See Carter 1955: 27, and Acres 1934.

141. See Giuseppi 1962, and Giuseppi 1955. The foremost army contractor in Flanders between 1707 and 1711 was Sir Solomon de Medina, a Jewish international financier (Rabinowicz 1974: 38).

142. Monter 1969; Dickson 1967: 293.

143. See Speck 1969: 136. Swift's *The Examiner*, no. 14 expresses this bafflement: ". . . yet through the Contrivance and Cunning of Stock-jobbers, there has been brought in such a Complication of Knavery and Couzenage, such a Mystery of Iniquity, and such an unintelligible Jargon of Terms to involve it in, as never were known in any other Age or Country of the World" (Ellis 1985: 7–8).

144. Examples of political commentary critical of the new financial system could be multiplied almost endlessly. Jonathan Swift's critique is typical: "The City Coffee-houses have been for some years filled with People, whose Fortunes depend upon the Bank, East-India, or some other Stock: Every new fund to these, is like a new Mortgage to a Usurer, whose Compassion for a young Heir is exactly the same with that of a Stockjobber to the Landed Gentry" (*The Conduct of the Allies*, 2d ed.). Swift's *The History of the Four Last Years of the Queen*: 160–62, Defoe's *The Anatomy of Exchange-Alley*: 13, 15, and *The Freeholders Plea Against Stock-Jobbing Elections of Parliament Men*: 20, 22 recapitulate the same idea. In his *The Villainy of Stock-jobbers detected . . .*, Defoe writes that ". . . these People [stock-jobbers] can ruin Men silently, undermine and impoverish by a sort of impenetrable Artifice, like Poison that works at a distance, can wheedle Men to ruin them-selves, and Fiddle them out of their Money" (p. 22). The stock market was spoofed in Thomas Shadwell's 1693 play *The Volunteers, or the Stock Jobbers* (see Summers 1927, 5: 188). An otherwise sedate textbook on accounting describes stocks and stockjobbing in a colorful manner: "And the way is, to cast the Interest in the Stock, and Profit in Proportion, into Shares, which are called Stocks, such as the Bank, Indian Company, Sword-Blade-Company, South-Sea, &c. which Shares in Stocks are Vendible, as in a Market, and have a Nation of Brokers, that live upon them; who are to Knaves, as Pimps to Whores. And the whole Influence of this invisible Traffick, is secret Confederacy, and no Truth, or what they call Intrinsick, governs any thing, and as Stocks run High or Low, so are the Heavans like to Stand or fall" (North 1714, Vocabulary). The aura of disrespectability that surrounded the stock market did not dissipate quickly. Even a promoter like Mortimer could use a term as pungent as "the Mammon of unrighteousness" to characterize stockjobbers (Mortimer 1785: xix). See also Bowen 1993.

145. See Wykes 1990: 39, and De Krey 1978: 103. De Krey (1985: 75) estimates that there were around 100,000 dissenters in London at the end of the seventeenth century.

146. Dickinson 1967a.

147. See Brewer 1989: 153.

148. Elsewhere, Swift concluded that ". . . whoever were Lenders to the Govern-ment would by the surest Principle be obliged to support it" (Davis 1951: 68). In his 1699 essay, *An Essay upon the Probable Methods to Make a People Gainers in the Balance of Trade*, Charles Davenant also makes this point (Davenant 1771, vol 2: 267).

149. Years later in his *Some Reflections on the Present State of the Nation*, Boling-broke was making the same argument: "It was said that a new government, estab-lished against the ancient principles and actual engagements of many, could not be so effectually secured any way, as it would be if the private fortunes of great numbers were made to depend on the preservation of it, and that this could not be done unless they were induced to lend their money to the public, and to accept securities under

the present establishment. Thus the method of funding and the trade of stock-jobbing began. Thus were great companies created, the pretended servants, but in many respects the real masters, of every administration" (Bolingbroke 1841: 443). See also Dickinson 1977: 151.

150. The idea that a monarch would intentionally go into debt in order to "capture" his creditors was posed after the Stop of the Exchequer: "Charles . . . falls upon new Councels, he considered he had to do with a people that dealt much in Money, and were generally great Bankers, and Merchants, and therefore concluded that if by extraordinary Usuries he could allure their Money into his Exchequer, he should then be in possession of the best Hostages they could give him for their Fidelity and Observance" (Turner 1674). Kidnappers usually hold people hostage in order to obtain money, but according to this analysis, Charles II held money hostage in order to obtain people.

151. See Lenman 1980; Harris 1993: 208–33; and Colley 1992: 24. Furthermore, as Colley points out, there were Jacobite invasion scares in 1717, 1719, 1720–21, 1743–44, and 1759.

152. See Jones 1994: 68.

153. Indeed, every Jacobite invasion threat was met with falling share prices on the London stock market (see Sperling 1955: iii). More generally, share prices reflected how the war with France was going, with military failure leading to falling prices (see Clapham 1945: 57). Dutch investors, shrewd as always, stayed away from English joint-stock company shares in the early eighteenth century because of fears of Jacobitism and worries about the Hanoverian Succession. Once the 1715 Jacobite invasion was crushed, and after the success of the Hanoverian Succession, Dutch investors became more enthusiastic about British government securities.

154. See Colley 1992: 76–77.

155. "The notorious 'monied interest' spawned by a combination of commercial growth and fiscal innovation posed an undeniable, perhaps even insurmountable challenge to the defenders of the land" (Langford 1991: 58).

156. See Speck 1969: 140–45.

157. This Act, 9 Anne, c.5, stipulated that only persons with estates worth at least £600 per annum were qualified for county seats in the Commons, while the requirement for a borough seat was an estate worth a minimum of £300 per annum.

158. See Beckett 1986: 10, 128, 406; Colley 1992: 61. According to Cain and Hopkins (1986: 513), it wasn't until later in the eighteenth century that the landed interest reconciled politically with the monied interest.

159. Swift's *Examiner* no. 14 stated that ". . . Power, which according to the old Maxim, was us'd to follow Land, is now gone over the Money" (Ellis 1985: 4–5), while Henry St. John observed in a letter to the Earl of Orrery: "The men of estates have, generally speaking, neither served in the fleets nor armies, nor meddled in the public fonds, and management of the treasure. A new interest has been created out of their fortunes, and a sort of property, which was not known twenty years ago, is now encreased to be almost equal to the terra firma of our island. The consequence of all this is, that the landed men are become poor and dispirited. . . . In the mean while those men are become their masters, who formerly would with joy have been their servants" (Dickinson 1975: 146). See also Dickinson 1977: 107, 170, and De Krey 1985: 111.

160. See Jones 1994: 70.

161. Parker 1988: 61.

162. See the figures in Jones 1988: table 2.1.

163. See the estimates in Tilly 1990: 79.

164. These figures are drawn from Ehrman 1953: xx; Childs 1987: appendix c; Childs 1976: appendix g; Childs 1980: 1; Childs 1991: 73; and Jones 1988: 29.

165. A large standing army always raised the specter of absolutism.

166. See Brewer 1989: 141; Colley 1992: 3–4; and Bosher 1994.

167. See Tilly 1990: 30–31, 61, 85–86, 117.

168. Ibid.: 157. For the early seventeenth century, Aylmer estimates the total number of local government officials over the entirety of England and Wales in the hundreds, while the number of officials in a single French province, Normandy, as between three and four thousand. See Aylmer 1961: 440, and Tomlinson 1979: 116. For a comparison of England and Brandenburg-Prussia, see Braun 1975. For more comparisons of the English state bureaucracy with other countries, see Fischer and Lundgreen 1975.

CHAPTER FOUR
BRITAIN IN COMPARATIVE PERSPECTIVE

1. See Root 1994: 11, 19–20, 94.

2. See Lundkvist 1973: 20, and Roberts 1979: 1.

3. See de Vries 1984: table 3.6, and Lundkvist 1973: 21. Roberts (1992, p. 13) puts the population of Sweden and Finland together at only 1.3 million in 1611.

4. See de Vries 1984: table 3.7.

5. See Dahlgren 1973: 104.

6. See Roberts 1979: 49.

7. See Roberts 1992: 111. The king received more butter, fish, iron, copper, and tar, than specie, and Sweden was hard-pressed to come up with the 1 million *riksdaler* in cash necessary to ransom the fortress of Älvsborg in 1613. In kind revenues were advantageous in one respect, however. Crown revenues were insulated from the effects of inflation.

8. For example, Gustavus Adolphus recognized how advantageous flourishing towns were, both for economic growth and for tax revenues, and so tried to encourage their expansion. See Roberts 1992: 115, and Åström 1973: 73.

9. See Downing 1992: 190, and Roberts 1992: 18. Despite its political importance, the *riksdag* was unlike the late seventeenth-century English Parliament because of the absence of political parties. Sweden's first party system, involving the Hats and the Caps, didn't emerge until the eighteenth century. See Metcalf 1977, 1981.

10. See Upton 1990; Upton 1987: 281–82, and Downing 1992: 189. Lindegren (1985, p. 308) argues that the *riksdag* was generally dominated by the Crown, but acknowledges that the latter's role in granting taxes gave it growing political importance.

11. Illegal taxes, i.e., those established without the consent of the *riksdag*, were a rarity in Sweden. See Roberts 1967: 34.

12. See Åström 1973: 79.

13. See Ågren 1973: 238–39; Lindegren 1985: 320–21; and Upton 1987: 285.

14. Charles XI systematically built up a strategic reserve of silver, twenty tons of it sitting in the vault of a Stockholm castle.

15. Roberts 1992: 111.

16. See Dahlgren 1973: 196.

17. Åström 1973: 87; Dahlgren 1973: 106, and Lindegren 1985: 324.

18. See Upton 1990: 114–15; Upton 1987: 289–303; and Ågren 1976.

19. As Ågren explained: "The diminution [in the debt] was accounted for, to a large extent, by the fact that estates which had been pawned or sold by the crown had been reckoned as part of the debt: many of them had now reverted to the crown without any compensation" (Ågren 1973: 247).

20. Some opponents argued against the *reduktion* in 1686 on the grounds that it violated the sanctity of contract. See Upton 1990: 116.

21. Although the nobility were the biggest losers from this measure, by granting exemptions to the *reduktion*, the King was able to maintain close ties to selected aristocrats and thus retain their support.

22. See Ågren 1973: 239, and Downing 1992: 203.

23. Roberts 1992: 100.

24. Roberts 1967: 215.

25. See Roberts 1992: 122; Roberts 1979: 52; and Lundkvist 1973: 22.

26. These figures are from Roberts 1992: 123.

27. See Lindegren 1985: 317.

28. Roberts 1992: 100.

29. See Casey 1985: 209.

30. It had the largest armies in Christendom (see Thompson 1976: 103).

31. Kamen 1991: 256.

32. See de Vries 1984: table 3.6.

33. Lynch 1992: 63–64.

34. These estimates are from de Vries 1984, appendix 1.

35. Kamen 1980: 89; Lynch 1992: 2.

36. See, e.g., Kamen 1980: 67, 70–74. Even in its trade with the New World, Spain was unable to export manufactures and concentrated instead on agricultural products. See Lynch 1992: 1.

37. Part of the reason for this was the extremely low social status accorded trade. Commercially successful families were quick to abandon trade and try to acquire noble status. See Kamen 1991: 170; Lynch 1992: 191–92; and Lynch 1991: 148.

38. See Kamen 1980: 144; Kamen 1991: 228; and Lynch 1992: 116.

39. Lynch 1991: 164; Kamen 1991: 166.

40. Lynch 1992: 42–43.

41. See Thompson 1982.

42. See Jago 1981: 310, 317. The Spanish aristocracy and church dealt directly with the Crown, and did not seek representation through the *cortes*. Although it was a representative body, one should not overstate the similarity between the *cortes* and Britain's parliament. Most important: "There were, of course, no political parties [in the *cortes*]" (Lynch 1992: 35).

43. Kamen 1991: 139–40.

44. Parker 1972: 145. Tax receipts demonstrate clearly the fiscal effects of the Dutch revolt. In 1570–71, the Netherlands treasury received 8.8 million florins from

local taxes, and 1.1 million from Castile. In 1572–73, local taxes provided only 1.8 million florins, and Castile had to remit 6.9 million (Parker 1985: 162).

45. Under Carlos II, the last of the Habsburg kings, the aristocracy became so powerful that Lynch characterizes this reign as an "aristocratic republic." See Lynch 1992: 354.

46. Kamen (1991, p. 155) cites the example of Salamanca, where 63% of the land and 60% of the people were subject to aristocratic jurisdiction, as illustrative of the more general pattern.

47. The crown did not passively accept the political power of the aristocracy. Jago (1973) provides a fascinating account of how private debts were used to give the crown leverage over aristocrats. Most aristocratic estates were subject to the *mayorazgo*, an imbarrable entail. This made it difficult, if not impossible, for the nobility to borrow on the security of their own land. The king could, however, suspend the entail and permit the estate owner to borrow money. Such a favor always had a price. See also Kamen 1980: 230.

48. Seigneurial jurisdiction over peasants included the right to collect the *alcabala*, which was one reason why the shift of so much of the Spanish populace from royal to aristocratic jurisdiction was fiscally consequential.

49. See Lynch 1992: 47–48, and Thompson 1976: 81.

50. Kamen 1991: 49.

51. See the discussion in Motomura 1991: 64–65.

52. Parker 1972: 148.

53. *Juros* could be for lives (i.e., interest payments would continue until the death of the holder) or in perpetuity. See Parker 1972: 149; Motomura 1991: 65; and Lynch 1991: 78.

54. A patent of nobility brought social status and a variety of privileges, including exemption from some taxes. On the sale of nobility, see Thompson 1979.

55. See Lynch 1991: 274.

56. See Kamen 1991: 167.

57. Recourse to venal offices was common in Spain, but not on the same scale as France. See Bonney 1991: 340.

58. See Thompson 1976: 5–7, 262.

59. Ibid.: 7.

60. The importance of financial considerations is revealed by the fact that after every bankruptcy, when the burden of debt was lifted, the shift toward subcontracting halted. See Thompson 1976: 274.

61. See Lynch 1991: 404–5, and Parker 1985: 164.

62. For example, repayment of *juros* absorbed 36% of the ordinary revenues in 1522, 65% in 1543, and 68% in 1556. Total debt repayments absorbed a whopping 84% of all public revenue in 1565 (Kamen 1991: 89, 167). Castilian debts went from 36 million ducats' worth in 1557 to 85 million in 1598, and to 112 million in 1667 (Lynch 1991: 472).

63. Lovett (1980) provides a useful analysis of the bankruptcy of 1575.

64. See Motomura 1991: 66.

65. Kamen 1991: 90; Lynch 1992: 116.

66. See Thompson 1994: 161–62.

67. See Lynch 1991: 148.

68. Kamen 1991: 246.

69. Among other things, this helped ensure the perpetuation of extraordinary taxes such as the *millones*. As the state went increasingly into debt, the *millones* was earmarked for repayment of *juros*. The holders of *juros* tended to be the same elites who were in control of the *cortes* which voted the *millones* in the first place. See Jago 1981: 324.

70. See also Ardant 1975: 166, 176, 199.

71. Casey puts the blame squarely on the Spanish economy: "... Spain's peculiar failure was an inability to complete the transition to a more urbanised economy" (Casey 1985: 224).

72. See de Vries 1984: tables 3.6, 3.7. Note that de Vries' population threshold for "urban" is set at 10,000, a relatively high level. Thus, 31.7% is a conservative estimate.

73. 't Hart 1989: 665.

74. See Wallerstein 1974: chapter 4, and Wallerstein 1980: chapter 2.

75. See Roorda 1964.

76. See Israel 1989b, and de Vries 1976: 117–23.

77. This figure is derived from Israel 1989b: table 6.5. Consider another example from the Baltic trade: in 1662 there were 1,199 ships sailing eastward into the Baltic through the Danish Sound. Of these, 740 were Dutch (see Israel 1989b: table 6.4).

78. See van Houtte 1977: 191–92, and Wilson 1968: 74. The rise of Holland was greatly assisted by the decline of Antwerp as a commercial center, and the growth in trade with the East Indies was largely at the expense of the Portuguese. See Israel 1989b: 247–49.

79. Parker 1985: 25.

80. Israel 1989b: 35.

81. See Barbour 1963: 33; Van Dillen 1934: 105; and Israel 1989b: 73–79. It also made Amsterdam a center for the exchange of information; see Smith 1984.

82. Van Dillen 1934; Barbour 1963: 43.

83. See Van Der Wee 1977: 339–40.

84. As in the London financial market, there was a significant number of Sephardi Jews who were active in the Amsterdam stock market. See Israel 1990: 444–45.

85. As Israel points out: "The merchant elite of Holland and Zeeland had at their disposal financial institutions and resources, and a degree of specialization in financial, brokerage, and insurance techniques, such as none of their rivals possessed and which together afforded an immense and continuous advantage in the international arena" (Israel 1989b: 79).

86. See 't Hart 1993: 4.

87. See Grever 1982 and Grever 1984. As a contemporary put it: "... All the Provinces must concur [in decisions], Plurality being not at all weighed or observed" (Temple 1972 [1673]: 64).

88. In the early seventeenth century, the total number of persons working directly for the central state was no more than 200 ('t Hart 1993: 197).

89. The Dutch nobility, for example, had little involvement in either commerce or politics, and so was deprived of both economic and political influence. See Van Nierop 1993: 217–18, and 't Hart 1993: 18. The position of *stadtholder*, usually held by a member of the House of Orange, was the closest thing to a monarch.

90. Haley 1972: 52, 72; Wilson 1968: 42–44. Temple described Amsterdam's city government thus: "So as ever since, when any one of their numbers dies, a new one

is chosen by the rest of the Senate, without any intervention of the other Burghers; Which makes the Government a sort of Oligarchy" (Temple 1972 [1673]: 53–54).

91. See 't Hart 1993: 192, 219.

92. Ibid.: table 3.1.

93. See Wilson 1968: 232, and 't Hart 1993: 137, 149.

94. See 't Hart 1993: table 5.2. Direct taxes on property were more important in the peripheral Dutch provinces.

95. 't Hart 1993: 123.

96. Ibid.: 192; Swart 1949: 71.

97. See 't Hart 1993: 164–65.

98. See Dickson and Sperling 1970: 298. Recourse to lottery loans in 1711, 1712, and 1713 was a sign of how desperate Holland had become, and this perilous financial state explains the post-1713 policy of neutrality: the Netherlands could simply not afford any more wars. See Aalbers 1977, and Riley 1980: 78.

99. See Tracy 1985: 194, and Fryde and Fryde 1963: 492.

100. There seemed to be greater supply than demand in the Dutch capital market, and so public borrowers could almost always sell off their bonds and annuities. As Temple put it: "Whoever is admitted to bring in his money, takes it for a great deal of favour; And when they pay off any part of the principal, those it belongs to, receive it with tears, not knowing how to dispose of it to interest with such safety and ease" (Temple 1972 [1673]: 130).

101. See Parker 1973: 51–52. Despite the large sums borrowed by the United Provinces, interest rates actually dropped over the long run. See Riley 1980: 72.

102. See 't Hart 1993: 162, and 't Hart 1989b: 121.

103. Ibid.: 173–74.

104. As 't Hart put it: ". . . the Dutch success must be explained by the fact that the chief investors [in Dutch public debt] were magistrates and politicians themselves" ('t Hart 1993: 178). See also Parker 1973: 50.

105. See Burke 1974: 57–58, and appendix.

106. Tracy 1985: 217.

107. See Van Nierop 1993: x, and Tracy 1985: 147.

108. See Tracy 1985: 156–57.

109. See Veenendaal 1994: 126.

110. See de Vries 1984: tables 3.6, 3.7. Some population estimates are slightly higher. Riley (1986: 5) puts the French populace at 21.5 million in 1700, and suggests that it may have been even larger.

111. See, e.g., Schaeper: 33.

112. See Mousnier 1979: 662, 665.

113. For a discussion of the theory of absolutism, see Parker 1989.

114. See Bonney 1991: 317.

115. See Morrill 1978.

116. See Kettering 1986: 7, 232. There was a basic division between *pays d'élection* and *pays d'états*, and generally the later a province was incorporated into France, the more likely it was to have kept its own institutions and privileges. See Bonney 1981: 15.

117. See Bien 1987; Bossenga 1989: 584, and Bossenga 1986: 613.

118. Kettering 1986: 6.

119. See the discussion of intendants in Mousnier 1984: 60–64, 78, and Kettering 1986: 226.

120. See Kettering 1986: 76, 142.

121. As Bossenga points out, it was socially dishonorable to be liable to pay the *taille* (Bossenga 1989: 582). See also Behrens 1963: 458.

122. See Bonney 1992: 162–67, and Root 1987: 25.

123. See Matthews 1958: 77–116, and Bossenga 1989: 584.

124. See Bossenga 1989: 585.

125. See Matthews 1958: 11, 13, 17, 248.

126. See Mathias and O'Brien 1976.

127. According to Parker, between 1610 and 1789, the only time the French national budget was in surplus was from 1662 until 1671. See Parker 1973: 53.

128. Lynn (1993) shows how the French army sustained itself given the perpetual inadequacy of the monies raised or borrowed to fund it.

129. Miron stated in 1605 that "Kings cannot be coerced . . . to repay debts to their subjects" (quoted in Bonney 1981: frontispiece). See also Root 1994: 167.

130. See Bonney 1991: 358.

131. See Bonney 1981: 274. Murphy (1986: 56–57) describes in detail the *chambre de justice* established in March 1716. Many others were held through the seventeenth century (Mousnier 1984: 485).

132. See Bonney 1981: 278.

133. See Parker 1973: 45–46.

134. See Dickson and Sperling 1970: 300–301.

135. Matthews 1958: 31; Bossenga 1989: 587.

136. See Doyle 1984: 853, and Matthews 1958: 30.

137. See Bonney 1991: 340, 343. At the end of the eighteenth century, the number of offices was calculated to be over 50,000, which was certainly an underestimate (see Doyle 1984: 832). During periods of financial duress, the incentives to create new offices were overwhelming. Between 1689 and 1715, 2,461 new offices were created on the quays and markets of Paris alone and sold to raise over 80 million livres (Behrens, 1985: 75).

138. See Mousnier 1984: 28.

139. See Bossenga 1986: 616, and Bien 1987: 97.

140. See De Vries 1976: 220–21.

141. This is Colbert's estimate. See Bonney 1992: 153. For an estimate of the total worth of offices at the end of the eighteenth century, see Taylor 1967: 477, and Giesey 1977: 287.

142. See Moote 1964, and Matthews 1958: 31.

143. See the general discussions in Doyle 1984 and Bien 1987.

144. For example, the offices of *secrétaires du roi* paid only about 2–3% interest on the capital. See Bien 1989: 447.

145. See Giesey 1983: 203.

146. See Giesey 1977; Bien 1987: 94–95; Swart 1949: 9; and Taylor 1967: 471.

147. See Collins 1988: 86.

148. Beik 1985: 245.

149. See also Riley 1986: 43, 71.

150. See Weir 1989: table 1, and Mathias and O'Brien 1976.

151. Venal offices were much less common in Britain than in France, but they were not completely absent. Commissions in the army, for example, were bought and sold until well into the nineteenth century (Bruce 1980). For some interesting ideas about why venal offices were so common in France, but not in Britain, see Ertman 1994a; Aylmer 1980; and Tomlinson 1975.

152. See Beik 1985: 245, 251; Hoffman 1994: 230; and Collins 1988: 6.

153. In this respect, the sheer size of the tax system was advantageous. Collins estimates that between 150,000 and 175,000 persons had some official role in the tax system, or about 2–3% of the adult male population of France (Collins 1988: 16). The similarities with England become apparent in Braddick's (1994) discussion of parliamentary taxation.

154. See Swart 1949: 11; Collins 1988: 96–97, 106; and Waquet 1982: 667.

155. See Tilly 1986: 91–100, 115, 120–27.

156. Root 1987: 26; Tilly 1986: 132.

157. See also Brewer 1989: 16. Weir (1989: 123) even suggests that tontine loans were offered to the public at especially attractive rates in order to forge an alliance between the French government and the urban middle class, the main purchasers of tontines.

158. Similarly, Eumenes' life would be in danger again if someone agreed to pay off his debts on his behalf.

159. See Doyle 1984: 848; Giesey 1983: 207; and Pinaud 1991. Pinaud explains that the deputies of the convention: ". . . decided to honour the debts of the previous regime, a measure which appears to have been taken in the interests of preserving national unity" (Pinaud 1991: 425). From my perspective, the revolutionaries successfully "bought off" those with a vested financial interest in the old regime.

160. See De Long and Schliefer 1993. For more on the structural dependence of the capitalist state, see Steinmetz 1993; Block 1977; and Przeworski and Wallerstein 1988.

161. Or, in the language of economics: ". . . issuing debts creates a constituency in favor of repaying it" (Tabellini 1993: 69). See Alesina and Tebellini 1990; Alesina and Perotti 1995; and van Velthoven, Verbon, and van Winden 1993.

162. Tocqueville posed this connection in the context of political upheaval. "Any revolution is more or less a threat to property. . . . Therefore the more widely personal property is distributed and increased and the greater the number of those enjoying it, the less is a nation inclined to revolution" (Tocqueville 1969: 636–37).

CHAPTER FIVE
FINANCIAL PROPERTY RIGHTS AND THE STATE

1. For example, the total tonnage of English merchant shipping went from about 162,000 tons in 1660 to 340,000 tons in 1686 (Holmes 1993: 442).

2. As Grassby puts it: "Active businessmen did not concentrate their passive investments in land. Their investment capital either circulated in goods or was held in short-term credits, assignable shares, ships and Company stocks" (Grassby 1970: 105).

3. Money to ransom a captured king and money for the dowry of a princess were the two other situations where traditionally a monarch could claim special taxes.

4. Involuntary loans are really a form of taxation.

5. This is why the earmarking of funds can be so effective politically. Twentieth-century campaigns to sell war bonds illustrate this as they typically played upon nationalistic and patriotic themes to induce citizens to lend money to their government.

6. This is the familiar trade-off between risk and return.

7. See MacNeil 1974: 790, and Karpoff and Rice 1989. On the attractiveness of assignability for seventeenth-century shareholders, see Chaudhuri 1978: 420.

8. In early modern Spain, for example, the estates of the nobility were typically protected by an imbarrable entail (the *mayorazgo*) which forbade selling of the land, even by the nobleman himself (Jago 1973). These restrictions sharply curtailed the market for real estate.

9. See Stigler and Becker, 1977.

10. North and Weingast 1989: 831. See also Field 1991; North and Thomas 1973; and North 1981.

11. For other economic studies of property rights and their significance, see Alchian and Demsetz 1973; Anderson and Hill 1975, 1990; Barzel 1989; Coase 1960; De Alessi 1980; Greif 1994; Libecap 1986, 1989; and Milgrom, North, and Weingast 1990.

12. "The rise in the relative numbers of contract actions—assumpsit, convenant and especially debt sur obligation—confirm the importance of economic factors" (Francis 1983: 43).

13. Transaction costs: ". . . consist of the costs of arranging a contract *ex ante* and monitoring and enforcing it *ex post*, as opposed to production costs, which are the costs of executing the contract. To a large extent transaction costs are costs of relations between people and people" (Matthews 1986: 906). For some criticisms of the new institutional economics, see Field 1981, and Hodgson 1988.

14. See Levi 1988: 96–97, 113, and Root 1994: 11, 22, 47.

15. See North and Weingast 1989: 803, and North 1991: 107.

16. Extra-legal means, involving the use of coercive force, was also out of the question because of the state monopoly on the means of violence.

17. North and Weingast 1989: 810.

18. Like the right to issue royal proclamations and to remove judges from office, and the court of Star Chamber. See North and Weingast 1989: 813–14.

19. As Richard Lachmann has pointed out (personal communication), one important qualification is in order: the Crown's ability to interfere with property rights in land had diminished by the early seventeenth century.

20. North and Weingast 1989: 817.

21. See Havighurst 1950, 1953.

22. See North and Weingast 1989: 822–23.

23. Ibid.: 819, 831.

24. For an analysis of how a market for a commodity can precede (private) property rights, see Demsetz's (1988) discussion of land and the fur trade in Quebec.

25. See North and Weingast 1989: 805.

26. See the *Calendar of Treasury Books*, vol. 3: xlviii. The 1677 total includes accrued interest.

27. See the text of the official announcement of the Stop in Browning 1953: 352–53.

28. See Jones 1987: 7–8, and Lee 1965: 3.

29. Wilson 1978: 77.

30. Jones 1987: 81.

31. See the discussion in chapter 3 above; Roseveare 1973: 39, and Chandaman 1975: 224–25.

32. See Browning 1951: 93. Shaftesbury, the former Anthony Ashley-Cooper, was one of the five Cabal ministers.

33. See Henning 1940: 37; Lee 1965: 145; and also Grey's *Debates of the House of Commons*, vol. 1: 273–74. Goldsmith-bankers were criticized in such pamphlets as *The Mystery of the New Fashioned Goldsmiths*, printed in 1676. They were accused of being responsible for coin-clipping and numerous other illegal practices.

34. See Lee 1965: 159. The insulation of the market for mortgages from public finance may also have prevented the Stop from having more generally disastrous financial effects.

35. See *Cobbett's Parliamentary History of England*: 505–6, 586.

36. See Turnor 1674: introduction.

37. "For indeed the Common Law is not more solicitous of any one thing than to preserve the property of the Subject from the inundation of the Prerogative" (Turnor 1674: sect. 2).

38. As Turnor puts it: ". . . it is a Fundamental Law of this Realm, that the Subject's propriety is not violable, no not in cases of National Danger, without his own free and voluntary consent" (1674: sect. 5).

39. "I will suppose that the King owes a Banker 1000 l. this Banker owes me the like summ, I owe as much to a third, he to a fourth, and so in *infinitum*, and the Banker, my Self, and the third person, have little else to satisfie our Creditors than this 1000 l. which is owing severally to us. . . . In this case then I say, it will be most evident, that if the King never payeth the Banker, the Banker can never pay me, or I the third person, or he the fourth, so that by a necessary chain of consequences, the 4th person and his Creditors in *infinitum*, are as much grieved by the King's non-payment of the Banker, as I my self, who am the Bankers immediate Creditor" (Turnor 1674: introduction). In other words, illiquidity ramifies throughout the network of debtors and creditors, and has a kind of multiplier effect.

40. Turnor 1674: section 7.

41. Horsefield 1982: 514.

42. Letters patent were a formal legal letter issued by the Crown.

43. See *His Majesty's Gracious Patent to the Goldsmiths, for Payment and Satisfaction of Their Debt*: 8.

44. See Turnor's *The Joyful News of Opening the Exchequer . . .* (1677), especially pp. 7–8, which states that the payment of interest goes a long way to restoring the compromised property rights of Crown creditors.

45. See Horsefield 1982: 517. A 1689 petition (*The Case of the Assignees of the Goldsmiths*) complained that interest was paid during James II's reign for only three-quarters, and that "by the Advice of Papists, or other wicked persons . . . the Creditors aforesaid were denied payment of what was justly due to them."

46. This was generally true in Western Europe. See Fryde and Fryde 1963: 436.

47. See Holdsworth 1944: 8–15, 22–23.

48. There were two other speedier alternatives to the petition of right, the *monstrans de droit* and the traverse (Holdsworth 1944: 26, 28). However, these were applicable only under very special conditions. The petition of right remained the general procedure.

49. See Holdsworth 1944: 33, and *Howell's State Trials* 1816: 3. Also noteworthy was the question of whether a sovereign could alienate revenue, in this case the hereditary excise, in such a way that would bind his successors. In other words, if Charles II alienated a portion of his revenue to satisfy the bankers' debt, were James II and William and Mary also bound by Charles's decision? See *Howell's State Trials* 1816: 42, and more generally Fryde and Fryde 1963: 430.

50. Somers was one of the Whig Junto.

51. See Campbell 1880: 7, and Sachse: 75. Somers's justification for his ruling is set forth in detail in *Howell's State Trials*, vol. XIV, cols. 39–105.

52. See *Howell's State Trials*, vol. XIV, col. 3.

53. See Horsefield 1982: 519–20. Somers's ruling later haunted him. His reversal of the Court of Exchequer decision was the basis of one of the articles of impeachment during his impeachment in 1701. See *Howell's State Trials*, vol. XIV, cols. 261–62.

54. See H.M.C. *Manuscripts of the House of Lords*, new series, vol. 3: 407–9.

55. In 1700 the Commons again appropriated the Hereditary Excise for current expenses, instead of setting it aside for interest payments. See *The Case of Several Thousands of His Majesty's Subjects Entitled under the Letters Patents of King Charles the Second, to Annual Sums out of the Hereditary Revenue of Excise*.

56. See Horsefield 1982: 523.

57. See Turnor's *The Case of the Bankers and Their Creditors Stated and Considered . . .*, section 2, and *The Case of many thousands of His Majesty's subjects, who for valuable considerations are entitled under the Letters patents of King Charles the Second, to annual sums out of the hereditary revenue of excise*. Somers denied the relevance of property. In justifying his decision to rule against the bankers and their assignees, Somers argued that the case was not really about property rights. See *Howell's State Trials* 1816: 44–45.

58. In 1699, Davenant stated that "a stop there [the Exchequer] would at once pull down all our civil rights. Nay, to stop the principal only, though the payments of the interest should be continued, would be fatal to our constitution" (Davenant 1771: 287).

59. "There is no other public Credit in England, but that of the Parlament. The Bankers, and all concern'd with them, well remember King Charles II's shutting up of the Exchequer" (Toland 1701: 125).

60. Defoe asserted: "Let any man view the public credit in its present flourishing circumstances, and compare it with the latter end of the years of King Charles II after the Exchequer had been shut up, parliamentary appropriations misapplied, and, in a word, the public faith broken; who would lend? Seven or eight per cent. was given for anticipations in King William's time, though no new fraud had been offered, only because the old debts were unpaid; and how hard was it to get any one to lend money at all!" (Defoe 1987 [1726]: 239–40).

61. They mention the Stop (p. 820), but do not treat it at length.

62. See Campbell 1874: 38, and *Howell's State Trials*, vol. XIV, cols. 261–62.

63. See Bailey 1932a: 254–55, and Holdsworth 1937a: 539.

64. The King could, however, expressly empower the assignee to be able to assign the debts further.

65. See Bailey 1932a: 261–62.

66. See Roseveare 1973: 24.

67. For a thirteenth-century statement of the Law Merchant, see Teetor 1962. Rogers (1995) has recently taken exception to the received account of the relationship between the Law Merchant and the Common Law. See Rogers 1995: 1–2, 252.

68. Josiah Child complained about English commercial law: "I could say much more of the damage this Nation sustains by the want of a Law-Merchant, but that is so evident to all men's experience, that I shall no longer insist upon it" (Child 1740: 145).

69. See Holdsworth 1937b: 113.

70. Holden 1955: 30, and Rogers 1995: 94.

71. Once again, merchants in Amsterdam and Antwerp were ahead of the English in regard to the assignability and liquidity of financial assets. See Van Der Wee 1977: 304, 329.

72. In a similar fashion, the securitization of bank loans during the 1980s and 1990s erodes the "banking relationship" and makes debtor-creditor relations more formal, explicitly contractual, and anonymous. See Cumming 1990: 25–27.

73. The reason is simple. Liquidity means that the creditor can exit the relationship at any point, so it becomes less risky to lend to unfamiliar debtors.

74. Richards 1929: 40.

75. They were also called "running-cash notes."

76. As Lewis put it: "A Bill of Exchange, Or a Bill of Credit that is transferable upon a good man that cannot easily fail, is as good as Mony" (Lewis 1678: 1).

77. See Postan 1973: 54–64. Bills of exchange were also used to evade the prohibition against usury.

78. See Tigar and Levy 1977: 49–50.

79. However, the law merchant was not as distinct from common law as, for example, the canon law of the ecclesiastical courts. See Sutherland 1934: 153.

80. See Coquillette 1981: 347–48, and Baker 1979b: 107–9. Of course, this doesn't imply that merchants only used the law merchant, or that they didn't use the central courts. Cf. Baker 1979a: 302, and Rogers 1995: 20.

81. See Baker 1979a: 299, and Teeter 1962: 182–83.

82. See Holden 1955: 17, and Holdsworth 1937a: 520, 534.

83. See Holden 1951: 230, and Holdsworth, 1937b: 159.

84. The contrast between English and Dutch law was highlighted when colonial New Amsterdam was taken by the English from the Dutch to become New York. English law replaced Dutch law, but this had little effect on commerce only because colonial English law was more advanced than regular Common Law in the treatment of financial instruments and debtor-creditor relations. See Johnson 1963: 20–35.

85. See Holdsworth 1937a: 516; Holdsworth 1915; Postan 1973: 43; Cook 1916; and Sweet 1894: 304. Blackstone explained: "Having thus considered the several divisions of property in possession, which subsists there only, where a man hath both the right and also the occupation of the thing; we will proceed next to take a short

view of the nature of property in action, or such where a man hath not the occupation, but merely a bare right to occupy the thing in question; the possession whereof may however be recovered by a suit or action at law: from whence the thing so recoverable is called a thing or chose, in action. Thus money due on a bond is a chose in action" (Blackstone 1766 vol. 2: 396–97).

86. See Holdsworth 1937a: 518–20, and Bailey 1932b: 548–49. Again, Blackstone explains: "First then it [a contract] is an agreement, a mutual bargain or convention; and therefore there must at least be two contracting parties, of sufficient ability to make a contract: as where *A* contracts with *B* to pay him 100 l. and thereby transfers a property in such sum to *B*. Which property is however not in possession, but in action merely, and recoverable by suit at law; wherefore it could not be transferred to another person by the strict rules of the antient common law: for no chose in action could be assigned or granted over, because it was thought to be a great encouragement to litigiousness, if a man were allowed to make over to a stranger his right of going to law" (Blackstone 1766 vol. 2: 442).

87. Sweet 1894: 311–12.

88. On the history of the Admiralty Courts, see Laing 1946.

89. Steckley says that "the records of the 1530s reveal that the Admiralty was hearing a wide variety of shipping and commercial disputes" (Steckley 1978: 141). He lists several advantages for merchants of Admiralty over common law on pp. 171–73, but this should not be taken to mean that merchants never used common-law courts (see Baker 1979a: 302). In general, the law merchant was sympathetic to mercantile custom, and so let merchants do what they wanted.

90. See Steckley 1978: 169.

91. See Coquillette 1981: 322–23; Trakman 1983: ‘26; and Plucknett 1956: 662. North and Thomas (1973, pp. 147–48) grant considerable importance to Coke's tenure in relation to the development of property rights favorable to economic growth.

92. Writs of prohibition were a device mostly used by common-law judges to defend their jurisdiction from ecclesiastical courts.

93. Steckley 1978: 143–44, 146.

94. See Coquillette 1981: 362–64.

95. Holden 1955: 31–32, 35.

96. For example, Woodward v. Rowe (1666); Williams v. Williams (1693); and Bromwich v. Loyd (1698).

97. See Richards 1929: 44.

98. Holdsworth 1937b: 163–64.

99. Holden 1955: 74, 77.

100. Holdsworth 1937b: 172.

101. The notes issued by the Bank of England were by statute legally assignable from the outset. But their negotiable status was not completely certain until after the passage of the 1704 act (Holdsworth 1937b: 191).

102. Consider the resulting difficulties if a father tried to transfer his paternal relationship to his son to another man. Social relationships are inherently hard to alienate. For an insightful discussion of the problems associated with making a relationship legally transferrable, see MacNeil 1974: 791–92.

103. As the name of this act suggests, it was passed in the aftermath of the South Sea Bubble.

104. According to one estimate, there were almost 150 joint-stock companies in existence by 1695, with about 85% of them having been established after 1688. See Scott 1912, vol. 1: 327–28.

105. See Carr 1913: xvii.

106. See Holdsworth 1937b: 206.

107. The regulated company form was not without its advocates. Sir Henry Pollexfen, a seventeenth-century merchant, thought it better that every man trade with his own personal money and credit, and thus "every man knowing his creditor and his debtor" (quoted in Shammas 1975: 102). For Pollexfen, the joint-stock company form resulted in too much anonymity and impersonality.

108. Company shares were different from debts. When a debtor doesn't repay a debt, the creditor can sue, whereas when a company doesn't pay out dividends to shareholders, the latter have no similar right to sue (they can, of course, try to replace the management at the next shareholders' meeting). Nevertheless, shares were lumped together with debts as "choses in action." See Sweet 1894: 303, 312, and Holdsworth 1937a: 516.

109. Unless shareholders can pass their shares on to someone else, a company would cease to exist with the eventual death of all its owners.

110. See Carr 1913: xlvi–xlvii; Holdsworth 1937b: 203; and Sweet 1894: 312. The Act establishing the South Sea Company made provision for the assignment of company shares, and stated that ". . . all Assignments and Transferrences [of stock] made in such manner, and no other, shall be good and available in the Law" (*An Act for making good Deficiencies, and satisfying the Public Debts; And for Erecting a Corporation to Carry on a Trade to the South-Seas*, 9 Anne c.21).

111. Mortimer described in detail how an individual could buy and sell shares on the London market without the assistance of a broker (Mortimer 1785: 122–32), and concluded by asking rhetorically: "I must here appeal to the candid and judicious, and beg leave to ask, if there is any thing in nature more easy and simple than the transacting this business?" (Mortimer 1785: 141).

112. See Jones 1970: 233–34.

113. See Cooke 1951: 70.

114. Ibid.: 26–27, 31, 56.

115. See Holdsworth 1937b: 194, and Scott 1912, vol. 1: 152.

116. This is explicitly stated in the East India Company's Court of Committee meeting in late March 1669. See Sainsbury 1929: 182.

117. See Carr 1913: xlix, and Chaudhuri 1965: 33.

118. See Cooke 1951: 59; Shammas 1975: 97; and Ekelund and Tollison 1980.

119. On occasion, shareholders were refused permission to transfer their stock. See Davies 1952: 294.

120. See Cooke 1951: 76, and Shammas 1975: 96.

121. This is the Salmon v. Hamborough Company case of 1671. See Shammas 1975: 104–5.

122. In two cases, the Bank of England and the East India Company, the stock ledgers from this period have survived. These documents give a complete listing of share owners and share transfers.

123. When Jonathan Swift's stockbroker failed in early 1712, he worried that he

didn't have secure title to the shares his broker bought on his behalf, and that his money was lost: "And Stratford had near four hundred pounds of mine, to buy me five hundred pounds in the South-Sea company. . . . This morning I sent for Tooke, whom I had employed to buy the stock of Stratford, and settle things with him. He told me, I was secure; for Stratford had transferred it to me in the form of the South-Sea house, and he had accepted it for me, and all was done on stampt parchment" (Williams 1948: 463). Consider also the letter from Hoare's Bank to William Betts, dated January 1701 (Peregrine and Hoare 1955: 22–23).

124. One economic explanation for the change was that because share owners had ". . . wealth-maximizing incentives to seek the development of a legal form of organization under which they could more easily trade their property rights in these firms" (Ekelund and Tollison 1980: 717), restraints on trading in shares were removed. Limited alienability of company shares was inefficient, and eventually was replaced by full alienability.

125. On this point generally, see Roseveare 1991.

126. This difference has been highlighted in work on contracts, another important part of the legal framework for markets. Like property rights, the enforcement of contracts is a function of the legal system. Enforceable contracts allow business-people to make "credible commitments" to one another. Yet, in contemporary practice, formal contracts are often not used, and even if signed, are seldom litigated (Macaulay 1963, Macaulay 1977: 507; Vincent-Jones 1989: 173; Beale and Dugdale 1975; Bernstein 1992; Charny 1990; and Winn 1994). The full legal apparatus of contract is frequently dispensed with, and transactions occur on a more informal basis.

CHAPTER SIX
POLITICS AND THE JOINT-STOCK COMPANIES

1. North and Weingast 1989: 831.

2. As he put it: "The key to the London merchants' politics in the later sixteenth and early seventeenth centuries was to be found in the nature of their relationship with the royal government" (Brenner 1993: 199).

3. Brenner terms these privileges "politically constituted forms of private property" (Brenner 1993: 652).

4. See Brenner 1993: 54–56, 83, 91, 203–4, 238.

5. See De Krey 1985: 75, and Harris 1993: 11, 66–67.

6. See De Krey 1985: 101–2.

7. Ibid.: 108–9, and Harris 1993: 198–99.

8. See Harris 1993: 152–57.

9. See also Haley 1988: 162, and Clapham 1945: 2.

10. See Horwitz 1977: 73, 129. Previous financial proposals involving the capitalization of future tax revenues were obviously relevant. See Horsefield 1960: 114–24.

11. See Clapham 1945: 17; Horwitz 1968: 149; Horwitz 1977: 130–31, and Sundstrom 1992: 64.

12. See Horwitz 1977: 145. The Bank's own Minutes of the Courts of Directors refer to a petition against the Bank delivered to the House of Commons at almost

exactly the same time as Nottingham's assault. The Bank took the attack seriously enough to order its directors to attend the Commons in order to muster a defense. See Bank of England Archives G4/1 f. 143.

13. The Duke of Leeds, a prominent Tory member of William's ministry and one who opposed the Bank, later ordered his banker to subscribe to £1,000 worth of shares. Leed's letter to his banker suggests that he hesitated at first (perhaps for political reasons), but upon seeing the quick subscription and undoubted success of the enterprise, decided to get in: "I am informed that the subscriptions to the Bank do fill so fast, that there is at this day near £700,000 subscribed, so that it must now necessarily be a bank: I therefore desire that you will subscribe for one thousand pounds for me" (Royal Bank of Scotland Archives, CH/315/1). See also Browning 1951: 508.

14. The reduction of trade brought about by the Bank is discussed in John Briscoe's pamphlet (1694: 14), and an anonymous one entitled *Some considerations offered against the continuance of the Bank of England*: 6. See Horsefield 1960: 137.

15. See Habakkuk 1952: 26–27.

16. ". . . for the Bank having engrossed the Money and Credit . . . have thereby put the Landed-men, who are the greatest part of the Kingdom under the utmost Extremity." *An Argument, Proving, that the Reason Given by the Directors of the Bank of England, Against Settling any other Bank . . . is the Highest Reason For It* 1695: 2.

17. ". . . it [the Bank] has given a mighty damp to Commerce," *Angliae Tutamen* 1695: 6. See as well Davenant 1771: 292. Concerns about the effects of the Bank on trade were present from the outset. In its passage through parliament, the original act establishing the Bank was amended to prohibit the Bank from engaging directly in any trade except in bills of exchange or bullion. See Clapham 1945: 18.

18. See *Some considerations offered against the continuance of the Bank of England*: 6. On the importance of credit, see Earle 1989: 115–18, and Hoppit 1987: 25, 134, 160.

19. As D. W. Jones has shown, investment in Bank stock was more an effect than a cause of the decline in international trade in the 1690s. The war interfered with trade and left many merchants with balances of idle money. Many of them invested in stocks, which promised capital growth and liquidity. See Jones 1988: 249–50.

20. See Godfrey 1695: 1–2, 4, and Paterson 1694: 15.

21. See Horwitz 1977: 180, and De Krey 1978: 69. De Krey reports that the number of goldsmith-bankers keeping "running cashes" (i.e., issuing their own bank notes) declined from 44 in 1677 to 24 in 1725, perhaps because of Bank competition. See De Krey 1985: 157–58.

22. Evidently, Land Bank schemes ran in Chamberlen's family as both his father and brother also proposed them. See Horsefield 1960: 156.

23. See also *A Proposal for Erecting a General Bank; Which may be fitly called the Land Bank of England* 1695: 2.

24. William may also have become disillusioned with the Bank because of problems with remittances. See Sundstrom 1992: 73.

25. See Horwitz 1977: 166–67.

26. See Hill 1988: 44. This group included Robert Harley, who as Queen Anne's chief minister later applied the lessons of the failed Land Bank when he successfully

launched the South Sea Company in 1711. Other supporters of the Land Bank scheme included Sir Thomas Cooke and Sir Josiah Child, both prominent within the old East India Company. See Rubini 1970: 702.

27. The price of Bank of England shares fell in response to parliamentary endorsement of the Land Bank. See Scott 1912 vol. 3: 208; Rubini 1970: 704; and Sundstrom 1992: 74.

28. See the Minutes of the Court of Directors, Bank of England Archives, G4/2 ff. 102–4.

29. See Bank of England Archives, G4/2 ff. 104, 107, 123.

30. Bank of England Archives, G4/2 f. 107.

31. See Horwitz 1977: 167. John Briscoe argued that the Bank's counteroffer ought to be rejected precisely because it was made: "To prevent the Establishment of the Land Bank, I am informed the Bank of England purpose to take the following Methods. First; As one of their Members advised them to make a bold Offer, to furnish the Government with Two Millions at 5 l. per Cent per Annum. This . . . I take to be a strong Reason why another Bank ought to be establish'd; for as the fear of the Establishment of another Bank has been some check to their Arbitrary Inclinations, and hath brought them to any Bounds of Reason, so nothing will keep them within such Bounds but the Establishment of another Bank, which may stand in competition with them" (Briscoe 1696: 2).

32. See Jones 1988: 22.

33. See Horsefield 1960: 207.

34. See Horwitz 1977: 218. It also discredited Land Bank schemes. See Scott 1912 vol. 3: 252.

35. See Clapham 1945: 47.

36. See Godolphin's letter to Marlborough, 22 February 1709 (Snyder 1975: 1231).

37. On the fight with the Hollow Sword Blade Company in 1704, see Bank of England Archives G4/6 ff. 27, 62, 154, 197.

38. See Clapham 1945: 151, and Price 1992: 92–93.

39. See Clapham 1945: 116–17.

40. See Price 1992: 96, and Clapham 1945: 117–18. For a contemporary account, see Defoe 1701a: 6–8.

41. See Holmes 1973: 156, 168.

42. As Sir David Hamilton expressed it in his diary: "That the fear of the City, was the loss of my Lord Godolphin, because he had been a great support to the Bank" (Roberts 1975: 11). See Hill 1971: 400; Roberts 1982: 82–83; and Clapham 1945: 74–75. On other occasions as well, Heathcote wasn't shy about stating his political opinions. For example, when negotiating with the Lord Treasurer in September of 1709 over the circulation of £600,000 worth of Exchequer Bills, Heathcote expressed strong support for the Whig position over the war in Spain, insisting that there should be no peace with France until Spain was secured for the allies. See Snyder 1975: 1371.

43. The Bank's refusal was interpreted in highly partisan terms, as John Drummond's letter of November 7, 1710 to Robert Harley attests: "I hope you will find some way to make the Bank discount foreign bills for money, as they have done all this war; . . . which can be of no more hindrance and prejudice to them than

it was before the change of the ministry, and it is only pique and revenge of Heathcote's and his party who now govern the Bank absolutely" (*H.M.C. Portland Vol. IV*: 618).

44. Godolphin wrote in a letter of June 1711: "The rumour that wee are to have a new Parliament continues so strong, that besides the generall uneasyness it gives people's minds, the creditt begins now also to bee affected by it" (Snyder 1975: 1547). Tories blamed the decline in government credit on Whig financial manipulations. For example: ". . . we may also take notice of the Practices of some of their [the Whig Junto's] private Agents in Exchange-Alley; who upon the Removal of the E. of Sunderland, and the Report that the Lord Treasurer would soon follow, brought all the Stocks they, or their Friends had by them to Market; so that there being more Sellers than Buyers, the Stocks fell gradually, that of the Bank in particular, from 123 1/2 to 107" (*An Essay Towards the History of the Last Ministry and Parliament* 1710: 69–70).

45. See De Krey 1985: 224, and Hill 1971: 401–2. Evidently, Godolphin's dismissal worried the financial community as the price of Bank stock went from 113 to 108 3/4 in response to the news. See Sundstrom 1992: 258.

46. It was deliberately spread by Robert Harley, among others. See *H.M.C. Portland Vol. IV*: 545.

47. See Holmes 1967: 174. Pamphleteers such as Broughton and Defoe were clearly worried about the power possessed by the Bank by virtue of its near monopoly position as provider of financial services to the government (Broughton 1710: 44; Defoe 1710: 10). Swift's *The Examiner* no. 38 put it thus: "What People then, are these in a corner, to whom the Constitution must truckle? If the whole Nation's Credit cannot supply Funds for the War, without humble Application from the entire Legislature to a few Retailers of Mony, 'tis high time we should sue for a Peace. What new Maxims are these, which neither We nor our Forefathers ever heard of before, and which no wise Institution would ever allow? Must our Laws from henceforth pass the Bank and the East-India Company, or have their Royal Assent before they are in force?" (Ellis 1985: 376).

48. Dr. Stratford railed in his correspondence against the "insolence of these fellows" (*H.M.C. Portland Vol. VII*: 1).

49. See Clapham 1945: 111.

50. This was well understood at the time: ". . . 'tis plain that those who have the Major Part of the Stock, have the Major Part of the Votes, and may make what Directors they please; who by virtue of such Election will have the Government, and consequently the Power of the Cash and Credit of the Bank in their Hands" (Briscoe 1696: 1–2).

51. Given that the number of shareholders was relatively stable over this period of time, higher numbers mean a more contested election. See Sutherland 1952: 41.

52. Clapham 1945: 112.

53. On the eve of the 1711 company election, Lady Hervey wrote to her husband the Earl of Bristol, who was horse racing, to ". . . beg you would come to Town by Wednesday night, and bring everybody with you that has any votes in the Bank. Thursday is the day of election, and she [the Duchess of Marlborough] says it is a terrible reflection upon any body that can stay to see a horse race though there were but a possibility of having the Bank of England put into ill hands by it, and if the

Tories get the better (as they threaten), Mr. Hopkins says you may all make use of your horses to run away" (Jackson 1894: 287).

54. A variety of sources were used to determine the political allegiances of each director (see appendix).

55. De Krey does a slightly different analysis, and examines the number of "City Leaders" with corporate directorships but his results point in the same direction. Of the thirty-three city leaders who were also Bank directors between 1694 and 1715, thirty were Whigs. See De Krey 1985: 125.

56. The seven companies are the Bank of England, Million Bank, New East India Company, Old East India Company, United East India Company, Royal Africa Company, and South Sea Company.

57. This may explain the sympathy shown by the Bank's directors toward French Huguenots. At several points during 1698, for example, the Bank loaned substantial sums to "poor French Refugees" and "French Protestants" by discounting tallies. See Bank of England Archives, G4/4 f. 90, 134.

58. See, for example, Godolphin's letter to Marlborough of 29 August 1710, in which he points out that good news from the war in Spain raised Bank share prices by 5% (Snyder 1975: 1618).

59. The Bank also endeavored to remain on good terms with public officials. From the beginning, it was paying various gratuities to Exchequer employees and parliamentary servants (see, e.g., Bank of England Archives G4/2 ff. 85, 98, G4/7 ff. 15, 189).

60. Of course, in earlier times it was still heavily involved in politics. See Brenner 1993 for a discussion of the early seventeenth century, and Lougheed (1980: 112–21) for his analysis of Charles II's changing relations with the company during the 1670s.

61. Even before then, the Company managed to make its rivalry with the Dutch East India Company (the VOC) a foreign policy issue. See Sherman 1976.

62. According to one estimate, the number of shareholders in 1688 was only 320, expanding to 482 in 1693 (Scott 1912, vol. 3: 467). *A List of the Names of all the Adventurers in the Stock of the Honourable East-India Company* names 461 shareholders in April 1691.

63. Chaudhuri (1978: 421), puts the price of stock in the £80 range in 1664, and at around £365 per share in 1681.

64. See Lougheed 1980: 314–15.

65. See Scott 1912 vol. 1: 302–3, 317. East India Company bonds paid 5% interest in the 1678–81 period, while company stocks paid an average annual dividend of 27.5%. In 1686–91, bonds were still paying 5% while stocks were up to over 29% annually. Clearly it was much more profitable to own stocks than bonds. See Chaudhuri 1978: 422.

66. Elsewhere it was argued that ". . . there is every day Stock to be bought on the Exchange . . . so that no Man but may when he pleaseth come into the Company, and have what share in the Trade he pleaseth, so far as he is able to purchase" (*A modest and just apology for, or defense of the present East-India-Company* 1690: 14). There was turnover of company shares, but most of the buying and selling occurred between people who were already shareholders. See Jones 1988: 288.

67. Critics certainly thought so: "Another Evidence that their Stock is too little for their Trade, may be their borrowing six hundred thousand Pounds at Interest, which

besides the unmerchantlike way of Trading, by preferring a Dead to a Quick Stock, and electing rather to Trade with Money at Interest, than to inlarge their Stock by new subscriptions, is also a Publique danger to the Nation" (*The Allegations of the Turky Company and others Against the East-India-Company* . . . 1681: 5–6).

68. See Scott 1912, vol. 1: 304–5.

69. See Chaudhuri and Israel 1991: 433; Wood 1935: 102; Lougheed 1980: vii, 4, 209; and Scott 1912, vol. 1: 307–8. "The East-India Company on the other side, manage their Trade by a Joint Stock, confined to the narrow compass of some few persons, exclusive to all others, under the penalty of Mulcts, Fines, Seizures, and other extraordinary proceedings. And upon an exact inquiry it will be found, that this Stock is so ingrossed, that about ten or twelve men have the absolute management of the whole Trade (there being one who hath at least Eight Votes [Josiah Child]) and about forty men do not only divide the Major part of the gains, but not content therewith, do also indirectly appropriate to themselves a greater profit in a separate Trade" (*The Allegations of the Turky Company and others Against the East-India-Company* . . . 1681: 2).

70. For example, in 1688 the East India Company made such an arrangement with a group of Armenian merchants. See Jones 1970: 289–90.

71. See Kearney 1958: 485–86. In January 1697, rioting London weavers attacked the East India Company headquarters. See the Court Minutes, India Office Library B/41, ff. 286–87.

72. See Chaudhuri 1978: 70.

73. See Jones 1970: 312–13.

74. Ibid.: 303, 320, and Jones 1988: 289–92.

75. For listings of such gifts and loans, see Chaudhuri and Israel 1991: 430, 433; Scott 1912, vol. 2: 143; and Lougheed 1980: 97, 122–23.

76. His shareholdings were worth £7,000. See Scott 1912, vol. 2: 149.

77. See Jones 1970: 325, 328, and Jones 1988: 294.

78. The Company was severely criticized for the association with James: "This very Society [the old East India Company] was of the first that made Addresses to the late King [James II], with a promise of slavish complyance to that illegal arbitrary demand of continuing the Customs then expired, to the encouraging and setting up of Popery and Tyranny, and was a leading Card to the rest of the lesser Companies, and particular Merchants to a tame submission to that Badge of Slavery, Raising Money by Proclamations, and of this Action they publickly and highly boasted, valuing themselves mightily thereon. But how much favour and respect they or their Introducers deserve of the Nation on that account, is soon cast up: and more particularly divers of them have declared themselves, upon all Accounts, Friends to Arbitrary Power and Tyranny, and have been paltry Tools of State in the late Reigns" (*Reasons humbly offered against grafting or splicing, and for dissolving this present East-India-Company* . . . 1690: 5–6). On the Tory leanings of company shareholders and the Whiggishness of the opposition, see De Krey 1985: 25.

79. The company received early warning of its troubles when Parliament censured it on the grounds that martial law commissioners and other quasi-sovereign powers exercised by the company ought not to be granted by the Crown except by Act of Parliament. See Horwitz 1977: 315, and Horwitz 1978: 2.

80. See the list of names in Jones 1970: 335.

81. See Horwitz 1978: 3–5.

82. Not coincidentally, the Bank's backers included a number of East India Company interlopers. See Horwitz 1978: 6–7.

83. See, for example, reports of its efforts in early 1697 in the Court Minutes, India Office Library, B/41, ff. 99–100, 107, 113.

84. See Court Minutes, India Office Library, B/41 f. 311, and Horwitz 1978: 9.

85. See Minute Books, India Office Library, B/41 f. 334.

86. See Horwitz 1977: 149, and Horwitz 1978: 7. The Speaker of the House, Sir John Trevor, was expelled for taking bribes from the company. See Brewer 1989: 151.

87. See Court Minutes, India Office Library B/41 ff. 540–43.

88. See Court Minutes, India Office Library B/41 f. 562.

89. See Horwitz 1978: 10–11.

90. See Court Minutes, India Office Library B/41 ff. 570–71, 574.

91. Court Minutes, India Office Library B/41 ff. 578–79.

92. Court Minutes, India Office Library B/41 f. 680.

93. See De Krey 1985, table 4.2.

94. De Krey 1985, table 3.8. This religious association was used to criticize the interlopers who formed the new company on the grounds that they were antimonarchy. ". . . the Chief Men among the Dissenters from our Church are deeply concern'd in the New Subscription, which might give no unreasonable Jeolousie that that Party may have form'd this Design to change the Government hereafter into a Commonwealth, which they have so long, and so continually thirst after'" (*Advice about the New East-India stock, in a letter to a friend* 1691: 1).

95. See Price, 1992: 96; Scott 1912, vol. 1: 367–68, vol. 2: 184–85, vol. 3: 217; and Clapham 1945: 117–18, 226.

96. See Court Minutes, India Office Library B/41 ff. 715, 719, 724, and Court Minutes of the New Company, India Office Library B/42, ff. 65, 150.

97. See Horwitz 1977: 239–40, 265, and Horwitz 1978: 12–13.

98. For a discussion of these electoral efforts, see Walcott 1956b, and Horwitz 1978: 13–14. Defoe observed that ". . . they suppose which Company so ever gets most Friends in the House, will be most likely to be farther Established, to the Ruin of the other, and therefore they make such a stir to get Friends there" (Defoe 1701b: 12).

99. See Jones 1988: 140.

100. For details, see Scott 1912, vol. 2: 169–77.

101. See De Krey 1985: 241–42.

102. Internal conflict notwithstanding, the Company did "take care of business." Like the Bank of England it helped smooth its relations with significant departments of government by offering various blandishments to public servants. There is a surviving 1710 account (India Office Library D/92 f. 54) that details all the payments made at Christmastime to the officers of the Customs (patent searchers, patent waiters, patent officers, cashiers, warehouse surveyors, secretaries, and ushers). These totaled over £197 and, no doubt, were made to help celebrate the holiday season.

103. As Bowen explains: "Of equal importance in analysis of stock turnover is consideration of the political use that was made of the Company's stock, particularly between 1760 and 1774. This is because possession of stock was not judged by con-

temporaries in financial terms alone; it also had important political applications within the Company's General Court. At a time of fierce and protracted struggle for control of the Company, and during a period when the Company itself became a subject for parliamentary examination, many individuals sought a voice and a vote within the General Court" (Bowen 1989: 197). See also Bowen 1989: 187, and Sutherland 1952: 19, 22, 29–30, 33, 35.

104. See Flinn 1960: 55, 57.

105. See Hill 1988: 143.

106. Ibid.: 137–38, and De Krey 1985: 162.

107. This included such things as discounting bills and issuing notes. When the Hollow Sword Blade Company also purchased land in Ireland, the Bank of England accused it of acting as a Land Bank, and thus violating the Bank's own monopoly privileges. See Sperling 1962a: 5; Carswell 1960: 35–38; and Scott 1912, vol. 3: 435–38.

108. See Sperling 1961: 194.

109. See Court Minutes, India Office Library, B/51 f. 432.

110. Ibid., ff. 440–42.

111. See Bank of England Archives, Minutes of the Courts of Directors, G4/7 ff. 152–53, 155.

112. See Sperling 1961, and Hill 1989: 63.

113. See Sperling 1962a: 7.

114. See *Abstract of the Charter of the Governour and Company of Merchants of Great Britain, trading to the South-Seas* 1711: 2, and De Krey 1985: 242.

115. See Carswell 1993: 54.

116. See Scott 1912, vol. 3: 295, and Flinn 1960: 59.

117. There was a lot of money to be made by those who knew early about the deal, for they could buy navy bills at the fully discounted price and enjoy a quick profit as prices rose in reaction to the South Sea scheme. See Carswell 1960: 55.

118. See Brewer 1989: 120, 161; Hill 1971: 410; and McInnes 1970: 129. The Tory newspaper the *Post-Boy* (no. 2493, May 3–5, 1711) reported the news of the Company: "The Parliament beyond all Expectation having found a Fund to satisfy the Great Debt upon the nation, amounting to above Nine Millions, and to settle a Trade to the South Seas in the Spanish West-Indies, which must be of the highest Advantage to the Nation; the Universal Joy of this, was express'd by Bonefires and ringing of Bells, last Thursday night." Despite this celebration, in the long run the South Sea Company never supplanted the Bank. Especially after the Bubble, it was obvious that the South Sea Company was never going to amount to much as a trading company, and so by the middle of the eighteenth century, the Bank was more centrally involved in government finance and debt than ever before. See Clapham 1945: 103–4.

119. Sixteen percent of South Sea Company directors were dissenters, as compared to 43% and 30% for the Bank and East India Company, respectively. See De Krey 1985: 109.

120. Ibid.: 125.

121. See Clapham 1945: 85, and Richards 1932: 352.

122. See Brewer 1989: 126. Borrowing from a few large-scale organizations attracted political attention in a way that borrowing from a diffuse and unorganized group of individuals would not.

123. For instance, by 1712, 31% of the United East India Company directors, and almost 25% of Bank directors, had been or were active politicians (i.e., were peers or MPs).

124. See Carswell 1993: 58.

125. It was not possible to include the South Sea Company in the analysis because the necessary documents, in particular the company stock ledgers, have not survived.

126. It would be a serious mistake to conclude that the "unknowns" were politically indifferent, simply because their loyalties could not be ascertained. Late Stuart England was a period of intense partisanship, and it is likely that most of the unknowns were like everyone else: Whig or Tory supporters.

127. Among wealthy shareholders and active traders, the dominance of the Whigs gets even stronger. For example, among the 5% wealthiest Bank shareholders, 56.4% were Whigs and only 12.3% were Tories. Similarly, among the wealthiest East India Company shareholders, 57.3% were Whigs as compared to 14.5% for the Tories. If we consider trading activity, the pattern is repeated. Among the 5% most active traders in Bank stock, 46.3% were Whigs and 14.7% were Tories. Among active traders in East India stock, 57.9% were Whigs and 14.9% were Tories. Among shareholders at large, the Whig-Tory ratio is on the order of two-to-one. Among important selected groups (wealthy and active shareholders), however, this ratio increases to between three and four to one.

128. In these tables, "other" refers to corporate or collective shareholders who do not belong to either sex. The "Corporation of ye Amicable Society for a Perpetual Assurance" owned £5,060 worth of Bank stock, but was neither a man nor a woman.

129. According to 't Hart (1993), Dutch women were much more frequently investors in public debt. The important connection between gender, family structure, and financial involvement in the Dutch state is raised and discussed by Julia Adams (1994). There are, however, no comparable studies of England.

130. See also Beckett 1986: 86.

CHAPTER SEVEN
TRADING ON THE LONDON STOCK MARKET

1. For the classic analysis, see Akerloff 1970.

2. Consider the difference between the market for home mortgages (highly standardized) and that for commercial mortgages (unstandardized). Presently, the former is a much more liquid market than the latter.

3. Jevons was not the first to suggest that rational traders are willing to overlook a lot in the pursuit of profit. As the Roman poet Juvenal expressed it in his *Satires*: "The smell of profit is clean/ And sweet, whatever the source."

4. See Cooter and Landa 1984: 15, and Landa 1981: 351.

5. This follows from Friedkin 1981: 44, and Baker 1990: 595.

6. See also Walras 1954: 83–84.

7. See also Telser 1981.

8. See also Weber 1968: 83–84, 164, 937; Weber 1981: 276; and Haskell and Teichgraeber 1993: 1.

9. For example, "The defining social characteristic of a market is the impersonal relation between buyer and seller. . . . As long as a buyer has the purchasing power

to pay the highest price, his or her identity is of no concern to the seller" (Lazonick 1991:'59). For more on the anonymous and "asocial" quality of capitalist markets, see Anderson 1993: 144–45; Parsons 1982: 314; Smelser 1963: 92; Barber 1977: 26; Berger, Berger, and Kellner 1973: 31, 125; Bowles and Gintis 1993: 85–86; Granovetter 1992: 5; Silver 1990: 1482–83; Hirschman 1977: 61, 66; North 1990: 117, 121; Holton 1992: 28; Walzer 1983: 31, 104; and Smith 1989.

10. Ensminger also suggests that ". . . self-interest dominates in markets where competition punishes those who ignore narrow goals" (Ensminger 1992: 14).

11. This result is related to the older idea that commerce, and economic rationality in general, is inherently dispassionate and attenuates strong political preferences. As Tocqueville put it: "Trade is the natural enemy of all violent passions" (Tocqueville 1969: 637). See also Hirschman 1977.

12. Arrow 1972: 92; Cain 1986: 715.

13. See Carr and Landa 1983; Landa 1981; and La Croix 1989.

14. This is consistent with Macaulay's (1963) findings.

15. Ben-Porath discusses the important role played by familial ties in reducing the transaction costs of nonmarket transactions. In his argument, institutional features of modern markets (e.g., money) act as substitutes for familial ties in resolving transaction cost problems (Ben-Porath 1980: 13). The logic of his analysis is similar to that of Homogeneous Middleman Group theory.

16. Cooter and Landa 1984: 22.

17. Without any explicit mention of Homogeneous Middleman Group theory, Jacob Price discusses early modern mercantile correspondent networks in a way consistent with the theory: "Reflecting the need for trust, many networks of correspondence followed family and religious-ethnic connections" (Price 1991: 279).

18. See, for example, Mingione 1991; Holton 1992; Swedberg 1991; Zukin and DiMaggio 1990; and Etzioni 1988.

19. Zelizer (1989, 1994) argues this for the case of money, while Sahlins (1976) takes the extreme culturalist position that even such basic elements as "utility" and "needs" are culturally constituted.

20. Of course, there is no more consensus in anthropology than in the other social sciences. The now antique "formalist-substantivist" debate marked a sharp disagreement among anthropologists about the usefulness of formal economics to the study of preindustrial societies. For recent treatments, see Orlove 1986 and Plattner 1989; and for a not-so-recent reenactment, see Scott (1976) v. Popkin (1979).

21. Studies have shown the importance of social factors for economic behavior. Podolny (1993) notes the role that status rankings played in competition among American investment banks. Biggart (1989) shows how gender and family relations shape the marketing strategies of direct selling organizations. How culture influenced market prices is Zelizer's focus in her study of insurance (1979). Even money, the primary agent of abstract, rational calculation, is imbued with social meaning (Zelizer 1989, 1994). See also Child 1964.

22. See Anderson 1970: 98.

23. Sperling 1962b.

24. See Kerridge 1988: 40–41, and chapter 4 above.

25. By the end of the century, the alternatives also included public lotteries, annuities, tallies, and Exchequer bills.

26. Coleman 1951: 224, and Stone and Stone 1984: 11.

27. Earle 1989: 152, and Grassby 1969: 739.

28. There were a number of different ways in which to configure a mortgage. For a discussion of their legal evolution, see Anderson 1969: 12.

29. See Jones 1988: 281.

30. Their traditional job involved drawing up legal documents (often for the mortgaging or conveyancing of land), but they branched out as brokers for mortgages. Some scriveners even took deposits and acted as bankers, although most confined their financial activities to mortgages. See Melton 1986: 9, 33, and Coleman 1951: 221.

31. For a discussion of these bankers' notes, see Richards 1929: 40–43.

32. Horsefield 1977: 121.

33. In a sample of business inventories, Earle found that the median proportion of liabilities to total assets was about 25%. This is likely to be an underestimate, but it shows how much businessmen depended upon credit (Earle 1989: table 4.4).

34. Ships were usually owned by partnerships, not single owners. To minimize risks, the partnerships usually consisted of between ten and twenty partners (Davis 1962: 82, 87).

35. See Davis 1954: 150. Investment in shipping was especially risky during war. Witness the fate of the Turkey Fleet, and all those with a financial interest in it, when it was attacked in 1693 by the French Navy. Total losses were estimated at around £600,000 (Jones 1972: 320).

36. Bonds were usually repayable at three or six months, but given the paucity of long-term investment opportunities bondholders were frequently willing to extend the term of their loan and reinvest in more bonds (Davies 1952: 289).

37. Until the Glorious Revolution, the East India Company raised additional capital through bonds rather than by enlarging its capital stock (Khan 1923: 172).

38. These figures are from Scott 1912, vol. 2: 230.

39. The biggest increase in trading came between 1679–81 and 1682–84. Perhaps not coincidentally, these are the years of the Exclusion Crisis and the emergence of Whig-Tory conflict. Political conflict was reflected inside the East India Company, in the controversy over whether or not to expand the capital of the company with a new stock subscription. Those opposed tended to be Tories, like Josiah Child, while those in favor tended to be Whigs, like Thomas Papillon (Lougheed 1980: 166, 169, 173). The latter group lost, and most liquidated their holdings of company stock.

40. Davies 1952: 292.

41. See Scott 1912, 1: 327. Most of the fourteen were small operations.

42. See Jones 1972: 320, and Davis 1954: 161.

43. This was especially true of merchants who specialized in the wine trade. Their trade declined because of the war, but they generally suffered no fatal losses that would have extinguished their capital. See Jones 1988: 249–50, 276.

44. See also Swift's *Examiner* no. 13 (Davis 1940: 6).

45. See, e.g., Parsons 1974: 4, and Smith 1929: 207.

46. See also Clay 1984: 276.

47. See Scott 1912, 1: 345. In 1669, the busiest trader in East India Company stock traded only 19 times: not enough work to constitute a full-time job. In contrast,

the busiest trader in East India stock in 1712 traded 128 times, while the busiest trader in Bank stock was even more active, trading a total of 301 times.

48. Davies 1952: 294. For example, the *Post Boy* of June 5–7, 1711 features an advertisement by a Mr. John Taylor, whose office was next to Jonathan's Coffeehouse in Exchange Alley, offering to buy or sell various "Publick Securities."

49. Half a century later, brokers were still being blamed for causing the South Sea Bubble of 1720. See Mortimer 1785: xii.

50. This bill was ineffectual, and the issue of how to control brokers in the stock market was revived from time to time.

51. Morgan and Thomas 1962: 20.

52. See Dickson 1967: 490.

53. See Cope 1978: 3. Morgan and Thomas claim that most trading was done through brokers (pp. 55–58), and my own analysis indicates that about half of all trades involved a broker directly.

54. Mortimer (1785) goes into excruciating detail on the mechanics of share transfers (see pp. 122–32). Traders of company shares did not always have to go to the company office, for occasionally a company would bring the transfer book to them. For example, on 28 July 1710, the Court of Directors of the East India Company "Ordered that Mr. Waters have liberty to carry the Transferr Booke to Mrs. Martha Bridge widow she being lame of the palsey" (Minutes of the Court of Directors, India Office Library, B/51 f. 98). In hardship cases, it was not necessary for the trader to be physically at the company office. The transfer books were open for most of each trading day, with a break for lunch. They were closed on holidays and during the period before company elections or payment of dividends.

55. Consider the resolution of the Court of Directors of the East India Company on 4 May 1709: "Ordered that it be a direction to the Accomptants to take special care that all Persons who come to Transfer any part of the Company's Stock be the very Persons to whom the Stock belongs which they would Transfer way before such a Transfer be made" (Minutes of the Court of Directors, India Office Library B/49 f. 513). In the case of the Bank of England, there is only one mention of a discussion among the General Court of fraudulent transfers of stock between 1694 and 1723 (Minutes of the General Court, Bank of England Archives, G7/2 f. 207), which suggests that it was not a large problem. Records of each transaction were made for the company and the transacting parties: "Ordered . . . that every Transferrer shall give the Transferee a printed receipt to be attested by Mr. Mercer [the Bank's chief clerk]" (Minutes of the Court of Directors, Bank of England Archives, G4/1 f. 125).

56. For an interesting discussion of the general significance of preprinted forms, see Yates 1989: 80–85.

57. In the 22 June 1694 edition of his *A Collection for Improvement of Husbandry and Trade*. See Dickson 1967: 491.

58. In fact, they were expressly forbidden in the 1697 Act passed to regulate brokers and stockjobbers (8 & 9 William III, c.32, sect. X).

59. Fama 1970: 383.

60. See Gilson and Kraakman 1984: 593, 610.

61. Mortimer's advice to the would-be trader in stock was first to learn share prices from the newspapers. See Mortimer 1785: 122–23.

62. See Neal 1988: 165. According to Price (1954: 244) Whiston began listing information for the East India, Royal Africa, and Hudson's Bay Companies in October 1681.

63. By the 1700s, share prices were also being published by the *Post Boy*, the *British Mercury*, and *Dawks's Newsletter*.

64. See the Sun Insurance Office General Committee Minute Books, Guildhall Library 11,931 vol. 1, ff. 23, 34.

65. Guildhall Library Mss. 11,931, vol. 1, f. 17. In January of the next year, the directors again ordered that ". . . no party matter or Comment to be put in the Mercury. . . ." (f. 24).

66. There was not perfect agreement among different sources on what prices were, even for the same shares on the same day. Over a seven-month period from January through July of 1712, both the *Course of the Exchange* and the *British Mercury* published prices for Bank, East India Company, and South Sea Company stock. The agreement between the two sources was high, but not perfect. For example, the correlation between the price of Bank stock as reported by the *Course* and that reported by the *Mercury* was 0.9418. For the two versions of the price of East India Company stock, the correlation was equal to 0.9749, while for the South Sea Company it was 0.9872. Prices can change within a day, or even an hour, but it is not clear what accounts for the discrepancy between the different sources.

67. See Morgan and Thomas 1962: 37. Carswell estimates its total size as "rather smaller than a football pitch" (Carswell 1993: 13).

68. In a 1710 petition, the inhabitants of the area around Exchange Alley claimed that ". . . by the daily Resort and Standing of Brokers and Stock-Jobbers in the same Alley, not only the common Passage to and from the Royal-Exchange is greatly obstructed, but Incouragement is given by the tumultuary Concourse of People attending the said Brokers, to Pick-Pockets, Shop-lifters, and other Idle and Disorderly People to mix among them . . . to the great Damage and Detriment of all Passengers going through the said Alley about their Lawful Occasions, as well as of the Petitioners" (*Levet Mayor*). Later in the eighteenth century, Mortimer characterized life in the stock market as consisting ". . . of such a medley of news, quarrels, prices of different funds, calling of names, adjusting of accounts, &c. &c. continually circulating in an intermixed chaos of confusion" (Mortimer 1785: 98).

69. Dickson 1967: 490.

70. See Earle 1989: 54, 70, 120. Lillywhite (1963: 20) points out that coffeehouses competed for business by providing newspapers, bulletins, and information sheets to their commercially minded clientele.

71. This point was raised in the defense of the old East India Company, when it was asserted that the Company ". . . refuse admittance to no Christians of any Nation to buy Stock, neither to Turks, Jews nor Infidels, the more the better" (*Answer to all the material Objections against the present East-India-Company*, 1688).

72. Cope 1977: 213.

73. Some examples include Sir Josiah Child's *Brief Observations Concerning Trade, and Interest of Money*, and Charles Davenant's *An Essay upon Ways and Means*.

74. See De La Vega 1688: 5, 9, 12, 35.

75. Ibid.: 35, and Mortimer 1785: 66–68.

76. In appendix D, Dickson (1967) provides tables that show how the growth in market activity continued until at least 1754.

77. See Dickson 1967: 459.

78. As Mirowski points out (1987: 117), there were no transfer taxes, differential taxation of dividends and capital gains, investment controls, or other forms of government financial regulation.

79. Others also asserted the primacy of profits, ranging from Wheeler in his *A treatise of Commerce* (1601) that ". . . there is nothing in the world so ordinarie, and naturall unto men, as to contract, truck, merchandize, and traffike one with an other" (quoted in Appleby 1978: 94), to Child (". . . Shop-Keepers are, like all other men, led by their profit" [Child 1740: 116]).

80. In 1720, a journalist commented that "when we come to Exchange Alley [the stock market] We hear Whigs and Tories . . . like People in a General Business, all their Animosities are laid aside" (quoted in Colley, 1982: 10). When they took office, directors of the Bank of England swore in their oath of office to: "be indifferent and equall to all manner of persons" (Bank of England Archives M5/448).

81. Also recall the argument made in defense of the old East India Company that anyone could buy company shares, regardless of who they were.

82. See Haley 1972: 95. When Jews were readmitted into England during the Commonwealth, and when Charles II showed them some favor, it was partly for economic reasons. See Perry 1984: 2, and Ross 1970: 63.

83. See Riley 1980: 60, and Haley 1972: 46.

84. See Barbour 1963: 40.

85. An efficient market is one in which security prices fully reflect all available information. See Fama 1970: 383; Firth 1977: 105; and Elton and Gruber 1987: 361.

86. Fama 1970: 383. For recent surveys of the efficient markets hypothesis and related evidence, see LeRoy 1989, and Fama 1991.

87. See Parsons 1974; Neal 1987: 105, 113; and Neal 1990. The evidence is not unequivocal, however, for on the basis of a different but more controversial test (the Schiller test), Mirowski found that the market sometimes diverged from efficiency. He attributes these divergences to specific organizational features and political events. See Mirowski 1987: 127.

88. See Fama 1991: 1575.

89. For an insightful discussion of markets and discrimination, see Sunstein 1991.

90. By yet another measure, the ratio of range to median, East India share prices are still more variable than Bank prices (0.125 versus 0.082).

91. Using a standard financial measure, the beta weight, Neal (1990) also concludes that East India Company shares were a riskier investment than Bank stock.

92. For example, between January and the end of July, the correlation between Bank and East India Company stock was -0.3406, while for the August to December period it was +0.7242. The correlations between South Sea Company and East India Company stock followed a similar pattern.

93. See Hoppit, 1986.

94. This discrepancy continued further out into the tails of the distribution of shareholdings. The 95th percentile for the East India Company was £5,478, while for the Bank it was £4,592. The 99th percentile for the East India Company was £18,217, while for the Bank it was only £12,161.

95. This is consistent with the fact that price-volatility was greater for East India shares than for Bank shares. Changing prices encourage more buying and selling.

96. The stock ledgers distinguished between regular share transfers and those which occurred after a shareholder died, as his or her estate was divided among the heirs. Inheritance practices did not produce the pattern of share transfers among Whigs, Tories, and Unknowns.

97. Since the most frequent combination involves Whigs and Unknowns, it is worth considering who got classified in the latter category. Given the available documentary sources, it is highly likely that many party supporters could not be tracked down. In other words, "unknowns" includes many Whigs and Tories, as well as those who were truly apolitical.

98. For advice on data analysis, I thank Stephen Stigler, Peter McCullagh, David Wallace, and Per Myklund, from the Department of Statistics, University of Chicago.

99. "Quasi-independence" (Goodman 1984, appendix A) refers to independence models of triangular contingency tables. For more details on the statistical models used here, see Carruthers 1991, chapter 7.

100. I have not done formal significance tests of these results for three reasons. All transactions in Bank and East India Company stock are in the data set, so the data represent a population, not a sample, and thus sampling theory is not very relevant. Second, the improvements in fit are so substantial that no test is necessary to see the differences between models. For instance, the G^2 statistic drops from 15.78 to 2.14 between the quasi-independence and endogamy models. For nested models, this difference is chi-square distributed with 1 degree of freedom and is significant at the 0.0005 level. Third, these data probably violate the assumption of independence since the likelihood that person A trades with person B could well be affected by whether or not A traded with person C.

101. Residuals are simply the difference between the actual counts in the table and the values predicted by particular models. Large residuals mean a poor fitting model and a high value for the G^2.

102. Analysis of two-by-two tables of trades excluding the political Unknowns gives the same result: a strong tendency for trading to occur within parties.

103. Cartels become harder to organize and maintain the larger the number of conspirators.

104. This particular cutoff point corresponded to the 95th-percentile for shareholdings. There were 110 shareholders owning more than £5,477 of East India Company shares.

105. This is not an unproblematic argument for this period. As critics of Walcott (1956a) have pointed out (e.g., Holmes 1967; Holmes 1993; Speck 1970), party politics in the reign of Anne are generally not explicable in terms of family groupings in court or parliament. There were too many instances of political families split between the Whigs and Tories.

106. An endogamy model would use up the last degree of freedom, and would reproduce the data perfectly, so I did not bother to fit it. I also did an analysis with four groups: nonminorities, Jews, Huguenots, and other minorities. As with the simpler analysis, the quasi-independence model underestimated the extent to which each group traded with itself.

107. Pursuing the economic risk argument, one might account for the absence

of endogamy among active East India Company traders and its presence among inactive traders, on the grounds that, as repeat transactors, big traders could establish cooperative and trustworthy relations among themselves (Axelrod 1984; Taylor 1987). While plausible, this still leaves open the important question of why small traders used political parties as the basis for endogamy rather than some other social institution.

108. See Ashton 1979: 46–47, 51–52, and Doolittle 1982: 4.

109. See Beier 1986: 157, and Kellett 1958: 384, 388–89. In the early eighteenth century, for example, London guilds vigorously enforced their right to search and collect quarterage (Kellett 1958: 386). Early modern London guilds look weak compared to medieval London guilds, but that is not a relevant comparison. As organizations to be harnessed for the reduction of transaction costs in the stock market, they were superior to political parties.

110. They might also have used clubs, for as Brewer (1982) points out, clubs and lodges were important organization bases for mobilization of capital and credit. Unfortunately, there are no data on the club memberships of shareholders, so I cannot explore this possibility.

111. For the Bank of England shareholders, additional guild memberships were obtained from the Bank Stock Alphabet. There were sixty liveried companies, but to analyze a sixty-by-sixty contingency table would have been much too cumbersome. I therefore partitioned traders into eighteen groups (twenty was the maximum for the software I used): 1) others, 2) apothecaries, 3) clothworkers, 4) cordwainers, 5) coopers, 6) drapers, 7) dyers, 8) fishmongers, 9) goldsmiths, 10) grocers, 11) haberdashers, 12) mercers, 13) poulters, 14) salters, 15) skinners, 16) stationers, 17) merchant-taylors, and 18) vintners. These companies were the most numerous and/or active and so accounted for more of total trading than any others. In the case of the Bank, it is interesting that the goldsmiths were relatively numerous, for they were among the most vocal political opponents of the Bank and were economic rivals to the Bank in the provision of financial services. Apparently, some goldsmiths considered it prudent to hedge their bets and purchase a piece of the opposition.

112. One might argue that the true reason for the absence of endogamy was that there were too few guild members. There were, however, as many guild members as there were London Whigs and Tories since to vote in the London parliamentary elections one had to be a member of a guild. Of course, on average each of the guilds had fewer members than the Whig or Tory parties had supporters, but the smaller numbers are exactly what would make them more useful for reducing transaction costs: it is easier to monitor and control behavior when fewer people are involved.

113. Grief (1989, 1993) shows how social solidarities were used by medieval Jews trading in the Levant.

114. The model fits and residuals showed that the quasi-independence model underestimated within-group trading and overestimated trading between groups, suggesting that an endogamy process was at work.

115. These results differ from Baker's study of the modern stock-options market. Differences in price volatility did not correspond systematically with differences in the level of endogamy or "cliqueness." Baker argued that greater price volatility resulted from a market fragmented into separate cliques. This happens for party

trading in East India Company and Bank shares, but not for guild or ethnic-religious trading. Furthermore, Baker's transaction cost explanation applies to active traders, whose high number of trades is sufficient for bounded rationality and opportunism to act as constraints (Baker 1984: 777). The absence of party endogamy among active traders in East India stock, and its presence among the small traders, is contrary to this.

116. Endogamous trading may also have been a way to affirm political allegiances or bolster party solidarity.

117. Unfortunately, existing price data are daily prices, and are not transaction specific. Companies recorded share transfers, but not the price paid by the buyer. Thus for a given share and fixed time one cannot measure the price differences between a Tory sale to another Tory, and a Tory sale to a Whig.

118. Lease, McConnell, and Mikkelson (1983) show in a modern setting how the value of shareholder voting rights is reflected in share prices.

119. Although the proportion of Whig-to-Tory shareholders was about the same in the two companies, the proportions for directors were quite different.

120. See, e.g., Ashenfelter 1989; Isard 1977; Marvel 1976; Rothschild 1973; and Telser 1973. Maynes et al. (1984) found that even for homogeneous commodities in the same urban area at the same time, the ratio of highest to lowest price sometimes exceeded four-to-one. That is, some sellers were offering goods at a price four times higher than other sellers of the very same good.

121. If sale prices are randomly distributed, then a buyer will be interested in the first order statistic of the sample of prices drawn from the market (i.e., the lowest price). The distribution of order statistics, and their expected values, is well understood, and in general the larger the sample, the lower the expectation of the first order statistic (Stigler 1968; David 1970; see the tables in Harter 1969). Similarly, a seller would want to get the highest price, i.e., the n-th order statistic of the sample of n offer prices received from the market. The larger the sample n, the higher the expectation of the n-th order statistic. In other words, to get on average a lower purchase price, or a higher offer price, a trader needs a bigger sample. Thus, someone who refuses to buy from half of the sellers in the market can expect to pay a higher price, even if the buyer picks the lowest price from the subsample. Likewise, someone who refuses to sell to half of the buyers in the market can expect to sell at a lower price.

122. This is why Defoe is partly right in his characterization of the stock market: politics didn't affect the trades of the most active traders.

123. Thanks to Ken Dauber for raising this issue.

124. There appear to be two distinct groups in the stock market: fully rational arbitrageurs, and (financially) irrational traders. Recent "noisy trader" models of financial markets (Grossman and Stiglitz 1980; De Long, Shleifer, Summers, and Waldmann 1990; and Shleifer and Summers 1990) posit a similar distinction in which the market is populated by a small number of rational traders and a large number of traders who do not respond to the underlying fundamentals of the securities they trade, and there is a suggestive congruence between the models and the results presented here. These newer financial models differ from older ones by showing that the "rational" traders need not drive the "irrational" ones out of the market, and so

their coexistence is not a temporary aberration. Early eighteenth-century noisy traders may have been irrational from an economic standpoint, but may have had very good reasons, albeit noneconomic ones, for doing what they did.

125. By my definition, traders who sat in the Commons or the House of Lords, or who were company directors, were politically active.

126. There is another reason why such evidence may be scarce, and this has to do with the idiom of motivation. When people reflect on why they have done something, and record or communicate their thoughts in a form accessible to later generations, they usually draw upon socially constituted idioms. Such reflections on motive are in part rationalizations, and are done with an eye to casting actions in a reasonable or legitimate light. In the early eighteenth century, there was one good reason to avoid framing motives in political terms, and there may have been another recommending economic motives. Although parties were real facts of political life, they were very new and not fully legitimate. Parties were denounced as factions, as representing particular interests rather than the general interest. The idea of institutionalized political conflict had not yet taken hold. All this meant that it was not entirely legitimate to openly embrace political parties. One could not comfortably cast one's motives in a partisan mold. This would make people hesitant to represent their motives as partisan motives, even if that were true (if anything, people were likely to label the motives of their political opponents as partisan). There may have been another reason why economic motives for economic behavior would be stressed. Although the stock market was new, markets in general were not, and the profit motive was widely recognized. To appear reasonable in their financial dealings, people might have preferred to stress their economic motives. This would be particularly true among the mercantile and commercial groups who dominated the stock market.

127. See Harris 1991: 115–16, 227.

128. See Rabb 1967: 31, 36, 41, 69.

129. See also Brenner 1993: 149, 153.

130. See Sutherland 1962: 2.

131. Legal records provide ample evidence of the importance of credit relationships, as Muldrew (1993b) shows.

132. See Muldrew 1993a: 163, 177–81, and Tittler 1994.

133. Johnson 1987: 276–77.

134. See Johnson 1987: 278, 282; Pollins 1982: 34–35; Endelman 1990: 21–22; and Henriques 1908: 188–89. The political rights of Jews were restricted, but no more than anyone else who wasn't a member of the Church of England. Before they were banished by Edward I, Jews enjoyed better property rights, in some respects. For example, according to Routledge (1982: 100) Jews could buy and sell choses in action at a time when others could not.

135. Huguenots and Jews were not peculiar in this respect. Both taxation and loans were viewed as measures of political support for the regime. Braddick (1994: 152) points out that some opponents of Parliament during the interregnum period refused to support it with taxes. In the eighteenth century, "In every war the alacrity with which government loans were taken up was watched even more closely than the process by which Parliament levied taxes to pay the interest on them. It was the crucial test of propertied people's faith in their governors" (Langford 1991: 116–17).

136. On Huguenots in the military, see Brewer 1989: 56, and Cottret 1991: 216.

---

137. See Carter 1955: 41; Dickson 1967: 267; and Gwynn 1985: 150–57.

138. Israel 1985: 161–63.

139. As Israel concludes: "Dutch Sephardi Jewry, then, was intimately involved in almost every aspect of the Dutch and allied war-effort between 1702 and 1713. Perhaps no other comparable group had as great a preoccupation with the course of the war or interest in its outcome" (Israel 1989b: 134). See also Israel 1985: 124, 127, 133, and Johnson 1987: 256, 281.

140. See Israel 1989a: 119.

141. See Schumpeter 1990: 101.

CHAPTER EIGHT
GOVERNMENT BONDS AND POLITICAL BONDS

1. See Sahlins 1976; Appadurai 1986; and Douglas 1982.

2. The anthropologist Belshaw says that ". . . the impersonality of the market is an element in economic and sociological theory which requires much modification" (p. 79), but then makes a telling exception: "True, there are important sectors in which men make decisions on the basis of technical factors alone, and especially on price, supply, and demand alone. *The stock market is the prime example*" (Belshaw 1965: 114, my emphasis). The willingness to make this distinction was greatest among the substantivists, as Granovetter (1993: 11) points out.

3. A notable exception is O'Barr and Conley 1992a, 1992b.

4. Following Roseveare (1991), one must not overexaggerate the Glorious Revolution as an event initiating changes in the public financial system, nor should one underestimate the ability of the Crown to influence Parliament, even after 1688 (see Clark 1986: 71, 74–75).

5. This was one reason why ministers like Godolphin and Harley worked so hard to construct a government that combined moderate elements from both parties.

6. See Brewer 1989: 88–89, 114.

7. See Holmes 1993: 334, and Langford 1991: 121.

8. My thanks to Michael Burawoy for raising this point.

9. See, e.g., Clark 1986: 80, 145.

10. Brewer 1989: 137.

11. See the discussion of France in chapter 4.

12. Collins 1988: 64, 96.

13. Ibid. 1988: 103, 217.

14. See Meuvret 1970: 323; Van Der Wee 1977: 378; and Dickson and Sperling 1970: 314.

15. One difference was that the provincial gentry were more willing to deposit money with a goldsmith banker than to buy joint-stock company shares.

16. 't Hart 1989a: 664, 678.

17. Ibid.: 663, 669.

18. Through local and county governments, traditional elites maintained their control of local public policy.

19. See Cain and Hopkins (1986) for an interesting discussion of how the monied interest was brought into the British polity during the course of the eighteenth century.

20. See Root 1994: 94, 181, 190–91.

21. We may call it the "Eumenes strategy," in honor of the Alexandrian general who used it to protect his own life from jealous rivals.

22. On this point, see Root's insightful analysis of old-regime France (Root 1994: 205).

23. For more on the political ends of government borrowing during the Civil War, see Larson 1936: 120; Davis 1910: 36, 90, 111; Stabile and Cantor 1991: 55; and Bensel 1990: 14, 111, 114, 161.

24. See the discussion of the English national debt in chapters 2 and 3.

25. Marx and Engels 1947: 79–80.

26. To understand how attractive a feature liquidity was, consider the fact that in 1672 it was the chief advantage investors gained by depositing their money with a goldsmith-banker rather than with the Treasury directly.

27. See Marx's famous discussion of commodity fetishism, Marx 1976: 163–77.

28. As Marx said: "It is nothing but the definite social relation between men which assumes here, for them, the fantastic form of a relation between things" (Marx 1976: 165).

29. To give an example, suppose that A and B are father and son. As a father, A has certain obligations to B, but B cannot transfer those obligations to a third party. The obligation arises out of the particular father-son relationship, and is not alienable.

30. See Smelser 1959: 1–3, 29–42.

31. See Thompson 1971. As well, during the seventeenth century the economy became understood as an autonomous realm with laws and regularities of its own that politicians ought not to tamper with. See Appleby 1978: 26, 47, 193.

32. See Blee 1991: 147–53.

APPENDIX

1. See Bank of England Archives, AC28/1534, 1536–38, and India Office Library L/AG/14/5/2. In the case of the East India Company, the accounts were balanced on October 3, 1711, so I used this sum for the amount of the shareholder's stock. In the case of the Bank, there had been no general recent balance of accounts, so I calculated the size of each account based on the individual balance carried forward from the previous ledger and on all transactions up to the start of 1712. Unfortunately, the stock ledgers for the South Sea Company have not survived, so similar information cannot be obtained for it.

2. Although both companies kept their stock ledgers this way, the books of the East India Company are much more systematic and better organized than the Bank books. I have no idea what accounts for the superior bookkeeping of the East India Company.

3. These names could be checked against standard sources like Cockayne (1912, 1900–1906) and Clay (1894).

4. See Dickson 1967: 256–57.

5. The full title is: *The Poll of the Livery-Men of the City of London at the election for Members of Parliament: Begun Monday, October 9th, 1710, and ended the Saturday following.*

6. The two poll books were used in sequence, not simultaneously. I used the 1713

poll book first because it was readily available. Later, after having transcribed the 1710 poll book, I was able to code those additional shareholders as Whigs or Tories who voted in 1710, but failed to vote in 1713. The coding was done at the most simple level: a person who voted for four Whigs (or Tories) was coded a Whig (or Tory); a person who split his vote disproportionately, either by voting for three Whigs and one Tory, or for three Tories and one Whig, was coded according to his majority preference; persons supporting fewer than four candidates were coded accordingly (e.g., someone who voted for only two persons, both Whigs, would be coded a Whig); a person who split his vote evenly was coded a Split Vote. There were very few of the latter.

7. See Henning 1983, for the years 1660–90, and Sedgwick 1970, for the years 1715–54.

8. The full title is: *A True and Impartial Account of the Poll of the Inhabitants of the Ward of Broad Street, Upon the Nomination of an Alderman in the Room of Sir Joseph Woolfe, deceased. Begun the 13th of September 1711.*

9. See Dickson 1967: 265.

10. See Giuseppi 1962. Persons not already identified as Jewish by Giuseppi, but possessing a Jewish family name, were also coded as Jewish.

11. See Shaw 1911, and Shaw 1923. Aliens could be denized by the monarch, or naturalized by parliament (the difference is discussed by Statt [1989]). Naturalization conferred a fuller set of rights than denization. As with Jews, persons possessing a Huguenot family name were coded as Huguenot, even if they were not explicitly listed as such. Carter (1975) also matches names in this fashion to determine ethnicity.

12. India Office Library, B/255.

13. Directors sat on the all-important standing committees. The structure of these committees reflected the different organizational concerns of the two companies. For example, the East India Company standing committees were entitled "For Accompts," "For Correspondence," "For Buying," "For Shipping," "For the Treasury," "For Law Suits," "For Private Trade," and "For Warehouses" (see *Minutes of the Court of Directors*, India Office Library, B/51, ff. 433–34). The Bank's standing committees were: "For Accompts," "For ye House and Servants," "To Attend ye Lords of the Treasury," "For Discounting Tallys," and "For Exchanges" (see *Minutes of the Court of Directors*, Bank of England Archives, G4/7, f. 143). The trading emphasis of the East India Company was as obvious from its committee structure as was the financial emphasis of the Bank.

BIBLIOGRAPHY

PRIMARY AND PRINTED SOURCES

Abstract of the Charter of the Governour and Company of Merchants of Great Britain, trading to the South-Seas. 1711. London.

Advice about the new East-India stock, in a letter to a friend. 1691. London.

The Allegations of the Turky Company and others Against the East-India-Company . . . . 1681. London.

Angliae Tutamen: or, the safety of England. Being an account of the banks, lotteries, mines . . . and many pernicious projects . . . . 1695. London.

Answer to all the material Objections against the present East-India-company. 1688. London.

An argument, proving, that the reason given by the directors of the Bank of England, against settling any other bank, viz. Because they are already settled, is the highest reason for it. 1695. London.

Bank of England Archives. AC28/1534, 1536–38. *Bank Stock Transfer Ledgers*. London.

Bank of England Archives. G7/2. *Minutes of the General Court of the Governor and Company of the Bank of England*. London.

Bank of England Archives. G4/6–7. *Minutes of the Court of Directors*. London.

Briscoe, John. 1694. *A discourse on the late funds of the Million-Act, Lottery-Act, and Bank of England*. London.

———. 1695. *Reasons humbly offered for the establishment of the National Land-Bank*. London.

———. 1696. *Reasons humbly offered for the establishment of the National Land-Bank*. London.

Broughton, John. 1705. *Remarks Upon the Bank of England With Regard more Especially to our Trade and Government*. London.

———. 1710. *The Vindication and Advancement of our National Constitution and Credit*. London.

The Case of many thousands of His Majesty's subjects, who for valuable considerations are entitled . . . to annual sums out of the hereditary revenue of excise. 1700. London.

The Case of several Thousands of His Majesty's Subjects, Entituled under the Letters Patents of King Charles the Second, to Annual Sums out of the Hereditary Revenue of Excise. 1700. London.

The Case of the Assignees of the Goldsmiths. 1688. London.

Castaing, John. *The Course of the Exchange*. London.

Child, Josiah. 1668. *Brief Observations Concerning Trade, and Interest of Money*. London.

———. 1740. *A New Discourse of Trade*. 4th ed. London.

Cobbett's Parliamentary History of England. Vol. 4. 1808. London.

A Collection of the Names of Merchants Living in and about the City of London. 1677. London.

Davenant, Charles. 1771. *The Political and Commercial Works of the Celebrated Writer Charles D'Avenant.* 5 Vols. Sir Charles Whitworth, ed. London.

Defoe, Daniel. 1701a. *The Villainy of Stock-jobbers Detected . . . .* London.

————. 1701b. *The Freeholders Plea Against Stock-jobbing Elections of Parliament Men.* London.

————. 1710a. *An Essay Upon Loans.* London.

————. 1710b. *An Essay Upon Publick Credit.* London.

————. 1719. *The Anatomy of Exchange-Alley: Or, A System of Stock-Jobbing.* London.

————. 1987 [1726]. *The Complete English Tradesman.* London: Alan Sutton.

De La Vega, Joseph. 1957 [1688]. *Confusion de Confusiones.* Hermann Kellenbenz, trans. Cambridge: Kress Library of Business and Economics Publication No. 13.

An Essay Towards the History of the Last Ministry and Parliament. 1710. London.

Godfrey, Michael. 1695. *A Short Account of the Bank of England.* London.

Great Britain, House of Commons. 1857–58. *Parliamentary Papers.* Vol. 33. London: H.M.S.O.

Great Britain, House of Commons. 1858. *Return of the Whole Amount of the National Debt of Great Britain and Ireland.* London: H.M.S.O.

Great Britain, Public Record Office. *Calender of Treasury Books.* Vols. 1, 3, 25. W. A. Shaw, ed. London: H.M.S.O.

Grey, Anchitell. 1769. *Debates of the House of Commons.* 10 Vols. London.

His Majesty's Gracious Patent to the Goldsmiths, for Payment and Satisfaction of Their Debt. 1677. London.

Historical Manuscripts Commission. 1905. *Manuscripts of the House of Lords, 1697–1699.* New series. Vol. 3. London: H.M.S.O.

Historical Manuscripts Commission. *The Manuscripts of the Duke of Portland.* Vols. 4, 7. London: H.M.S.O.

Howell's State Trials. Vol. 14. 1816. London.

The Importance of Public Credit. 1699. London.

India Office Library. L/AG/14/5/2. *Stock Transfer Alphabet and Ledger,* Ledger D. London.

India Office Library. B/49–51. *Minutes of the Court of Directors.* London.

India Office Library. B/255. *Minutes of the General Court Meetings.* London.

King, A. T., ed. 1898. *History of the Earlier Years of the Funded Debt, From 1694 to 1786.* London: H.M.S.O.

Levet Mayor. 1710. London.

Lewis, M. 1678. *Proposals to the King and Parliament, or a large model of a bank . . . .* London.

A List of the Names of all the Adventurers in the Stock of the Honourable East-India Company. 1691. London.

A modest and just apology for, or defense of the present East-India-Company. 1690. London.

Mortimer, Thomas, Esq. 1785. *Every Man His Own Broker: Or, A Guide to Exchange-Alley.* 10th ed. London.

The Mystery of the New Fashioned Goldsmiths or Bankers. 1676. London.

North, Hon. Roger. 1714. *The Gentleman Accomptant*. London.

Papillon, Thomas. 1677. *The East-India-Trade a Most Profitable Trade to the Kingdom, and Best Secured and Improved in a Company and a Joint-Stock . . . .* London.

Paterson, William. 1694. *A Brief Account of the Intended Bank of England*. London.

The Poll of the Livery-Men of the City of London at the election for Members of Parliament . . . . 1710. London.

A Proposal for Erecting a General Bank: Which may be fitly called the Land Bank of England. 1695. London.

Public Record Office. E/406/27–32. *Bankers' Assignment Books*. London.

Reasons for Passing the Bill, for the better Preserving Publick Credit, by reviving and continuing the Act . . . to restrain the Number and Ill Practices of Brokers and Stock-Jobbers . . . 1711. London.

Reasons humbly offered against grafting or splicing, and for dissolving this present East-India Company . . . . 1690. London.

Sainsbury, Ethel B., ed. 1929. *A Calendar of the Court Minutes of the East India Company*. Vol. 8. Oxford: Clarendon Press.

The Secret History of the October Club. Part 2. 1711. London.

Some Considerations offered against the continuance of the Bank of England. 1694. London.

Swift, Jonathan. 1711. *The Conduct of the Allies*. 2d ed. London.

———. 1738. *The History of the Four Last Years of the Queen*. London.

Temple, Sir William. 1673. *Observations upon the United Provinces of the Netherlands*. London.

Toland, John. 1701. *The Art of Governing by Partys . . . .* London.

A True and Impartial Account of the Poll of the Inhabitants of the Ward of Broad Street . . . . 1711. London.

Turnor, T. 1674. *The Case of the Bankers and Their Creditors Stated and Examined*. London.

———. 1677. *The Joyful News of Opening of the Exchequer to the Goldsmiths of Lombard-Street, and Their Creditors*. London.

<h2 style="text-align:center">SECONDARY SOURCES</h2>

Aalbers, J. 1977. "Holland's Financial Problems (1713–1733) and the Wars against Louis XIV," in *Britain and the Netherlands*. Vol. VI. A. C. Duke and C. A. Tamse, eds. The Hague: Martinus Nijhoff.

Acres, W. Marston. 1931. *The Bank of England from Within, 1694–1900*. Vol. 1. London: Oxford University Press.

———. 1934. "Huguenot Directors of the Bank of England," *Proceedings of the Huguenot Society of London* 15: 238–48.

———. 1940. "Directors of the Bank of England," *Notes and Queries* 179: 38–41.

Adams, Julia. 1994. "The Familial State: Elite Family Practices and State-Making in the Early Modern Netherlands," *Theory and Society* 23: 505–39.

Addison, Joseph, and Richard Steele. 1982. *Selections from The Tatler and The Spectator*. Angus Ross, ed. London: Penguin.

Agnew, Jean-Christophe. 1986. *Worlds Apart: The Market and the Theater in Anglo-American Thought, 1550–1750*. Cambridge: Cambridge University Press.

Ågren, Kurt. 1973. "The *Reduktion*," in *Sweden's Age of Greatness 1632–1718*. Michael Roberts, ed. London: Macmillan.

———. 1976. "Rise and Decline of an Aristocracy," *Scandinavian Journal of History* 1: 55–80.

Akerlof, George. 1970. "The Market for Lemons: Qualitative Uncertainty and the Market Mechanism," *Quarterly Journal of Economics* 84: 485–500.

Alchian, Armen A. 1950. "Uncertainty, Evolution and Economic Theory," *Journal of Political Economy* 58: 211–21.

Alchian, Armen A., and Harold Demsetz. 1973. "The Property Rights Paradigm," *Journal of Economic History* 33: 16–27.

Alesina, Alberto, and Roberto Perotti. 1995. "The Political Economy of Budget Deficits," *IMF Staff Papers* 42: 1–31.

Alesina, Alberto, and Guido Tabellini. 1990. "A Positive Theory of Fiscal Deficits and Government Debt," *Review of Economic Studies* 57: 403–14.

Allen, David. 1976. "Political Clubs in Restoration London," *Historical Journal* 19 (3): 561–80.

Alter, George, and James C. Riley. 1986. "How to Bet on Lives: A Guide to Life Contingent Contracts in Early Modern Europe," *Research in Economic History* 10: 1–53.

Anderson, B. L. 1969. "Provincial Aspects of the Financial Revolution of the Eighteenth Century," *Business History* 11 (1): 11–22.

———. 1970. "Money and the Structure of Credit in the Eighteenth Century," *Business History* 12 (2): 85–101.

Anderson, Elizabeth. 1993. *Value in Ethics and Economics*. Cambridge: Harvard University Press.

Anderson, Perry. 1974. *Lineages of the Absolutist State*. London: NLB.

Anderson, Terry L., and Peter J. Hill. 1975. "The Evolution of Property Rights: A Study of the American West," *Journal of Law and Economics* 18: 163–79.

———. 1990. "The Race for Property Rights," *Journal of Law and Economics* 33: 177–97.

Appadurai, Arjun, ed. 1986. *The Social Life of Things: Commodities in Cultural Perspective*. Cambridge: Cambridge University Press.

Appleby, Joyce. 1976. "Ideology and Theory: The Tension between Political and Economic Liberalism in Seventeenth-Century England," *American Historical Review* 81: 499–515.

———. 1978. *Economic Thought and Ideology in Seventeenth-Century England*. Princeton: Princeton University Press.

Ardant, Gabriel. 1975. "Financial Policy and Economic Infrastructure of Modern States and Nations," in *The Formation of National States in Western Europe*. Charles Tilly, ed. Princeton: Princeton University Press.

Arrow, Kenneth. 1972. "Models of Job Discrimination," in *Racial Discrimination in Economic Life*. Anthony Pascal, ed. Lexington: Lexington Books.

Ashenfelter, Orley. 1989. "How Auctions Work for Wine and Art," *Journal of Economic Perspectives* 3: 23–36.

Ashton, Robert. 1960. *The Crown and the Money Market, 1603–1640*. Oxford: Clarendon Press.

_____. 1979. *The City and the Court 1603–1643*. Cambridge: Cambridge University Press.

Åström, Sven-Erik. 1973. "The Swedish Economy and Sweden's Role as a Great Power 1632–1697," in *Sweden's Age of Greatness 1632–1718*. Michael Roberts, ed. London: Macmillan.

Axelrod, Robert. 1984. *The Evolution of Cooperation*. New York: Basic Books.

Aylmer, G. E. 1961. *The King's Servants: The Civil Service of Charles I, 1625–1642*. New York: Columbia University Press.

_____. 1980. "From Office-Holding to Civil Service: The Genesis of Modern Bureaucracy," *Transactions of the Royal Historical Society*. 5th ser. 30: 91–108.

Bailey, S. J. 1931. "Assignment of Debts in England from the Twelfth to the Twentieth Century, I," *Law Quarterly Review* 47: 516–35.

_____. 1932a. "Assignment of Debts in England from the Twelfth to the Twentieth Century, II," *Law Quarterly Review* 48: 248–71.

_____. 1932b. "Assignment of Debts in England from the Twelfth to the Twentieth Century, III," *Law Quarterly Review* 48: 547–82.

Baird, Douglas, and Thomas Jackson. 1984. "Information, Uncertainty, and the Transfer of Property," *Journal of Legal Studies* 13: 299–320.

Baker, J. H. 1979a. "The Law Merchant and the Common Law Before 1700," *Cambridge Law Journal* 38: 295–322.

_____. 1979b. *An Introduction to English Legal History*. 2d ed. London: Butterworths.

Baker, Wayne E. 1984. "The Social Structure of a National Securities Market," *American Journal of Sociology* 89: 775–811.

_____. 1990. "Market Networks and Corporate Behavior," *American Journal of Sociology* 96: 589–625.

Barber, Bernard. 1977. "Absolutization of the Market," in *Markets and Morals*. Gerald Dworkin, Gordon Bermant, and Peter G. Brown, eds. Washington, D.C.: Hemisphere.

Barbour, Violet. 1963. *Capitalism in Amsterdam in the Seventeenth Century*. Ann Arbor: University of Michigan Press.

Baron, James N., and Michael T. Hannan. 1994. "The Impact of Economics on Contemporary Sociology," *Journal of Economic Literature* 32: 1111–46.

Barzel, Yoram. 1989. *Economic Analysis of Property Rights*. Cambridge: Cambridge University Press.

_____. 1992. "Confiscation by the Ruler: The Rise and Fall of Jewish Lending in the Middle Ages," *Journal of Law and Economics* 35: 1–13.

Baskin, Jonathan Barron. 1988. "The Development of Corporate Financial Markets in Britain and the United States, 1600–1914: Overcoming Asymmetric Information," *Business History Review* 62: 199–237.

Basu, Kaushik, Eric Jones, and Ekkehart Schlicht. 1987. "The Growth and Decay of Custom: The Role of the New Institutional Economics in Economic History," *Explorations in Economic History* 24: 1–21.

Baxter, Stephen B. 1957. *The Development of the Treasury 1660–1702*. London: Longmans, Green and Co.

Beale, Hugh, and Tony Dugdale. 1975. "Contracts Between Businessmen: Planning and the Use of Contractual Remedies," *British Journal of Law and Society* 2: 45–60.

Becker, Gary S. 1968. "Economic Discrimination," in *International Encyclopedia of the Social Sciences*. D. L. Sills, ed. New York: Macmillan.

———. 1971. *The Economics of Discrimination*. 2d ed. Chicago: University of Chicago Press.

———. 1976. *The Economic Approach to Human Behavior*. Chicago: University of Chicago Press.

———. 1981. *A Treatise on the Family*. Cambridge: Harvard University Press.

Beckett, J. V. 1985. "Land Tax or Excise: the levying of taxation in seventeenth- and eighteenth-century England," *English Historical Review* 100: 285–308.

———. 1986. *The Aristocracy in England 1660–1914*. Oxford: Basil Blackwell.

de Beer, E. S. 1933–34. "Members of the Court Party in the House of Commons, 1670–1678," *Bulletin of the Institute of Historical Research* 11: 1–23.

———. 1970. "The English Revolution," in *The New Cambridge Modern History*. Vol. 6. J. S. Bromley, ed. Cambridge: Cambridge University Press.

Behrens, Betty. 1963. "Nobles, Privileges and Taxes in France at the end of the Ancien Régime," *Economic History Review* 15: 451–75.

Behrens, C.B.A. 1985. *Society, Government, and the Enlightenment*. New York: Harper and Row.

Beier, A. L. 1986. "Engine of Manufactures: the trades of London," in *London 1500–1700*. A. L.Beier and Roger Finlay, eds. London: Longman.

Beik, William. 1985. *Absolutism and Society in Seventeenth-Century France: State Power and Provincial Aristocracy in Languedoc*. Cambridge: Cambridge University Press.

Belshaw, Cyril S. 1965. *Traditional Exchange and Modern Markets*. Englewood Cliffs, N.J.: Prentice Hall.

Benjamin, Roger, and Raymond Duvall. 1985. "The Capitalist State in Context," *The Democratic State*. Roger Benjamin and Stephen L. Elkin, eds. Lawrence: University of Kansas Press.

Bennett, G. V. 1969. "Conflict in the Church," in *Britain After the Glorious Revolution*. Geoffrey Holmes, ed. New York: St. Martin's Press.

Ben-Porath, Yoram. 1980. "The F-Connection: Families, Friends and Firms and the Organization of Exchange," *Population and Development Review* 6: 1–30.

Bensel, Richard Franklin. 1990. *Yankee Leviathan: The Origins of Central State Authority in America, 1859–1877*. Cambridge: Cambridge University Press.

Beresford, John. 1925. *The Godfather of Downing Street: Sir George Downing 1623–1684*. London: Richard Cobden-Sanderson.

Berger, Peter, Brigette Berger, and Hansfried Kellner. 1973. *The Homeless Mind: Modernization and Consciousness*. New York: Vintage.

Bernstein, Lisa. 1992. "Opting Out of the Legal System: Extralegal Contractual Relations in the Diamond Industry," *Journal of Legal Studies* 21: 115–57.

Bien, David D. 1987. "Offices, Corps, and a System of State Credit: The Uses of Privilege under the Ancien Régime," in *The Political Culture of the Old Regime*. Keith Baker, ed. Oxford: Pergamon Press.

_____. 1989. "Manufacturing Nobles: The Chancelleries in France to 1789," *Journal of Modern History* 61: 445–86.

Biggart, Nicole Woolsey. 1989. *Charismatic Capitalism: Direct Selling Organizations in America*. Chicago: University of Chicago Press.

Blackstone, Sir William. 1765. *Commentaries on the Laws of England*. Vol. 2. Oxford: Clarendon Press.

Blee, Kathleen M. 1991. *Women of the Klan: Racism and Gender in the 1920s*. Berkeley: University of California Press.

Block, Fred. 1977. "The Ruling Class Does Not Rule," *Socialist Revolution*, 33: 6–28.

Bolingbroke, Lord [Henry St. John]. 1841. *The Works of Lord Bolingbroke*. Vol. 2. Philadelphia: Carey and Hart.

Bonney, Richard. 1981. *The King's Debts: Finance and Politics in France 1589–1661*. Oxford: Clarendon Press.

_____. 1991. *The European Dynastic States 1494–1660*. Oxford: Clarendon Press.

_____. 1992. "The State and its Revenues in *ancien-régime* France," *Historical Research* 65: 150–76.

Bosher, J. F. 1994. "The Franco-Catholic Danger, 1660–1715," *History* 79: 5–30.

Bossenga, Gail. 1986. "From *Corps* to Citizenship: The *Bureaux des Finances* before the French Revolution," *Journal of Modern History* 58: 610–42.

_____. 1987. "City and State: An Urban Perspective on the Origins of the French Revolution," in *The Political Culture of the Old Regime*. Keith Baker, ed. Oxford: Pergamon Press.

_____. 1989. "Taxes," in *A Critical Dictionary of the French Revolution*. François Furet and Mona Ozouf, eds. Cambridge: Belknap Press.

Bowen, H. V. 1989. "Investment and Empire in the Later Eighteenth Century: East India Stockholding, 1756–1791," *Economic History Review* 42: 186–206.

_____. 1993. "'The Pests of Human Society': Stockbrokers, Jobbers and Speculators in Mid-eighteenth-century Britain," *History* 78: 38–53.

Bowles, Samuel, and Herbert Gintis. 1993. "The Revenge of Homo Economicus," *Journal of Economic Perspectives* 7(1): 83–102.

Braddick, M. J. 1994. *Parliamentary Taxation in Seventeenth-Century England: Local Administration and Response*. Woodbridge: Boydell Press.

Braun, Rudolph. 1975. "Taxation, Sociopolitical Structure, and State-Building," in *The Formation of National States in Western Europe*. Charles Tilly, ed. Princeton: Princeton University Press.

Brenner, Reuven. 1980. "Economics—An Imperialist Science?" *Journal of Legal Studies* 9: 179–88.

Brenner, Robert. 1976. "Agrarian Class Structure and Economic Development in Pre-Industrial Europe," *Past and Present* 70: 30–75.

_____. 1993. *Merchants and Revolution: Commercial Change, Political Conflict, and London's Overseas Traders, 1550–1653*. Princeton: Princeton University Press.

Brewer, John. 1982. "Commercialization and Politics," in *The Birth of a Consumer Society*. Neil McKendrick, John Brewer, and J. H. Plumb, eds. Bloomington: Indiana University Press.

_____. 1988. "The English State and Fiscal Appropriation, 1688–1789," *Politics and Society* 16(2–3): 335–85.

Brewer, John. 1989. *The Sinews of Power: War, Money and the English State, 1688–1783*. New York: Knopf.

———. 1994. "The Eighteenth-Century British State," in *An Imperial State at War: Britain from 1689 to 1815*. Lawrence Stone, ed. London: Routledge.

Brooks, Colin. 1974. "Public Finance and Political Stability: The Administration of the Land Tax, 1688–1720," *Historical Journal* 17(2): 281–300.

———. 1984. "The Country Persuasion and Political Responsibility in England in the 1690s," *Parliaments, Estates and Representation* 4(2): 135–46.

Browning, Andrew. 1948. "Parties and Party Organization in the Reign of Charles II," *Transactions of the Royal Historical Society*. 4th Series 30: 21–36.

———. 1951. *Thomas Osborne Earl of Danby and Duke of Leeds, 1632–1712*. Vol. 1. Glasgow: Jackson, Son and Co.

———, ed. 1953. *English Historical Documents 1660–1714*. Oxford: Oxford University Press.

Bruce, Anthony. 1980. *The Purchase System in the British Army, 1660–1871*. London: Royal Historical Society.

Burke, Peter. 1974. *Venice and Amsterdam: A study of seventeenth-century elites*. London: Temple Smith.

Burton, I. F., P.W.J. Riley, and E. Rowlands. 1968. *Political Parties in the Reigns of William III and Anne: The Evidence of Division Lists*. London: The Athlone Press.

Cain, Glen G. 1986. "The Economic Analysis of Labor Market Discrimination," in *Handbook of Labor Economics*. Vol. 1. Orley Ashenfelter and Richard Layard, eds. Amsterdam: North-Holland.

Cain, P. J., and A. G. Hopkins. 1986. "Gentlemanly Capitalism and British Expansion Overseas I: The Old Colonial System, 1688–1850," *Economic History Review* 39: 501–25.

Campbell, John Lord. 1874. *The Lives of the Chief Justices of England*. Vol. 3. New York: James Cockroft.

———. 1880. *Lives of the Lord Chancellors and Keepers of the Great Seal of England*. Vol. 5. Jersey City: Frederick Linn and Co.

Carr, Cecil T., ed. 1913. *Select Charters of the Trading Companies*. Vol. 28. London: Selden Society Publications.

Carr, Jack L., and Janet T. Landa. 1983. "The Economics of Symbols, Clan Names, and Religion," *Journal of Legal Studies* 12: 135–56.

Carruthers, Bruce G. 1991. *State-Building and Market-Making: The Politics of Public Debt in the English Financial Revolution, 1672–1712*. Ph.D. dissertation. Chicago: University of Chicago.

Carswell, John. 1960. *The South Sea Bubble*. London: Cresset Press.

———. 1993. *The South Sea Bubble*. Rev. ed. London: Alan Sutton.

Carter, A. C. 1955. "The Huguenot Contribution to the Early Years of the Funded Debt, 1694–1714," *Proceedings of the Huguenot Society of London* 19(3): 21–41.

———. 1968. *The English Public Debt*. London: Historical Association.

———. 1975. *Getting, Spending and Investing in Early Modern Times*. Assen, The Netherlands: Van Gorcum.

Carter, Jennifer. 1969. "The Revolution and the Constitution," in *Britain After the Glorious Revolution*. Geoffrey Holmes, ed. New York: St. Martin's Press.

———. 1979. "Law, Courts and Constitution," in *The Restored Monarchy 1660–1688*. J. R. Jones, ed. London: Macmillan.

Casey, James. 1985. "Spain: a Failed Transition," in *The European Crisis of the 1590s*. London: George Allen & Unwin.

Chandaman, C. D. 1975. *The English Public Revenue 1660–1688*. Oxford: Clarendon Press.

Charny, David. 1990. "Nonlegal Sanctions in Commercial Relationships," *Harvard Law Review* 104: 373–467.

Chase, Salmon. 1862. *Report of the Secretary of the Treasury*. Washington, D.C.: Government Printing Office.

Chaudhuri, K. N. 1965. *The English East India Company: The Study of an Early Joint-Stock Company 1600–1640*. London: Frank Cass.

———. 1978. *The Trading World of Asia and the English East India Company 1660–1760*. Cambridge: Cambridge University Press.

———. 1985. *Trade and Civilisation in the Indian Ocean*. Cambridge: Cambridge University Press.

Chaudhuri, K. N., and Jonathan I. Israel. 1991. "The English and Dutch East India Companies and the Glorious Revolution of 1688–9," in *The Anglo-Dutch Moment*. Jonathan I. Israel, ed. Cambridge: Cambridge University Press.

Child, John. 1964. "Quaker Employers and Industrial Relations," *Sociological Review* 12: 293–315.

Childs, John. 1976. *The Army of Charles II*. London: Routledge and Kegan Paul.

———. 1980. *The Army, James II, and the Glorious Revolution*. New York: St. Martin's.

———. 1987. *The British Army of William III, 1689–1702*. Manchester: Manchester University Press.

———. 1991. *The Nine Years' War and the British Army 1688–1697: the operations in the Low Countries*. Manchester: Manchester University Press.

Clapham, Sir John. 1945. *The Bank of England*. Vol. 1. Cambridge: Cambridge University Press.

Clark, J.C.D. 1986. *Revolution and Rebellion: State and society in England in the seventeenth and eighteenth centuries*. Cambridge: Cambridge University Press.

Clay, C.G.A. 1984. *Economic Expansion and Social Change: England 1500–1700*. Vol. 2. Cambridge: Cambridge University Press.

Clay, Christopher. 1978. *Public Finance and Private Wealth: The Career of Sir Stephen Fox, 1627–1716*. Oxford: Clarendon Press.

Clay, John W. 1894. *Familiae Minorum Gentium*. 4 Vols. London: Harleian Society Publication No. 37.

Coase, R. H. 1937. "The Nature of the Firm," *Economica* 4: 386–405.

———. 1960. "The Problem of Social Cost," *Journal of Law and Economics* 3: 1–44.

Cohen, G. A. 1978. *Karl Marx's Theory of History*. Princeton: Princeton University Press.

Cohen, Jacob. 1953. "The Element of Lottery in British Government Bonds, 1694–1919," *Economica* 20: 237–46.

Cokayne, G. E. 1900–1906. *The Complete Baronetage*. 5 Vols. Exeter: William Pollard and Co.

———. 1912. *The Complete Peerage*. 13 Vols. London: St. Catherine Press.

Coleman, D. C. 1951. "London Scriveners and the Estate Market in the Later Seventeenth Century," *Economic History Review* 4(2): 221–30.

Coleman, James S. 1990. *The Foundations of Social Theory*. Cambridge: Harvard University Press.

Colley, Linda. 1982. *In Defiance of Oligarchy: The Tory Party 1714–60*. Cambridge: Cambridge University Press.

———. 1992. *Britons: Forging the Nation 1707–1837*. New Haven: Yale University Press.

Collins, James B. 1988. *Fiscal Limits of Absolutism: Direct Taxation in Early Seventeenth-Century France*. Berkeley: University of California Press.

Cook, Walter Wheeler. 1916. "The Alienability of Choses in Action," *Harvard Law Review* 29: 816–37.

Cooke, C. A. 1951. *Corporation Trust and Company: An Essay in Legal History*. Cambridge: Harvard University Press.

Cooter, Robert, and Janet T. Landa. 1984. "Personal versus Impersonal Trade: The Size of Trading Groups and Contract Law," *International Review of Law and Economics* 4: 15–22.

Cooter, Robert, and Thomas Ulen. 1988. *Law and Economics*. Glenview: Scott, Foresman and Co.

Cope, S. R. 1977. "The Stock-brokers find a home," *Guildhall Studies in London History* 2(4): 213–19.

———. 1978. "The Stock Exchange Revisited: A New Look at the Market in Securities in London in the Eighteenth Century," *Economica* 45: 1–21.

Coquillette, Daniel R. 1981. "Legal Ideology and Incorporation II: Sir Thomas Ridley, Charles Molloy, and the Literary Battle for the Law Merchant, 1607–1676," *Boston University Law Review* 61: 315–71.

Cottret, Bernard. 1991. *The Huguenots in England: Immigration and Settlement c. 1550–1700*. Peregrine and Adriana Stevenson, trans. Cambridge: Cambridge University Press.

Cumming, Christine M. 1990. "The Economics of Securitization," in *Asset Securitization: Principles and Practice*. David M. Morris, ed. New York: Executive Enterprises.

Dahlgren, Stellan. 1973. "Estates and Classes," in *Sweden's Age of Greatness 1632–1718*. Michael Roberts, ed. London: Macmillan.

David, H. A. 1970. *Order Statistics*. New York: Wiley.

Davies, K. G. 1952. "Joint-Stock Investment in the Later Seventeenth Century," *Economic History Review* 4(3): 283–301.

———. 1957. *The Royal Africa Company*. London: Longmans, Green and Co.

Davis, Andrew McFarland. 1910. *The Origins of the National Banking System*. Washington, D.C.: National Monetary Commission.

Davis, Herbert, ed. 1940. *The Examiner and Other Pieces Written in 1710–11*. From *The Prose Works of Jonathan Swift*. Vol. 3. Oxford: Basil Blackwell.

Davis, Ralph. 1954. "English Foreign Trade, 1660–1700," *Economic History Review* 7: 150–66.

———. 1962. *The Rise of the English Shipping Industry in the Seventeenth and Eighteenth Centuries*. Newton Abbot: David and Charles.

De Alessi, Louis. 1980. "The Economics of Property Rights: A Review of the Evidence," *Research in Law and Economics* 2: 1–47.

De Krey, Gary S. 1978. *Trade, Religion, and Politics in London in the Reign of William III*. Ph.D. dissertation. Princeton University.

———. 1983. "Political Radicalism in London after the Glorious Revolution," *Journal of Modern History* 55: 585–617.

———. 1985. *A Fractured Society: The Politics of London in the First Age of Party 1688–1715*. Oxford: Clarendon Press.

De Long, J. Bradford, and Andrei Shleifer. 1993. "Princes and Merchants: European City Growth Before the Industrial Revolution," *Journal of Law and Economics* 36: 671–702.

De Long, J. Bradford, Andrei Shleifer, Lawrence H. Summers, and Robert J. Waldmann. 1990. "Noise Trader Risk in Financial Markets," *Journal of Political Economy* 98: 703–38.

Demsetz, Harold. 1988. *Ownership, Control, and the Firm*. Oxford: Basil Blackwell.

Dent, Julian. 1973. *Crisis in Finance: Crown, Financiers and Society in Seventeenth Century France*. Newton Abbot: David and Charles.

Dibble, Vernon K. 1965. "The Organization of Traditional Authority: English County Government 1558–1640," *Handbook of Organizations*. James March, ed. Chicago: Rand McNally.

Dickinson, H. T. 1967a. "The Tory Party's Attitude to Foreigners," *Bulletin of the Institute of Historical Research* 40: 153–65.

———. 1970. "The October Club," *Huntington Library Quarterly* 33(2): 155–73.

———. 1977. *Liberty and Property: Political Ideology in Eighteenth-Century Britain*. London: Weidenfeld and Nicolson.

———, ed. 1967b. *The Correspondence of Sir James Clavering*. Vol. 178. Surtees Society Publication.

———, ed. 1975. "The Letters of Henry St. John to the Earl of Orrery, 1709–1711," *Camden Miscellany Vol. XXVII*. 4th series, vol. 14. London: Royal Historical Society.

Dickson, P.G.M. 1967. *The Financial Revolution in England*. London: Macmillan.

Dickson, P.G.M., and John Sperling. 1970. "War Finance, 1689–1714," in *New Cambridge Modern History*. Vol. VI. J. S. Bromley, ed. Cambridge: Cambridge University Press.

Van Dillen, J. G. 1934. "The Bank of Amsterdam," in *History of the Principal Public Banks*. J. G. Van Dillen, ed. The Hague: Martinus Nijhoff.

DiMaggio, Paul. 1990. "Cultural Aspects of Economic Action and Organization," in *Beyond the Marketplace*. Roger Friedland and A. F. Robertson, eds. New York: Aldine de Gruyter.

Doolittle, I. G. 1982. *The City of London and its Livery Companies*. Dorchester: Gavin Press.

Douglas, Mary. 1982. "Goods as a System of Communication," in *In the Active Voice*. London: Routledge and Kegan Paul.

Downie, J. A. 1976. "The Commission of Public Accounts and the formation of the Country Party," *English Historical Review* 91: 33–51.

Downing, Brian. 1992. *The Military Revolution and Political Change*. Princeton: Princeton University Press.

Downs, Anthony. 1957. *An Economic Theory of Democracy*. New York: Harper and Row.

Doyle, William. 1984. "The Price of Offices in Pre-revolutionary France," *Historical Journal* 27: 831–60.

Earle, Peter. 1989. *The Making of the English Middle Class*. Berkeley: University of California Press.

Eggertsson, Thráin. 1990. *Economic Behavior and Institutions*. Cambridge: Cambridge University Press.

Ehrman, John. 1953. *The Navy in the War of William III 1689–1697*. Cambridge: Cambridge University Press.

Ekelund, Robert B. Jr., and Robert D. Tollison. 1980. "Mercantilist Origins of the Corporation," *Bell Journal of Economics* 11: 715–20.

Ellis, Frank H., ed. 1985. *Swift vs. Mainwaring: The Examiner and The Medley*. Oxford: Clarendon Press.

Elton, Edwin J., and Martin J. Gruber. 1987. *Modern Portfolio Theory and Investment Analysis*. New York: John Wiley and Sons.

Endelman, Todd M. 1990. *Radical Assimilation in English Jewish History 1656–1945*. Bloomington: Indiana University Press.

Ensminger, Jean. 1992. *Making a Market: The Institutional Transformation of an African Society*. Cambridge: Cambridge University Press.

Ensminger, Jean, and Andrew Rutten. 1991. "The Political Economy of Changing Property Rights: Dismantling a Pastoral Commons," *American Ethnologist* 18: 683–99.

Epstein, Leon D. 1967. *Political Parties in Western Democracies*. New York: Frederick A. Praeger.

Ertman, Thomas. 1994a. "*The Sinews of Power* and European State-Building Theory," in *An Imperial State at War: Britain from 1689 to 1815*. Lawrence Stone, ed. London: Routledge.

———. 1994b. "Rethinking Political Development in Medieval and Early Modern Europe," presented at the 1994 American Political Science Association Meetings.

Etzioni, Amitai. 1988. *The Moral Dimension: Toward a New Economics*. New York: Free Press.

Ewen, C. L'Estrange. 1932. *Lotteries and Sweepstakes: An Historical, Legal, and Ethical Survey of their Introduction, Suppression and Re-establishment in the British Isles*. London: Heath, Cranton.

Fama, Eugene. 1970. "Efficient Capital Markets," *Journal of Finance* 25: 383–417.

———. 1991. "Efficient Capital Markets: II," *Journal of Finance* 46: 1575–1617.

Farrell, Joseph. 1987. "Information and the Coase Theorem," *Journal of Economic Perspectives* 1: 110–25.

Field, Alexander James. 1981. "The Problem with Neoclassical Institutional Economics," *Explorations in Economic History* 18: 174–98.

———. 1991. "Do Legal Systems Matter?" *Explorations in Economic History* 28: 1–35.

Firth, Michael. 1977. *The Valuation of Shares and the Efficient-Markets Theory*. London: Macmillan.

Fischer, Wolfram, and Peter Lundgreen. 1975. "The Recruitment and Training of Administrative and Technical Personnel," in *The Formation of National States in Western Europe*. Charles Tilly, ed. Princeton: Princeton University Press.

Flandrin, Jean-Louis. 1979. *Families in Former Times*. Richard Southern, trans. Cambridge: Cambridge University Press.

Fletcher, Anthony. 1983. "National and Local Awareness in the County Communities," in *Before the English Civil War*. Howard Tomlinson, ed. New York: St. Martin's Press.

Fligstein, Neil. 1990. *The Transformation of Corporate Control*. Cambridge: Harvard University Press.

Flinn, Michael W. 1960. "Sir Ambrose Crowley and the South Sea Scheme of 1711," *Journal of Economic History* 20: 51–66.

Forster, G.C.F. 1983. "Government in Provincial England Under the Later Stuarts," *Transactions of the Royal Historical Society*. 5th series. 33: 29–48.

Foster, Joseph., ed. 1887. *The Visitation of Middlesex, 1663*. London.

Francis, Clinton W. 1983. "The Structure of Judicial Administration and the Development of Contract Law in Seventeenth-Century England," *Columbia Law Review* 83: 35–137.

Friedkin, Noah E. 1981. "The Development of Structure in Random Networks," *Social Networks* 3: 41–52.

Friedland, Roger, and A. F. Robertson, eds. 1990. *Beyond the Marketplace*. New York: Aldine de Gruyter.

Friedman, Milton. 1962. *Capitalism and Freedom*. Chicago: University of Chicago Press.

Fryde, E. B. and M. M. Fryde. 1963. "Public Credit," in *Cambridge Economic History of Europe*. Vol. III. M. M. Postan, E. E. Rich, and Edward Miller, eds. Cambridge: Cambridge University Press.

Geary, Patrick. 1986. "Sacred Commodities: the Circulation of Medieval Relics," in *The Social Life of Things*. Arjun Appadurai, ed. Cambridge: Cambridge University Press.

Giesey, Ralph E. 1977. "Rules of Inheritance and Strategies of Mobility in Prerevolutionary France," *American Historical Review* 82: 271–89.

———. 1983. "State-Building in Early Modern France: The Role of Royal Officialdom," *Journal of Modern History* 55: 191–207.

Gilson, Ronald J., and Reinier H. Kraakman. 1984. "The Mechanisms of Market Efficiency," *Virginia Law Review* 70(4): 549–644.

Giuseppi, J. A. 1955. "Sephardi Jews and the early years of The Bank of England," *Transactions of the Jewish Historical Society of England* 19: 53–63.

———. 1962. "Early Jewish Holders of Bank of England Stock (1695–1725)," *Jewish Historical Society of England, Miscellanies*. Part 6.

Glassey, Lionel K. J. 1979. *Politics and the Appointment of Justices of the Peace 1675–1720*. Oxford: Oxford University Press.

Goldin, Claudia. 1990. *Understanding the Gender Gap: An Economic History of American Women*. New York: Oxford University Press.

Goldstone, Jack. 1986. "State Breakdown in the English Revolution," *American Journal of Sociology* 92(2): 257–322.

Goldstone, Jack. 1991. *Revolution and Rebellion in the Early Modern World*. Berkeley: University of California Press.

Goodman, Leo A. 1984. *The Analysis of Cross-Classified Data Having Ordered Categories*. Cambridge: Harvard University Press.

Goody, Jack. 1966. "Introduction," in *Succession to High Office*. Jack Goody, ed. Cambridge: Cambridge University Press.

Goubert, Pierre. 1970. *Louis XIV and Twenty Million Frenchmen*. Anne Carter, trans. New York: Pantheon.

Granovetter, Mark. 1985. "Economic Action, Social Structure, and Embeddedness," *American Journal of Sociology* 91: 481–510.

———. 1992. "Economic Institutions as Social Constructions," *Acta Sociologica* 35: 3–11.

———. 1993. "The Nature of Economic Relationships," in *Explorations in Economic Sociology*. Richard Swedberg, ed. New York: Russell Sage.

Grassby, Richard. 1969. "The Rate of Profit in Seventeenth-Century England," *English Historical Review* 84: 721–51.

———. 1970. "English Merchant Capitalism in the Late Seventeenth Century," *Past and Present* 46: 87–107.

Gregg, Edward. 1980. *Queen Anne*. London: Routledge and Kegan Paul.

Gregory, Chris. 1983. "Kula gift exchange and capitalist commodity exchange: a comparison," in *The Kula*. Jerry W. Leach and Edmund Leach, eds. Cambridge: Cambridge University Press.

Greif, Avner. 1989. "Reputation and Coalitions in Medieval Trade: Evidence on the Maghribi Traders," *Journal of Economic History* 49: 857–82.

———. 1993. "Contract Enforceability and Economic Institutions in Early Trade: The Maghribi Traders' Coalition," *American Economic Review* 83: 525–48.

———. 1994. "On the Political Foundations of the Late Medieval Commercial Revolution," *Journal of Economic History* 54: 271–87.

Grever, John H. 1982. "The Structure of Decision-Making in the States General of the Dutch Republic 1660–68," *Parliaments, Estates and Representation* 2: 125–53.

———. 1984. "The French Invasion of the Spanish Netherlands and the Provincial Assemblies in the Dutch Republic 1667–1668," *Parliaments, Estates and Representation* 4: 25–35.

Grierson, Philip. 1959. "Commerce in the Dark Ages," *Transactions of the Royal Historical Society* 9: 123–40.

Grossman, Sanford J., and Joseph E. Stiglitz. 1980. "On the Impossibility of Informationally Efficient Markets," *American Economic Review* 70: 393–408.

Gwynn, Robin D. 1985. *Huguenot Heritage: The History and Contribution of the Huguenots in Britain*. London: Routledge and Kegan Paul.

Habakkuk, H. J. 1952. "The Long-Term Rate of Interest and the Price of Land in the Seventeenth Century," *Economic History Review* 5(1): 26–45.

Haley, K.H.D. 1953. *William of Orange and the English Opposition 1672–4*. Oxford: Clarendon Press.

———. 1968. *The First Earl of Shaftesbury*. Oxford: Clarendon Press.

———. 1970. "Shaftesbury's Lists of the Lay Peers and Members of the Commons, 1677–8," *Bulletin of the Institute of Historical Research* 43: 86–105.

_____. 1972. *The Dutch in the Seventeenth Century*. New York: Harcourt, Brace Jovanovich.

_____. 1988. *The British and the Dutch*. London: George Philip.

Hampsher-Monk, Iain. 1991. "The Market for Toleration: A Case Study in an Aspect of the Ambiguity of 'Positive Economics,'" *British Journal of Political Science* 21: 29–44.

Harper, W. Percy. 1929. "The Significance of the Farmers of the Customs in Public Finance in the Middle of the Seventeenth Century," *Economica* 25: 61–70.

Harris, Frances. 1991. *A Passion for Government: The Life of Sarah, Duchess of Marlborough*. Oxford: Clarendon Press.

Harris, Tim. 1987. *London Crowds in the Reign of Charles II*. Cambridge: Cambridge University Press.

_____. 1993. *Politics Under the Later Stuarts: Party Conflict in a Divided Society, 1660–1715*. London: Longman.

't Hart, Marjolein C. 1989a. "Cities and Statemaking in the Dutch Republic, 1580–1680," *Theory and Society* 18: 663–87.

_____. 1989b. "Public Loans and Moneylenders in the Seventeenth Century Netherlands," *Economic and Social History in the Netherlands* 1: 119–40.

_____. 1991. "'The Devil or the Dutch': Holland's Impact on the Financial Revolution in England, 1643–1694," *Parliaments, Estates and Representation* 11: 39–52.

_____. 1993. *The Making of a Bourgeois State: War, Politics and Finance during the Dutch Revolt*. Manchester: Manchester University Press.

Harter, H. Leon. 1969. *Order Statistics and Their Use in Testing and Estimation*. Vol. 2. Washington, D.C.: Aerospace Research Laboratories, United States Air Force.

Haskell, Thomas L., and Richard F. Teichgraeber III. 1993. "Introduction," in *The Culture of the Market*. Thomas L. Haskell and Richard F. Teichgraeber III, eds. Cambridge: Cambridge University Press.

Havighurst, Alfred F. 1950. "The Judiciary and Politics in the Reign of Charles II," *Law Quarterly Review* 66: 62–78, 229–52.

_____. 1953. "James II and the Twelve Men in Scarlet," *Law Quarterly Review* 69: 522–46.

Hayton, David. 1990. "Moral Reform and Country Politics in the Late Seventeenth-Century House of Commons," *Past and Present* 128: 48–91.

Hayton, David, and Clyve Jones, eds. 1979. *A Register of Parliamentary Lists 1660–1761*. Leicester: University of Leicester History Department Occasional Publication #1.

Heal, Ambrose. 1935. *The London Goldsmiths 1200–1800*. Cambridge: Cambridge University Press.

Hechter, Michael. 1987. *Principles of Group Solidarity*. Berkeley: University of California Press.

Henning, B. D., ed. 1940. *The Parliamentary Diary of Sir Edward Dering 1670–1673*. New Haven: Yale University Press.

_____. 1983. *The House of Commons 1660–1690*. London: Secker and Warburg.

Henriques, H.S.Q. 1908. *The Jews and the English Law*. Oxford: Oxford University Press.

Hill, B. W. 1971. "The Change of Government and the 'Loss of the City', 1710–1711," *Economic History Review* 24(3): 395–413.

Hill, B. W. 1976. *The Growth of Parliamentary Parties, 1689–1742*. Hamden, U.K.: Archon Books.

———. 1988. *Robert Harley: Speaker, Secretary of State and Premier Minister*. New Haven: Yale University Press.

———. 1989. *Sir Robert Walpole: 'Sole and Prime Minister'*. London: Hamish Hamilton.

Hilton, Rodney. 1976. "Introduction," *The Transition from Feudalism to Capitalism*. Rodney Hilton, ed. London: Verso.

Hintze, Otto. 1975. *The Historical Essays of Otto Hintze*. Felix Gilbert, ed. New York: Oxford University Press.

Hirschman, Albert O. 1970. *Exit, Voice and Loyalty*. Cambridge: Harvard University Press.

———. 1977. *The Passions and the Interests: Political Arguments for Capitalism before its Triumph*. Princeton: Princeton University Press.

Hirst, Derek. 1975. *The Representative of the People? Voters and Voting in England under the Early Stuarts*. Cambridge: Cambridge University Press.

Hoadley, John F. 1980. "The Emergence of Political Parties in Congress, 1789–1803," *American Political Science Review* 74: 757–79.

Hodgson, Geoffrey M. 1988. *Economics and Institutions*. Oxford: Polity Press.

Hoffman, Philip T. 1994. "Early Modern France, 1450–1700," in *Fiscal Crises, Liberty, and Representative Government 1450–1789*. Philip T. Hoffman and Kathryn Norberg, eds. Stanford: Stanford University Press.

Holden, J. Milnes. 1951. "Bills of Exchange During the Seventeenth Century," *Law Quarterly Review* 67: 230–48.

———. 1955. *The History of Negotiable Instruments in English Law*. London: Athlone Press.

Holdsworth, William. 1915. "The Origins and Early History of Negotiable Instruments," *Law Quarterly Review* 31: 12–29.

———. 1937a. *A History of English Law*. Vol. 7. 2d ed. London: Methuen and Co.

———. 1937b. *A History of English Law*. Vol. 8. 2d ed. London: Methuen and Co.

———. 1944. *A History of English Law*. Vol. 9. 3d ed. London: Methuen and Co.

Holmes, Geoffrey. 1967. *British Politics in the Age of Anne*. London: Macmillan.

———. 1969. "Harley, St. John and the Death of the Tory Party," in *Britain After the Glorious Revolution*. Geoffrey Holmes, ed. New York: St. Martin's Press.

———. 1973. *The Trial of Doctor Sacheverell*. London: Eyre Methuen.

———. 1993. *The Making of a Great Power: Late Stuart and Early Georgian Britain, 1660–1722*. London: Longman.

Holton, R. J. 1985. *The Transition from Feudalism to Capitalism*. London: Macmillan.

———. 1992. *Economy and Society*. London: Routlege and Kegan Paul.

Hoppit, Julian. 1986. "Financial Crises in Eighteenth-century England," *Economic History Review* 39: 39–58.

———. 1987. *Risk and Failure in English Business 1700–1800*. Cambridge: Cambridge University Press.

Horsefield, J. Keith. 1960. *British Monetary Experiments 1650–1710*. London: G. Bell and Sons.

———. 1977. "The Beginnings of Paper Money in England," *Journal of European Economic History* 6(1): 117–32.

_____. 1982. "The 'Stop of the Exchequer' Revisited," *Economic History Review* 35(4): 511–28.

Horwitz, Henry. 1968. *Revolution Politicks: The Career of Daniel Finch Second Earl of Nottingham, 1647–1730*. Cambridge: Cambridge University Press.

_____. 1977. *Parliament, Policy and Politics in the Reign of William III*. Newark: University of Delaware Press.

_____. 1978. "The East India Trade, The Politicians, and the Constitution: 1689–1702," *Journal of British Studies* 17(2): 1–18.

Houblon, Lady Alice A. 1907. *The Houblon Family*. London: Archibald Constable.

van Houtte, J.A. 1977. *An Economic History of the Low Countries 800–1800*. New York: St. Martin's.

Hughes, Edward. 1934. *Studies in Administration and Finance 1558–1825*. Manchester: Manchester University Press.

Hume, David. 1955. "Of Public Credit," in *Writings on Economics*. Eugene Rotwein, ed. London: Nelson.

Hutton, Ronald. 1985. *The Restoration: A Political and Religious History of England and Wales 1658–1667*. Oxford: Oxford University Press.

Inikori, Joseph. 1990. "The Credit Needs of the African Trade and the Development of the Credit Economy in England," *Explorations in Economic History* 27: 197–231.

Isard, Peter. 1977. "How Far Can We Push the 'Law of One Price'?" *American Economic Review* 67: 942–48.

Israel, Jonathan I. 1985. *European Jewry in the Age of Mercantilism, 1550–1750*. Oxford: Clarendon Press.

_____. 1989a. "The Dutch Republic and its Jews During the Conflict over the Spanish Succession (1699–1715)," in *Dutch Jewish History*. Jozeph Michman, ed. Maastricht: Van Gorcum.

_____. 1989b. *Dutch Primacy in World Trade, 1585–1740*. Oxford: Clarendon Press.

_____. 1990. *Empires and Entrepots: The Dutch, the Spanish Monarchy and the Jews, 1585–1713*. London: Hambledon Press.

Jackson, Earnest, ed. 1894. *Letter-Books of John Hervey, First Earl of Bristol*. Vol. 1. Wells: E. Jackson.

Jago, Charles. 1973. "The Influence of Debt on the Relations between Crown and Aristocracy in Seventeenth-Century Castile," *Economic History Review* 26: 218–36.

_____. 1981. "Habsburg Absolutism and the Cortes of Castile," *American Historical Review* 86: 307–26.

Jennings, Robert M., and Andrew P. Trout. 1982. *The Tontine*. Philadelphia: S. S. Huebner Foundation University of Pennsylvania.

Jevons, W. Stanley. 1931. *The Theory of Political Economy*. 4th ed. London: Macmillan & Co.

John, A. H. 1953. "Insurance Investment and the London Money Market of the 18th Century," *Economica* 20: 137–58.

Johnson, Herbert Alan. 1963. *The Law Merchant and Negotiable Instruments in Colonial New York 1664 to 1730*. Chicago: Loyola University Press.

Johnson, Paul. 1987. *A History of the Jews*. New York: Harper and Row.

Jones, Clyve. 1976. "Debates in the House of Lords on 'The Church in Danger' 1705, and on Dr. Sacheverell's Impeachment, 1710," *Historical Journal* 19(3): 759–71.

Jones, D. W. 1970. *London Overseas-Merchant Groups at the end of the Seventeenth Century and the Moves Against the East India Company*. Ph.D. dissertation. Oxford University.

––––––. 1972. "London Merchants and the Crisis of the 1690s," in *Crisis and Order in English Towns 1500–1700*. Peter Clark and Paul Slack, eds. Toronto: University of Toronto Press.

––––––. 1988. *War and Economy in the Age of William III and Marlborough*. Oxford: Basil Blackwell.

––––––. 1991. "Sequel to Revolution: The economics of England's emergence as a Great Power, 1688–1712," in *The Anglo-Dutch Moment*. Jonathan I. Israel, ed. Cambridge: Cambridge University Press.

Jones, J. R. 1961. *The First Whigs: The Politics of the Exclusion Crisis 1678–1683*. Oxford: Oxford University Press.

––––––. 1978. *Country and Court: England 1658–1714*. London: Edward Arnold.

––––––. 1979. "Parties and Parliament," in *The Restored Monarchy 1660–1688*. J. R. Jones, ed. London: Macmillan.

––––––. 1987. *Charles II, Royal Politician*. London: Allen and Unwin.

––––––. 1994. "Fiscal Policies, Liberties, and Representative Government during the Reigns of the Last Stuarts," in *Fiscal Crises, Liberty, and Representative Government 1450–1789*. Philip T. Hoffman and Kathryn Norberg, eds. Stanford: Stanford University Press.

Jones, S.R.H. 1993. "Transaction costs, institutional change, and the emergence of a market economy in later Anglo-Saxon England," *Economic History Review* 46: 658–78.

Jones, Stephen R. G. 1984. *The Economics of Conformism*. Oxford: Basil Blackwell.

Kamen, Henry. 1980. *Spain in the Later Seventeenth Century, 1665–1700*. London: Longman.

––––––. 1991. *Spain 1469–1714*. 2d ed. London: Longman.

Karpoff, Jonathan M., and Edward M. Rice. 1989. "Organizational Form, Share Transferability, and Firm Performance," *Journal of Financial Economics* 24: 69–105.

Kearney, H. F. 1958. "The Political Background to English Mercantilism, 1695–1700," *Economic History Review* 11: 484–96.

Kellett, J. R. 1958. "The Breakdown of Gild and Corporation Control Over the Handicraft and Retail Trade in London," *Economic History Review* 10: 381–94.

Kenyon, J. P. 1966. *The Stuart Constitution 1603–1688*. Cambridge: Cambridge University Press.

Kerridge, Eric. 1988. *Trade and Banking in Early Modern England*. Manchester: Manchester University Press.

Kettering, Sharon. 1986. *Patrons, Brokers, and Clients in Seventeenth-Century France*. New York: Oxford University Press.

Khan, Shafaat Ahmad. 1923. *The East India Trade in the XVIIth Century*. Oxford: Oxford University Press.

Kindleberger, Charles P. 1984. *A Financial History of Western Europe*. London: George Allen & Unwin.

Kishlansky, Mark A. 1986. *Parliamentary Selection: Social and Political Choice in Early Modern England*. Cambridge: Cambridge University Press.

Knight, Jack. 1992. *Institutions and Social Conflict*. Cambridge: Cambridge University Press.

Krasner, Stephen D. 1978. "United States Commercial and Monetary Policy," in *Between Power and Plenty*. Peter J. Katzenstein, ed. Madison: University of Wisconsin Press.

Lachmann, Richard. 1987. *From Manor to Market: Structural Changes in England, 1536–1640*. Madison: University of Wisconsin Press.

La Croix, Sumner J. 1989. "Homogeneous Middleman Groups: What Determines the Homogeneity?" *Journal of Law, Economics, and Organization* 5: 211–22.

Laing, Lionel H. 1946. "Historic Origins of Admiralty Jurisdiction in England," *Michigan Law Review* 45: 163–82.

Lambert, Sheila. 1990. "Committees, Religion, and Parliamentary Encroachment on Royal Authority in Early Stuart England," *English Historical Review* 414: 60–95.

Landa, Janet T. 1981. "A Theory of the Ethnically Homogeneous Middleman Group: An Institutional Alternative to Contract Law," *Journal of Legal Studies* 10: 349–62.

Landau, Norma. 1979. "Independence, Deference, and Voter Participation," *Historical Journal* 22(3): 561–83.

Landes, David S. 1969. *The Unbound Prometheus*. Cambridge: Cambridge University Press.

Lane, Frederic C. 1958. "Economic Consequences of Organized Violence," *Journal of Economic History* 18: 410–17.

Langford, Paul. 1991. *Public Life and the Propertied Englishman, 1689–1798*. Oxford: Clarendon Press.

La Palombara, Joseph. 1966. "The Origin and Development of Political Parties," in *Political Parties and Political Development*. Joseph La Palombara and Myron Weiner, eds. Princeton: Princeton University Press.

Larson, Henrietta M. 1936. *Jay Cooke, Private Banker*. Cambridge: Harvard University Press.

Lazonick, William. 1991. *Business Organization and the Myth of the Market Economy*. Cambridge: Cambridge University Press.

Lease, Ronald C., John J. McConnell, and Wayne H. Mikkelson. 1983. "The Market Value of Control in Publicly-Traded Corporations," *Journal of Financial Economics* 11: 439–71.

Lee, Maurice Jr. 1965. *The Cabal*. Urbana: University of Illinois Press.

Lenman, Bruce. 1980. *The Jacobite Risings in Britain, 1689–1746*. London: Eyre Methuen.

LeRoy, Stephen F. 1989. "Efficient Capital Markets and Martingales," *Journal of Economic Literature* 27: 1583–1621.

Letwin, William. 1963. *The Origins of Scientific Economics: English Economic Thought 1660–1776*. London: Methuen.

Levi, Margaret. 1988. *Of Rule and Revenue*. Berkeley: University of California Press.

Libecap, Gary D. 1986. "Property Rights in Economic History," *Explorations in Economic History* 23: 227–52.

———. 1989. *Contracting for Property Rights*. Cambridge: Cambridge University Press.

Lillywhite, Bryant. 1963. *London Coffee Houses*. London: George Allen & Unwin.

Lindegren, Jan. 1985. "The Swedish 'Military State,' 1560–1720," *Scandinavian Journal of History* 10: 305–36.

Lossky, Andrew. 1970. "International Relations in Europe," *The New Cambridge Modern History*. Vol. 6. J. S. Bromley, ed. Cambridge: Cambridge University Press.

Lougheed, Peter. 1980. *The East India Company in English Domestic Politics, 1657–1688*. Ph.D. dissertation. Oxford University.

Lovett, A. W. 1980. "The Castilian Bankruptcy of 1575," *Historical Journal* 23: 899–911.

Lundkvist, Sven. 1973. "The Experience of Empire: Sweden as a Great Power," in *Sweden's Age of Greatness 1632–1718*. Michael Roberts, ed. London: Macmillan.

Lynch, John. 1991. *Spain 1516–1598: From Nation State to World Empire*. Oxford: Blackwell.

———. 1992. *The Hispanic World in Crisis and Change 1598–1700*. Oxford: Blackwell.

Lynn, John A. 1993. "How War Fed War: The Tax of Violence and Contributions during the *Grand Siècle*," *Journal of Modern History* 65: 286–310.

Macaulay, Stewart. 1963. "Non-Contractual Relations in Business," *American Sociological Review* 28: 55–69.

———. 1977. "Elegant Models, Empirical Pictures, and the Complexities of Contract," *Law and Society Review* 11(3): 507–28.

MacLachlan, A. D. 1969. "The Road to Peace 1710–13," in *Britain After the Glorious Revolution*. Geoffrey Holmes, ed. New York: St. Martin's Press.

MacNeil, Ian R. 1974. "The Many Futures of Contract," *Southern California Law Review* 47: 691–816.

Mandeville, Bernard. 1970 [1723]. *The Fable of the Bees*. Philip Harth, ed. Harmondsworth: Penguin Books.

Mann, Michael. 1984. "The Autonomous Power of the State," *Archives Européenes de Sociologie* 25: 185–213.

———. 1986. *The Sources of Social Power*. Vol. 1. Cambridge: Cambridge University Press.

Marshall, Alfred. 1938. *Principles of Economics*. 8th ed. London: Macmillan and Co.

Marvel, Howard P. 1976. "The Economics of Information and Retail Gasoline Price Behavior: An Empirical Analysis," *Journal of Political Economy* 84: 1033–60.

Marx, Karl. 1973. *Grundrisse*. Martin Nicolaus, trans. New York: Vintage Books.

———. 1976. *Capital*. Vol. 1. Ben Fowkes, trans. New York: Vintage Books.

———. 1978. "Wage Labour and Capital," in *The Marx-Engels Reader*. Robert C. Tucker, ed. New York: Norton.

Marx, Karl, and Frederick Engels. 1947. *The German Ideology*. C. J. Arthur, ed. New York: International Publishers.

Mathias, Peter, and Patrick O'Brien. 1976. "Taxation in Britain and France, 1715–1810," *Journal of European Economic History* 5: 601–50.

Matthews, George T. 1958. *The Royal General Farms in Eighteenth-Century France*. New York: Columbia University Press.

Matthews, R.C.O. 1986. "The Economics of Institutions and the Sources of Growth," *Economic Journal* 96: 903–18.

Maynes, E. Scott, Robin A. Douthitt, Greg J. Duncan, and Loren V. Geistfeld. 1984. "Informationally Imperfect Markets," in *The Collection and Analysis of Economic and Consumer Behavior Data*. Seymour Sudman and Mary A. Spaeth, eds. Urbana: University of Illinois.

McAdam, Doug. 1982. *Political Process and the Development of Black Insurgency 1930–1970*. Chicago: University of Chicago Press.

McInnes, Angus. 1970. *Robert Harley, Puritan Politician*. London: Victor Gollancz.

Meekings, C.A.F. 1969. "The City Loans on the Hearth Tax, 1664–1668," in *Studies in London History*. A.E.J. Hollaender and William Kellaway, eds. London: Hodder and Stoughton.

Melton, Frank T. 1986. *Sir Robert Clayton and the Origins of English Deposit Banking, 1658–1685*. Cambridge: Cambridge University Press.

Metcalf, Michael F. 1977. "The First 'Modern' Party System? Political parties, Sweden's Age of Liberty and the historians," *Scandinavian Journal of History* 2: 265–87.

———. 1981. "Structuring Parliamentary Politics: Party Organization in Eighteenth-century Sweden," *Parliaments, Estates and Representation* 1: 35–49.

Mettam, Roger. 1990. "France," in *Absolutism in Seventeenth-Century Europe*. John Miller, ed. London: Macmillan.

Meuvret, Jean. 1970. "The Condition of France, 1688–1715," in *The New Cambridge Modern History*. Vol. 6. J. S. Bromley, ed. Cambridge: Cambridge University Press.

Milgrom, Paul R., Douglass C. North, and Barry R. Weingast. 1990. "The Role of Institutions in the Revival of Trade," *Economics and Politics* 2: 1–24.

Miller, John. 1973. *Popery and Politics in England 1660–1688*. Cambridge: Cambridge University Press.

———. 1984. "The Potential for Absolutism in Later Stuart England," *History* 69: 187–207.

Milsom, S.F.C. 1981. *Historical Foundations of the Common Law*. 2d ed. Toronto: Butterworths.

Mingione, Enzo. 1991. *Fragmented Societies: A Sociology of Economic Life beyond the Market Paradigm*. Paul Goodrick, trans. Oxford: Basil Blackwell.

Minowitz, Peter. 1993. *Profits, Priests, and Princes: Adam Smith's Emancipation of Economics from Politics and Religion*. Stanford: Stanford University Press.

Mirowski, Philip. 1981. "The Rise (and Retreat) of a Market: English Joint Stock Shares in the Eighteenth Century," *Journal of Economic History* 41: 559–77.

———. 1987. "What Do Markets Do? Efficiency Tests of the 18th-Century London Stock Market," *Explorations in Economic History* 24(2): 107–29.

Mitchell, B. R. 1962. *Abstract of British Historical Statistics*. Cambridge: Cambridge University Press.

———. 1988. *British Historical Statistics*. New York: Cambridge University Press.

Monter, E. William. 1969. "Swiss Investment in England, 1697–1720," *Rev. Int. D'Hist. De La Banque* 2: 285–98.

Moote, A. Lloyd. 1964. "The French Crown Versus its Judicial and Financial Officials, 1615–83," *Journal of Modern History* 34: 146–60.

Morgan, E. Victor, and W. A. Thomas. 1962. *The Stock Exchange*. London: Elek Books.

Morrill, J. S. 1978. "French Absolutism as Limited Monarchy," *Historical Journal* 21: 961–72.

Motomura, Akira. 1991. *War, Money, and Sovereign Policy: Early Modern Spain's Public Finance and Currency Policies*. Ph.D. dissertation. Evanston: Northwestern University.

Mousnier, Roland E. 1979. *The Institutions of France Under the Absolute Monarchy 1598–1789*. Vol. 1. Brian Pearce, trans. Chicago: University of Chicago Press.

———. 1984. *The Institutions of France Under the Absolute Monarchy 1598–1789*. Vol. 2. Arthur Goldhammer, trans. Chicago: University of Chicago Press.

Mueller, Dennis C. 1989. *Public Choice II*. Cambridge: Cambridge University Press.

Muldrew, Craig. 1993a. "Interpreting the Market: the ethics of credit and community relations in early modern England," *Social History* 18: 163–83.

———. 1993b. "Credit and the Courts: Debt Litigation in a Seventeenth-Century Urban Community," *Economic History Review* 46: 23–38.

Murphy, Antoin E. 1986. *Richard Cantillon: Entrepreneur and Economist*. Oxford: Clarendon Press.

Neal, Larry. 1987. "The Integration and Efficiency of the London and Amsterdam Stock Markets in the Eighteenth Century," *Journal of Economic History* 47: 97–115.

———. 1988. "The Rise of a Financial Press: London and Amsterdam, 1681–1810," *Business History* 30(2): 163–78.

———. 1990. *The Rise of Financial Capitalism: International Capital Markets in the Age of Reason*. Cambridge: Cambridge University Press.

Newman, A. N. 1970. "Political Parties in the Reigns of William III and Anne: the Evidence of Division Lists: a Supplementary Note," *Bulletin of the Institute of Historical Research* 43: 231–33.

Nichols, Glenn O. 1971. "English Government Borrowing, 1660–1688," *Journal of British Studies* 10(2): 83–104.

———. 1987. "Intermediaries and the Development of English Government Borrowing," *Business History* 29(1): 27–46.

North, Douglass C. 1981. *Structure and Change in Economic History*. New York: Norton.

———. 1990. *Institutions, Institutional Change and Economic Performance*. Cambridge: Cambridge University Press.

North, Douglass C., and Robert Paul Thomas. 1973. *The Rise of the Western World*. Cambridge: Cambridge University Press.

North, Douglass C., and Barry R. Weingast. 1989. "Constitutions and Commitment: The Evolution of Institutions Governing Public Choice in Seventeenth-Century England," *Journal of Economic History* 49: 803–32.

O'Barr, William M., and John M. Conley. 1992a. *Fortune and Folly: The Wealth and Power of Institutional Investing*. Homewood, Ill.: Business One Irwin.

———. 1992b. "Managing Relationships: The Culture of Institutional Investing," *Financial Analyst's Journal* September/October: 21–27.

O'Brien, Patrick K. 1985. "Agriculture and the Home Market for English Industry, 1660–1820," *English Historical Review* 100: 773–99.

———. 1988. "The Political Economy of British Taxation, 1660–1815," *Economic History Review* 41(1): 1–32.

Ogg, David. 1955. *England in the Reign of Charles II*. 2d ed. Oxford: Clarendon Press.

Orlove, Benjamin. 1986. "Barter and Cash Sale on Lake Titicaca: A Test of Competing Approaches," *Current Anthropology* 27: 85–98.

Padgen, Anthony. 1988. "The Destruction of Trust and its Economic Consequences in the Case of Eighteenth-century Naples," in *Trust: Making and Breaking Cooperative Relations*. Diego Gambetta, ed. Oxford: Basil Blackwell.

Papillon, A.F.W. 1887. *Memoirs of Thomas Papillon of London Merchant*. Reading: Joseph Beecroft.

Parker, David. 1989. "Sovereignty, Absolutism and the Function of the Law in Seventeenth-Century France," *Past and Present* 122: 36–74.

Parker, Geoffrey. 1972. *The Army of Flanders and the Spanish Road 1567–1659*. Cambridge: Cambridge University Press.

————. 1973. *The Emergence of Modern Finance in Europe 1500–1730*. London: Fontana.

————. 1985. *The Dutch Revolt*. Rev. ed. London: Penguin.

————. 1988. *The Military Revolution*. Cambridge: Cambridge University Press.

Parsons, Brian. 1974. *The Behavior of Prices on the London Stock Market in the Early Eighteenth Century*. Ph.D. dissertation. University of Chicago.

Parsons, Talcott. 1982. *Institutions and Social Evolution*. Leon H. Mayhew, ed. Chicago: University of Chicago Press.

Peregrine, Henry, and Rennie Hoare. 1955. *Hoare's Bank: A Record 1672–1955*. London: Collins.

Perry, Norma. 1984. "Anglo-Jewry, the Law, Religious Conviction, and Self-interest (1655–1753)," *Journal of European Studies* 14: 1–23.

Pinaud, Pierre-François. 1991. "The Settlement of the Public Debt from the *Ancien Régime*, 1790–1810," *French History* 5: 414–25.

Pitt, H. G. 1970. "The Pacification of Utrecht," in *The New Cambridge Modern History*. Vol. 6. J. S. Bromley, ed. Cambridge: Cambridge University Press.

Plattner, Stuart. 1989. "Introduction," in *Economic Anthropology*. Stuart Plattner, ed. Stanford: Stanford University Press.

Plucknett, T. F. Theodore. 1956. *A Concise History of the Common Law*. 5th ed. Boston: Little, Brown, and Co.

Plumb, J. H. 1956. *Sir Robert Walpole: The Making of a Statesman*. London: Cresset Press.

————. 1967. *The Growth of Political Stability in England 1675–1725*. Atlantic Highlands, N.J.: Humanities Press.

————. 1969. "The Growth of the Electorate in England from 1600 to 1715," *Past and Present* 45: 90–116.

Plutarch. 1989. *Plutarch's Lives*. Vol. VIII. Bernadotte Perrin, trans. Cambridge: Harvard University Press.

Pocock, J.G.A. 1979. "The Mobility of Property and the Rise of Eighteenth-Century Sociology," in *Theories of Property: Aristotle to the Present*. Anthony Parel and Thomas Flanagan, eds. Waterloo: Wilfrid Laurier University Press.

Podolny, Joel. 1993. "A Status-based Model of Market Competition," *American Journal of Sociology* 98: 829–72.

Polachek, S. W., and W. S. Siebert. *The Economics of Earnings*. Cambridge: Cambridge University Press.

Polanyi, Karl. 1944. *The Great Transformation*. Boston: Beacon Press.

Pollins, Harold. 1982. *Economic History of the Jews in England*. Rutherford, N.J.: Fairleigh Dickinson University Press.

Popkin, Samuel L. 1979. *The Rational Peasant*. Berkeley: University of California Press.

Posner, Richard A. 1986. *Economic Analysis of Law*. 3d ed. Boston: Little, Brown, and Co..

Postan, M. M. 1973. *Medieval Trade and Finance*. Cambridge: Cambridge University Press.

Poulantzas, Nicos. 1975. *Political Power and Social Classes*. Timothy O'Hagan, trans. London: Verso.

Price, Jacob. 1954. "Notes on Some London Price-Currents, 1667–1715," *Economic History Review* 7(2): 240–50.

———. 1991. "Transaction Costs: a note on merchant credit and the organization of private trade," in *The Political Economy of Merchant Empires*. James D. Tracy, ed. Cambridge: Cambridge University Press.

———. 1992. "The Bank of England's Discount Activity and the Merchants of London, 1694–1773," in *Industry and Finance in Early Modern History*. Ian Blanchard, Anthony Goodman, and Jennifer Newman, eds. Stuttgart: Franz Steiner Verlag.

Przeworski, Adam, and Michael Wallerstein. 1988. "Structural Dependence of the State on Capital," *American Political Science Review* 82: 11–29.

Rabb, Theodore K. 1967. *Enterprise and Empire: Merchant and Gentry Investment in the Expansion of England, 1575–1630*. Cambridge: Harvard University Press.

Rabinowicz, Oskar K. 1974. *Sir Solomon de Medina*. London: Jewish Historical Society of England.

Rasler, Karen A., and William R. Thompson. 1985. "War Making and State Making: Governmental Expenditures, Tax Revenues, and Global Wars," *American Political Science Review* 79: 491–507.

Reddy, William M. 1987. *Money and Liberty in Modern Europe*. Cambridge: Cambridge University Press.

Reitan, E. A. 1970. "From Revenue to Civil List, 1689–1792," *Historical Journal* 13(4): 571–88.

Richards, James O. 1972. *Party Propaganda Under Queen Anne*. Athens: University of Georgia Press.

Richards, R. D. 1929. *The Early History of Banking in England*. Westminster: P. S. King and Son.

———. 1932. "The Bank of England and the South Sea Company," *Economic History* 7: 348–74.

———. 1934. "The First Fifty Years of the Bank of England (1694–1744)," in *History of the Principal Public Banks*. J. G. Van Dillen, ed. The Hague: Martinus Nijhoff.

Riker, William H., and Itai Sened. 1991. "A Political Theory of the Origin of Property Rights: Airport Slots," *American Journal of Political Science* 35: 951–69.

Riley, James C. 1980. *International Government Finance and the Amsterdam Capital Market, 1740–1815*. Cambridge: Cambridge University Press.

_____. 1986. *The Seven Years War and the Old Regime in France: The Economic and Financial Toll*. Princeton: Princeton University Press.

Robert, R. 1952. "A Short History of Tallies," *Accounting Research* 3: 220–29.

Roberts, Clayton. 1977. "The Constitutional Significance of the Financial Settlement of 1690," *Historical Journal* 20(1): 59–76.

_____. 1982. "The Fall of the Godolphin Ministry," *Journal of British Studies* 22: 71–93.

Roberts, Michael. 1967. *Essays in Swedish History*. London: Weidenfeld and Nicolson.

_____. 1979. *The Swedish Imperial Experience 1560–1718*. Cambridge: Cambridge University Press.

_____. 1992. *Gustavus Adolphus*. 2d ed. London: Longman.

Roberts, Philip, ed. 1975. *The Diary of Sir David Hamilton 1709–1714*. Oxford: Clarendon Press.

Rogers, J. E. Thorold. 1887. *The First Nine Years of the Bank of England*. Oxford: Clarendon Press.

Rogers, James Steven. 1995. *The Early History of the Law of Bills and Notes: A Study of the Origins of Anglo-American Commercial Law*. Cambridge: Cambridge University Press.

Roorda, D. J. 1964. "The Ruling Classes in Holland in the Seventeenth Century," *Britain and the Netherlands* 2: 109–32.

Root, Hilton L. 1987. *Peasants and King in Burgundy: Agrarian Foundations of French Absolutism*. Berkeley: University of California Press.

_____. 1994. *The Fountain of Privilege: Political Foundations of Markets in Old Regime France and England*. Berkeley: University of California Press.

Roseveare, Henry. 1962. *The Advancement of the King's Credit 1660–1672*. Ph.D. dissertation. Cambridge University.

_____. 1969. *The Treasury*. New York: Columbia University Press.

_____. 1973. *The Treasury 1660–1870*. London: George Allen and Unwin.

_____. 1987. *Markets and Merchants of the Late Seventeenth Century: The Marescoe-David Letters, 1668–1680*. Oxford: Oxford University Press.

_____. 1991. *The Financial Revolution 1660–1760*. London: Longman.

Ross, J. M. 1970. "Naturalisation of Jews in England," *Transactions of the Jewish Historical Society of England* 24: 59–72.

Rothschild, Michael. 1973. "Models of Market Organization with Imperfect Information," *Journal of Political Economy* 81: 1283–1308.

Routledge, R. A. 1982. "The Legal Status of the Jews in England 1190–1790," *Journal of Legal History* 3: 91–124.

Rubini, Dennis. 1970. "Politics and the Battle for the Banks, 1688–1697," *English Historical Review* 85: 693–714.

Russell, Conrad. 1983. "The Nature of a Parliament in Early Stuart England," in *Before the English Civil War*. Howard Tomlinson, ed. New York: St. Martin's Press.

Sachse, William L. 1975. *Lord Somers: A Political Portrait*. Manchester: Manchester University Press.

Sahlins, Marshall. 1976. *Culture and Practical Reason*. Chicago: University of Chicago Press.

Sainty, J. C. 1965. "The Tenure of Offices in the Exchequer," *English Historical Review* 80: 449–75.

Sandbrook, Richard. 1986. "The State and Economic Stagnation in Tropical Africa," *World Development* 14(3): 319–32.

Sartori, Giovanni. 1976. *Parties and Party Systems*. Vol. 1. Cambridge: Cambridge University Press.

Schaeper, Thomas J. 1990. "The Economic History of the Reign," in *The Reign of Louis XIV*. Paul Sonnino, ed. Atlantic Highlands, N.J.: Humanities Press.

Schattschneider, E. E. 1942. *Party Government*. New York: Holt, Rinehart and Winston.

Schofield, R. S. 1965. "The Geographical Distribution of Wealth in England, 1334–1649," *Economic History Review* 18: 483–510.

———. 1988. "Taxation and the Political Limits of the Tudor State," in *Law and Government Under the Tudors*. Claire Cross, David Loades, and J. J. Scarisbrick, eds. Cambridge: Cambridge University Press.

Schotter, Andrew. 1981. *The Economic Theory of Social Institutions*. Cambridge: Cambridge University Press.

Schumpeter, Joseph A. 1991. "The Crisis of the Tax State," in *The Economics and Sociology of Capitalism*. Richard Swedberg, ed. Princeton: Princeton University Press.

Schwoerer, Lois G. 1977. "Propaganda in the Revolution of 1688–89," *American Historical Review* 84(4): 843–74.

Scott, James C. 1976. *The Moral Economy of the Peasant*. New Haven: Yale University Press.

Scott, W. R. 1912. *The Constitution and Finance of English, Scottish and Irish Joint-Stock Companies to 1720*. 3 Vols. Cambridge: Cambridge University Press.

Seaward, Paul. 1988. *The Cavalier Parliament and the Reconstruction of the Old Regime, 1661–1667*. Cambridge: Cambridge University Press.

Sedgwick, Romney. 1970. *The House of Commons 1715–1754*. New York: Oxford University Press.

Selznick, Philip. 1949. *TVA and the Grass Roots*. Berkeley: University of California Press.

Shammas, Carole. 1975. "The 'Invisible Merchant' and Property Rights: The Misadventures of an Elizabethan Joint Stock Company," *Business History* 17: 95–108.

Shammas, Carole, Marylynn Salmon, and Michel Dahlin. 1987. *Inheritance in America: From Colonial Times to the Present*. New Brunswick: Rutgers University Press.

Shapiro, Barbara. 1975. "Law Reform in Seventeenth Century England," *American Journal of Legal History* 19: 280–312.

Sharpe, Kevin. 1986. "Crown, Parliament and Locality: Government and Communication in Early Stuart England," *English Historical Review* 399: 321–50.

Sharpe, Reginald R. 1894. *London and the Kingdom*. Vol. 2. London: Longmans, Green and Co.

Shavell, Steven. 1987. *Economic Analysis of Accident Law*. Cambridge: Harvard University Press.

Shaw, W. A., ed. 1911. "Letters of Denization and Acts of Naturalization for Aliens in England and Ireland, 1603–1700," *Publications of the Huguenot Society of London* 18.

―――. 1923. "Letters of Denization and Acts of Naturalization for Aliens in England and Ireland, 1701–1800," *Publications of the Huguenot Society of London* 27.

Sheffrin, Steven M. *Rational Expectations*. Cambridge: Cambridge University Press.

Sherman, Arnold A. 1976. "Pressure from Leadenhall: The East India Company Lobby, 1660–1678," *Business History Review* 50: 1–35.

Shleifer, Andrei, and Lawrence H. Summers. 1990. "The Noise Trader Approach to Finance," *Journal of Economic Perspectives* 4: 19–33.

Silver, Allan. 1990. "Friendship in Commercial Society," *American Journal of Sociology* 95: 1474–1504.

Simpson, A.W.B. 1986. *A History of the Land Law*. 2d ed. Oxford: Clarendon Press.

Sims, John, ed. 1984. *A Handlist of British Parliamentary Poll Books*. Leicester: University of Leicester Occasional Publication No. 4.

Skocpol, Theda. 1992. *Protecting Soldiers and Mothers*. Cambridge: Harvard University Press.

Smelser, Neil. 1959. *Social Change in the Industrial Revolution*. Chicago: University of Chicago Press.

―――. 1963. *The Sociology of Economic Life*. Englewood Cliffs, N.J.: Prentice-Hall.

Smelser, Neil J., and Richard Swedberg. 1994. "The Sociological Perspective on the Economy," in *The Handbook of Economic Sociology*. Neil J. Smelser and Richard Swedberg, eds. Princeton: Princeton University Press.

Smith, Adam. 1976 [1790]. *The Theory of Moral Sentiments*. Indianapolis: Liberty Classics.

Smith, C. F. 1929. "The Early History of the London Stock Exchange," *American Economic Review* 19: 206–16.

Smith, Charles W. 1989. *Auctions: The Social Construction of Value*. Berkeley: University of California Press.

Smith, Woodruff D. 1984. "The Function of Commercial Centers in the Modernization of European Capitalism: Amsterdam as an Information Exchange in the Seventeenth Century," *Journal of Economic History* 44: 985–1005.

Snyder, Henry L. 1972. "Party Configurations in the Early Eighteenth-century House of Commons," *Bulletin of the Institute of Historical Research* 45: 38–72.

―――. ed., 1975. *The Marlborough-Godolphin Correspondence*. 3 Vols. Clarendon Press: Oxford.

Speck, W. A. 1969. "Conflict in Society," in *Britain After the Glorious Revolution 1689–1714*. Geoffrey Holmes, ed. London: Macmillan.

―――. 1970. *Tory and Whig: The Struggle in the Constituencies 1701–1715*. London: Macmillan.

―――. 1972. "Political Propaganda in Augustan England," *Transactions of the Royal Historical Society* 5th series 22: 17–32.

―――. 1988. *Reluctant Revolutionaries: Englishmen and the Revolution of 1688*. Oxford: Oxford University Press.

Speck, W. A., and W. A. Gray. 1970. "Computer Analysis of Poll Books: an Initial Report," *Bulletin of the Institute of Historical Research* 43: 105–12.

Speck, W. A., and W. A. Gray, eds. 1981. *London Politics 1713–1717*. London: London Record Society.

Speck, W. A., W. A. Gray, and R. Hopkinson. 1975. "Computer Analysis of Poll Books: A Further Report," *Bulletin of the Institute of Historical Research* 48: 64–90.

Sperling, John G. 1955. *Godolphin and the Organization of Public Credit, 1702–1710.* Ph.D. dissertation. Cambridge University.

———. 1961. "The Division of 25 May 1711, on an Amendment to the South Sea Bill," *Historical Journal* 4: 191–217.

———. 1962a. *The South Sea Company.* Boston: Baker Library, Harvard Graduate School of Business Administration.

———. 1962b. "The International Payments Mechanism in the Seventeenth and Eighteenth Centuries," *Economic History Review* 14(3): 446–68.

Stabile, Donald R., and Jeffrey A. Cantor. 1991. *The Public Debt of the United States.* New York: Praeger.

Statt, Daniel. 1989. "The Birthright of an Englishman: the practice of naturalization and denization of immigrants under the later Stuarts and early Hanoverians," *Proceedings of the Huguenot Society* 25: 61–74.

———. 1990. "The City of London and the Controversy over Immigration, 1660–1722," *Historical Journal* 33: 45–61.

Steckley, George F. 1978. "Merchants and the Admiralty Court During the English Revolution," *American Journal of Legal History* 22: 137–75.

Steinmetz, George. 1993. *Regulating the Social: The Welfare State and Local Politics in Imperial Germany.* Princeton: Princeton University Press.

Stigler, George J. 1968. *The Organization of Industry.* Homewood, Ill.: Richard Irwin.

Stigler, George J. and Gary S. Becker. 1977. "De Gustibus Non Est Disputandum," *American Economic Review* 67: 76–90.

Stinchcombe, Arthur L. 1983. *Economic Sociology.* New York: Academic Press.

Stone, Lawrence. 1994. "Introduction," in *An Imperial State at War: Britain from 1689 to 1815.* Lawrence Stone, ed. London: Routledge.

Stone, Lawrence, and Jeanne C. Fawtier Stone. 1984. *An Open Elite? England 1540–1880.* Oxford: Clarendon Press.

Summers, Montagu, ed. 1927. *The Complete Works of Thomas Shadwell.* 5 Vols. London: Fortune Press.

Sundstrom, Roy A. 1992. *Sidney Godolphin: Servant of the State.* Newark: University of Delaware Press.

Sunstein, Cass R. 1991. "Why Markets Don't Stop Discrimination," *Social Philosophy and Policy* 8: 22–37.

Sutherland, L. S. 1934. "The Law Merchant in England in the Seventeenth and Eighteenth Centuries," *Transactions of the Royal Historical Society.* 4th series 17: 149–76.

———. 1952. *The East India Company in Eighteenth-Century Politics.* Oxford: Clarendon Press.

———. 1962. *A London Merchant, 1695–1774.* New York: Barnes and Noble.

Swart, K. W. 1949. *Sale of Offices in the Seventeenth Century.* The Hague: Martinus Nijhoff.

Swedberg, Richard. 1991. "Major Traditions of Economic Sociology," *Annual Review of Sociology* 17: 251–76.

Swedberg, Richard, and Mark Granovetter. 1992. "Introduction," in *The Sociology of Economic Life*. Mark Granovetter and Richard Swedberg, eds. Boulder: Westview.

Sweet, Charles. 1894. "Choses in Action," *Law Quarterly Review* 10: 303–17.

Swift, Jonathan. 1951. *Political Tracts*. Herbert Davis, ed. Oxford: Basil Blackwell.

Szechi, Daniel. 1986. "The Tory Party in the House of Commons 1710–1714," *Parliamentary History* 5: 1–16.

———. 1984. *Jacobitism and Tory Politics 1710–14*. Edinburgh: John Donald.

Tabellini, Guido. 1993. "The Politics of Intergenerational Redistribution," in *The Political Economy of Government Debt*. H.A.A. Verbon and F.A.A.M. van Winden, eds. Amsterdam: Elsevier.

Taylor, George V. 1967. "Noncapitalist Wealth and the Origins of the French Revolution," *American Historical Review* 72: 469–96.

Taylor, Michael. 1987. *The Possibility of Cooperation*. Cambridge: Cambridge University Press.

Teetor, Paul R. 1962. "England's Earliest Treatise on the Law Merchant," *American Journal of Legal History* 6: 178–210.

Telser, Lester G. 1973. "Searching for the Lowest Price," *American Economic Review* 63(2): 40–49.

———. 1981. "Why There Are Organized Futures Markets," *Journal of Law and Economics* 24: 1–22.

Telser, Lester G., and Harlow N. Higinbotham. 1977. "Organized Futures Markets: Costs and Benefits," *Journal of Political Economy* 85: 969–1000.

Temple, Sir William. 1972 [1673]. *Observations Upon the United Provinces of the Netherlands*. Sir George Clark, ed. Oxford: Clarendon Press.

Thompson, E. P. 1971. "The Moral Economy of the English Crowd in the Eighteenth-Century," *Past and Present* 50: 76–136.

Thompson, I.A.A. 1976. *War and Government in Habsburg Spain 1560–1620*. London: Athlone Press.

———. 1979. "The Purchase of Nobility in Castile, 1552–1700," *Journal of European Economic History* 8: 313–60.

———. 1982. "Crown and Cortes in Castile, 1590–1665," *Parliaments, Estates and Representation* 2: 29–45.

———. 1994. "Castile: Polity, Fiscality, and Fiscal Crisis," in *Fiscal Crises, Liberty, and Representative Government 1450–1789*. Philip T. Hoffman and Kathryn Norberg, eds. Stanford: Stanford University Press.

Thrupp, Sylvia L. 1948. *The Merchant Class of Medieval London*. Ann Arbor: University of Michigan Press.

Tigar, Michael E., and Madelaine R. Levy. 1977. *Law and the Rise of Capitalism*. New York: Monthly Review Press.

Tilly, Charles. 1975. "Reflections on the History of European State-Making," in *The Formation of National States in Western Europe*. Charles Tilly, ed. Princeton: Princeton University Press.

———. 1985. "War Making and State Making as Organized Crime," in *Bringing the State Back In*. Peter Evans, Dietrich Rueschemeyer, and Theda Skocpol, eds. Cambridge: Cambridge University Press.

———. 1986. *The Contentious French*. Cambridge: Belknap Press.

Tilly, Charles. 1990. *Coercion, Capital, and European States, A.D. 990–1990*. Cambridge: Basil Blackwell.

Tittler, Robert. 1994. "Money-Lending in the West Midlands: the Activities of Joyce Jefferies, 1638–49," *Historical Research* 67: 249–63.

de Tocqueville, Alexis. 1969. *Democracy in America*. J. P. Mayer, ed. George Lawrence, trans. New York: Anchor Books.

Tomlinson, Howard. 1975. "Place and Profit: An Examination of the Ordnance Office, 1660–1714," *Transactions of the Royal Historical Society*. 5th ser. 25: 55–75.

———. 1979. "Financial and Administrative Developments in England, 1660–88," in *The Restored Monarchy 1660–1688*. J. R. Jones, ed. London: Macmillan.

Tracy, James D. 1985. *A Financial Revolution in the Habsburg Netherlands: Renten and Renteniers in the County of Holland, 1515–1565*. Berkeley: University of California Press.

Trakman, Leon E. 1983. *The Law Merchant: The Evolution of Commercial Law*. Littleton, Colo.: Fred Rothman.

Upton, A. F. 1987. "The Riksdag of 1680 and the Establishment of Royal Absolutism in Sweden," *English Historical Review* 102: 281–308.

———. 1990. "Sweden," in *Absolutism in Seventeenth-Century Europe*. John Miller, ed. London: Macmillan.

Van Der Wee, Herman. 1977. "Monetary, Credit and Banking Systems," in *Cambridge Economic History of Europe*. Vol. 5. E. E. Rich and C. H. Wilson, eds. Cambridge: Cambridge University Press.

Van Nierop, H.F.K. 1993. *The Nobility of Holland: From Knights to Regents, 1500–1650*. Maarten Ultee, trans. Cambridge: Cambridge University Press.

Vandevelde, Kenneth J. 1980. "The New Property of the Nineteenth Century: The Development of the Modern Concept of Property," *Buffalo Law Review* 29: 325–67.

Veenendaal, A. J. 1970. "The War of the Spanish Succession in Europe," in *The New Cambridge Modern History*. Vol. 6. J. S. Bromley, ed. Cambridge: Cambridge University Press.

———. 1994. "Fiscal Crises and Constitutional Freedom in the Netherlands, 1450–1795," in *Fiscal Crises, Liberty, and Representative Government 1450–1789*. Philip T. Hoffman and Kathryn Norberg, eds. Stanford: Stanford University Press.

Veitch, John. 1986. "Repudiations and Confiscations by the Medieval State," *Journal of Economic History* 46: 31–36.

Veljanovski, Cento G. 1985. "The Role of Economics in the Common Law," *Research in Law and Economics* 7: 41–64.

van Velthoven, Ben, Harrie Verbon, and Frans van Winden. 1993. "The Political Economy of Government Debt: A Survey," in *The Political Economy of Government Debt*. H.A.A. Verbon and F.A.A.M. van Winden, eds. Amsterdam: Elsevier.

Vincent-Jones, Peter. 1989. "Contract and Business Transactions: A Socio-Legal Analysis," *Journal of Law and Society* 16(2): 166–86.

Voltaire. 1926 [1733]. *Letters Concerning the English Nation*. London: Peter Davies.

de Vries, Jan. 1976. *The Economy of Europe in an Age of Crisis, 1600–1750*. Cambridge: Cambridge University Press.

———. 1984. *European Urbanization 1500–1800*. Cambridge: Harvard University Press.

Walcott, Robert. 1956a. *English Politics in the Early Eighteenth Century*. Cambridge: Harvard University Press.

———. 1956b. "The East India Interest in the General Election of 1700–1701," *English Historical Review* 71: 223–39.

Wallerstein, Immanual. 1974. *The Modern World System I*. New York: Academic Press.

———. 1980. *The Modern World System II*. New York: Academic Press.

Walras, Léon. 1954. *Elements of Pure Economics*. William Jaffé, trans. Homewood, Ill.: Richard Irwin.

Walzer, Michael. 1983. *Spheres of Justice*. New York: Basic Books.

Waquet, Jean-Claude. 1982. "Who Profited from the Alienation of Public Revenues in Ancien Régime Societies?" *Journal of European Economic History* 11: 665–73.

Ward, W. R. 1953. *The English Land Tax in the Eighteenth Century*. London: Oxford University Press.

Ware, Alan. 1988. *Citizens, Parties, and the State: A Reappraisal*. Princeton: Princeton University Press.

Weakliem, David L. 1989. "The Employment Contract: A Test of the Transaction Cost Theory," *Sociological Forum* 4: 203–26.

Weber, Max. 1946. *From Max Weber*. H. H. Gerth and C. Wright Mills, eds. New York: Oxford University Press.

———. 1968. *Economy and Society*. Guenther Roth and Claus Wittich, eds. Berkeley: University of California Press.

———. 1981. *General Economic History*. Frank H. Knight, trans. New Brunswick: Transaction Books.

Weir, David R. 1989. "Tontines, Public Finance, and Revolution in France and England, 1688–1789," *Journal of Economic History* 49: 95–124.

White, Harrison C. 1981. "Where Do Markets Come From?" *American Journal of Sociology* 87: 517–47.

Williams, Harold, ed. 1948. *A Journal to Stella*. Oxford: Clarendon Press.

Williamson, Oliver E. 1975. *Markets and Hierarchies*. New York: The Free Press.

———. 1981a. "The Economics of Organization: The Transaction Cost Approach," *American Journal of Sociology* 87: 548–77.

———. 1981b. "The Modern Corporation: Origins, Evolution, Attributes," *Journal of Economic Literature* 19: 1537–68.

———. 1985. *The Economic Institutions of Capitalism*. New York: The Free Press.

Willman, Robert. 1974. "The Origins of 'Whig' and 'Tory' in English Political Language," *Historical Journal* 17(2): 247–64.

Wilson, Charles. 1968. *The Dutch Republic*. New York: McGraw-Hill.

———. 1978. *Profit and Power: A Study of England and the Dutch Wars*. The Hague: Martinus Nijhoff.

Winn, Jane Kaufman. 1994. "Relational Practices and the Marginalization of Law: Informal Financial Practices of Small Businesses in Taiwan," *Law and Society Review* 28: 193–232.

Witcombe, D. T. 1966. *Charles II and the Cavalier House of Commons, 1663–1674*. Manchester: Manchester University Press.

Wolfe, Alan. 1989. *Whose Keeper? Social Science and Moral Obligation*. Berkeley: University of California Press.

Wood, Alfred C. 1935. *A History of the Levant Company*. Oxford: Oxford University Press.

Woodhead, J. R. 1965. *The Rulers of London 1660–1689*. London: London and Middlesex Archaeological Society.

Wykes, David L. 1990. "Religious Dissent and the Penal Laws," *History* 75: 39–62.

Yates, JoAnne. 1989. *Control Through Communication: The Rise of System in American Management*. Baltimore: Johns Hopkins University Press.

Zelizer, Viviana A. 1979. *Morals and Markets: The Development of Life Insurance in the United States*. New York: Columbia University Press.

———. 1985. *Pricing the Priceless Child*. New York: Basic Books.

———. 1989. "The Social Meaning of Money," *American Journal of Sociology* 95(2): 342–77.

———. 1994. *The Social Meaning of Money: Pin Money, Paychecks, Poor Relief, and Other Currencies*. New York: Basic Books.

Zukin, Sharon, and Paul DiMaggio. 1990. "Introduction," in *Structures of Capital: The Social Organization of the Economy*. Cambridge: Cambridge University Press.

INDEX

absolutism, 15, 98, 106, 215n.43, 236n.113
Act of Settlement, 43
Act of Union, 43
Adams, Julia, 253n.129
Addison, Joseph, 6, 215n.63
Admiralty Courts, 129–30. *See also* Lex
   Mercatoria
Adolphus, Gustavus, 96, 232n.8. *See also*
   Sweden
Alexander the Great, 3
alienability, 117, 204–5, 229n.125. *See also*
   liquidity
Amsterdam, 102, 201
Anne, Queen of Great Britain, 15, 42–46
annuities. *See* financial instruments
Aragon, 99
Asgill, John, 141
assumpsit, 129

Backwell, Edward, 63–64
Baker, Wayne, 260n.115
Bank of England, 8, 14, 18–19, 24–25, 45, 53,
   76–77, 80, 82–83, 85, 88–89, 132, 139–46,
   197, 209; directors' elections, 144, 211,
   248n.53; effects on trade and land prices,
   140, 2246nn.16, 17; loans to the government, 140, 142–43; opposition to the Land
   Bank, 141, 158, 247n.31; politics and company directors, 144–45, 248n.44; politics
   and shareholders, 155–56, 187, 189–90;
   religion and company directors, 145–46;
   and share prices, 173–75; share trading in,
   185–87, 189–90; shareholdings in, 177–78;
   Whigs and, 141, 143
Bankers' Assignments, 64–65
Bankers' Case, 24, 125, 134, 199
Barbon, Dr. Nicholas, 141
Becker, Gary, 7, 162, 164, 188
bills of exchange. *See* financial instruments
Blackstone, Sir William, 13, 115, 242n.85,
   243n.86
Blunt, John, 153
Bolingbroke, Henry St. John Viscount, 49, 86
Bourbons, 42
boycotts, 26, 207
Brenner, Robert, 9, 114, 138, 191–92

Brewer, John, 54
Bridgeman, Sir Orlando, 122, 218n.40
Briscoe, Robert, 141
Bubble Act, 131
Bucknall, Sir William, 58, 69

Cabal, 32, 34, 218n.36
capital markets, 11, 105, 112, 201. *See also*
   efficient markets hypothesis; stock
   market
Castaing, John, 169, 173
Castile, 99
Caswall, George, 152–53
catholicism, 33, 218n.52; and influence at
   court, 33, 38
Cavalier Parliament, 34–35, 41
Chamberlen, Dr. Hugh, 141
Charles I, King of England, 31
Charles II, King of England, 11, 15, 21, 31,
   36, 55
Charles V, King of Spain, 98, 224n.11
Charles XI, King of Sweden, 233n.14
Chase, Salmon, 203
Child, Sir Josiah, 146, 213n.4, 247n.26
choses in action, 129, 131–32, 134, 204,
   242n.85, 244n.108
Civil War, 22, 120
Clarendon, Edward Hyde Earl of, 31–32, 61
Clifford, Thomas, 122
Coke, Sir Edward, 129–30
Commission of Public Accounts, 69, 220n.89
company shares. *See* financial instruments
contracts, 245n.126
Court of Exchequer, 124
Crowley, Ambrose, 152
customs tax, 40, 56, 58, 69–70, 83. *See also*
   taxes

Danby, Thomas Osborne Earl of, Marquess
   of Carmarthen, Duke of Leeds, 34–35, 49,
   68, 218n.45
Danzig, 97
Dartmouth, William Legge Earl of, 143
Davenant, Charles, 54, 86
debtor-creditor relations, 3, 9–10, 82, 127,
   135, 192, 199–200, 204–5

Bruce G. Carruthers is Assistant Professor of Sociology at
Northwestern University.